Internet Management Issues: A Global Perspective

John D. Haynes
Universal College of Learning, New Zealand
and
University of Central Florida, USA

 **Idea Group**
Publishing

 **Information Science**
Publishing

Hershey • London • Melbourne • Singapore • Beijing

Acquisition Editor: Mehdi Khosrowpour
Managing Editor: Jan Travers
Development Editor: Michele Rossi
Copy Editor: Maria Boyer
Typesetter: LeAnn Whitcomb
Cover Design: Deb Andre
Printed at: Integrated Book Technology

Published in the United States of America by
        Idea Group Publishing
        701 E. Chocolate Avenue, Suite 200
        Hershey PA 17033-1240
        Tel: 717-533-8845
        Fax: 717-533-8661
        E-mail: cust@idea-group.com
        Web site: http://www.idea-group.com

and in the United Kingdom by
        Idea Group Publishing
        3 Henrietta Street
        Covent Garden
        London WC2E 8LU
        Tel: 44 20 7240 0856
        Fax: 44 20 7379 3313
        Web site: http://www.eurospan.co.uk

Library of Congress Cataloging-in-Publication Data

Internet management issues : a global perspective / [edited by] John Haynes.
        p. cm.
    Includes bibliographical references and index.
    ISBN 1-930708-21-1 (paper)
      1. Internet. 2. Telecommunication policy. 3. Internet--Management. I. Haynes, John.

    TK5105.875.I57 I5625 2001
    004.67'8--dc21

                                                                    2001039386

eISBN 1-59140-015-5

British Cataloguing in Publication Data
A Cataloguing in Publication record for this book is available from the British Library.

NEW from Idea Group Publishing

Internet Management Issues: A Global Perspective

Table of Contents

Section V: Internet Health and Banking Issues

In loving memory of

Harry Frederick Haynes and

Gwendoline Pearl Haynes,

both of whom, as far as I am aware,

never used a computer.

Their world was not our world.

Preface

It is tempting to think that, in the year 2001, our technology is very sophisticated and accordingly, it is very tempting to believe that present-day computer technology is "very advanced" (begging the question of to what?). The fact is that we have only just begun to develop computer technology, and the recent implementation of the Internet brings us to a special threshold in that development. Development stages require very careful and thoughtful management. What we do now in this present development stage will be profoundly important for future generations. The management of the foundation for the 'evolution' of computer technology is a very special case because it will also become intimately connected with the management of mankind itself, not only in groups or collectively but also, eventually, as a species.

The Internet is a vast multi-disciplined array of information that potentially *invades* and affects the very *essence* of our lives. It is no thundering insight to say that we all have to manage our lives. But at the *beginning* of the twenty-first century–for those of us who consider information, knowledge, global third-dimensional communication and local and global business important–our lives are becoming inextricably bound into the Internet: we now need to manage our lives and our interests vis-à-vis the Internet. Accordingly, any collection of papers about 'management issues' arising out of the use of the Internet should be, given the prior basis, to some degree multi-disciplined in nature.

This book extends the *existing* discipline of information systems insofar as it has been put together as a collection of chapters with what is anticipated to be elements of the future discipline of information systems in mind. Most of the chapters have been contributed by academics from within the area of information systems, but importantly, in addition, there is one chapter on Internet data mining from two mathematicians, one chapter on on-line data from two psychologists and two chapters from academics working in the area of the philosophy of information technology. Another two chapters elucidate the theme of sustainability on the Internet.

As a collection of papers, this book is intended to be directed at all of the following categories interested in management issues relating to the use of the Internet: academics, students, managers, business people, the informed general public and future aspects of these foregoing groups. The Internet will either work for us or it will work against us. It makes sense then to consider a number of different perspectives on what the Internet may do to us, as well as what it will do for us.

The 19 chapters have been organized into five groups. In one sense all of the groups offer different perspectives on Internet management issues, and all chapters within the various groups carry, thematically, a global message. The authors of the chapters collectively come from England, USA, Germany, Australia and New Zealand. Some of the chapters are somewhat technical and a few of the chapters may be difficult conceptually, but all of the chapters, it is hoped, will have satisfied, by their own perspective, the aim of the book. This provides a number of advantages for the reader.

To begin with, the initial group, Section 1, "e-Commerce, e-Business and Web Page Design Issues," covers the bulk of assumptions and implications of the latest information available to us on culturally informed Web interfaces, the power of the mobile Internet, issues relating to the user and e-Commerce in terms of interface design, the implications for global e-Commerce and issues relating to international user interfaces. All contributors to Section 1 are information systems academics.

Section 2 is a blend of contributions from management systems, communication and journalism, marketing, management and information systems and management science and information. The underlying theme of Section 2 is strategic Internet management issues. Its authors cover issues as diverse as electronic business strategic orientation; human factors and e-Commerce, virtual absenteeism and systems thinking and the Internet.

Section 3 considers more deeply the underlying assumptions of our interaction with the Internet and how we manage that interaction from the perspective of "Internet Management, Sustainability and Philosophical Issues." Its opening chapter considers the Internet in relation to sustainable development and ecosystems and is written by three management information systems academics at the cutting edge of this topic. The second chapter deepens the theme elucidated in the previous chapter with "The Internet and Intercultural Communication and the Idea of Sustainability." The remaining three chapters in Section 3 are all single authored. Two of these chapters treat the philosophical nature of 'lived experience' in one chapter and "Heidegger on the essence of information technology" in relation to the Internet in the other chapter. The third considers the critical nature of change inherent in the topic of "The Internet: An End to Classical Decision Modeling." Perhaps the most difficult chapter in the book, especially for those not schooled in philosophical writings, is the 'Heidegger and essence' topic, but it is worth the effort for those who genuinely seek an answer to some of the most pertinent questions in this epoch on our *real* relationship to the Internet. It also serves as an academic grounding for previous chapters in this section.

Section 4 opens up the topic of Internet online data. The first chapter, by two mathematicians both very familiar with computer science, covers Internet data mining, and the second chapter, from two psychologists, examines the implications of their combined current research topic in relation to questionnaires on the Internet. Both of these chapters explore important topics that should appeal across all of the above-mentioned book readership groupings.

Section 5 covers the area of on-line health (one chapter) and on-line banking (two chapters). Consider that e-Commerce has spread to the health and banking fields, and already the Internet has had a significant impact on both industries, with Internet health and banking sites growing at an exponential rate. Clearly health and banking are, and will continue to be, lucrative e-Businesses. For example in e-health, currently there are over 20,000 health sites on the Internet offering information, expert advice and even drug prescriptions. While the majority of sites provide health information in the form of fact sheets, frequently asked questions, expert opinions, bulletin boards and chat rooms, there is a growing trend toward provision for full online consultations. As an emerging field, e-health offers many exciting prospects, to both the health professionals as well as to the health consumer.

We are moving into an era where information and its higher co-relative knowledge, are no longer sufficient for nurturing–in terms of learning–an effective life, let alone an academic life. Information and knowledge have given way to, or perhaps more precisely, are beginning to embrace, 'connectedness.' In this respect, it is instructive to note that the Internet is a concrete example of connectedness. If information on the Internet comes to be treated as an artefact, then the danger is that knowledge, and self-knowledge in particular, may be construed in the same way (available and in no need of deeper thought). Good management, especially management that needs to manage the process of change, critically relies on thought that itself recognises the connections between things, not only for their own sake, but also for the clarity which is afforded of the whole *implicated* 'picture.' Effective communication is an effective understanding of the notion and power inherent in 'connect-edness.' It is becoming increasingly evident that information and knowledge are given clarity via their thematic underpinning among many disciplines. Just under one-third of this book draws upon interdisciplinary subject matter to create a mix that is thematically appropriate for a study of management issues on the Internet, especially management issues that are conditioned by a global perspective.

The clear advantage for the reader of this book is the reward offered by a diversity of topics within the theme of management issues from a global perspective. All chapters were subject to at least four blind reviews with the exception of one specialist chapter. I feel confident that the range of topics presented in this book is sufficient for the reader.

John D. Haynes
Faculty of Humanities and Business
UCOL, Universal College of Learning
Palmerston North, New Zealand
and
MIS Department, College of Business Administration
University of Central Florida, Orlando, USA
August 8, 2001

Section I

e-Commerce, e-Business and Web Page Design Issues

Chapter I

A Model for Culturally Informed Web Interfaces

Brian Corbitt
Deakin University, Australia

Theerasak Thanasankit
University of Melbourne, Australia

INTRODUCTION

This chapter will challenge the accepted notions of cultural vanilla applications for e-Commerce and e-Business on the Web. The approach taken suggests that national culture exists at all levels from the visual to the implicit behaviors that frame interpretation of business process when undertaking e-Commerce. Studies done show quite clearly that culture distorts the relationships in any trading and business situation in ways that are not always obvious. We will explore the in-depth nature of the trading relationships and demonstrate the impact of cultural practice on the trading interface both on the Web and in the negotiations for business.

Globalization, Culture and e-Business

Note that e-Commerce and e-Business are challenging the very fabric of business. Jim Harkness, the Vice President of the TIAA-CREF Insurance Co., said in 2000 that "there is almost nothing you're doing that you can't figure out some way to do better, faster, cheaper using the Internet." The world of e-Commerce and e-Business has gone global. No longer is business localized to geographical areas. With the exception of a few countries, any business anywhere in the world can exchange products, trade, negotiate, invoice and conduct payments for goods and services in real time over the Internet. While the acceptance of Internet commerce at all levels of business is slow, since many small and medium enterprises see Internet commerce as a challenge in terms of their skills and in terms of its impact on costs, there is growth and change across all parts of the world. Internet commerce is beginning to frame new ways of conducting business.

However, this raises a challenge for business. Global business creates situations where culture can affect the nature of business and the nature of trade. In management studies there has been an acceptance for a long time that culture does impact on the way management processes happen in the same organization in different countries across the globe. This was demonstrated very clearly by very large studies done by Hofstede (1991) and Trompenaars (1993). It is from their work that we are beginning to see the impact of culture on e-Business and the impact of that culture on the interface for e-Business produced by the World Wide Web.

The Culture Paradigm in e-Business

A culture cannot, as one might naively expect, be defined simply in terms of the nation in which it exists. Examination of only cross-national differences misses a wide range of characteristics that distinguish people and therefore might be useful for predicting their needs (Ankomah, 1985; Negandhi, 1985). There are several models of national culture suggested in the literature (Parson and Shils, 1951; Kluckhohn and Strodtbeck, 1961; Rokeach, 1973; McClelland, 1961; Glenn and Glenn, 1981; Hofstede, 1991). All of these models are structural and therefore prescriptive constructs. Hofstede's framework has been widely accepted by many researchers attempting to understand culture differences between nations, especially in management research (Shore and Venkatachalam, 1996; Sekaran and Snodgras, 1986; Kedia and Bhagat, 1988; Kogut and Singh, 1988; Tricker, 1988; Rodriguez, 1991; Ueno and Sekaran, 1992; Morris et al., 1994; Shane, 1994). The popularity of the Hofstede model comes from its large sample and use of empirical data to demonstrate cultural difference. However, alternative frameworks are emerging (e.g., Burn, Davison and Jordan, 1998) which enrich the detail present in existing models.

There is also substantial empirical research, which suggests that national culture can be used to indicate differences in behavioural patterns in different countries (Komin 1990). Robbins (1989 in Komin, 1990, p. 215) defines national culture as "primary values and practices that characterize a particular country." However, there are many different views on culture, on what culture is and on its implications (Deal and Kennedy, 1982; Molin, 1987; Peters and Waterman, 1982; Pettigrew, 1979; Schein, 1984). Whilst there is no commonly accepted definition of culture, for this chapter the definition of culture relies on Hofstede's concept of "software of the mind" (Hofstede, 1991, p. 4) which he defines as "the source of one's mental programs lie within the social environments in which one grew up and collected one's life experiences. The programming starts within the family; it continues within the neighbourhood, at school, in youth groups, at the workplace and in the living community."

In a more precise way, Komin (1990, p. 17) identifies culture as "the end product of society, generally refers to the total patterns of values, ideas, beliefs, customs, practices, techniques, institutions, objects and artifacts which make a society distinctive... Therefore, people are culturally conditioned."

Culture then is a shared belief within a country or community where a person lives. Culture is learned and cannot be inherited (Hofstede, 1991). It reflects the ability of humans to feel, communicate and learn. If we agree that culture is learned, then it will affect personality at the individual level. Therefore, culture imposes rules, values and practices for societies.

Hofstede (1991) argues that at the human nature level, traits inherited in human genes determine human physical and basic psychological functions. The culture level is created in the social environment and is not inherited from human genes. Hofstede (1991, p. 5) suggests that culture "is always a collective phenomenon, because it is at least partly shared with people who live or lived within the same social environment, which is where it was learned."

However, culture introduces the notion of a social personality–a personality of shared behaviours and attitudes. These shared phenomena distinguish differences between societies and affect the way people do business. In the world of e-Business such cultural behaviour is challenged by the structures and norms, and sometimes standards, established on the World Wide Web. These Web norms and structures have created a new Web culture. It is a derived and emerging culture, informed essentially by western notions of interface interaction as the World Wide Web which has developed out of the west and been adopted across other cultures.

At the cultural level, there are four elements that can be used to identify differences from one country to another. They include:

- power distance–used to indicate the dependence relationships in a particular country (Hofstede, 1991);
- individualism and collectivism–collectivism is concerned with group interest rather than individual interest (Hofstede, 1991; Trompenaars, 1993);
- uncertainty avoidance–"the extent to which the members of a culture feel threatened by uncertain or unknown situations" (Hofstede, 1991); and
- dominance and subserviance–the extent to which dominance is used and perceived in a society (Hofstede, 1991; Trompennars, 1993).

These conceptualizations, which Hofstede argues differentiate different cultures, have supported most research on the impact of culture both in management studies (Nelson and Clark, 1994) and Information Systems (Palvia and Palvia, 1992). However, the model also has been widely criticized for using a single organization (IBM) and for suggesting that the four dimensions alone are sufficient enough to frame all aspects of culture differences (Thanasankit, 1999a and 1999b; Shore and Venkatachalam 1996). Burn et al. (1998) suggest that Hofstede's research is dated and has not been substantiated within the context of the 1990s and after 20 years of innovation and information technology diffusion through societies. Some (e.g., Alcoff, 1995) would argue that it is essential that studies in culture or gender have to be engaged by those who are part of that culture or gender. Hofstede is European and the construct is essentially European and represents his own European value systems. As a tool used across multiple cultures, it represents a unitarian conceptualisation rather than a pluralistic one where difference is recognized and accepted.

Burn, Davison and Jordan (1998) have recently reviewed the existing culture literature and have argued for a culturally informed information acceptance model. They argue that the way in which information is accepted is central to the way information systems are used within an organization or in a society. Understanding the impact of societal culture and the cultural assumptions that frame that society impacts on the way society and those individuals and organizations within it accept and thus use information. They suggest that a change may have to be effected in the information culture before the innovation can produce the expected results (Burn et al., 1998). Corbitt (1997) has suggested that in such circumstances individuals and organizations recontextualise information and adapt to their cultural mores and values. In terms of e-Business they adapt it to their traditional patterns of behaviour.

The core of culture is formed by values (Rokeach, 1973; Komin, 1990; Hofstede, 1991). Values are expressed a symbolic form and include words, gestures, pictures or objects that have certain meaning and have understanding accepted by members in that society. Often these symbols are acted out as ritual (Hofstede, 1991, p. 8). To illustrate this we seek an understanding of those values in society, which frame many of the rituals and symbols which act to frame behaviour and which will impact on a process like e-Business.

Values are core conceptions of desirable behaviour by individuals and within society (Komin, 1990). Values act as guidelines or standards for members of the society through actions, judgment, attitudes, evaluation, ideology and presentations of self to others. Rokeach (1973, p. 25) argues that "to say that a person has a value is to say that he has an enduring prescriptive or proscriptive belief that a specific mode of behaviour or end-state of existence is preferred to an opposite mode of behaviour or end-state. This belief transcends attitudes toward objects and toward situations; it is a standard that guides and determines action, attitudes toward objects and situations, ideology, presentations of self to others, evaluation. Values serve adjustive, ego-defensive, knowledge and self-actualizing functions. Instrumental and terminal values are related yet are separately organized into relatively enduring hierarchical organizations along a continuum of importance."

Values are used to guide what action is desirable or undesirable depending on situations. Values provide a common mechanism (Burn et al., 1998) for individuals and a society to interpret information and share understanding about the way that society operates. Values also "reflect a culture's view toward such central issues as politics, economics, religion, aesthetics, interpersonal relationships, morality and the environment" (Komin, 1990, p. 26). Values differ according to their importance, the order of which is created by both individuals and by society (Komin, 1990). Values represent real cultural differences. This conceptualisation will be discussed further in relation to Thai culture following a review of the impact of culture on systems development and its use in the development of e-Business solutions on the World Wide Web.

As a means to support the adoption of culturally informed and suitable interfaces for e-Business, we propose a model (Figure 1) which reflects the parameters which designers of e-Business systems should use as part of the development process. The model is based on other information systems research relating to requirements elicitation for business projects (Thanasankit, 1999), and its applicability to understanding Web-based interfaces is just as relevant. The model suggests that the front stage of the e-Business interface, the obvious, is in reality differentiated from the back stage of that interface which is informed by culture and its component parts. The elements of culture, we argue, are infused in the background of both customer and supplier behavior in e-Commerce. Without understanding the essential component parts of any culture will in effect reduce the impact of any new strategy to adopt e-Commerce.

In the remainder of this chapter we will use the components of this model, as they apply in the Thai e-Commerce context, to demonstrate the practicalities of developing a culturally informed e-Business.

Influence of Culture on Systems Development and e-Business

Organizational theories acknowledge that indigenous culture plays an important role in managing organizations. Culture influences individual and group values, belief systems, symbols and deep assumptions held by members in the particular

Figure 1: Design parameters

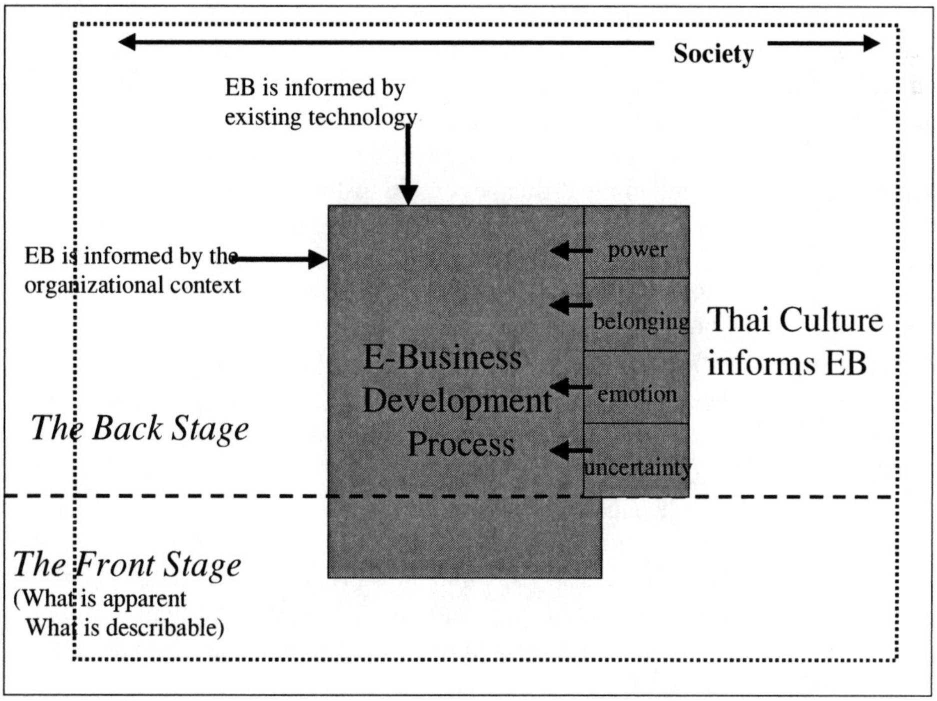

society (Deal and Kennedy, 1982; Ott, 1989; Peter and Waterman, 1982; Schein, 1984; Smircich, 1983). Many difficulties have been faced when implementing and using western technologies, management processes, information systems methods and Information Systems techniques in developing countries (Malling, 1998). This is akin to studies in international management, which suggest that there is no one best way to manage people and organizations (Hofstede, 1991; Mendoza, 1992; Trice and Beyer, 1993; Trompenaars, 1993). Management styles and methodologies have to be designed to suit different organizational cultures and indigenous peoples. These studies universally conclude that implementation of management process should respect different social and cultural values and beliefs.

Information systems and e-Business research has investigated how culture has an impact upon information (Odedra, 1993), implementation (Burn, Davidson and Jordan, 1998), requirements analysis (Hunter and Beck, 1996) and information systems failure (Hales, 1995). There are many social variables, which influence the successful use and implementation of information systems. These can include culture (Malling, 1998), local society values and beliefs (Rohitratana, 1998), economic issues (Palvia and Hunter, 1996), political issues (Palvia and Hunter, 1996) and local government policy (Nulens, 1998). Accepting the impact of these variables, it becomes significant to suggest that each of these is part of a social/cultural whole which impacts across and within society and its constituent parts. Information systems is an integral part of society and therefore they too must be embedded within the social system, as a means of solving problems (Stamper, 1994) rather than creating rejection and more confusion. In relationships to e-Business, the relationship is the same. E-Business conducted in any culture will be informed by that culture and affect the way the user interacts with the interface (World Wide Web) and the others in the business transaction. The World Wide Web introduces an intermediary in the interface of business when applied to e-Commerce. There is another element added to the traditional face-to-face business process, and this just makes the interface process more complex as different cultures try and adapt to the same interface presented in the e-Business relationship.

A limited number of researchers have investigated how culture influences the use, development, implementation and adoption of western-designed information systems (Malling, 1998), information technology (Burn et al, 1998; Jirachiefpattana, 1996a; Hall et al., 1996; Korpela, 1994; Mouritsen et al., 1991) and methodologies (Janczewski, 1992; Odedra, 1993). Their research has increased our understanding about how culture has affected information systems and information technology in developing countries where cultures are different from initiator countries. Janczewski (1992) suggests that computer products are developed within a 'western' context. For adopters of those technologies to be able to use them in other countries, indigenous people must adjust to the culture of the developers. This outcome, it is argued, would lead to increased stress within the workplace. As culture impacts on individual behavior within systems applications (Adler 1983), system developers must be sensitive toward their clients' cultures when designing information systems (Ankomah, 1985; Sauter, 1992).

Cultural differences between countries affect individual personality and behavior and organizational culture (Hofstede, 1991; Karpatschof, 1984). Each country has its own ways of expressing feelings, showing emotions, solving problems and constructing its society. Hales (1995, p. 103) asks, "Does it help to think 'culture' when addressing multinational practices of information systems strategy?" The appropriate application and implementation of computer information technology is an important issue for organizations because of both their internal cultural differences and because of the increasing existence of overseas branches. Hales (1995, p. 105) states that "... 'culture' approaches to computing technologies are rather high-profile." In a world with fewer and fewer barriers to communication, information transfer and development of information systems between countries, especially with the rapid development of e-Commerce and e-Business, developers should look at information systems as they could be influenced by national culture including methodologies, development, transferring of information technology and implementation.

Methodologies

The methodologies of information systems development, e-Business and the World Wide Web, are invented in the West and are considered as universal rules, but the application of these rules is not. Developers should apply these rules according to a particular country when developing successful information systems and search the appropriateness of the methodologies and adapt them to suit the local culture (Korpela et al., 1998). Palvia and Hunter (1996) suggest that promoting one methodology and single technique for development of information systems within a multinational organization, or similarly an e-Business established for international trade, is not necessarily a good idea, because of culture differences between headquarters and branches in other countries. Furthermore, the use of different methods and different uses of the same methods in countries can be caused by cultural differences (Palvia and Hunter, 1996). Korpela et al. (1998) suggest that African countries need their own ISDM[1] (Information Systems Development Methodology). They argue that the ISDM that has been taught in industrialized countries may not be appropriate for use in developing countries without adjustment. Therefore, it can be argued that localised ISD practices and methodologies are needed for better development of information systems (Avgerou, 1996; Liebenau, 1992).

Organizational issues, social issues and political issues in a country are important and influence the development of information systems (Waema, 1996; Walsham, 1992). Korpela et al. (1998, p. 276) suggest that: "the nuts and bolts of information systems are likely to be the same in industrialized and developing countries, but the uses and preconditions differ. In other words, the software engineering methods of technological implementation are likely to be the same in different countries, but the ISD methods and methodologies need to be adjusted from country to country to take the infrastructure, organizational, social and political differences into account."

The methodologies and methods employed during information systems development are tested within western countries where differences of culture between countries are low (Hofstede, 1991). Hunter and Beck (1996) suggest that variation of research findings in different countries may result from differences in culture and values of the societies. For example, JAD (Joint Application Development) is recommended as a very successful technique, which can be used for gathering requirements, for designing information systems, for getting agreement amongst stakeholders and to increase participation from users (Purvis and Sambamurthy, 1997). Users' involvement is highly regarded as an important element for development and implementation of information systems (Baronas and Louis, 1988; Baroudi et al., 1986; Ives and Olson, 1984; Sambamurthy and Poole, 1992) and increases the likelihood of success (Avison and Wood-Harper, 1991).

However, JAD has not been tested in developing countries, nor with the establishment of an e-Business, therefore the finding of Purvis and Sambamurthy (1997) may not be valid when tested and applied in South East Asia. JAD involves intensive communication and negotiations between system analysts and clients. It was argued earlier in this chapter that culture influences personality and behaviour (Karpatschof, 1984), therefore, western behaviour and eastern behaviour should be different during JAD sessions. Some adjustment of JAD methodologies may be needed to be successfully used in developing countries or in those countries of Asia considered to be developed.[2]

Development

Information systems are mainly designed and used by the 'West' and this leads to lack of consideration of different users in different cultures in designing such technologies and systems. We would argue that developing an e-Business should take national culture as well as organizational culture and institutionalised information technology practice into account, because each organization and society has its own values, heroes and heroines. Avoidance of cultural influences may lead to more likelihood of rejection of information systems in organizations (Odedra, 1993). Odedra (1993, p. 143) argues that information technologies designed for the West are difficult to apply to African societies. He says that "so far, the technology has been resisted by many as it is considered a threat to the existing system. As the use of technology would require some formalisation and adoption of unfamiliar techniques, the technology is viewed an alien force brought in to break-up the system."

It is fair to say that culture would affect the design and development of an e-Business. Each country needs specific information technology and systems to achieve its goals and objectives at both national and organizational levels. Information system techniques are portable across international boundaries and are those always applied in the development of most e-Businesses. However, such techniques need to be modified by local practitioners for suitability to use in the relevant society (Hunter and Beck, 1996). Therefore, information system techniques *should be* developed or modified to cater to the needs of that particular culture to reduce resistance of rejection of technologies and systems and utilize the most benefits from the information systems. This would assist an e-Business in one culture attract business to their Web site. Gill et al. (1993) support Odedra's arguments that it is important to understand indigenous culture before transferring and implementation of information technology.

For example, the Nepalese concept of information is to give it away in return for getting something back. Lower rank employees will provide information to their superiors in return of their protection (Bista, 1994; Burbank, 1992). Information systems provide Nepalese managers with access to all information within their organizations. If the system creates conflict with Nepalese culture or any uncertainty, there could be some disturbance within a Nepalese organization. Malling (1998, p. 123) suggests that the "safest way to secure full rights over the information is naturally not to externalise it at all." This means that information is not exposed as information on paper, or in electronic storage or through the Internet (Malling, 1998). Malling reported facing some difficulties when working with the Nepalese because he "never received a written agenda for a meeting, neither were minutes from meetings prepared. Most communication took place orally. Often meetings would be called in a rather informal way–with a very short notice and still the participants would display an impressing flexibility to order to appear for the meetings" (Malling, 1998, p. 123).

In Nepal, information is considered as a commodity, which should not be distributed freely. Therefore, Nepalese culture imposes limitations on externalising information, especially in a networked computerized system (Malling, 1998). Such research would then suggest that before systems analysts start to gather requirements for the establishment of an e-Business, they need to have a comprehensive understanding about how people in that society behave and what are the common values in the society. Such knowledge it can be argued enables better understanding of how systems will be used and thus how they might most effectively be developed.

Transferring Information Technology

In many Asian countries, the use of information systems has significantly increased over the past two decades. Information use has emerged and strengthened within development of these highly industrialized societies (Malling, 1998). This process of transferring information technology is simply the process of moving western technologies and systems to be used in Asian countries. However, the full potential of using such technologies and systems are very limited, even in developed Asian countries like Japan (Schatzberg et al., 1997; Steffensen, 1996a, 1996b). Vozakis et al. (1992) suggest that there are many issues involved in information systems transfer. However, when transferring information systems across culture, Vozakis et al. (1992) identify three main important factors, which influence the cross-culture transfer process. These factors include national culture of the organizations (headquarters and host), the competitive environment; and the methods of organization for transfer process (task congruency). Kedia and Bhagat (1988) argue that studying the role of culture identified that the factors which may constrain the transferring process include the characteristics of the technology involved, societal culture-based differences, organizational culture differences and the absorptive capacity of recipient organizations. Shore and Venkatachalam (1996) suggest that by using Hofstede's concept of power distance and uncertainty avoidance, the nature of problems, which may occur during the transfer of information technology (Table 1), can be identified.

Uncertainty avoidance is also used to investigate information technology diffusion. Straub (1994) suggests that culture plays an important role in the predisposition toward, and selection of, electronic communication media. By using the uncertainty avoidance concept (Hofstede, 1991), Straub (1994) finds that Japanese culture (high uncertainty avoidance culture) has a: "proclivity to avoid uncertainty by relying on traditional, information-rich channels for communication work against the acceptance of asynchronous, lean electronic channels such as e-mail. Second, the nature of the Japanese language gives certain structural advantages to facsimile and image-based communication media" (Straub, 1994, p. 26).

Table 1: Information technology transfer process and national culture consequences (constructed from Shore and Venkatachalam, 1996)

Hofstede's concept	Consequences
High power distance culture	"Applications which impose new work practices and require independent actions may directly conflict with core cultural values. As a result, subordinates may be as culturally unprepared to accept new authority relationships as their superiors" (Shore & Venkatachalam, 1996, p. 24).
Low power distance culture	"...users may now wield significant influence in the transfer process. They may feel entitled to express their views on the new application, not only to host management but to headquarters as well. Accordingly, users may be instrumental in the systems' acceptance, rejection and critical evaluation... Low power distance may also suggest that certain methods or procedures, with which the host organization is familiar, may have to be accommodated to win management and user support" (Shore and Venkatchalam, 1996, p. 24).
High uncertainty avoidance	Staff will "show concern over the uncertainty of new methods and procedures associated with the new application and will be particularly resistant to the abandonment of systems with which they are familiar and feel secure" (Shore & Venkatchalam, 1996, p. 24).
Low uncertainty avoidance	Staff have "somewhat greater willingness to take risks associated with new methods and procedures" (Shore & Venkatchalam, 1996, p. 24).

Earlier research has found that culture differences between Asia and the West can be pronounced (Ho et al., 1989). Therefore, failure, limited use and development of information systems can be partly explained by contradiction between indigenous culture and inventors culture (Malling, 1992), and between headquarters and their overseas branches (Vozakis et al., 1992).

Implementation

Implementation of the systems that make up an e-Business are constructed by societal and cultural norms. Cooper (1994, p. 18) states that: "a realignment of status, power and working habits which can accompany the implementation of new technologies may violate some of a group's shared values and meanings, and result in culture-based resistance."

Robey and Rodriguez-Diaz (1989) argue that social factors such as culture affect the successful implementation of information systems. They contend that culture can either be well managed and/or mismanaged during the implementation process and this will impact on the effectiveness of the implementation process. Social norms are very complex. Significantly, they are difficult to uncover and be made explicit by systems developers during implementation (Stamper, 1994). Therefore, implementation of an e-Business is messy, complex and very hard to manage (Corbitt and Brown-Parker, 1996; Goodman and Griffith, 1991). Aydin and Rice (1991) suggest that individual behaviour and personality also influence the implementation of information systems, because of individual cognitive style of thinking (Zmud, 1979), where some individuals might feel comfortable with one logical way of structuring problems (thinking type). They will then feel more comfortable in using an associated information system. However, some individuals might feel more uncomfortable using information systems or an e-Business on the World Wide Web if their operation relies on systems developed in other cultures using different assumptions and talking the interface between the computer and the systems user as one that anyone can use. As we can see from the above arguments, culture influences the development, methodology use and implementation of information systems and e-Businesses in all countries. In the remainder of this chapter we will apply these principles to the Thai e-Business context. We will investigate what Thai culture is, how Thai culture differs from western culture, and we will present an analytical framework on how Thai culture influnces the use of the interface of e-Business, the World Wide Web.

The Nature of Thai Culture

Rohitratana (1998) argues that Thai values shape and control the direction of information systems and thus also e-Business implementation. They influence the way people think, tackle problems and make decisions. Rohitratana (1998, p. 199) also suggests that Thai values "must be taken into consideration because no system is run in a vacuum. It needs people to operate and become involved with the system in order to control the operational process. Since the people who use the system carry values, perceptions and attitudes influenced by their own culture, it would be beneficial to consider their cultural perspective in order to overcome many possible difficulties which may occur during and after the implementation period."

The following discussion will examine Thai culture with a framework, which examines those elements of social construction, power, control, legitimacy, privilege, justice and equity. Within the context of Thai understanding of these western-derived concepts, we have reframed the terminology to better reflect their meaning in Thai. The ensuing discussion will deal with power (power, control, legitimacy), emotion, belonging (both of which embrace privilege, justice and equity) and uncertainty–the four components of the proposed model (Figure 1) as the basis for understanding the backstage, or cultural impact of the Web on users' reactions to e-Business interfaces.

The Concept of Power in Thai Culture

Hofstede used IBM employees, who work in similar positions in different countries, to investigate power distance, focusing on employee fear, superior autocratic or paternalistic management style and preferred working environment. The result was the development of a power distance index (PDI),[3] indicating the dependence relationships in a particular country. The PDI score for Thailand indicates that Thai society has high power distance, which can be interpreted that Thais accept wide differences in power in their organizations (Komin, 1990) and subordinates will not influence their superior's ideas or decisions (Holmes and Tangtongtavy, 1995). In Thai society, a person's power normally comes with his/ her title, rank and status. Australia, New Zealand, the USA and the UK are low power distance societies. Hofstede (1991) suggests that, for a low power distance society, the members of that society tend to prefer consultation when conflict arrives. Therefore, subordinates are more likely to contradict their superiors' ideas and are willing to present their ideas for consideration.

High power distance creates tall organizational structures for most Thai organizations. The high power-oriented culture tends to create respect for the leader as the father figure of the organization (Trompenaars, 1993), e.g., the current King of Thailand is respected and is accepted as the father figure for the country. Rohitratana (1998, p. 190) suggests that "due to paternalism and dependence, the concept of a 'flat structure' in an organization, which entails speedy decisions, cannot effectively take place. The reason is that only those at the top can possibly make decisions; that is their obligation, to operate as 'fathers.' Thais perceive the role of 'leader' as a controller rather than a colleague. This may be called the 'superior-inferior' concept, which is dominant in Thailand."

Therefore, without superior's directions and guidance, effectiveness may be reduced within the organization. McKenna (1995 in Rohitratana, 1998, p. 190) suggests the superiors' role "are almost like those in a family. There is respect and obligation. This is how things get done." If a superior figure is used in an e-Business context, it will have more power and influence than a non-descript symbol of figure.

Face saving or the criticism avoidance value plays a very important role in Thai culture. Thais try to avoid conflict and criticism at all times because of the face saving value. Komin (1990, p. 135) suggests that "the 'face' is identical with 'ego' and is very sensitive. Since the Thais place tremendous emphasis on 'face' and 'ego,' preserving one another's 'ego' is the basic rule of all Thai interactions both on the continuum of familiarity-unfamiliarity, and the continuum of superior-inferior, with difference only in degree."

Therefore, whenever there is a problem to be solved, Thais would find softer approaches or tone down the negative messages used, avoiding confrontation in public, such as during meetings. Thais try to avoid making a person "lose face" at all cost. Losing face also means that a person is being insulted by the other party. This leads to criticism avoidance. Komin (1990, p. 135) suggests that Thais "are very 'ego' oriented, to the extent that it is very difficult for the Thai to dissociate one's ideas and opinions from the 'ego' self." This is why a person who presents the ideas and gets criticism for the ideas will take the criticisms personally and not as criticism of the ideas themselves. Criticism creates insulting situations (Mulder, 1978). Using the interface of the World Wide Web challenges this concept of face. How do Thais deal with the prospect of loss of face with an impersonal interface? How do they avoid the process other than not use it?

An 'idea' in Thailand means knowledge gained from one's experience. In situations where criticism or questioning of a Pu Yai (superior, elder, authority-power figure) occurs, the interpretation is one of an insult. In the e-Business development process in Thailand, there is great deal of questioning by systems analysts of clients. In the Thai context such questioning must not engage or create criticism of senior staff. Questioning the way a Pu Yai works means insulting their knowledge and experience. Such behaviour is avoided in Thai organizational processes. Significant withdrawal by clients would occur if the situation arose resulting in ineffective and incomplete gathering of information or requirements, resulting in effective development of e-Businesses.

Power in the Thai context is constructed not by influence or personality, rhetoric or education, rather it is created by position and the status associated with position and rank. Superior/inferior relationships are clearly defined by acceptance and implicit recognition of rank and status. Thai culture accepts that power relations are implicitly constructed in all organizations and at levels of Thai society by appointment to a position, title or status.

In Thai culture power and authority are gained in a way that respects positions and rank. In Thai business Web sites and in Thai information Web sites, the user at the World Wide Web interface is shown the deference and respect that is appropriate to the context, e.g., in the example of the Bangkok Bank (http://www.bbl.co.th/creditcard/index.html), the user is greeted with the Thai 'wei' (joining hands in a greeting), designating respect and making the customer feel comfortable.

This is in direct contrast to western banks where the interface reflects a different culture and ideology. The Wood and Huston Bank in Missouri in the United States reflects the desire to show strength and confidence being 125 years old. There are no visuals used (http://www.woodhustonbank.com).

There is no sense of having that formal relationships symbol exposed in the American example. But it is fundamental in the Thai Web site.

The Concept of Belonging in Thai Culture

Fieg (1989, p. 33) states that "individualism has generally been played down by Thai culture in favour of group harmony, including especially close family ties and smooth interpersonal relations…While Thais have the freedom to follow a wide variety of lifestyles–from banker to artist to politician–once the Thai is in a certain milieu, he or she generally tries to fit into that environment and get along harmoniously with the group. Socialisation in group harmony begins at an early age in Thailand, just as pressure to think independently begins early in the U.S. In both cases the societies trying to encourage their young to act maturely according to values of the society."

Collectivism is concerned with group interest rather than individual interest (individualism) (Hofstede, 1991). Collective societies usually support structures where people are born and live in extended families. Relationships between subordinates and superiors are perceived in moral terms, like family links. Decision making, management and promotions are based on group performance (Hofstede, 1991; Trompenaars, 1993). Hofstede (1991) and Trompenaars (1993) suggest that Thailand is a collective society and Australia, New Zealand, the UK, the USA and Canada are individualist societies. In individualist societies everyone grows up to look after himself/herself. The relationship between superiors and subordinates is based on contract and mutual advantage, and promotion is based on individual performance and rules (Hofstede, 1991). Hendon et al. (1996, p. 199) suggest that "Australians are known to be rugged, direct, and tough-minded people, quick to assert what they perceive as their rights–occasionally, at the expense of others. They have very strong positive feelings for egalitarianism."

Previous research on IS development in Australia found that it was normal for each member of an organization to express their opinions about the information system because it was their performance that was going to be directly affected (Thanasankit, 1997). On the other hand, when an individualist works extensively with collectivists, he/she should:

- pay attention to every group member and notice their behaviour which take place;
- develop long-term relationships with collectivists;
- not criticize collectivists in the public for making them lose their face; and
- take note on collectivists' status hierarchies (Seelye and Seelye-James, 1996).

In essence working with the World Wide Web interface to e-Business is easier. There is an individual challenge only. The collective responsibility to the society, or the state, is not evident. Gratification and rewards are personal rather than collective, and trade in an e-Business environment reflects any user's desire to take economic advantage from the interface being used.

However, in the Thai context, the situation is significantly different. Jirachiefpattana (1996, p. 105) suggests that "personal and family connections play an integral part in operations of Thai business. Views and opinions have a greater impact on business management when expressed by members of family or in-group members." In Thailand it is normal for the owner of an organization to have family members hold very high managerial positions, even if they lack experience. Kinship values play an important role in Thai organizations (Rohitratana, 1998). Relationship and trust within a group plays an important role in Thai society. Before starting to design a successful information system/e-Business, developers would need to establish good relationships with management of a project. Trust and relationships with others are the basis of the Thai culture and values. Relationship-orientation behaviour happens more commonly than work-oriented behaviour both within Thai society and Thai organizations (Sorod, 1991). Komin's (1990) research shows that Thais value social relationships more than they do ambition or working hard. The Thais of Chinese descent rank social relationships higher than working hard and ambition, even though the Chinese in Thailand has been known to be hard workers and there are many success stories of Chinese migrants climbing from "rags-to-riches" (Komin, 1990).

Thais prefer to have stable social relationships and maintain surface harmony (Rohitratana, 1998). Personal image is important and plays a key role in surface harmony. The characteristics of surface harmony are that a person prefers to be smooth, kind, pleasant, conflict-free, non-assertive, polite and humble (Rohitratana, 1998). These characteristics appear in Thais' appearance, manners, and interpersonal approach (Rohitratana, 1998).

The lack of close relationships between management and subordinates has been shown to influence executive information systems development and methodology in Thailand (Jirachiefpattana, 1996), and it is not unreasonable to suggest, also in e-Business. In western countries such as Australia, employees believe in personal achievement and that they should be rewarded according to their contributions to projects. Emotional interaction with other employees or their superiors is kept to a minimum. Therefore, achievements are the priority in gaining recognition and advancement in their careers. These differences would be expected to influence the initial stages of any user's interaction with the e-Business interface, the World Wide Web. Thais do not want to be confronted or challenged. Rather, they want support from the interface, just as they gain support from their traditional business relationships. They use images of the monarchy and national symbols to represent this in the Web interface.

In Thai culture, power, confidence and respect are associated with symbols of important kings of the past or with the current monarch and queen. Such symbols not only represent the hierarchical nature of Thai society, but also the importance of respect to gain confidence (http://amarin.co.th). In business the interface uses the national colours of Thailand, even symbolically and uses a great deal of visual graphics to gain respect showing what they do and how well they do it. It is a visual rather than text-based representation (http://www.fti.or.th/nfti/index_n.htm).

Such concepts of belonging in Thai culture frame interpersonal interaction and interpersonal relationships. This sense of belonging frames how business is conducted, how meetings are conducted and how clients interact with businesses. Requirements engineering is an interactive process between people, both systems analyst and client. It then is also subject in Thailand to these same frames of reference, belongingness and power relationships, which are constructed and implicitly created and accepted within Thai organizations and society. The complexities such relationships create are enriched and made more complex by the nature of emotional engagement in these relationships.

The Concept of Emotion in Thai Culture

Emotion in culture refers to the nature of relationships. Emotion seeks to describe dominance, influence, equity and toughness amongst a variety of descriptors. Hofstede (1991, p. 83) defines masculinity as 'toughness' and femininity as 'tenderness.' The Masculinity index (MAS) (Hofstede, 1991, p. 84) shows that Thailand's MAS is 34. According to Hofstede (1991), the Thais are thus more likely to be a society where tenderness in relationships is the characteristic emotional trait. Such relationships are based on trust and emotional stability. Conflict between individuals is kept to a minimum or is avoided if possible. The Thais believe that "being nice helps people like you and builds the kind of long-term obligation to provide service which just does not follow from blasting an unseen ear over the telephone" (Cooper, 1991, p. 40). The important elements that differentiate a masculinity and femininity society are shown in Table 2 below.

Many Thai values play an important role in establishing the degree of femininity or tenderness evident in Thai society. These include *Bun Khun* (an etiquette or transactional relationship) and *Kreng Jai* (consideration), which are often used to keep good relationship between people. The Thais believe in *Bun Khun* which can be described as "... indebted goodness, is a psychological bond between someone who, out of sheer kindness and sincerity, renders another person the needed help and favor, and the latter's remembering of the goodness done and his ever-readiness to reciprocate the kindness" (Holmes and Tangtongtavy, 1995, p. 30).

This *Bunkhun* would be used for the base relationship between two people to

Table 2: The differences of important elements between masculinity and femininity society (adapted from Hofstede, 1991, pp. 81-82)

Masculinity Society	Femininity Society
Earnings–Have an opportunity for high earnings.	Manager–Have a good working relationship with your direct superior.
Recognition–Get the recognition you deserve when you do a good job.	Cooperation–Work with people who cooperate well with one another
Advancement–Have an opportunity for advancement to higher level jobs.	Living area–Live in an area desirable to you and your family.
Challenge–Have challenging work to do–work from which you can get a personal sense of accomplishment.	Employment security–Have the security that you will be able to work for your company as long as you want.

respect and/or 'do favors for' each other. Bun Khun "must be returned, often on a continuous basis and in a variety ways, because *Bun Khun* should not and cannot be measured quantitatively in material terms. It is an ongoing, binding of good reciprocal feelings and lasting relationship… the Thais are brought up to value this process of gratefulness—the process of reciprocity of goodness done, and the ever-readiness to reciprocate. Time and distance are not the factors to diminish the *Bun Khun*" (Komin, 1990, p. 139).

For subordinates to create conflict or influence their superiors in meetings or public places would be considered as not respecting them and not returning *Bun Khun*. However, it is important to understand that superiors build/create *Bun Khun* (*Saang Bun Khun*) toward their subordinates in the first instance, before they can expect to get back reciprocal gratitude from their subordinates. When a subordinate makes a mistake in their work or creates negative messages towards clients, his/her superior then will try to cover up for them. Therefore, not returning *Bun Khun* may sour their relationship and may effect their mutual cooperation. *Saang Bun Khun* can also be exploited and used in establishing power in Thai society (Rohitratana 1998). This power and connections sometimes can build an empire for that person. Subordinates, under their superior's empire, might then gain a certain degree of protection and benefits in return (Komin, 1990; Rohitratana, 1998). This process may create job security for subordinates and good relationships with their superiors. They will work in a group and share their success. This is difficult in the use of the interface of e-Business, the World Wide Web. How can the Thai gain the sorts of relationship *Bun Khun* represent? At this stage in the development of e-Business Web sites, it does not.

The concept of *Bun Khun* plays an important role throughout all levels in the Thai social hierarchy. *Bun Khun* creates a behavioural pattern, which enables different levels of people at different social levels to interact in a friendly manner (Holmes and Tangtongtavy, 1995). *Bun Khun* would thus impact significantly in an e-business when the actual user's requirements may not be the same as their superiors'. None of the subordinates would want to contradict their superiors and thus their declaration of requirements would be the ones accepted.

Another representation of Thai culture is its reflection not of dominance but cooperation, respect and tending towards the submissive. In the examples below the Krung Thai Bank interface feelings of submission to the customer are represented. Respect is gained by offering service to what the customer wants. It is structured in an open manner and uses pale colours (http://www.ktb.co.th). The respect element and the symbol of strength is gained by the use of the Eagle. This is in contrast to the ASP Bank interface in New Zealand which is more formal, more structured by frames and uses bold colours (http://www.asp.co.nz).

Kreng Jai (consideration) is defined by Klausner (1981, p. 199), who is an American social scientist and long-time resident in Thailand, as "… to be consid-erate, to feel reluctant to impose upon another person, to take another person's feelings (and 'ego') into account, or to take every measure not to cause discomfort or inconvenience for another person." *Kreng Jai* behaviour can be observed by all superiors, equals, and inferiors and includes intimate relationships between husband and wife, and between close friends. The only differences is the degree of *Kreng Jai*. Komin (1990, p. 136) suggests that "a Thai knows how far he/she can go in displaying the degree of *Kreng Jai* in accordance to different degree of status discrepancy, degree of familiarity and different situations. It is a basic rule to *Kreng Jai*." Showing *Kreng Jai* towards one who is higher in rank and seniority also means showing consideration merged with respect (Klausner, 1981).

The emotional nature of Thai culture and the importance of feelings is often displayed in Web interfaces with the use of symbols. This is well illustrated in the SmileHomes Web site where the interface uses graphic display, photographics, people and a mixture of both Thai and English to reinforce and show feelings of satisfaction (http://www.smilehomes.com).

Even for the young the emphasis of the interface is about symbols, colour and emotions (http://www.lemononline.com). With power distance relationships significantly high and with the concept of a submissive society existing strongly in Thailand, one could suggest that establishing good relationships with customers/ clients will play an important role during development of an e-Business relationship. However, such relationships have to be tempered with some understanding of the role of uncertainty in Thai culture.

The Concept of Uncertainty in Thai Culture

Hofstede (1991, p. 113) defines uncertainty avoidance as "the extent to which the members of a culture feel threatened by uncertain or unknown situations." Countries that have high uncertainty avoidance tend to avoid or dislike uncertain situations. This uncertainty is not just for individuals but it can be shared within the community or across society as a whole. The UAI (Uncertainty Avoidance Index) (Hofstede, 1991) score for Australia is 51 and for Thailand is 64, indicating a higher degree of congruence than for the other culture elements. But one can observe that the Thais have a higher tendency to dislike uncertainty or unpredictable situations. The fear of insecure Web transaction in Thailand, and their almost universal refusal to use credit cards as a means of payment on the World Wide Web testifies to the strength of this cultural impact.

In Thailand, subordinates tend not to get involved in decision-making processes, thus avoiding confrontation with their superiors or even with other employees at the same level. Involvement in decision-making processes may engage subordinates with unwanted responsibilities (Rohitratana, 1998). Thai culture does not encourage subordinates to dare to make mistakes, nor to take initiative. Thais avoid taking on more responsibility and avoid taking risks, because risk means bringing on more uncertainty situations and increasing their responsibilities. Thai culture encourages only a few people at the top of Thai organizations to make decisions and take risks (Holmes and Tangtongtavy, 1995, p. 84).

Decision making is made by high level management. Their subordinates believe that since the superiors are qualified for the top positions, they possess certain knowledge, wisdom or experience, which goes beyond their subordinates (Holmes and Tangtongtavy, 1995). It is fair to state that the decision-making system in Thailand is an "upward" delegation. "The result, of course, is a buildup of a myriad of major and minor decisions on the top person's desk" (Holmes and Tangtongtavy 1995, p. 63).

Thai decision-making is commonly not underataken as a team approach like in western countries or as in Japan. From a recent survey in Thailand, it was found that superiors in Thai organizations accept that they have to make decisions in an "authoritarian" way (Holmes and Tangtongtavy, 1995, p. 63). However, there is a fine line between an "authoritarian superior" and a "dictatorial manager." A dictatorial manager makes decisions without consulting anyone, but an "authoritarian manager" should nevertheless ask for subordinates' opinion and show some interest in their views (Holmes and Tangtongtavy, 1995). However, the authoritarian manager is entitled to make decisions about what he/she thinks is correct (Holmes and Tangtongtavy, 1995). It is his/her job to decide and guide their subordinates as he/she is their father/mother figure.

Most uncertainty avoidance in Thailand then is associated with avoidance of decision making. Decisions made might bring unwanted tasks and responsibilities, which subordinates do not want to take. Likewise, unsuccessful implementation of a decision may bring uncertainty for job security and blame to the subordinate. Thus decision making in Thailand is delegated upwards. Subordinates tend to avoid taking on more responsibilities, thus avoiding mistakes.

For the interface of e-Business, the World Wide Web, there is no escaping the uncertainty of not knowing who is at the other Web site, of not understanding the state of the other business, not being able to 'know' the other person in the other company, not be able to use 'guanxi' or relationships built up over a number of years of trading, thus establishing trust. Some Chinese proverbs aptly describe avoiding uncertainty in the Thai workplace. One is "one less responsibility is better than one more" and the other is "unnecessary efforts bring unnecessary problems" (in Chu, 1995, p. 234). Uncertainty avoidance means that the uncertainties of the World Wide Web challenge the use of e-Business as a strategy in the Thai context. How they are adapting to that challenge can best be seen in the use of Web sites and e-Business by Thais themselves.

The Nature of the Trading Relationship in Thailand–Some Challenges for the e-Business Model

Information systems and e-Commerce projects are difficult to develop and adopt because they always involve people, technology and the linkages and interactions between them. If we remove the technology, we are no longer studying information systems but are working in reference disciplines such as psychology, sociology, human communication, organizational behavior, philosophy, epistemology, ethics, logic, anthropology and theology. Similarly, if we remove the human aspects, we position ourselves in computer science, electronic engineering, communications technologies, physics, chemistry and other technological reference disciplines. IS and e-Commerce are semi-logical systems, mainly informal but supplemented by formalised messages. The nature of e-Business has both dimensions of formality and informality. How they are used at the interface of conducting e-Commerce, or making transactions, or engaging in trade, is informed by the culture it is operating in. These conceptualizations frame the following discussion of the use of the World Wide Web as the e-Business interface in Thailand.

What happens as a result of these interfaces is the acceptance or rejection of its use in e-Business. In the Thai context the take up rate of e-Commerce, as reported by the Thai Government, is very low. Why this is appears to be the result of a number of issues, some relating to the interfaces created for Thai businesses which do not reflect Thai culture but also to another set of factors derived from a recent two-year study (Thanasankit, 1999). The other set of issues relate to:

- Bricks and mortar seem to be important, knowing who you are trading with is fundamental.
- Trusting trading partners is better accepted culturally when face to face.
- Relationships are slow to form in the Thai business context and is slowed by the impersonal nature of the World Wide Web.
- Cash trading is preferred as a method of payment. There is little if any trust in credit card payment systems over the Internet.

One issue though is very significant. That is about transparency. The World Wide Web interface exposes businesses to everyone. Nothing can actually be hidden away from customers or trading partners. This transparency of business is not a good idea for Thai businesses, as business operations and stocks are still preferred to be kept within organizations. Differential pricing of goods is accepted practice, formed by years of relationship building and formal contacts. The very nature of what e-Business does and can do is subjected to open scrutiny and to an environment where accepted and traditional business practice is made available for all to see. This is a challenge for e-Business in the Thai context because business has always been built on relationships and 'knowing' building respect and trust. They are much more difficult to find, form and maintain in the impersonal interface for e-Business created on the World Wide Web.

The brief discussion and examples shown in the previous section support the other research reported earlier in the chapter that the interface created for e-Business by the World Wide Web is essentially a flaw in the implementation and adoption of e-Commerce when the interfaces designed do not reflect the variation in national culture. The demands of e-Commerce to become global and for e-Business to trade in that global context, is fraught with difficulties because of differences in the way people use the interface to interact, the different ways people in various cultures react to the interface.

E-Business designers must be able to reflect in the front stage component of the interface what is represented in the backstage. Without that representation the meanings given to the front stage might create various forms of entropy in their use.

Dissipated effort in establishing an EB will reflect on poor adoption of e-Commerce and a lack of use of the interfaces by customers and consumers. For e-Business to be a success, the barrier between the hidden (back stage) and the exposed form of the interface of the World Wide Web must be minimized and remain flexible enough to meet the varying demands of different users.

ENDNOTES

1 ISD methodology means to use "a systematic way of conducting ISD by using a set of procedures and methods which are based on a shared more or less explicit philosophy or approach" (Avison and Fitzgerald, 1995, pp. 10-12, 418-429).

2 Japan and Singapore

3 Hofstede method for calculating power distance index described in Hofstede (1991, pp. 24-25).

REFERENCES

Adler, N. J. (1983). Cross-cultural management research: The ostrich and the trend. *Academy of Management Review*, 33, 447-465.

Alcoff, L. (1995). The problem of speaking for others. In Roof, J. and Wiegman, R. (Eds.), *Who Can Speak? Authority and Critical Identity*. Urbana: University of Illinois Press.

Ankomah, K. (1985). African culture and social structures and development of effective public administration and management systems. *Indian Journal of Public Administration*, 31, 394-413.

Avgerou, C. (1996). Transferability of information technology and organizational practices. In Odedra-Straub, M. (Ed.), *Global Information Technology and Socio-Economic Development*, 106-115. Nashua, NH: Ivy League Press.

Avison, D. E. and Wood-Harper, A. T. (1991). Information systems development research: An exploration of ideas in practice. *The Computer Journal*, 34(2), 98-112.

Aydin, C. E. and Rice, R. E. (1991). Social worlds, individual differences and implementation: Predicting attitudes toward a medical information system. *Information & Management*, 20, 119-136.

Baronas, A. K. and Louis, M. R. (1988). Restoring a sense of control during implementation: How user involvement leads to system acceptance. *MIS Quarterly*, 12(1), 111-123.

Baroudi, J., Olson, M. H. and Ives, B. (1986). An empirical study of the impact of user involvement on system usage and information satisfaction. *Communication of the ACM*, 29(3), 232-238.

Bista, D.B. (1994). *Fetalism and Development*. UK: Orient Longman.

Burbank, J. (1992). *Culture Shock!* Nepal, UK: Times Books International.

Burn, J. M., Davison, R. and Jordan, E. (1998). The information society–A cultural fallacy? *Failure & Lessons Learned in Information Technology Management*, 1, 219-232.

Cooper, R. B. (1994). The inertial impact of culture on IT implementation. *Information & Management*, 27, 17-31.

Corbitt , B. J. (1997). Implementing policy for homeless kids in schools: Reassessing the micro and macro levels in the policy debate in Australia. *Journal of Education Policy*, 12(3), 165-176.

Corbitt, B. J. and Brown-Parker, J. (1996). *Change Factors and Management Issues in Electronic Commerce*. School of Business and Electronic Commerce, Monash University, Australia.

Deal, T. E. and Kennedy, A. A. (1982). *Corporate Cultures*. Reading, MA: Addison-Wesley.

Gill, K. S., Funston, T., Thorpe, J., Hijitaka, M. and Gotze, J. (1993). Individuals, culture and the design of information systems. In Beardon, C. and Whitehouse, D. (Eds.), *Computers and Society*. Oxford, UK: Intellect Press.

Glenn, E. S. and Glenn, C. G. (1981). *Man and Mankind: Conflict and Communication Between Cultures*. Norwood, NJ: Ablex.

Goodman, P. S. and Griffith, T. L. (1991). A process approach to the implementation of new technology. *Journal of Engineering and Technology Management*, 8, 261-285.

Hales, M. (1995). Information systems strategy. A cultural borderland, some monstrous behaviour. In Star, S. L. (Ed.), *The Cultures of Computing*, 103-117. Oxford, UK: Blackwell Publishers.

Hall, P., Hovenden, F., Rachel, J. and Robinson, H. (1996). *Postmodern Software Development*, Technical Report from the Computer Department of Open University, UK.

Ho, T. H., Raman, K.S. and Watson, R. T. (1989). Group decision support systems: the cultural factor. *Proceedings of the Tenth Annual International Conference on Information Systems*, Boston, MA, 119-129.

Hofstede, G. (1991). *Cultures and Organizations*. UK: McGraw-Hill.

Hunter, M. G. and Beck, J. E. (1996). A cross-cultural comparison of 'excellent' system analysts. *Information Systems Journal*, 6(4), 261-281.

Ives, B. and Olson, M. H. (1984). User participation and MIS success: A review of research. *Management Science*, 30(5), 586-603.

Janczewski, L. J. (1992). Factors of information technology implementation in under-developed countries: Example of the West African nations. In Palvia, S. and Palvia, P. (Eds.), *The Global Issues of Information Technology Management*. Hershey, PA: Idea Group Publishing.

Jirachiefpattana, W. (1996a). *An Examination of Some Methodological Issues in Executive Information Systems Development in Australia and Thailand*. Unpublished PhD Thesis, Department of Information Systems, Monash University, Australia.

Karpatschof, B. (1984). Gransen for automatisering–En virksomhedsteoretisk bestemmelse af informationsteknologien. (Limits for automation–A defini-tion of IT from activity theory). *Psyke & Logos*, 5(2), 201-220. Dansk Psykologisk Forlag.

Kedia, B. L. and Bhagat, R. S. (1988). Cultural constraints on transfer of technology across nations: Implications for research in international and comparative management. *Academy of Management Review*, 13(4), 559-571.

Kluckhon, F. and Strodtbeck, R. (1961). *Variations in Value Orientations*. IL: Evanston, Row Peterson.

Kogut, B. and Singh, H. (1988). The effect of national culture on the choice of entry model. *Journal of International Business Studies*, 19(3), 411-433.

Komin, S. (1990). *Psychology of the Thai People: Values and Behavioral Patterns*. NIDA (National Institute of Development Administration), Bangkok, Thailand.

Korpela, M. (1994). *Nigerian Practice in Computer Systems Development*. Helsinki University of Technology.

Korpela, M., Soriyan, H. A., Olufokunbi, K. C. and Mursu, A. (1998). Blueprint of an African systems development methodology: An action research project in the health sector. In Avgerou, C. (Ed.), *Proceedings of the Fifth International Working Conference of IFIP WG 9.4–Implementation and Evaluation of Information Systems in Developing Countries*, February 18-20, 273-285. London School of Economics and Political Science and Asian Institute of Technology Bangkok, IFIP.

Liebenau, J. (1992). Teaching information systems to students from developing countries. In Bhatnagar, S.C. (Ed.), *Information Technology Manpower: Key Issues for Developing Countries*, 137-144. New Delhi: Tata McGraw-Hill.

Malling, P. (1992). *Indfoerelse af Informationsteknologi i Thailand (Implementa-tion of Information Technology in Thailand)*. In Danish, Master's Thesis, University of Copenhagen.

Malling, P. (1998). Information systems and human activity in Nepal. In Avgerou, C. (Ed.), *Proceedings of the Fifth International Working Conference of IFIP WG 9.4–Implementation and Evaluation of Information Systems in Develop-ing Countries*, February 18-20, London School of Economics and Political Science and Asian Institute of Technology Bangkok, IFIP, 120-128.

McClelland, D. C. (1961). *The Achieving Society*. Princeton, NJ: Van Nostrand.

Mendoza, G. (1991). *Management the Asian Way*. Eddiplex Sdn. Bhd., Swlangor Darul Ehsan, Malaysia.

Molin, J. (1987). *Beyond Structure and Rationality*. Copenhagen: Akademisk Forlag.

Morris, M. H., Davis, D. L. and Allen, J. W. (1994). Fostering corporate entrepre-neurship: Cross-cultural comparisons of the importance of individualism versus collectivism. *Journal of International Business Studies*, 25(1), 65-89.

Mouritsen, J. and Bjoern-Anderson, N. (1991). Understanding third-world wave information systems. In Dunlop, C. and Kling, R. (Eds.), *Computerization and Controversy*. Academic Press.

Nelson, K. G. and Clark, T. D. (1994). Cross-cultural issues in information systems research: A research program. *Journal of Global Information Management*, 2(4), 19-29.

Negandhi, A. R. (1985). Management in the third world. In Joynt, P. and Warner, M. (Eds.), *Managing in Different Cultures*. Oslo, Norway: Universtetsforlaget, 69-97.

Nulens, G. (1998). Information technology in Africa. The policy of the World Bank. In Avgerou, C. (Eds.), *Proceedings of the Fifth International Working Conference of IFIP WG 9.4–Implementation and Evaluation of Information Systems in Developing Countries*, February 18-20, London School of Economics and Political Science and Asian Institute of Technology Bangkok, IFIP, 105-119.

Odedra, M. (1993). Enforcement of foreign technology on Africa: Its effect on society, culture and utilization of information technology. In Beardon, C. and Whitehouse, D. (Eds.), *Computers and Society*, Oxford, England: Intellect Press.

Ott, J. S. (1989). *The Organizational Culture Perspective*. Pacific Grove, CA: Broods Cole Press.

Palvia, P. C. and Palvia, S. (1992). MIS issues in India and a comparison with the United States. *International Information Systems*, April, 101-110.

Palvia, S. and Hunter, G. (1996). Information systems development: A conceptual model and a comparison of methods used in Singapore, USA and Europe. *Journal of Global Information Management*, 4(3), 5-16.

Parson, T. and Shils, E. A. (1951). *Toward a General Theory of Action*. New York: The Free Press.

Peters, T. J. and Waterman, R. H. (1982). *In Search of Excellence*. New York: Harper & Row.

Pettigrew, A. M. (1979). On studying organizational cultures. *Administrative Science Quarterly*, December, 24.

Purvis, R. and Sambamurthy, V. (1997). An examination of designer and user perceptions of JAD and the traditional IS design methodology. *Information & Management*, 32, 123 -135.

Robey, D. and Rodriguez-Diaz, A. (1989). The organizational and cultural context of systems implementation: Case experience from Latin America. *Information & Management*, 17, 229-239.

Rodriguez, C. (1991). The situation and national culture as contingencies for leadership behavior; two conceptual models. In Prasad, S. B. (Ed.), *Advances in International Comparative Management*, 5, Greenwich, CT: JAI Press.

Rohitratana, K. (1998). The role of Thai values in managing information systems; A case study of implementing an MRP systems. In Avgerou, C. (Ed.), *Proceedings of the Fifth International Working Conference of IFIP WG 9.4– Implementation and Evaluation of Information Systems in Developing Countries*, 188-201. February 18-20, London School of Economics and Political Science and Asian Institute of Technology Bangkok, IFIP.

Rokeach, M. (1973). *The Nature of Human Values*. New York: The Free Press.

Sambamurthy, B. and Poole, M. S. (1992). The effects of variations in GDSS capabilities on management of cognitive conflict in groups. *Information Systems Research*, 3(3), 224-251.

Sauter, V. L. (1992). Cross-culture aspects of model management needs in a transnational decision support system. In Palvia, S. and Palvia, P. (Eds.), *The Global Issues of Information Technology Management*. Hershey, PA: Idea Group Publishing.

Schatzberg, L., Keeney, R. and Gupta, V. K. (1997). Cultural and managerial comparisons: An analysis of the use of email and WWW in Japan and United States. In Khosrowpour, M. (Ed.), *Managing Information Technology Resources and Applications in the World Economy, Proceedings of the 1997 IRMA International Conference*, 296-300, Hershey, PA: Idea Group Publishing.

Schein, E. H. (1984). *Organizational Culture and Leadership-A Dynamic View*. San Francisco: Jossey-Bass.

Sekaran, U. and Snodgrass, C. R. (1986). A model for examining organizational effectiveness cross culturally. *Advances in International Comparative Management*, 1, 211-232.

Shane, S. (1994). The effect of national culture on the choice between licensing and direct foreign investment. *Strategic Management Journal*, 15(8), 627-642.

Shore, B. and Venkatachalam, A. R. (1996). Role of national culture in the transfer of information technology. *Strategic Information Systems*, 5, 19-35.

Smircich, L. (1983). Concepts of culture and organizational analysis. *Administrative Science Quarterly*, 339-358.

Stamper, R. (1994). Social norms in requirement analysis–An outline of MEASURE. In Jirotka, M. and Goguen, J. (Eds.), *Requirements Engineering–Social and Technical Issues*. London:Academic Press.

Steffensen, S. K. (1996a). *Managing New Types of Informational Business Networks and Network Businesses in Japan*. Copenhagen Business School.

Steffensen, S. K. (1996b). *Time of the Signs. Japanese Promotion of Next-Generation Information Infrastructures, Multimedia Network Business, and Informational Economy*. Copenhagen Business School.

Straub, D. W. (1994). The effect of culture on IT diffusion: E-Mail and FAX in Japan and the U.S. *Information Systems Research*, 5(1), 23-47.

Thanasankit, T. (1999). *Exploring Social Aspects of Requirements Engineering–An Ethnographic Study of Thai Systems Analysists*. Unpublished PhD Thesis, University of Melbourne.

Thanasankit, T. and Corbitt, B. J. (1999a). Understanding the impact of Thai culture on requirements engineering. In Corbitt, B. and Falvey, L. (Eds.), *The Melbourne Forum*. The University of Melbourne Press, Australia.

Thanasankit, T. and Corbitt, B. J. (1999b). Toward an understanding of the impact of Thai culture on requirements elicitation. In Harris, W. H. (Ed.), *Proceedings of the Conference on Information Technology in Asia*, Kuching, Sarawak, Malaysia, September 16-17, 420-440.

Trice, H. M. and Beyer, J. M. (1993). *The Cultures of Work Organizations*. NJ:

Prentice Hall.

Tricker, R. I. (1988). Information resource management–A cross-culture perspective. *Information and Management*, 15, 37-46.

Trompenaars, F. (1993). *Riding the Waves of Culture*. London, UK: Nicholas Brealey Publishing.

Ueno, S. and Sekaran, U. (1992). The influence of culture on budget control practices in the USA and Japan: An empirical study. *Journal of International Business Studies*, 23(4), 659-674.

Vozakis, G. S., Mescon, T. S. and Goss, E. (1992). Technical factors affecting international information and technology transfer. In Palvia, S., Palvia, P. and Zigli, R. (Eds.), *The Global Issues of Information Technology Management*. 450-462, Hershey, PA: Idea Group Publishing.

Waema, T. M. (1996). Implementation of information technology projects and economic development: Issues, problems and strategies. In Odedra-Straub, M. (Ed.), *Global Information Technology and Socio-Economic Development*, 106-115. Nashua, NH: Ivy League.

Walsham, G. (1992). Decentralization of information systems in DCs: Power to the people? In Bhatnagar, S.C. and Odedra, M. (Eds.), *Social Implications of Computers in Developing Countries, Proceedings*, 197-208. New Delhi:Tata McGraw-Hill.

Chapter II

From e-Commerce to m-Commerce: The Power of the Mobile Internet

Clarence N. W. Tan
Bond University, Australia

Tiok-Woo Teo
Bond University, Australia

INTRODUCTION

This chapter provides an overview of prevailing trends and developments shaping m-Commerce (mobile commerce) and the wireless economy. A detailed roadmap of the evolving mobile technology landscape is first presented. An intuitive review of the many basic underlying building blocks attempts to demystify the alphabet soup that wireless telecommunications infrastructure is often deemed to be. Interesting mobile Internet deployment and adoption demographics are highlighted. Commercial ramifications of actual and potential wireless application implementations are emphasized. Pertinent issues serving to promote or impede m-commerce take-off are examined. A case study is also included, profiling an industry-leading m-Commerce Web portal.

BACKGROUND

The World Wide Web and e-Commerce

The advent of the World Wide Web (WWW) provided the interface that made the Internet accessible to the mass market. Riding on the ubiquity and reach of the

WWW is commerce in its many forms: inter-business trade, intra-organizational transaction, purveyors of goods and services touting wares to potential customers and consumers soliciting purchases. Electronic commerce (e-commerce) is the primary propellant of Internet development today and is expected to continue driving innovation well into the new millennium.

For the business-to-business (B2B) e-Commerce sector alone, the Gartner Group forecast for the Asia-Pacific region excluding Japan is an impressive 155% compounded average growth from 1999–2004, growing in transaction value from US$9.2 billion to nearly US$1 trillion over the period to account for a 13.6% share of the US$7.3 trillion expected worldwide by 2004 (Asia/Pacific Business-To-Business e-Commerce to Reach $1 Trillion in 2004, 2000). The exponential growth pattern emulates that of the WWW upon inception.

From e-Commerce to m-Commerce

The wireless telecommunications market is exhibiting similarly impressive statistics. Conceived in the 1980s primarily to carry voice, the medium today also carries Internet data communications. The Cahners In-Stat Group forecasts the international wireless data market growing from 170 million subscribers to more than 1.3 billion between 2000–2004, equipping themselves with 1.5 billion wireless-capable handsets, personal digital assistants (PDA) and other Internet appliances by end 2004 (Wireless Data Users to Reach 1.3 Billion by 2004, 2000). The same study found in the United States with its high wired Internet penetration of 60 million connected households, some 100 million mobile phones—an enormous potential wireless market. Elsewhere around the world where wired Internet penetration is lower, mobile phones have actually become many subscribers' primary means of Internet access. The Strategis Group projects wireless Internet users in the Asia-Pacific region will rise ten-fold from 20 million in 2000 to 216.3 million by 2007 (Number of Wireless Internet Users in Asia-Pacific to Grow Ten-Fold by 2007, 2000).

The Gartner Group contends worldwide shipment of Web-enabled wireless devices rose 796% in 2000 alone over 1999 and predicts consumer transactions committed from such terminals would ring up a worldwide value of US$1.8 trillion by 2005 (The Shape of the Wireless Economy, 2000). As Internet and mobile communications converge, e-commerce evolves into mobile commerce (m-commerce). The potential of 'anytime' convenience and 'anywhere' mobility in carrying out everyday Internet transactions will spur many novel mobile services.

WIRELESS TELECOMMUNICATIONS TECHNOLOGY ROAD MAP

Television broadcasting inspired wireless communications architecture in the late 1940s: tall, centralized transmitter towers erected at select locales provided radio coverage to a region. Over time, system limitations like restricted mobility, low user capacity, poor voice quality and high cost saw the introduction of new cellular technology in late 1970s—a superior architecture persisting to this day.

First Generation—1G: Analogue network

Cellular Networks

Analogue technology characterized First Generation or '1G' cellular systems. A cellular mobile communications system employs a vast array of low-power antenna subsystems, dispersed in small, barely overlapping geographical units called cells. Cellular base stations provide individual local coverage and interconnect for a combined radio footprint that constitutes the wireless network. The cellular schema offers flexible network engineering: to match subscriber demand, cell size can be scaled by varying transmission power, while regional cell density can be increased to accommodate growth. Modern implementations are typified by larger, sparse cells in rural districts and small, dense ones in metropolitan areas.

Frequency Division Multiple Access (FDMA)

Inaugural cellular networks employed an analogue transmission scheme called Frequency Division Multiple Access (FDMA). Continuous radio signals are frequency modulated to carry information. Users accessing the network are each allotted a dedicated channel for the entirety of the connection. This simplistic algorithm hogged precious airtime even during momentary conversation lulls, eroding the absolute network capacity. Still, cellular technology superseded its analogue predecessors. Advancements in electronics manufacturing made cellular communication equipment more price accessible to consumers. Mass market acceptance launched the mobile telephony industry.

Advanced Mobile Phone Service (AMPS)

Early commercial cellular services included the European Nordic Mobile Telephone (NMT) system and the American Advanced Mobile Phone Service (AMPS)—the latter introduced in 1983. AMPS garnered extensive adoption throughout the Americas and across the Asia-Pacific to become the de facto standard, bringing unprecedented cross-border service compatibility for roaming subscribers. AMPS deficiencies included limited growth capacity, very poor data transport and inadequate transmission security. Despite technical imperfections, 1G systems maintained their popularity to the early 1990s—improved derivatives of AMPS are still deployed in analogue networks around the world today.

Second Generation—2G: Digital Network

Digital radio transmission heralded the 2G or Second Generation era in mobile telecommunications. Infrastructure providers needed scalable yet cost-effective solutions to address network saturation. Analogue coding schemes came to be supplanted by digital modulation that encoded transmission information into a stream of computer binary coded data packets for reassembly at the destination. Digital signaling is far less susceptible to radio interference and incorporates built-in error correction that enhanced coverage and improved voice quality. New features such as call encryption, short text messaging, fax and data transmission can also be added. By facilitating more simultaneous calls per channel, digital systems better optimize bandwidth utilization for large boosts in network capacity. Two competing signal digitization schemes dominate the marketplace: Time Division Multiple Access (TDMA) promoted by the Universal Wireless Communications Consortium (www.uwcc.org), and Code Division Multiple Access (CDMA) advo-cated by the CDMA Development Group (www.cdg.org).

Time Division Multiple Access (TDMA)

Under TDMA, each radio channel within a set bandwidth is divided into packet transmission time slots for unique assignment to individual users accessing the cellular network simultaneously. Concurrent connections can be supported with minimal interference since users are effectively 'time-sharing' bandwidth. TDMA can expand network capacity three to 15 times over that of analogue and was devised as an upgrade path from AMPS. The Europeans spearheaded the process to establish the Global System for Mobile (GSM) communications specifications based on TDMA. The first commercial service launched in 1991 acquired one million customers in two years. By late September 2000, GSM service spanned 158 countries with a subscriber base of 380 million (Footprint of World's Leading Wireless System Expands to 158 Countries, 2000), becoming the de facto interna-tional standard. Today, the GSM Association (www.gsmworld.com) is the global overseer of the GSM platform. The Americans operated an assortment of TDMA- and CDMA-based wireless systems under the Personal Communications Services (PCS) umbrella domestically. An adaptation of GSM called PCS 1900 was added in late 1995. This platform is presently administered by GSM North America (http://www.gsm-pcs.org/northamerica/gsmna.html).

Code Division Multiple Access (CDMA)

CDMA was originally devised for secure military telecommunications during World War II. CDMA tags each transmitted packet in the digital stream with unique identifying key codes that destination devices use to retrieve and decode intended packets. CDMA assigns neither a fixed frequency nor time slot to each user, transmitting simultaneously instead on multiple channels spanning the available spectrum. A CDMA-based network can expand call capacity eight to 15 times over that of AMPS.

The CDMA Development Group (CDG) established the IS-95 industry stan-dard in 1993. The world's first commercial rollout by Hutchison Telecom took place two years later in Hong Kong. The platform acquired the trade name of 'cdmaOne' in 1997 and user base rose to an estimated four million worldwide. By late October 2000, there were 71 million subscribers (More Than 71 Million Global Subscribers

Choose CDMA for Access to Mobile Communications, 2000) and cdmaOne had become the standard of choice in the Americas, Korea and Japan.

Digital technology exemplified Second Generation or '2G' mobile communication systems like GSM and CDMA, and represented the quantum leap that overcame the capacity, coverage and quality shortcomings of older infrastructures. Voice telephony remained the principal application, but demand for non-voice services such as fax, text messaging and data transmissions grew more prevalent.

2G Networks and Internet Access

The most common mode of Internet connection involves establishing an analogue data call using a conventional fixed telephone line to an Internet Service Provider (ISP). Data rates of up to 56 kbps (kilobits per second) are possible using industry standard V.92 protocol with V.44 data compression (Voiceband Modem Standards Take Another Significant Step Forward, 2000). A digital dial-up service like ISDN (Integrated Services Digital Network) offers data rates of 64-128 kbps. Access via optical fiber and Digital Subscriber Line (DSL) services are termed broadband as they deliver speeds of 256 kbps-1.5 Mbps (megabits per second).

Internet access has hitherto involved being tethered to some fixed line connection. Mobile users looking to recreate their Internet experience wirelessly found 2G mobile systems sub-optimized for data transmission. GSM networks in the early 1990s carried data at a dismal 9.6 kbps before climbing to 14.4 kbps in 1995. Subsequent High-Speed Circuit-Switched Data (HSCSD) specifications revved throughput fourfold to 57.6 kbps but limited network operator support stagnated transmission at slower rates in many GSM networks even to this day. CDMA networks did not fare much better with the first commercial 14.4 kbps data service launched as late as February 1998 (LG TeleCom Launches CDMA Wireless Data Service, 1998).

Many countries presently deploy both 1G and 2G systems concurrently to serve varying needs for capacity, mobility, coverage and service features. With demand for mobile Internet access growing rapidly, the market clearly needed a solution better optimized for wireless data transmission.

SECOND-AND-A-HALF GENERATION—2.5G

General Packet Radio Service (GPRS)

In 1996, the European Telecommunications Standards Institute or ETSI (www.etsi.org) rectified a new GSM standard that included a radical technology enhancement called General Packet Radio Service (GPRS) boasting a theoretical maximum data speed of 171.2 kbps—more than 10x times the average GSM rate and threefold that of analogue wired modems. While practical throughput may be considerably lower, the forecast is still for GPRS to offer at least 56 kbps connection in 2001, and double that the following year (Buckingham, Yes 2 GPRS, 2000). New handsets are required to exploit these advanced data features. British Telecom Cellnet inaugurated the world's first commercial GPRS service in June 2000 (BT Cellnet Rolls Out Nationwide GPRS Coverage, 2000).

GPRS overlays packet switching technology on top of GSM and TDMA cellular architectures, providing an upgrade path. Existing networks employ circuit switching whereby each conversation hogs the dedicated radio 'circuit' assigned until call termination. In contrast, packet switching conserves bandwidth in several ways. Data is transmitted in specially encoded packets that amalgamate multiple conversations to share radio bandwidth. No uninterrupted channels are set up among conversing parties and packets are simply sent into the network for routing to their destinations. Connections are maintained virtually and dynamically: access is instantaneous and established on-the-fly only when there is actual data traffic. High connection immediacy enables subscribers to maintain a virtual 'always online' status without a full-time wireless connection, resulting in considerable airtime cost savings. GPRS is especially useful in time-critical data applications like online e-commerce transactions and real-time credit authorization.

The Internet is perhaps the ultimate example of a packet switched network. GPRS embraces the industry standard Internet Protocol (IP) as its foundation. A GPRS network is subsumed in the Internet collective as yet another sub-network. GPRS mobile data devices function just like other wired Internet sub-nodes, inheriting seamless access to IP applications like the WWW, e-mail, Telnet and FTP (File Transfer Protocol). A GPRS terminal can stay wirelessly linked the whole day to a corporate intranet or to the Internet via an ISP, receiving transmissions automatically and initiating communications at will. Since data transmission may only be sporadic though a GPRS subscriber is always on air, entrenched pure time-based call tariff schemes need to be reviewed. However, charges based solely on transacted data volume would not allocate scarce bandwidth effectively over time. The optimal model could well be one that combines per-packet charges during peak times, and an unlimited volume flat fee off-peak (Buckingham, Yes 2 GPRS, 2000).

The GPRS data channel competes for bandwidth with voice calls, limiting average throughput and absolute network capacity. Packet switching incurs pro-cessing overhead associated with collecting and re-assembling received packets, causing slight transmission latency detrimental to a critically time-sensitive appli-cation like video decoding and playback. Hence, GPRS is not optimized for high quality wireless video conferencing. Another packet switching system artifact dissipates a data call if the intended recipient is offline during transmission—no store-and-forward mechanism exists to guarantee ultimate call delivery. Therefore, GPRS needs to be paired with a complementary network service such as Short Message Service (SMS), discussed later in this chapter.

CDMA IS-95B

The IS-95B CDMA standard mooted in mid-1997 extended the cdmaOne infrastructure to target ISDN-like data throughput. The technology made its commercial debut early in January 2000 in Japan with a sparkling 64 kbps data rate (IDO and DDI Establish Market Leadership with Motorola's 64kbps High-Speed Wireless Internet Access on cdmaOne Networks in Japan, 2000), besting prevailing GSM offerings and beating GPRS to market by some six months.

The systematic drive for improved data transmission laid the foundation for better wireless Internet access—the key to unleashing electronic commerce upon the mobile network. GPRS and CDMA IS-95B architectures mark the '2.5G' stage in the cellular telephony evolution.

'2.75G'

While wireless data infrastructure is finally delivering usable transmission speed, broadband connectivity was taking off in the realm of wired Internet access, raising the bar on throughput and user experience. Cellular network providers and standard bearers worked to meet rising subscriber expectations.

The Universal Wireless Communications Consortium (UWCC) and the GSM Association (GSMA) endorsed EDGE (Enhanced Data rates for Global Evolution), the penultimate extension to GSM technology that leverages installed TDMA and GPRS infrastructures to preserve past investments. Expected to be commercially available beyond 2001, EDGE requires upgraded cellular handsets to attain data transmission speeds of between 384-553.6 kbps. The CDMA Development Group had evolved its next-generation cdmaOne standard by July 1999. Called cdma2000 Phase 1 or 1XRTT, data speeds of between 144-614 kbps are possible. The first 144 kbps 1XRTT service was commercially launched in Korea by SK Telecom in October 2000 (SK Telecom Launches Commercial cdma2000 1x Service, 2000).

When EDGE and cdma2000 Phase 1 are in widespread deployment, high-speed mobile data connectivity rivaling the wired variety would become a reality and the era of wireless Internet access can be deemed to have truly arrived. Some have loosely demarcated this stage on the cellular technology road map as '2.75G.'

Third Generation—3G: Broadband Network

By the turn of the millennium, intense competition had consolidated the world cellular telecommunications market into regional blocs advocating divergent technologies and standards. While these infrastructures offered similar value-added voice and data services, many were technically incompatible across international boundaries and often even within a country. Subscribers committing to say, GSM handsets may access GSM networks at home and abroad but not CDMA ones and vice versa.

The International Telecommunications Union (www.itu.int) or ITU had working groups convened since the early 1990s in an attempt to propound a single global standard for telephony (Newly Created ITU Group on IMT-2000 to Develop Work Plans for Future Wireless Services and Systems, 2000). The first International Mobile Telecommunications 2000 (IMT-2000) recommendations were promulgated in late 1999. International participation was critical to producing a set of unified global guidelines, and submissions were exhaustively received from organizations as diverse as the UWCC, GSMA, CDG and the Third Generation Partnership Project or 3GPP (www.3gpp.org)—the association of national tele-communication standards authorities from the United States, Europe, China, Japan and South Korea.

IMT-2000 enables mobile service providers to evolve their cellular networks towards full inter-network compatibility independent of the underlying radio transmission technology. It is envisaged in the future for mobile devices to roam seamlessly on enabled networks across continents. TDMA, CDMA and GSM will be accommodated, integrating disparate systems to create borderless mobile services. IMT-2000 prescribes EDGE as enhancement to TDMA, cdma2000 as successor to CDMA, and UMTS (Universal Mobile Telecommunications System) as successor to GSM.

UMTS is advocated by the 3GPP and the UMTS Forum (www.umts-forum.org). UMTS protects existing investment in GSM and its derivatives like GPRS, and will employ a new radio transmission technology called Wideband-CDMA or W-CDMA (UMTS Forum Welcomes ITU Approval of IMT-2000 Radio Specifications, 2000).

IMT-2000 will offer unprecedented data rates scaling with the mobility of transmitting devices during communication: 144 kbps throughput for high velocity in-vehicle settings, 384 kbps for mobility below 120 kilometers per hour, and 2 Mbps under stationary indoor conditions (Buckingham, Data on 3G, 2000). To exploit the multimedia capabilities possible at these speeds, devices will sport cameras for image capture and bigger screens for video playback.

Harmonization and broadband connectivity differentiate Third Generation or '3G' mobile communication systems. The UMTS Forum projects more data than voice would be transported over wireless networks by 2005 (The UMTS Third Generation Market—Structuring the Service Revenues Opportunities, 2000).

Mobile network operators all over the world have been jostling for radio spectrum licenses to operate 3G services in their respective markets. The United States Federal Communications Commission (www.fcc.gov) 3G license auction commenced in mid-December 2000 offering a total of 422 licenses spanning 195 domestic markets (C and F Block Broadband PCS License Auction Fact Sheet, 2001). The launch of the first commercial 3G services was expected in May 2001 by NTT DoCoMo of Japan (DoCoMo Announces Service Brand Name of 3G Wireless System, 2000).

WIRELESS MESSAGING DEVELOPMENTS

SMS—Short Message Service

While bearer channels like HSCSD, GPRS and 3G differ in capacity and throughput, they all transmit over the central data conduit provided by the underlying bandwidth. One technology, however, is unique in this regard: data is instead borne by the signaling radio resources reserved in cellular networks for locating mobile devices and connecting calls. Short Message Service (SMS) is a wireless service conceived for the bi-directional exchange of short alphanumeric messages of up to 160[1] characters each among mobile devices. Introduced in 1991, SMS permeated the industry and has since grown in sophistication to support messaging among mobile devices and other enabled systems external to the cellular network such as Internet e-mail, the WWW, corporate intranets and private telephone exchange systems. Since data transmission occurs off the primary data channel, SMS messages can be sent or received concurrently even during a voice or data call.

A store-and-forward scheme guarantees delivery: sent messages pass through an electronic intermediary in the cellular network called a Short Message Service Center (SMSC) for routing to their destinations. A message gets successfully delivered if its intended recipient is immediately contactable. Otherwise, the SMSC stores it for subsequent delivery when the recipient next avails itself online. An undelivered message is purged from the system after the expiry of its validity period. A sender may request the SMSC to provide explicit notice of ultimate delivery success or failure through a SMS delivery report. This messaging methodology endears SMS as a complementary service to most digital infrastructures. A SMSC can also build reply mechanisms into messages it carries to create a feedback channel for recipients. For example, a user acknowledgment could be made to return a response code meaningful to the sender for follow-up. Properly encrypted and authenticated, secure interactive m-commerce services like banking and finance can be deployed using SMS.

Although multiple messages may be combined to form longer ones, the 160-character ceiling on each message is actually adequate for encapsulating succinct information. SMS began as a value-added service to voice calls, alerting subscribers to voice or fax messages recorded for them. Notification services today encompass paging alert, e-mail notification, calendar reminder and the like. Other one-way SMS information services include weather forecast, traffic watch, stock quotes, exchange rate pricing, flight schedules, sports statistics, gaming results and horoscope readings (Buckingham, Success 4 SMS, 2000).

Originating SMS notes from mobile handsets has traditionally been hampered by the cumbersome use of diminutive phone keypads, mitigated recently by availability of new devices sporting stylus input and miniature QWERTY keyboards. SMS messaging has also benefited from prevalent technologies like the T9 Text Input standard from Tegic Communications that speed entry efficiency by drastically reducing requisite keystrokes for message composition (T9 Text Input Licensed by Wireless Phone Manufacturers Representing More Than 90 Percent of Handset Shipments Worldwide, 1999). There is also a trend towards integrating SMS to e-mail systems for seamless duplex messaging, and SMS-enabling Web sites to extend their reach into the wireless domain. The case study at the end of this chapter profiles a firm that builds its business model around value-added SMS services and technology.

The functionality and convenience of SMS has popularized adoption. The Cahners In-Stat Group expects wireless messaging to explode from three billion messages sent monthly worldwide in December 1999 to 244 billion per month in 2004 (Fun Wireless Data Facts, 2000).

EMS—Enhanced Messaging Service

A minor extension to SMS promulgated by the ETSI, Enhanced Messaging Service (EMS) will imbue messages with a rich mix of formatted text, simple animations, tiny pictures and small melodies (ETSI TS 123 040 V3.4.1—Technical Realization of the Short Message Service, 2000). Such complexity increases message length considerably so EMS specifications provide for the concatenation of several classic SMS messages to convey the load. Given SMS has to compete for scarce radio resources within the cellular signaling band, a torrent of EMS messages can quickly degrade messaging service quality (Buckingham, Next Messaging: An Introduction to SMS, EMS and MMS, 2000). With SMS volume rising rapidly, a long-term growth strategy is crucial to securing the future of wireless messaging. It is fortunate a ready source of expanding bandwidth awaits in 2.5G and 3G technologies. EMS-enabled handsets are expected to be commercially available by the first half of 2001.

MMS—Multimedia Messaging Service

Multimedia Messaging Service (MMS) has been proposed by the 3GPP as the next-generation wireless messaging system (3G TS 22.140 V4.0.1—Stage 1 Multimedia Messaging Service: Release 2000, 2000). A single message can contain a myriad of elements such as text, audio clips, still pictures, animated images and full-motion video. As message size is much heftier than that of SMS or EMS, MMS transmits over the data and not signaling channel of cellular networks, tapping the broader bandwidth to deliver large messages expeditiously. MMS will also inherit the SMS store-and-forward schema, complete with delivery report confirmation.

MMS integrates fax, paging, voice mail and SMS legacy services and modern messaging platforms like Internet e-mail, chat and the WWW. Industry standards are embraced for compatibility. For example, MMS will support popular multimedia file formats such as JPEG for photographs, MP3 for audio and MPEG for video. Internet protocols such as MIME (Multipurpose Internet Mail Extension) and SMTP (Simple Message Transfer Protocol) will be used to encode multimedia messages and handle Internet e-mail.

Seamless and transparent service roaming among domestic and international networks is also targeted for truly universal messaging access. MMS services will be made accessible to all generations of cellular networks to cater to the eclectic mix of infrastructures across geographies. MMS will automatically re-purpose message content to fit target terminals, providing baseline messaging access to a broad range of devices. For example, a less graphics-intensive version of a multimedia message could be delivered to a terminal with limited screen real estate. A baseline security model is also in place to manage message encryption, authentication and privacy.

The 3GPP is collaborating with the WAP Forum (www.wapforum.org) to utilize the latter's Wireless Access Protocol (WAP) as the standard for encapsulating MMS messages (WAP MMS Message Encapsulation—Draft 0.8, 2000). WAP was selected for its extensibility and excellent technical fit. MMS is expected to dovetail on the gradual commercial rollout of 3G systems worldwide.

THE MOBILE INTERNET

WAP—Wireless Application Protocol

Cellular telecommunications vendors clamoring for market share often differentiated their products and services by taking proprietary and divergent routes, leaving a trail of fragmented standards and incompatible systems. Recognizing the need for a more coordinated strategy, Ericsson (www.ericsson.com), Motorola (www.motorola.com), Nokia (www.nokia.com) and Phone.com (www.phone.com) founded the WAP Forum (www.wapforum.org) in mid-1997 with a view to forging an open, extensible and unified industry standard for delivering sophisticated telephony services over wireless networks to mobile devices.

The Wireless Application Protocol or WAP architecture targets complete device and bearer independence: devices as diverse as mobile phones, alphanumeric pagers, PDAs and other wireless appliances are supported, as are practically all cellular network technologies from 2G to 3G. WAP specifications include frameworks defining the application development environment, data transmission protocols and transaction security (WAP Architecture, 1999).

At the core of the application development environment is the micro-browser or WAP browser, used to view content delivered wirelessly on demand from network servers. The facility to run applications under script control is also present like in conventional Internet Web browsers.

Data transmission scheme is Internet standards-based, adapted to the special constraints of the wireless domain—an environment exemplified by generally low bandwidth, high latency, connection instability and unpredictable availability. WAP encodes content using the lightweight Wireless Markup Language (WML) and transmits compressed binary code data in place of plain text. WML optimizes content for viewing on small screen displays typical of wireless terminals and facilitates easy, one-hand operation of the built-in micro-browser. The WAP framework is capable of data push: a network server can proactively initiate the sending of content wirelessly to a target device (WAP Push Architectural Overview, 1999), allowing for automated dispatch of time-critical information like alerts and notifications to subscribers.

Security framework is based again on Internet standards, optimized for response speed over wireless networks. Authentication and encryption is implemented to provide privacy and data integrity for secure communications and transactions. Support is being added for Public Key Infrastructure (PKI) cryptography. These measures enhance the viability of WAP as a platform for secure access to sensitive data stores like corporate intranets and databases.

Potential WAP applications include m-commerce transactions, online banking, stock trading and retail directory listings. The takeoff of WAP has thus far been hampered by the low immediacy and performance of 2G cellular systems, but the gradual worldwide rollout of high data rate networks such as GPRS should provide the necessary impetus (Yes 2 WAP, 2000). WAP-enabled handsets have been available from 2000, many commanding a price premium due to the necessary enhancements to device screen size, processing power, memory and battery life needed to create a satisfactory user experience.

With the WAP Forum industry alliance standing at some 500 members comprising the world's foremost telecommunications stakeholders, and more than 90% of mobile handset manufacturers committed to releasing WAP devices (The Wireless Application Protocol: Wireless Internet Today, 2000), WAP has become the de facto standard for wireless data services. Its continued development is supported by the close collaboration among global telecommunications and Internet standards authorities like the ETSI, Telecommunications Industry Association (www.tiaonline.org), World Wide Web Consortium (www.w3.org) and Internet Engineering Task Force (www.ietf.org). A recent Gartner Dataquest survey of the Asia-Pacific market found WAP to be the dominant mobile Internet platform supported by the majority of network operators in the region (Asia/Pacific Mobile Internet Service Dominated by WAP in First Quarter 2000, 2000).

MOBILE COMMERCE

Innovative M-Commerce Applications

The sheer success of the mobile telephone as a consumer electronic device cannot be disputed. Industry trends are pointing to the likelihood for wireless access via mobile terminals to eventually outstrip its cabled counterpart. In fact, this is already the case in Japan where a study had shown, while 25% of households had access to the Internet, only about 11% of them had a personal computer (Fun Wireless Data Facts, 2000). As mobile networks converge with the Internet, the spillover of Internet e-commerce fuels m-commerce take-off. The Aberdeen Group predicts by 2004, 74 million users or one-third of all wireless subscribers will access the mobile Internet (Mobile E-Commerce to Reach 74 million Wireless Users by 2004, 2000). There are reasons to believe that the arrival of wireless broadband technology will not only enable better versions of pre-existing Web applications to be deployed but fundamentally new ones, creating new value proposition for consumers and revenue streams for vendors. The true power of the mobile Internet lies in the innovative m-commerce applications that will be spawned.

Location-Based Services

The technology exists for mobile telephone service operators to place to within some accuracy the physical location of a subscriber roaming inside the coverage footprint. Several positioning strategies yielding varying accuracy may be deployed. One technique adds traditional Global Positioning System (GPS) hardware to handsets to relay satellite-placed locations back to service providers (Hayes, 2000). Most strategies, however, involves detecting a mobile terminal's interactivity with cellular base stations in its vicinity. Pinpoint precision may not be necessary for network operators to offer subscribers value-added services based on their location.

Many new commercial applications can capitalize on this previously unavailable subscriber detail (Buckingham, Mobile Positioning, 2000). Medical emergency and roadside assistance may be wirelessly requested. By homing in on the targeted recipient's location within a cellular network, such services may be rendered in a more timely manner. Mobile service providers may introduce location-based billing, charging subscribers at a residential rate when handsets are used at home[2], and a different tariff when they roam to other locations on the network. Commercial courier services can wirelessly track and manage their delivery fleets as each vehicle roams within the network coverage equipped with an in-vehicle mobile terminal. Advertising can become highly targeted and personalized to a subscriber's location, e.g., notifying an individual of a special discount on his or her favorite items as that person passes within the vicinity of the associated retail outlet. Even an information service as benign as helping subscribers find the nearest public washroom can be implemented (Taggart, 2000).

Multimedia Entertainment

The higher data bandwidth afforded by 2.5G and 3G networks will create new distribution channels for multimedia content like computer games, music and video.

Wireless Games

Some mobile handsets have a handful of rudimentary games embedded in them. Game play is very basic without lush graphics and choice of games were fixed for the lifetime of the device. In September 2000, the French company In-Fusio (www.in-fusio.com) launched its ExEn (ExecutionEngine) technology, a platform for sophisticated game development on mobile devices (Mobile Phones Finally Become Real Hand-Held Game Consoles Thanks to In-Fusio's ExEn Technology, 2000). ExEn game play is rich with real-time 3D graphics, animation, music and sound effects. Users can download games of their choice from a huge library over the cellular network for play on their enabled phones or play interactively against one another wirelessly, using data bearers such as SMS, GSM and GPRS. Users also receive embedded advertising in some game programs, creating a new real-time promotional channel for advertisers. The company expected to have more than 100 ExEn games by late 2001 and several major mobile handset manufacturers have committed to ExEn-enabling their phones.

Wireless Streaming Media

Streaming media enables the real-time playback of audio or video clips as they are being retrieved without waiting for the entirety to be downloaded and stored. Nielsen/NetRatings was reported to have found a 65% jump in the number of U.S. home Internet users accessing streaming content in the one year from 1999-2000, increasing from 21 to 35 million (Mariano, 2000).

PacketVideo Corporation (www.packetvideo.com) offers a platform optimized for deploying multimedia content over wireless communications networks. The technology employs high data compression and built-in error correction to deliver quality full-motion video and audio content to mobile devices (Motorola and PacketVideo Demonstrate Streaming Video and Audio for Mobile Devices, 2001). Another company, TuneTo.com, Inc. (www.tuneto.com), supplies a platform for broadcasting near-CD-quality music even over present-day, limited-bandwidth wireless networks (TuneTo.com Breaks the Wireless Barrier, Enabling Delivery of High Bandwidth Media Streams over Current 19.2 kbps CDPD Networks, 2000).

Conventional radio broadcasters have the opportunity to tap into the vast wireless subscriber base while music vendors can offer, for online purchase and instant delivery, songs from their music libraries. Location-based services can even be integrated to target subscribers with location-sensitive streaming content such as audio jingles promoting offers at retail outlets in the vicinity or movie trailer previews for films screening at the nearest theatre.

Wireless Telemetry

Wireless telemetry provides two-way communication between remote equipment and a central facility over the footprint of a mobile telephone system for the purpose of gathering data or remotely controlling devices. As conventional cellular infrastructure is utilized without significant modification, implementation benefits from low cost and fast turnaround (Cellemetry Data Service Via Cellular, 2000). A device can have its functionality remotely directed by the central facility through an embedded cellular communication module. It can also wirelessly relay crucial status information back in real time or batch mode for recording and follow-up. A popular control function is the instant remote activation and suspension of public utility supply to subscribers. Other commercial applications include the monitoring of security alarms, climate control systems, utility meter readings and vending machines service status (Telemetry: Red Hot in Ice Distribution, 2000).

Wireless telemetry drives supply chain efficiency and productivity through large-scale automation of data capture, improved billing timeliness and accuracy, reduced overheads associated with the manual alternative and increased customer satisfaction through service responsiveness. For example, vending machines can be kept replenished and in reliable operation by wirelessly polling inventory and service status continually to avert costly machine downtime. There were 5.4 million vending machines in the United States by the end of 1997, presenting a sizeable market for wireless telemetry deployment (Felps, 1999).

Wireless Electronic Payment Systems

Wireless payment systems transform mobile phones into secure, self-contained purchasing tools capable of instantly authorizing payment over the cellular network for goods and services consumed. In Finland, SMS messages sent from GSM handsets are already being used to pay for food and drinks at some outlets, initiate a car wash and trigger vending machines into dispensing goods, all simply by dialing special phone numbers posted for the purpose (Buechner, 2000).

An Israeli firm, TeleVend, Inc. (www.televend.com), has pioneered a secure platform that allows subscribers to make payments using mobile phones of any make on any cellular infrastructure (TeleVend, Inc. Introduces m-ABLE Technology at DEMO 2000, 2000). A customer making an impending purchase places a conventional mobile phone call to a number stipulated by the merchant. Connecting to a TeleVend server, the user selects the appropriate transaction option to authorize payment. Upon approval, the server finally alerts the merchant to complete the sale. Billing can be made to the customer's bank or credit card account, or even the mobile phone bill. This technology has wide-ranging application, such as payment collection of parking charges, restaurant or grocery bills and public utility tariffs.

Telematics

Telematics refers to the integration of wireless communications, vehicle monitoring systems and vehicle location devices. MobileAria (www.mobilearia.com) is a proposed standards-based telematics platform designed to bring multimedia services and m-commerce to automobiles. A cellular phone, a hand-held computer like a PDA and other appropriate hardware are integrated to provide personal information management, mobile Internet services and entertainment right on the vehicle dashboard. Sophisticated text-to-speech and voice recognition capabilities minimize driver distraction during use. For example, a user can compose and send e-mail by dictation, have news read aloud and easily voice navigate among system features hands-free.

A host of online information services such as news, weather report, stock quotes, flight schedule, traffic information and route assistance are accessible initially. Higher bandwidth m-commerce applications, rich messaging, streaming media and location-based services will follow as transmission bandwidth improves. People whom spend an inordinate amount of time daily inside their vehicles due to traffic congestion or long commute journeys may then use that time more productively. MobileAria is expected to ship commercially in the United States during the second quarter of 2001 (Delphi Automotive, Palm and Mayfield Fund Launch MobileAria to Bring Hands-Free Internet to the Automobile, 2000).

Wireless Telemedicine

Wireless telemedicine refers to the use of mobile telecommunication infrastructures and multimedia technologies to provide medical information and deliver health care services remotely. It facilitates the continuous monitoring of a patient's vital signs and condition by a hospital physician.[3] This would allow a medical situation to be managed even as a patient is attended to by a paramedic enroute to a hospital in an ambulance fitted with a wireless transmission system. Research experiments have demonstrated the feasibility of simple implementations over 2G infrastructure (Gagliano, 1998).

Teleconsultations have traditionally been conducted between doctors and patients in distant, rural areas over fixed-line ISDN networks. With the impending introduction of broadband 3G mobile systems, the concept of mobile medical clinics on wheels may become commercially realizable leveraging 3G multimedia capabilities, potentially reducing costs and improving delivery of quality health care in remote regions (Versweyveld, 1999).

CURRENT ISSUES IN MOBILE COMMERCE

Wireless Privacy

With improving location technology, it is plausible subscribers could soon be placed with near pinpoint accuracy. Consumer advocates view this to be a threat to personal privacy, raising issues of undue surveillance, spam and profiling (Privacy on Mobile Internet Studied, 2000). Location data could be collected to track the physical movement of a particular subscriber within the network. This could affect personal safety if the information fell into the wrong hands through inadvertence or malicious theft. Companies marketing location-sensitive products and services might flood mobile handsets with advertising material every time subscribers passed within range of retail outlets. Firms could, without user authorization, merge data on past Web usage habits and purchasing patterns with new location information to build even more detailed consumer profiles to glean previously obscured patterns and generate new promotional ideas.

The wireless marketing industry segment is still in its infancy, and stakeholders may yet stave off potential privacy disputes by concerted discussions at the onset. Stringent industry self-regulation proposed includes using low granularity location information when precision is not critical nor desirable, obtaining explicit user consent before releasing location details to advertisers and guaranteeing user anonymity even when data is used by applying only aggregate information without identifying specific individuals. Subscribers ought to stay vigilant by getting acquainted with the privacy policies of their service providers, whom in turn should have strict measures in place for securing user profile databases to prevent misuse or abuse.

Wireless Payment Systems

Encryption technology has largely contained the risks inherent in sending credit card payment information over the Internet. Authentication systems that verify the identities of transacting parties further fortify security. Advocated by credit card vendors Visa (www.visa.com) and MasterCard (www.mastercard.com), the Secure Electronic Transaction (www.setco.org) online payment system is supported by major banks but has been relatively costly for merchants to implement, delaying its widespread adoption. Its biggest shortcoming by far is the expensive fixed transaction overheads that favor higher value transactions, precluding cost-effective use for smaller value online payments.

Internet payment systems today must also accommodate sophisticated online tariff schemes like payment per access, by data volume or elapsed usage time. An ideal system must handle payment values large and small, cope well with high transaction volume, track billing comprehensively, adapt to complex pricing structures and interface seamlessly with diverse payment platforms like mobile phones and wireless terminals.

A new secure Internet payment platform called Jalda (www.jalda.com) has been formulated by EHPT (www.ehpt.com), a joint venture between Ericsson and Hewlett-Packard (www.hp.com). Jalda is an open system that enables Internet purchasing from stationary computers, mobile phones or any device with Internet connectivity (Jalda: A Quick Look at Payments on the Internet, 2000). A payment intermediary called an Internet Payment Provider (IPP)—which could be a bank, a credit card issuer, an ISP or a telecommunications network provider—arbitrates transactions between buyers and sellers, and bills customers on behalf of merchants. This value-added service earns the IPP an added revenue stream. Jalda handles payments for goods and services down to fractions of a cent, billed in any combination of vendor pricing schemes, accruing charges for single billing to the customer. Merchants and content providers gain from outsourcing billing logistics and much improved charging granularity and flexibility. Consumers benefit from a secure payment system that facilitates small purchases from wireless terminals with low administrative charges, potentially boosting the volume of micro-transactions online.

Wireless Security

A reader survey of 101 information technology and business managers by *InternetWeek* (www.internetweek.com) in December 2000 found security concerns to be delaying wider deployment of wireless Web technologies (Violino and Webster, 2000). Respondents found the early WAP specifications immature and relatively insecure for enterprise class deployment. The WAP Forum has committed to further improvement, enabling end-to-end transmission security and Public Key Infrastructure (PKI) cryptography (Yes 2 WAP, 2000). WAP digital certificates can be used to authenticate transacting parties and enable encrypted communications so that Web merchants can conduct secured transactions with mobile customers (Entrust Technologies First to Deliver Digital Certificates to Enable Trusted Wireless Transactions, 1999).

Computer viruses have begun the migration to hand-held devices like PDAs and even mobile phones as such terminals gain more processing power and intelligence. The Gartner Group was reported to have estimated the proliferation of viruses afflicting hand-held computers to occur by late 2001 and mobile phones soon after by mid-2002 (Kessler, 2000). This presents a significant security risk to mobile users growing increasingly reliant on wireless devices for voice and data services.

The first computer virus known to have specifically targeted mobile phones was isolated in Spain in mid-2000 (Security Experts Intercept Cell Phone Virus, 2000). The virus was spread as an e-mail enclosure on conventional computers but was also designed to send prank SMS text messages to randomly selected mobile phone numbers on a particular cellular network in the country. Had the outbreak not been contained early, the flood of messages could potentially have crippled the network. Few mobile phones today handle e-mail attachments but subsequent generations of better equipped Internet-enabled devices will be more vulnerable. Anti-virus vendors have already begun shipping anti-virus programs for hand-held computers but the onus remains on users to be vigilant.

Wireless Emission and Public Health

The mobile telecommunications industry has long grappled with cellular radio frequency (RF) emission and the impact on public health. There is fear that wireless handset and cellular base station emission may be cancer inducing, sparking public outcry for manufacturers to be more forthright with the implications, given the rapid increase in mobile phone use. A recent comprehensive study by the Independent Expert Group on Mobile Phones (www.iegmp.org.uk) in the United Kingdom reported no general risk to the health of people living near cellular base stations nor conclusive evidence that linked handset emission directly to health effects. The study did urge the public to adopt a more precautionary approach in using mobile phones pending more detailed research (Mobile Phones and Health, 2000).

Studies by the World Health Organization (www.who.int) had arrived at largely similar conclusions, noting that while some scientists have reported changes in brain activity, reaction times and sleep patterns in some human subjects, these effects are small and have no apparent health significance. Research had however clearly demonstrated an increase in traffic accidents when mobile phones are operated while driving—even using so-called hands-free kits. There was also evidence to suggest possible electromagnetic interference from the use of cellular phones near sensitive medical devices such as pacemakers and hearing aids, and aircraft avionics. The Organization is presently conducting coordinated research in more than 10 countries to study if cellular phone usage led to head and neck cancers. The project is expected to be completed in 2003 (Electromagnetic Fields and Public Health, 2000).

The Cellular Telecommunications and Internet Association (www.wow-com.com) in the United States mandated in June 2000 that every new mobile phone sold in the country carry information about its radiation emission rate to enable consumers to make an informed choice among different models (CTIA Certification Requirement to Provide Consumer Information About SARs, 2000). Public concern does not appear to have been quickly allayed: as of late December 2000, at least

10 lawsuits seeking compensation totaling billions of dollars were being prepared against cellular network providers in the U.S., charging that mobile phone radiation directly causes brain cancer (Borland, 2000). High-profile legal action could prove a public relations debacle for the wireless telecommunications industry. Negative publicity could potentially stunt subscriber growth, lower investor confidence, reduce investment in future infrastructure and affect the long-term outlook on mobile commerce.

3G License Auctions

The world's first 3G license auction was concluded in the United Kingdom in April 2000 and reaped the British government US$30 billion—four times more than was expected (Woffenden, 2000). A similar sale soon followed in Germany fetching US$45 billion. Telephone companies that won the bidding frenzies have since had their stock value traded down, punished by negative market perception that they might have overpaid for the rights to set up next-generation mobile infrastructures. There is fear that these licensees may ultimately be unable to return enough profits for sustainable growth, having to pass the significant license costs on to subscribers whom might balk at the high price for 3G services.

Rationality prevailed in many subsequent auctions around the world: one in Italy brought US$24 billion and another in Switzerland fetched US$113 million. Yet others have experienced delays and even cancellation: one in Poland was cancelled in December 2000 when only three bids were received. A 3G license auction slated for February 2001 in Singapore was postponed and subsequently canceled two months later (Tham). Yet another auction in the United States reaped the federal government US$16.86 billion (C and F Block Broadband PCS Auction Closes).The Yankee Group was reported to have estimated the final outcome to be a more conservative US$5 billion (Goodman, 2000).

A MOBILE PORTAL CASE STUDY— BLUESKYFROG PTY. LTD.

The Australian Mobile Phone Market

Australia has a mobile phone penetration rate exceeding 50% (Towards a National Mobile Phone Strategy, 2000). There are currently about 10.4 million mobile phones in total but only 15,000 are WAP-enabled. The majority are GSM-compatible, and practically all can send and receive SMS messages except the very early models. The CDMA network was introduced nationwide before analogue networks primarily serving rural Australia were decommissioned in October 2000.

Company Background

BlueSkyFrog.com (www.blueskyfrog.com) was founded in Australia in December 1999 with about 100 users initially to enable SMS interconnectibility among the three major mobile phone networks. Users grew to 1,000 within a week by word of mouth, proving the popularity of SMS services even then. By April 2000, the networks announced interconnectibility of their services and predicted the demise of SMS services companies like BlueSkyFrog. However, BlueSkyFrog membership had grown to almost 50,000 and the unique SMS functionalities it offered increased its user base to over one million by January 2001. The rapid growth was in part a result of active promotion and publicity by the local mobile network operators attempting to emulate European SMS success.

BlueSkyFrog also has a corporate division[4] responsible for marketing SMS and other wireless solutions to businesses. These include enabling SMS message broadcasting from corporate Internet Web sites or intranets, and providing the technology to develop m-commerce applications and mobile Web portals.

Demographics, Facts and Figures

BlueSkyFrog is among the most popular telecommunication Web portals in Australia and regularly features as one of the most visited consumer Web sites in the country as ranked by Top100.com.au (www.top100.com.au). About 15% of all Australians between 18-25 years old are BlueSkyFrog members. The phenomenon of higher overall SMS use by youths could stem from their lower technology aversion—the so-called 'Nintendo-generation' having grown up playing computer video games and the like. The lower cost of SMS messaging compared to voice calls is yet another draw.

About 75% of all BlueSkyFrog members are aged under 25, making the portal a very attractive advertising channel for retailers targeting the 'Generation-Y' market. Since each user is authenticated to his or her mobile telephone number, potential advertisers are assured of an audience made up of unique phone owners and mobile service subscribers. However, 35% of users are aged under 18, posing an issue with credit card payment administration. The acceptance of Internet currency Beenz[5] as payment has partly overcome this problem, making BlueSkyFrog one of the most popular online destinations for Beenz credits redemption.

Mobile Services

As at this writing in January 2001, BlueSkyFrog.com provides the following value-added SMS services:
- Mobile information services: News, finance, sports and entertainment.
- Personalization services: Composing and downloading phone ring tones; designing and downloading phone display logos and icons.
- Schedulers: Users may schedule information services for automatic delivery of SMS messages.
- Personal assistant and alerts: Short memos, to-do list, reminders, time sheet
- Games.
- Mail integration: Web-based e-mail with integrated SMS alerts.
- SMS-to-Web messaging: Sending SMS messages to/from mobile phones from/to the Internet.
- SMS-to-Web chat.

Mobile Commerce and the BlueSkyFrog Consumer Portal

New users are initially given a set number of message credits called "Bugz." More credits may be obtained as follows:

- Purchase credits on the Web.
- Earn credits by participating in online surveys and questionnaires.
- Earn credits by visiting sponsored Beenz sites and converting credited Beenz to Bugz.
- Earn credits by direct BlueSkyFrog membership referrals to friends and acquaintances.

The consumer portal also generates revenue from the following sources:

- Web banner advertisements.
- Sponsored SMS message transmission: A sponsor message is appended to BlueSkyFrog originated messages.
- Market research services: User response to online surveys are rewarded with Bugz. An actual survey conducted for a local mobile network reseller registered 16,000 responses to a questionnaire within an hour of its online posting.
- Target marketing channel: Corporations may target specific segments of the BlueSkyFrog user base for direct marketing by sponsoring e-mail or SMS messages to those interested in receiving them. For example, members can subscribe to an assortment of SMS information services, one of which is live surf reporting provided by Coastalwatch Technology.[6]
- Sale of Bugz to users.

The Future for BlueSkyFrog

BlueSkyFrog intends to maintain the popularity of its mobile portal through technological superiority. Its WAP site WAPMeBaby.com (www.wapmebaby.com) hosts a large number of WAP sites for its members. The BlueSkyFrog WAP gateway provides users the facility to go beyond the 'garden wall' that some mobile network operators have erected to restrict subscribers from accessing non-affiliated sites. WAPMeBaby has garnered about 50% market share of all WAP phone owners in Australia. BlueSkyFrog is poised to migrate the majority of its SMS users to WAP once the latter technology becomes more popular with the introduction of faster bandwidth technology such as GPRS.

BlueSkyFrog has patents pending on a filtering tool called FeedMeBaby that allows users to select text or image content on any Web site and customize it for delivery to their mobile phones via SMS or WAP. Other products in development include SMS Secure[7] and SMS Access. The former enables secure transactions on mobile phones via SMS without any hardware modification. It is a purely software-driven solution that verifies message receipt and authenticates the message sender to achieve non-repudiation in m-commerce transactions. SMS Access is a proprietary technology that SMS-enables conventional Web applications by providing online access to BlueSkyFrog's virtual SMS gateway via Microsoft SOAP (Simple Object Access Protocol) and COM (Component Object Model).

CONCLUSION

Mobile telecommunications has seen an evolution from a voice focus to data-centricity. The future along the development path continues down the multimedia route—plans are afoot to develop mobile technology into its Fourth Generation (4G) beyond 2007. A collaborative effort between NTT DoCoMo (www.nttdocomo.com) and Hewlett-Packard will research the next-generation wireless broadband multimedia delivery framework. Code-named MOTO-Media, the architecture is expected to enable high-performance streaming of multimedia content to mobile users based on intelligent agent technology, employing advanced scalable media encoding methodologies and optimally using scarce network resources (NTT DoCoMo, HP Announce Joint Research Effort, 2000).

Meanwhile, 3G networks will present a new channel for wirelessly distributing practically any content that can be digitized for delivery. Cellular handsets are expected to improve in form and function, a beneficiary of the many advancements in components technology coming on-stream. Organic Light-Emitting Diode (OLED) will displace conventional Liquid Crystal Display (LCD) screens, taking up less space and weight, and consuming far less power. New camera technologies with similar advantages will provide image and video capture on terminals. Low-cost, non-volatile storage media will offer cost-effective storage for mobile devices while drawing minimal power. New battery technologies will radically enhance battery life while reducing weight. As new handsets are required for each successive generation of wireless infrastructure, their timely availability in volume at mass market prices will be critical to the success of those networks.

The proliferation of mobile-enabled portable consumer electronics devices such as PDAs and other hand-held computers is expected to contribute significantly to the volume of m-commerce, further unleashing the power of the mobile Internet.

ENDNOTES

1 The decision to limit the number of characters to 160 was based on doubling the 80-character limitation of alphanumeric pagers.
2 Hutchison Telecommunications (www.orange.net.au) in Australia has already implemented this particular billing method on their CDMA network.
3 Micromedical Industries Limited (www.micromed.com.au) in Australia has successfully developed electrocardiograph (ECG) machines that are able to transmit recorded information via WAP from mobile devices to hospital centers.
4 The first author has been involved in the development of the BlueSkyFrog corporate division.
5 Beenz (www.beenz.com) is an Internet currency that functions like cash. Beenz can be earned by interacting with Web sites that reward visitors for browsing their content, and spent at sites like BlueSkyFrog and others that accept Beenz as online payment for goods and services.

6 Coastalwatch Technology (www.coastalwatch.com) provides surf reports on Internet platforms like the Web and e-mail, and mobile platforms like WAP and SMS.

7 The first author contributed to the development of the SMS Secure product.

REFERENCES

3G TS 22.140 V4.0.1– Stage 1 Multimedia Messaging Service: Release 2000 (2000). Third Generation Partnership Project. Available on the World Wide Web at: http://www.3gpp.org/ftp/TSG_T/WG2_Capability/SWG3/ SWG3_06_Duesseldorf/Docs/T2M010018%20Proposed%20CR%2022.140 %20MMS%20stage%201.zip. Accessed January 6, 2000.

Asia/Pacific Business-To-Business E-Commerce to Reach $1 Trillion in 2004. (2000). Gartner Group, Inc., February. Available on the World Wide Web at: http://www.dataquest.com/public/static/aboutgg/pressrel/pr021700.html. Accessed January 2, 2001.

Asia/Pacific Mobile Internet Service Dominated by WAP in First Quarter 2000. (2000). Gartner Group, Inc., September. Available on the World Wide Web at: http://www.dataquest.com/dq/static/about/press/pr-b09182000.html. Accessed January 3, 2001.

Borland, J. (2000). Cancer fears still dog wireless industry. *CNET News.com*. Available on the World Wide Web at: http://news.cnet.com/news/0-1004-200-4301323.html. Accessed January 7, 2001.

BT Cellnet Rolls Out Nationwide GPRS Coverage. (2000). *BT Cellnet Ltd.* Available on the World Wide Web at: http://www.btcellnet.net/cgi-bin/iminst2-1/zt/ show_pressrelease.jsp?cid=newsItem26. Accessed January 4, 2001.

Buechner, M. M. (2000). Cell phone nation. *TIME Digital Online*. May. Available on the World Wide Web at: http://www.time.com/time/digital/reports/ cellphonenation/index.html. Accessed January 7, 2001.

C and F Block Broadband PCS Auction Closes. (2001). *Federal Communications Commission*. January. Available on the World Wide Web at: http://www.fcc.gov/ wtb/auctions/c_f_blk/da010211.pdf. Accessed April 13, 2001.

C and F Block Broadband PCS License Auction Fact Sheet. (2001). *Federal Communications Commission*. January. Available on the World Wide Web at: http://www.fcc.gov/wtb/auctions/c_f_blk/c_f_fct.html. Accessed January 5, 2001.

Cellemetry Data Service Via Cellular. (2000). *Numerex Corp*, October. Available on the World Wide Web at: http://www.cellemetry.com/ Cell_White_Paper_10_00.pdf. Accessed January 6, 2001.

CTIA Certification Requirement to Provide Consumer Information About SARs. (2000). *Cellular Telecommunications and Internet Association*, July. Available on the World Wide Web at: http://www.wow-com.com/consumer/health/ sar/action.cfm. Accessed January 7, 2001.

Data on 3G. (2000). *Mobile Lifestreams Ltd*. March. Available on the World Wide Web at: http://www.mobileipworld.com/wp/threeg.htm. Accessed January 4, 2001.

Delphi Automotive, Palm and Mayfield Fund Launch MobileAria to Bring Hands-Free Internet to the Automobile. (2000). *MobileAria, Inc.*, October. Available on the World Wide Web at: http://www.mobilearia.com/ntopnav.html. Accessed January 7, 2001.

DoCoMo Announces Service Brand Name of 3G Wireless System. (2000). *NTT DoCoMo, Inc.*, November. Available on the World Wide Web at: http://www.nttdocomo.com/new/contents/00/whatnew1130a.html. Accessed January 4, 2001.

Electromagnetic Fields and Public Health. (2000). *World Health Organization*, June. Available on the World Wide Web at: http://www.who.int/inf-fs/en/fact193.html. Accessed January 7, 2001.

Entrust Technologies First to Deliver Digital Certificates to Enable Trusted Wireless Transactions. (1999). *Entrust Technologies Inc.*, December. Available on the World Wide Web at: http://www.entrust.com/news/files/12_16_99.htm. Accessed January 6, 2001.

ETSI TS 123 040 V3.4.1—Technical Realization of the Short Message Service. (2000). *European Telecommunications Standards Institute*, April. Available on the World Wide Web at: http://webapp.etsi.org/action\PU/20000523/ts_123040v030401p.pdf. Accessed January 5, 2001.

Felps, B. (1999). Huge potential remains for monitoring vending machines. *Wireless Week*, March. Available on the World Wide Web at: http://www.wirelessweek.com/index.asp?layout=story&articleId=CA3817&stt=001. Accessed January 7, 2001.

Footprint of World's Leading Wireless System Expands to 158 Countries. (2000). *GSM Association*, October. Available on the World Wide Web at: http://www.gsmworld.com/news/press_releases_77.html. Accessed January 3, 2001.

Fun Wireless Data Facts. (2000). *Cahners In-Stat Group*, July. Available on the World Wide Web at: http://www.instat.com/insights/wireless/2000/facts731.htm. Accessed January 3, 2001.

Gagliano, D. (1998). Wireless ambulance telemedicine may lessen stroke morbidity. *Telemedicine Today Magazine*, February. Available on the World Wide Web at: http://telemedtoday.com/articlearchive/articles/wirelessambulance.htm. Accessed January 7, 2001.

Goodman, P. S. (2000). U.S. set to start airwave auction. *The Washington Post Online*, December. Available on the World Wide Web at: http://washingtonpost.com/wp-dyn/articles/A56058-2000Dec11.html. Accessed January 7, 2001.

Hayes, S. (2000). Location services—Just a matter of time! February. *Third Generation Partnership Project*. Available on the World Wide Web at: http://www.3gpp.org/news/mobile_news_2000/lcs.htm. Accessed January 7, 2001.

IDO and DDI Establish Market Leadership with Motorola's 64kbps High-Speed Wireless Internet Access on cdmaOne Networks in Japan. (2000). *Motorola, Inc.*, January. Available on the World Wide Web at: http://www.motorola.com/NSS/Press/press_archive_2000/20000125.html. Accessed January 4, 2001.

Jalda: A Quick Look at Payments on the Internet. (2000). *EHPT*, January. Available on the World Wide Web at: http://www.jalda.com/home/downloads/Jalda_Whitepaper_000413.PDF. Accessed January 7, 2001.

Kessler, M. (2000). PDAs, cell phones vulnerable to viruses. *USATODAY.com*, December. Available on the World Wide Web at: http://www.usatoday.com/life/cyber/tech/cti956.htm. Accessed January 7, 2001.

LG TeleCom Launches CDMA Wireless Data Service. (1998). *LG TeleCom, Ltd.*, February. Available on the World Wide Web at: http://www.lg019.co.kr/english/news.html#2. Accessed January 3, 2001.

Mariano, G. (2000). Web surfers attracted to streamed content. *CNET News.com*, December. Available on the World Wide Web at: http://news.cnet.com/news/0-1005-200-4118543.html. Accessed January 8, 2001.

Mobile E-Commerce to Reach 74 million Wireless Users by 2004. (2000). *Aberdeen Group*, August. Available on the World Wide Web at: http://www.aberdeen.com/ab_company/press/08-08-00mcom.htm. January 6, 2001.

Mobile Phones and Health. (2000). *Independent Expert Group on Mobile Phones*, May. Available on the World Wide Web at: http://www.iegmp.org.uk/IEGMPtxt.htm. Accessed January 7, 2001.

Mobile Phones Finally Become Real Hand-Held Game Consoles Thanks to In-Fusio's ExEn Technology. (2000). *In-Fusio*, September. Available on the World Wide Web at: http://www.in-fusio.com/press/releases/pdf/release_exen.pdf. Accessed January 6, 2001.

Mobile Positioning. (1999). *Mobile Lifestreams Ltd.*, December. Available on the World Wide Web at: http://www.mobileipworld.com/wp/positioning.htm. Accessed January 6, 2001.

More Than 71 Million Global Subscribers Choose CDMA for Access to Mobile Communications. (2000). *CDMA Development Group*, October. Available on the World Wide Web at: http://www.cdg.org/press/2000/oct26_00c.asp. Accessed January 3, 2001.

Motorola and PacketVideo Demonstrate Streaming Video and Audio for Mobile Devices. (2001). *PacketVideo Corp*, January. Available on the World Wide Web at: http://www.packetvideo.com/press/pr01082001.htm. Accessed January 9, 2001.

Newly Created ITU Group on IMT-2000 to Develop Work Plans for Future Wireless Services and Systems. (2000). *International Telecommunication Union*, March. Available on the World Wide Web at: http://www.itu.int/newsroom/press/releases/2000/01.html. Accessed January 4, 2001.

Next Messaging: An Introduction to SMS, EMS and MMS. (2000). *Mobile Lifestreams Ltd.*, December. Available on the World Wide Web at: http://www.mobileipworld.com/wp/messaging.htm. Accessed January 5, 2001.

NTT DoCoMo, HP Announce Joint Research Effort. (2000). *NTT DoCoMo, Inc.*, December. Available on the World Wide Web at: http://www.nttdocomo.com/new/contents/00/whatnew1219.html. Accessed January 7, 2001.

Number of Wireless Internet Users in Asia-Pacific to Grow Ten-Fold by 2007. (2000). The Strategis Group, December. Available on the World Wide Web at: http://www.strategisgroup.com/press/pubs/ap-growth.html. Accessed January 2, 2001.

Perine, K. (2000). Talking about wireless privacy. *The Standard*, December. http://www.thestandard.com/article/display/0,1151,20860,00.htm. Accessed January 7, 2001.

Privacy on Mobile Internet Studied. (2000). *Singapore.CNET.com*, December. Available on the World Wide Web at: http://singapore.cnet.com/news/2000/12/13/20001213e.html. Accessed January 6, 2001.

Security Experts Intercept Cell Phone Virus. (2000). *USAToday.com*, June. Available on the World Wide Web at: http://www.usatoday.com/life/cyber/tech/cti031.htm. Accessed January 7, 2001.

The Shape of the Wireless Economy. (2000). *Gartner Group Inc.*, September. Available on the World Wide Web at: http://www.dataquest.com/public/static/aboutgg/pressrel/MobileRelease.html. Accessed January 2, 2001.

SK Telecom Launches Commercial cdma2000 1x Service. (2000). *SK Telecom Co., Ltd.*, October. Available on the World Wide Web at: http://www.sktelecom.com/cgi-bin/newnotice/notice_view_new.cgi?id=157&db=1. Accessed January 4, 2001.

Success 4 SMS. (2000). *Mobile Lifestreams Ltd.*, November. Available on the World Wide Web at: http://www.mobileipworld.com/wp/wp2.htm. Accessed January 4, 2001.

T9 Text Input Licensed by Wireless Phone Manufacturers Representing More Than 90 Percent of Handset Shipments Worldwide. (1999). *Tegic Communications*, November. http://www.tegic.com/pressreleases/pr_momentum.html. Accessed January 4, 2001.

Taggart, S. (2000). Skip to your loo with GPS. *Wired News*, November. Available on the World Wide Web at: http://www.wirednews.com/news/culture/0,1284,40331,00.html. Accessed January 2, 2001.

Telemetry: Red Hot in Ice Distribution. (2000). *Wireless Week*, July. Available on the World Wide Web at: http://www.wirelessweek.com/index.asp?layout=story&articleId=CA2859&stt=001. January 7, 2001.

TeleVend, Inc. (2000). Introduces m-ABLE technology at DEMO 2000. *TeleVend, Inc*, February. Available on the World Wide Web at: http://www.televend.com/pr.html. Accessed January 7, 2001.

Tham, I. (2001). Singapore cancels 3G auction. *Singapore.CNET.com*. Available on the World Wide Web at: http://singapore.cnet.com/news/communications/story/0,2000027545,10036267,00.htm. Accessed April 13, 2001.

Towards a National Mobile Phone Strategy. (2000). *Department of Communications, Information Technology and the Arts*, December. Available on the World Wide Web at: http://www.dca.gov.au/nsapi-text/?MIval=dca_dispdoc&ID=5487. Accessed January 7, 2001.

TuneTo.com Breaks the Wireless Barrier, Enabling Delivery of High Bandwidth Media Streams Over Current 19.2 kbps CDPD Networks. (2000). *TuneTo.com, Inc.*, December. Available on the World Wide Web at: http://www.tuneto.com/company/press_releases/_001211.cfm. Accessed January 9, 2001.

UMTS Forum Welcomes ITU Approval of IMT-2000 Radio Specifications. (2000). *UMTS Forum*, May. Available on the World Wide Web at: http://www.umts-forum.org/press/article035.html. Accessed January 4, 2001.

The UMTS Third Generation Market—Structuring the Service Revenues Opportunities. (2000). *UMTS Forum*, September. Available on the World Wide Web at: http://www.umts-forum.org/reports/report9.pdf. Accessed January 4, 2001.

Versweyveld, L. (1999). The newly emerging concept of next-generation wireless and mobile telemedicine systems. *Virtual Medical Worlds Monthly*, April. Available on the World Wide Web at: http://www.hoise.com/vmw/99/articles/vmw/LV-VM-05-99-16.html. Accessed January 7, 2001.

Violino, R. and Webster, J. (2000). Wireless slow to catch on. *InternetWeek Online*, December. Available on the World Wide Web at: http://www.internetweek.com/lead/lead121100.htm. Accessed January 7, 2001.

Voiceband Modem Standards Take Another Significant Step Forward. (2000). *International Telecommunication Union*, July. Available on the World Wide Web at: http://www.itu.int/newsroom/press/releases/2000/14.html. Accessed January 3, 2001.

WAP Architecture. (1998). *WAP Forum, Ltd.*, April. Available on the World Wide Web at: http://www1.wapforum.org/tech/documents/Technical_June2000-20010108.zip. Accessed January 6, 2001.

WAP MMS Message Encapsulation—Draft 0.8. (2000). *WAP Forum, Ltd.*, February. Available on the World Wide Web at: http://www1.wapforum.org/tech/documents/WAP-209-MMSEncapsulation-20000217-p.pdf. Accessed January 5, 2001.

WAP Push Architectural Overview. (1999). *WAP Forum, Ltd.*, November. Available on the World Wide Web at: http://www1.wapforum.org/tech/documents/Technical_June2000-20010108.zip. Accessed January 6, 2001.

The Wireless Application Protocol: Wireless Internet Today. (2000). *WAP Forum, Ltd.*, June. Available on the World Wide Web at: http://www.wapforum.org/what/WAP_white_pages.pdf. Accessed January 4, 2001.

Wireless Data Users to Reach 1.3 Billion by 2004. (2000). *Cahners In-Stat Group*, September. Available on the World Wide Web at: http://www.instat.com/pr/2000/md0003md_pr.htm. Accessed January 2, 2001.

Woffenden, C. (2000). Winners of 3G license auction revealed. *VNU Business Online*, April. Available on the World Wide Web at: http://www.vnunet.com/News/602583. Accessed January 7, 2001.

Yes 2 GPRS. (1999). *Mobile Lifestreams Ltd.*, August. Available on the World Wide Web at: http://www.mobileipworld.com/wp/wp3.htm. Accessed January 4, 2001.

Yes 2 WAP. (2000). *Mobile Lifestreams Ltd.*, May. Available on the World Wide Web at: http://www.mobileipworld.com/wp/wp4.htm. Accessed January 5, 2001.

Chapter III

Internet Interface Design: e-Commerce and the User

John D. Haynes
Universal College of Learning, New Zealand and
University of Central Florida, USA

Ahmed Mahfouz
Texas A&M University, USA

INTRODUCTION

Electronic commerce (e-Commerce) has exploded on the Internet over the past few years and is expected to continue growing at an exponential rate (Kannan, Chang and Whinston, 1998; Fellenstein and Wood, 2000). According to the GVU's 8th WWW User Surveys (1997), the most important issues facing online users are privacy (31%), censorship (24%) and navigation (17%). Since user interface design directly impacts navigation and affects the user's interaction with a Web site, this chapter will explore a number of different factors that affect user interface design on the World Wide Web. In all there are six factors that we explore in this chapter. They are the user's mental model as newly defined and focused upon perception and conception (Haynes and Mahfouz, 2001), the level of expertise of the user, the user's learning style, the richness of the media used, the organizational image and message, and the user's intentions. All these factors involve internal (to the Web page design) and external (to the user's environment) implications that impact user interface design on the Internet. Since all factors are external with the exception of the richness of the media used and, to some extent, the organizational image and message, it follows that we have chosen to emphasize in this chapter the external factors, namely those factors that directly relate to the user.

Consider the following view of the importance of the user interface on the World Wide Web and e-Commerce (Lohse and Spiller, 1998, p. 81):

"Issues of how people use the technology become critical as businesses and retailers attempt to exploit the boom in marketing. There are large differences between a physical store and its electronic counterpart. A help button on the home page of the Web shopping site replaces the sales clerk's friendly advice and service. The familiar layout of the physical store becomes a maze of pull-down menus, product indices and search features. Now more than ever, the promise of electronic commerce and online shopping will depend to a great extent upon the interface and how people interact with the computer."

USER INTERFACE MODELS

Four Types of User Interface

We can say that an interface is generally defined as the shared link that allows two independent systems to communicate or interact together. In computer-human interaction, it can be graphically expressed as the intersection overlapping human and computer systems. Specifically, the interface involves all the hardware input and output devices (such as the mouse, keyboard, computer monitor, etc.) and software (operating system, application, etc.) that allow the user and the system to interact.

The (human) user is flexible and adaptable (Mayhew, 1992). However, it is generally accepted that the system is neither flexible nor adaptable, which in turn places the responsibility of the initial successful connection on the interface designer. The continued interaction then falls into the "external factors of the user" (which we discuss later in the chapter). In order to maintain the interactive interest of the user, the external factors of the user are critical for the interface designer to second-guess or at least attempt to provide for. This second-guessing interface designer responsibility is the key, among other critical design considerations, to how users' perceive the system. Barki and Hartwick (1994) concluded that user participation and involvement towards a system affect their productivity and attitude in the workplace.

There are four types of user interface, as shown in Table 1: command-line, prompted, menu-driven and graphical (Parsons and Oja, 1998). Command-line interface requires typing a command that follows a specific syntax and punctuation, as used in Microsoft DOS and Unix. The prompted interface asks for input from the user through the use of messages. Wizards are dominating prompted interfaces through the use of multi-step sequences of screens that require a keyboard or mouse response. Menu-driven interface utilizes menus and submenus for ease of use. Graphical user interface allows the computer to be accessed through graphical objects like buttons, toolbars, etc., by the means of an input device, like the mouse, and the computer monitor (as output device).

Table 1: Four types of user interface (Parsons and Oja, 1998)

Type of Interface	Characteristics
Command-line	Typing of commands with specific syntax and punctuation
Prompted	Entering a required response via the use of wizards
Menu-driven	Utilizing menus and submenus for options
Graphical	Using graphical objects for ease of use and interaction

Gerlach and Kuo (1991) state that the user's involvement with the system can be expressed in two languages. This interaction has differences since the needs of the user are different from the system. This communication is expressed in two languages: action language and presentation language. The user utilizes action language to let the computer know what tasks or commands need to be done on various objects and components in the system or the software package. Presentation language is used by the system to ask about the tasks and objects and to respond to requests with the result of the operations. Both of these languages allow interaction and communication about common tasks and domains.

Four Levels of User Interface Model

Foley and van Dam (1982) devise a user interface model, based on four levels. The first level is the conceptual model, which describes the domain of tasks by which the human and system interact, such as objects manipulated, the relationships that exit among the objects and the operations performed on these objects. The remaining three levels describe the semantic, syntactic and lexical levels of both the action and presentation languages.

The semantic level defines what the words mean in the language, which is based on meanings taken from the conceptual model. This level incorporates objects that are part of the presentation language that deal with human interaction, such as menus, dialog boxes or prompts. The physical implementation of the interface starts at this level.

The third level is the syntactic level, which describes the grammar that allows combining words into a meaningful context of sentences. Syntax for the presentation language incorporates visual arrangements, such as shape and size, and temporal arrangement, such as the appearance and disappearance of objects on the screen. On the other hand, the syntax for the action language describes the order of actions done by the user to complete the messages.

The fourth level is the lexical level, which deals with how the words in the language are expressed. In the presentation language, displayed text or various symbols and combinations of different font types, colors, lines, etc., define the words. In the action language, a word may be expressed by what the user clicks on the screen or uses the mouse to manipulate a specific object on the computer screen.

Satzinger and Olfman (1998) show empirically that interface consistency is an important element in user interface design, based on the Foley and van Dam (1982) model described above. Consistency is somewhat difficult to define. Generally, it refs to how the interface is orderly, predictable and easily defined by elements of design that make the application easy to learn and change. Grudin (1989) classifies consistency into three levels: internal, analogical and external. Internal consistency refers to how the interface is consistent in design at any level of the interface inside the application itself. Analogical consistency refers to consistency of the system or the application with the user's task environment. When more than one application is involved, then external consistency refers to consistency across those applications, in all the four levels of interface design. For example, external consistency is evident in Microsoft applications, whereby Word, Excel and to a great extent Internet Explorer share the same "look and feel" when it comes to the menus, buttons, etc.

GOMS Model

Goals, operators, methods and selection (GOMS) rules cognitive model was developed by Card, Moran and Newell (1983). The model assumes that humans define goals, such as creating a document in a word processor, and subgoals, such as inserting words. These goals are attained by using methods or tasks, such as moving the cursor, using the four arrow keys. The operators on this context are tasks of the brain that include basic perceptual, motor or cognitive tasks. These tasks, such as recalling a filename, moving the mouse on the screen, etc., are important in changing the user's mental state or the task environment. The selection rules are the control mechanisms for selecting among the available methods for achieving a goal, such as erasing text in a document.

Object-Action Interface Model

Shneiderman (1998) redefines a user interface model he proposed earlier. The new model is called the object-action interface (OAI) model. The model emphasizes the manipulation of user objects and actions in a visual way. For example, folders of letters might be represented with envelopes (objects) and the deletion of these files (actions) could be represented with trashcans, like those first introduced in the Apple Macintosh.

In the OAI model, the first step is to understand the action or task to be carried out. The task in turn is broken further into intermediate goals and individual steps. Once the task objects and actions and their decomposition have been well defined, then a metaphor can be applied (metaphors will be discussed in a later section of the chapter). The designer must then represent the actions visually to the user, such as the movement of the mouse as the user clicks. Since the OAI model does not rely on syntax, it is easier to learn.

The OAI model supports two components in Web page design: metaphors and interface actions. Actions in Web sites can be represented using action handles: the labels, icons, buttons, images, etc., that allow the user the choice of clicks to start a specific action or sequence of actions. For example, navigation action can be represented by a turned page corner to indicate next-page action, or a magnifying glass to be used to zoom in or out of a page.

The OAI model (Shneiderman, 1998) specifies five main elements in Web page design: compactness and branching factors; sequencing, clustering and emphasis; support for universal access; good graphical design; and navigation support. The first is compactness and branching factors. These refer to page length and number of links, respectively. As Web pages grow and get more complex, the number of layers of index pages grows. Hence, an index is not appropriate. The solution is a higher branching factor. Good examples of Web page design are the Library of Congress (LOC) homepage (www.loc.gov) and Yahoo homepage (www.yahoo.com). The LOC page has a compact display with 31 links to specific services instead of the original seven links to general topics. The Yahoo Web site has over 100 links in a compact two-column format.

The second element is sequencing, clustering and emphasis. Internet users expect the most important item to be placed at the beginning of a page, which reflects the proper sequence of objects based on spatial importance. Clustering refers to grouping relevant items together to show their relationships. For emphasis, large fonts, coloring and drawing elements could be used to have certain items stand out.

Support for universal access is the third element. Different settings, such as resolution, color, refresh rate, bandwidth and type of browser must be taken into account by Web designers. That could be achieved by building two versions of Web sites: text only and graphical. This would accommodate users of differing computers and bandwidth, especially in developing countries lacking sufficient telecommunications infrastructure.

The fourth element is good graphical design. Tufte (1997) has written several books on information presentation. Each design philosophy must take into account the purpose of the site, as well the users who will be visiting it. For example, Wired magazine's Web site (www.wired.com) attracts attention to certain topics by using multiple colors and multiple font sizes.

The last element is navigation support. Many sites have a site map, showing the different sites in a diagram. Others use Java to expand items into submenus when the mouse pointer is placed on top of a specific item. As an example of educational software, Compton's Encyclopedia uses various types of multimedia and many windows to give a rich and interactive experience of information presentation. Tractinsky and Meyer (1999) show that information presentation and display formats clearly impact user preferences and decisions.

SIX FACTORS THAT AFFECT USER INTERFACE DESIGN

Factor 1: Mental Models

As explicated in Haynes and Mahfouz (2001, p. 33), Satzinger and Olfman (1998) describe mental models as what a user 'knows' and Ashcraft describes changes made to 'knowledge' generally as the source of mental models and an actual mental model as domain knowledge, constituted by "any body of information you have stored in memory about a situation, event, procedure" (Ashcraft, 1994, p. 561). Surely this describes only the surface level of a mental model? A more detailed viewing of a mental model comes from Maani et al. (2000, p.13), who embrace mental models as "based on beliefs, values, and assumptions that we (privately) hold." To illustrate the deeper point of beliefs and values conditioning knowledge, a restaurant customer, for example, has a mental model about restaurants that may include the following: menus to select food, waiters to take orders, cooks to prepare meals, etc. However from our perspective in this chapter if the perception (see next section) of the restaurant detail is flawed in some way, either by the user or by some incapacity of the restaurant, then the individual's mental model as defined above will also be applied in a flawed way. Similarly, if the individual is not able to invoke her conception based on her beliefs, values, etc., (see next section) then her aesthetic or imaginative sense may prevent her from staying at the restaurant. It is clear to us in this chapter that user perception and conception are critical elements in the application of the user's mental model.

In the following sections the above uses and definitions of mental models are given clarity via the distinction between (User) perception and (User) conception. This consequent clarity allows us to formulate a new definition of the User's Mental Model (see later in the chapter).

Perception and Conception

The differences between perception and conception are afforded by Haynes and Mahfouz (2001, p. 34) who refer to Don Ihde's distinction between perception and perception-in-a-gestalt (Haynes' notion of conception), as indicated in the following passage (Haynes, 2000, pp. 89, 90):

"Don Ihde ... described a shift from perception to a perception-in-a-gestalt when he spoke about words-in-a-text now being looked at from a bird's-eye-view. That bird's-eye-view or perception-in-gestalt is a mode which diffuses, like conceiving taken as a mode, a multiplicity of so-called interpretations into a modal shift. If one or the many so-called interpretations do not conform to a conception, i.e., leaving behind the perceiving of the words as objects or things, then we have a so-called interpretation which is still operating at the level of perceiving. But if we have an interpretation which is [legitimately] conceived, then we have made one modal shift to that of conception."

This point is made more forcefully by Don Ihde himself (Ihde, 1991, p. 138) in the following quotation:

"To see the moon through a telescope is to see it close up but also to lose it in its position in the sky. Lens technology transforms the very sense of space that I experience, in a significant modification of both bodily and world space. It transforms it into a kind of irreal, flattened and narrowed 'world.' Its distance is always a peculiar kind of near-distance. But we forget this as we learn to embody the technology into our familiar actions."

In other words, what is conceived either by ourselves (or others) is sooner or later perceived as a bodily experience. The cycle is perception to conception to perception. Perceiving always sees objects as objects, whereas conceiving is the process of creating a perspective. Creating a perspective leads to the further imaginative process of being perspectival. The critical importance of conceiving in terms of the distinction between perspective and "being perspectival" is made as follows (Haynes, 2001, p. 33):

"Making a perspective begins the process of the action of being-in-the-perspective or being perspectival. When we see things from the point-of-view of taking a perspective we are being perspectival (as distinct from, perhaps, taking things literally). Secondly, there needs to be some conceptual assistance in coming to terms with a perspective itself of perspectives. In taking this elevated sense, we are, again, being perspectival. When we are being perspectival in terms of our thinking, we are thinking conceptually, that is, if we consider ourselves, it is the concept of ourselves that is being considered, not ourselves [as objects, as such]. Similarly when we consider anything outside of ourselves [perspectivally], we are thinking in terms of the concept of that object."

To invoke in the user a sense of perspective out of the user's interaction with an interface is to have already captured the user's imagination. To have captured the user's imagination is to release in the user the potentially enormous energy of the action that flows on from thinking perspectivally. Fellenstein and Wood (2000, pp. 122-123) make the point that one way of "quantifying" "ease-of-use" of an interface is in terms of (1) payoff (does the content and function meets the users' diverse needs and expectations?), (2) courtesy (does the interface respect the user's time and avoid wasting it?), (3) trust (does the site work consistently?) and (4) intelligence (does the site proactively aid users to achieve their goals quickly?). Let us replace the term 'payoff' with relevance, and we now have the following four qualities (i.e. concepts)–as distinct from 'quantifying' terms–diagrammatically expressed with respect to a user's perception of the interface in Figure 1.

From Figure 1 as noted in Haynes and Mahfouz (2001, p. 34),the concepts of courtesy and intelligence are mutually reinforcing, that is, intelligence is required to perceive courtesy and what happens to be courteous derives from intelligence. Similarly we can perceive trust if the information is relevant, and it is relevant because we trust it. It follows that relevance enables courtesy and that courtesy and intelligence lead to trust. Finally, perception hinges on the dual connection between intelligence and relevance. In all of this analysis, "connectedness" is the theme, but it is a linear connectedness. That is, perception concentrates on objects, and from that, then, the linear connections between them are perceived. Perceptions are confused when there is too much object complexity within the interface design.

Figure 1: A map of user interface perception (Haynes et al., 2001)

Relevance
Courtesy
Trust
Intelligence

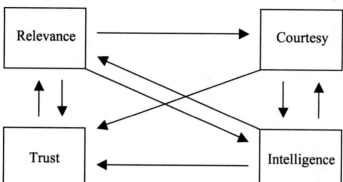

Figure 2: A map of user interface conception (similiar to Haynes et al., 2001)

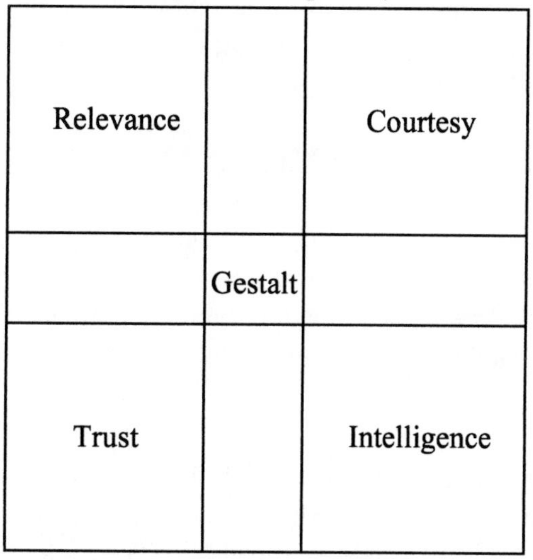

Relevance
Courtesy
Gestalt
Trust
Intelligence

As explicated in Haynes an Mahfouz (2001, p.35) the process of conceiving arises as a gestalt of what appears to perception (see Figure 2). In conceiving, a gestalt of what appears to perception takes place, such that objects (in the view of perception) are no longer seen as objects, but rather as connecting ideas (these are not the linear connections of perception mentioned above). Out of those connecting ideas comes a new conception (see Haynes, 1999, for an extension of conceiving as intuition). It may be that certain objects are lacking in "vitality" and actually turn off the possibility of conception. Yet conception is one of a human being's most powerful capacities. It is suggested that conception is more conductive to moving a user to action, and further, to repeated action, because the imagination is set into train. Once the imagination is unleashed, then a user will return again and again to explore the idealized theme of whatever it is that personally motivates that imagination.

The question then arises: what is necessary in an interface design to cause a shift in a user from perception into conception? That is, what could cause the user to cease merely seeing what is in front of the user and being driven by that, to conception? Here conception is understood to be the shift from seeing what is literally in front (because conception arises out of perception) and synthesizing that–out of the literal–into a user-conceived imaginative idea. One way for an interface design to invoke user conception is by use of interactive virtual reality, and another way is via Web cams and yet another is via metaphors as expanded in a later section. In Kendall and Kendall (1993, p. 149), we see metaphors described as "the cognitive lenses we use to make sense of all situations." The effective presentation of metaphors succeed in evoking user conception because their proper use eliminates a degree of screen complexity presented to the user. Maani and Cavana (2000, p. 54), note that "the human mind can deal with a limited degree of complexity. As the number of 'variables' in a system increase and their relationships become 'messier,' the human mind fails to 'see' the Web of relationships and the interplay among these variables." One way of keeping that complexity at a minimum and thereby allowing user conception to successfully emerge is via the effective use of metaphors.

A New Definition of the User Mental Model

From out of the previous discussion (directly above), we can now present a new definition of the user mental model: the user mental model is the user's system of beliefs and values underpinned by the user's perception and conditioned by the user's conception. It follows that if an interface design can affect the user's conception then it can condition the original belief and value system of the user.

Metaphors

Metaphors play an important role in defining a user's model since they represent computer components as real-world objects. One of the earlier metaphors is the ledger used in the first electronic spreadsheet, VisiCalc. One of the most prevalent metaphors is the desktop metaphor, which was introduced by Xerox PARC and later popularized by the Apple Macintosh and Microsoft Windows. The metaphor represents documents stored in a computer as pages of paper, and storage as a filing cabinet. Madsen (1994) noted that metaphors affect the ease of using and learning software.

However, Raskin (1997), who helped develop the Macintosh, criticizes the use of the desktop metaphor. First, he stated there are major problems to deal with, such as complaints from users about the functionality of the system, involving different settings that must be configured. In addition, Raskin (1997) cited cognitive psychology research that states humans can only deal with a few tasks at hand at one time. The desktop metaphor consumes many of the user's resources, such as attention, since the user has to be aware of the state of the operating system and the application, which results in frustration. The solution, according to Raskin, is an interface that is operated habitually and automatically that will not take away from human attention, and is also easy to learn and use. The research model proposed below takes into account the six factors that affect user interface, especially on the World Wide Web.

Interface Research Model

The major problem with many of the existing user interface models (Foley and van Dam, 1982; Card, Moran and Newell, 1983; Shneiderman, 1998) is that the focus is placed more on the system and not on the user. A new model as proposed here places greater emphasis on the user from a human interaction perspective.

The goal of this chapter is to discuss the factors that affect interface design on the World Wide Web, including the human interaction aspects that focus on the user (see Figure 3). However, the scope of the design is not limited, like in many studies, to the internal structure of the Web site design, but rather extends to the external factors (in addition to internal ones) that impact the design process. This is a macro-level approach rather than the limited micro-level approach that deals with objects and menus, which are still discussed in the chapter. It is the designer's responsibility to balance the design trade-offs and priorities of the Web site for optimum effect. For example, media richness of the site would be costly to add all the various multimedia and 3D effects so that customers could "experience a product" online by rotating it and viewing from different angles. However, a company like Black and Decker may not see cost as a priority as much as advertising its product line very well.

Figure 3: The research model of factors affecting the user interface

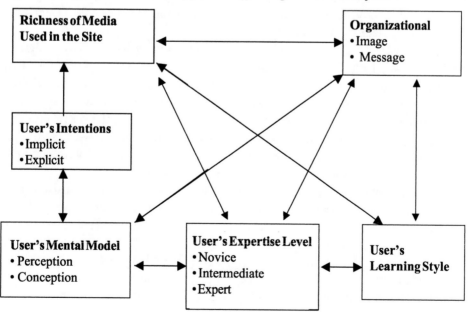

Factor 2: Level of Expertise of the User

Users respond differently to computer systems depending on their level of expertise and knowledge with computers (Hamlin, 1991). Users can be classified as novices with limited knowledge of the application and the domain of the system, or as experts with greater experience of the application and the domain of the system. Intermediate users would fall in the middle. Gillan et al. (1995) looked at how experts and novices interpret interface metaphors. They found that experts rely more on abstraction while novices rely more on the physical characteristics that are more concrete.

Ratner looked at novices' learning curve and found out that novices may not be able to distinguish the document on the Internet from the interface (Ratner, 1998). Using more concrete elements on a Web browser, like navigation buttons, would make it easier for novices since they need less abstraction. Since novices may get overwhelmed with many tasks, the interface must be simple, broken down into simpler subtasks; on the other hand, experts prefer faster response time and the ability to do multiple tasks simultaneously (Shneiderman, 1998).

Factor 3: User's Learning Style

Davis and Bostrom (1993) determined that learning style has an impact on how users learn and interact with the user interface. They discussed two types of learning according to Assimilation Theory: meaningful learning and rote learning (or memorization). Meaningful learning occurs when new knowledge is connected to existing information in a meaningful way to be applied to new situations and concepts. On the contrary, rote learning links old and new information in an arbitrary way, whereby memorization of new knowledge does not relate old and new knowledge in a new meaningful way. The learning style will affect how novice (versus expert) users learn and adapt to a new interface, and how they deal with its functionality.

Other learning theories, such as Kolb's learning style theory (as cited in Bostrom et al., 1990) classify learning style into a four-stage cycle across two modes: active experimenters (actives) and reflective observers (reflective). Kolb's cycle moves from concrete experience to reflective observation to formation of abstract concepts to testing hypotheses through active experimentation, resulting in four learning styles: diverger, assimilator, converger and accommodator. Here there is a parallel to how novice and expert users differ: novices start with concrete concepts and progress to abstract ideas as they become experts.

Satzinger and Olfman (1998) conclude that interfaces should be consistent and that a distinct visual appearance would aid users at the early stages of learning new applications. Therefore, they linked how transfer of learning would enhance a user's ability to work with a new interface or an exiting interface with new additional features. Transfer of learning refers to having knowledge of one application transferred to another application. For example, learning Microsoft Word would make it easier to learn PowerPoint since they share a common "look and feel."

Factor 4: Richness of the Media Used

Multimedia plays an important role in the design of a Web site since it adds interactivity. Eighmey (1997) determined that entertainment value is the main factor for a user's perception of a Web site. He also stated that users tend to favor sites that are exciting and interesting and would tend to visit them more often over poorly designed and uninteresting sites. It is not surprising then that according to media richness theory (Daft and Lengel, 1986), the richer or more varied the medium of communication, the richer the capabilities of information. For example, using hypermedia (audio, video and text) is an improvement over using just hypertext (plain text) to display information on a Web site.

Palmer and Griffith (1998) support the use of rich media with Web sites that provide information-intensive products and services. Information-intensive products and services include those provided by such companies like insurance firms, which require the firm and in turn its Web site to provide as much information as possible to assist the consumer in making a purchase decision. This allows customers to almost "test the products" online. For example, sites like Carpoint (www.carpoint.msn.com/gallery), a Microsoft site that sells cars online, and Sharperimage.com utilize 3-D graphics and animation so that consumers could "experience" products by viewing them from different angles by rotating them. Capabilities such as zooming in and out also allow customers to view the products from the inside, getting a closer look, such as purchasing a house online, using a company and its Web site like bamboo.com.

Factor 5: Organizational Image and Message

Organizational image should play a role in the design of the user interface. For example, a theme park like Six Flags (www.sixflags.com) would have a more playful and fun Web site and image than the CIA's more serious and informative Web site (www.cia.gov). A designer would need to take this into account in developing the site so that text, sound, animation, etc., are consistent with the company's image.

Eighmey states that metaphors "create a personality and inviting sense of place that is consistent with the company and its missions" (Eighmey, 1997, p. 64), and they clearly affect the user's perception and conception because the site is both attracting (conception) and attractive (perception). From the previous discussion, in our section 'Perception and Conception' explicating the user's conception, we can now appreciate that it is not only user perception that is affected, but also the more powerful capacity of user conception. In this case, user conception triggers the user's imagination to respond to that which is attracting because it was perceived, initially (prior to the shift to conception) to be attractive.

Another factor linked to the organization is the message. The message refers to the purpose or goal of the site. For example, an informative site, like the Texas A&M library homepage (http://library.tamu.edu), would tend to have different design characteristics from a commercial site, like eBay.com. Greater use of multimedia and interaction to sell a product or service would justify the added cost of these features since the business is trying to advertise products and attract and keep customers, a characteristic of a site called "stickiness." Yahoo and Excite (www.excite.com) have transformed their sites from search engines into portals with free services like email and personal homepages to attract customers.

Shneiderman (1998) stated there are two ways to classify sites based on message: top-level domain names and goals. Top-level domain names would indicate that a site is a commercial one (.com), an educational institute (.edu), a non-profit organization (.org), etc. The second way is to classify a site by its goal (see Table 2). A commercial site would be more eye catching in comparison with a site designed for non-profit purposes or one that is created for informative reasons.

Factor 6: Intentions of the User

In the chapter leading up to this point, much has been said about the flexibility of the user and degrees of inflexibility of the system. Harding (1995, p. 2), in relation to an explication of the "mechanology" of Gilbert Simondon, made the point in this context that "it is the object that creates the environment and not the other way around." In a very important sense, objects on the screen in the hands of the interface designer "create their own environment," but when the notion of user conception is considered we can see that what is conceived—because it becomes an idea—creates its own context (Haynes and Mahfouz, 2001 p. 35).

The attention of the user is largely based on the intention of the user. In terms of the intention of the user, we are going to distinguish between implicit (future) intentions and explicit (current) intentions of the user. We have presented the view (Haynes and Mahfouz, 2001 p. 36) that at the turn of the twenty-first century, it is generally well accepted that human beings have an unconscious or sub-conscious mind. What is also generally accepted is that interactions by human beings take place at two levels: (1) the unconscious or higher self, and (2) the conscious self. The current or explicit intentions of the user derive from the conscious self, whereas the likely or future implicit intentions are a product of the unconscious self. Thus conversations between one or more humans often take place on these two levels simultaneously, where something is said that may appear consciously to be unusual, if not paradoxical (Ascher, 1989). But to (at least) the unconscious self (or selves),

Table 2: Goals of Web sites (Shneiderman, 1998)

Goal	Organization
Sell products and services	Publishers, hotels, retail stores
Market products and services	Insurance companies, car dealers
Inform	Colleges, art galleries
Give access	Libraries, magazines
Provide services	Governments, public utilities
Discuss topics	Public interest groups, newsgroups
Care for community	Political groups, professional associations

if it is a genuine 'dual' conversation, it makes perfect sense. Of importance for this chapter is that the unconscious self is future-oriented, or more precisely: "Jung claims that the reason dreams [one of the 'expressions' of the unconscious] can occasionally be taken as a basis of prediction is that they express tendencies that are still only latent in the unconscious in advance of the time that they can be brought overtly into consciousness" (Progoff, 1953, p. 138). Clearly then, the task for interface design is to tap into the implicit unconscious intentions of the user, because these are the driving forces for future actions. In this respect interface design needs to apply itself to future orientations (see next section).

FUTURE TRENDS

Since online shopping lacks some of the aspects of shopping in a retail store such as experiencing the product physically, there is a need to incorporate as many of the user's five senses in an online shopping experience to bring that experience to life. The focus behind the research model proposed in this chapter is on the user, and consequently on the user's senses. A well-designed interface for a Web site that invokes many of the user's senses allows customers to experience products and services as close to the physical experience as possible.

For example, to include the sense of smell in the interface design, some companies, such as DigiScents (www.digiscents.com), have already developed fragrance cartridges that would be installed on computers and release odors depending on items shown on the screen. The Web site sends a message to the computer's chip to release the appropriate smell. A customer can experience the smell of a perfume or a grocery item. Other senses such as touch have allowed for tactile-based interaction with a Web site. With virtual reality, a user is fitted with attachments on the fingers that allow for feeling the softness of a piece of fabric or any other items intended for purchase. Better 3D interactive media as discussed earlier allows for greater emphasis on visual stimulation.

Also, the interface needs to have artificial intelligence capabilities that allows a "smart interaction" with the user, such as the case with adaptive hypermedia systems and conversational user interfaces. These future advances in interface design would do away with the keyboard and mouse with better advances in speech recognition and natural language processing, resulting in "smart interfaces" (Raskin, 1997). Finally, Internet interface design must go hand in hand with global strategies, such that when the future changes the global product, the interface must also change (Jeannet, 2000).

CONCLUSION

A physically perceived visit to a retail store is a perceived participation with actual objects and differs in this specific way from a visit to a Web site. Accordingly, a Web site must have a well-designed interface so that consumers can experience, not only as a perception but also as a conception, the products and services online.

Internal and external factors that affect Web site design were examined in this chapter. These six factors are the user's mental model, level of expertise of the user, the user's learning style, richness of the media used, the organizational image and message, and the user's intentions. A user's mental model will affect the user's online experience, and the online experience is a product of the user's perception and the user's conception. We have argued that the domain of user perception is no longer all encompassing enough for a user interface design to address itself to. The interface design must also consider user conceptions, because conceptions are future oriented. When we consider the notion of user intentions more deeply, we discover both conscious (explicit) current intentions and unconscious (implicit) future intentions. The future intentions of the user are clearly the driving forces of future user actions that the Web page design needs to focus upon. How a user learns an application and interacts with the interface will also need to be provided for as a design consideration. The richness of the media of a Web site, which would go hand-in-hand with the organization's image and message, is also a critical factor that interface designers must take into account in developing their Web sites.

REFERENCES

Ascher, L. M. (Ed.). (1989). *Therapeutic Paradox*. London, UK and New York, USA: The Guilford Press.

Ashcraft, M. H. (1994). *Human Memory and Cognition*. New York: Harper Collins College Publishers.

Barki, H. and Hartwick, J. (1994). Measuring user participation, user involvement and user attitude. *MIS Quarterly*, 18(1), 59-82.

Bostrom, R. P., Olfman, L. and Sein, M. K. (1990). The importance of leaning style in end-user training. *MIS Quarterly*, 14(1), 101-119.

Card, S., Moran, T. and Newell, A. (1983). *The Psychology of Human-Computer Interaction*. NJ: Lawrence Erlbuam Associates.

Daft, R. L. and Lengel, R. H. (1986). A proposed integration among organizational information requirements, media richness and structural design. *Management Science*, 32, 554-571.

Davis, S. A. and Bostrom, R. (1993). Training end users: An experimental investigation of the roles of computer interface training methods. *MIS Quarterly*, 17(1), 61-85.

Eighmey, J. (1997). Profiling user responses to commercial Web sites. *Journal of Advertising Research*, 37(3), 59-66.

Fellenstein, C. and Wood, R. (2000). *Exploring E-Commerce, Global E-Business and E-Societies*. Upper Saddle River, NJ: Prentice Hall PTR.

Foley, J. and van Dam, A. (1982). *Fundamentals of Interactive Computer Graphics*. Reading, MA: Addison-Wesley.

Gerlach, J. H. and Kuo, F. (1991). Understanding human-computer interaction for information systems design. *MIS Quarterly*, 15(4), 526-549.

Gillan, D. J., Fogas, B. S., Aberasturi, S. and Richards, S. (1995). Cognitive ability and computing experience influence interpretation of computer metaphors. *Proceedings of the Human Factors and Ergonomics Society 39th Annual Meeting*, 243-247.

Grudin, J. (1989). The case against user interface consistency. *Communications of the ACM*, 32(10), 1164-1173.

GVU's 8th WWW User Surveys. (1997). Available on the World Wide Web at: http://www.gvu.gatech.edu/use r_surveys/survey-1997-10/.

Hamlin, M. (1991). *Knowledge and Skill Components of Expert and Novice Software Users*. Washington: University of Washington.

Harding, A. (1995). *The Melancholy of Technology, Tekhnema 2 / "Technics and Finitude,"* Spring. Available on the World Wide Web at: http://tekhnema.free.fr/contents2.html.

Hardy, J. (1987). *A Psychology with a Soul: Psychosynthesis in Evolutionary Context*. London UK: Arkana, published by the Penguin Group.

Haynes, J. D. (1999). Practical and tacit knowing as a foundation of information systems. *Australian Journal of Information Systems*, May, 6(2), 57-64.

Haynes, J. D. (2000). *Perspectival Thinking: For Inquiring Organizations*. New Zealand: ThisOne and Company Limited.

Haynes, J. D. (2001). Churchman's Hegelian inquiring organizations and perspectival thinking. *Journal of Information Systems Frontiers*, 3(1), 29-39. The Netherlands: Kluwer Academic Publishers.

Haynes, J. D. and Mahfouz, A. (2001). Objects that create their own context: The inclusion of conception in the mental model of the user. In Kemp, Phillips, Kinshuk and Haynes (Eds.), *Proceedings of the Symposium on Computer Human Interaction,* 33-36. Palmerston North, New Zealand: Massey University Printery.

Idhe, D. (1991). Technology and the lifeworld. In Dunphy and Bilimoria (Eds.), *Proceedings of the 1990 Conference of the Australian Association for Phenomenology and Social Philosophy: Hermeneutics, Phenomenology and Technology*, 125-138. Victoria, Australia: Deakin University Press.

Jeannet, J. P. (2000). *Managing with a Global Mindset*. Great Britian: Pearson Educational Limited.

Kannan, P. K., Chang, A. and Whinston, A. B. (1998). Marketing information on the I-way. *Communications of the ACM*, 41(3), 35-43.

Kendall, J. E. and Kendall, K. E. (1993). Metaphors and methodologies: Living beyond the systems machine. *MIS Quarterly*, 17(2), 149-171.

Lohse, G. L. and Spiller, P. (1998). Electronic shopping: How do customer interfaces produce sales on the Internet. *Communications of the ACM*, 41(7), 81-87.

Maani, K. E. and Cavana, R.Y. (2000). *Systems Thinking and Modeling: Understanding Change and Complexity*. New Zealand: Prentice Hall, imprint of Pearson Education New Zealand Limited.

Madsen, K. H. (1994). A guide to metaphorical design. *Communications of the ACM*, 37(12), 57-62.

Mayhew, D. J. (1992). *Principles and Guidelines in Software User Interface Design*. Engelwood Cliffs, NJ: Prentice Hall.

Ngwenyama, O. K. and Allen, A. S. (1997). Communication richness in electronic mail: Critical social theory and the contextuality of meaning. *MIS Quarterly*, 21(2), 145-167.

Palmer, J. W. and Griffith, D. A. (1998). An emerging model of Web site design for marketing. *Communications of the ACM*, 41(3), 44-51.

Parons, J. J. and Oja, D. (1998). *Computer Concepts*. Cambridge, MA: Course Technology.

Progoff, I. (1953). *Jung's Psychology and its Social Meaning*. London UK: Routledge and Kegan Paul Ltd.

Raksin, J. (1997). Looking for a humane interface: Will computers ever become easy to use? *Communications of the ACM*, 40(2), 81-101.

Ratner, J. P. (1998). Easing the learning curve of novice Web users. In Forsythe, C., Grose, E. and Ratner, J. (Eds.), *Human Factors and Web Development*, 111-118. Mahwah, NJ: Lawrence Erlbaum Associates.

Satzinger, J. W. and Olfman, L. (1998). User interface consistency across end-user applications: The effects on mental models. *Journal of Management Information Systems*, 14(4), 167-193.

Shneiderman, B. (1998). *Designing the User Interface: Strategies for Effective Human-Computer Interaction*. Reading, MA: Addison-Wesley.

Tractinsky, N. and Meyer, J. (1999). Chartjunk or goldgraph? Effects of presentation objectives and content desirability on information presentation. *MIS Quarterly*, 23(3).

Tufte, E. (1997). *Visual Explanations*. Cheshire, CT: Graphics Press.

Chapter IV

Electronic Commerce (EC) Tools in Context: What Are the Implications for Global Electronic Commerce?

Deborah Bunker
University of New South Wales, Australia

INTRODUCTION

This chapter proposes the idea of electronic commerce (EC) systems as tools that are created within a given context. The implications of this view are discussed regarding implementation of these tools in the business-to-consumer marketplace (B2C) and their impact on consumer activities and B2C processes.

It is argued that EC systems by definition, are artefacts, tools that are made, used, inherited and studied within a cultural context. This context encompasses economic, historical, technical and social values and assumptions that are focused on particular ideas and definitions relating to B2C activities and processes. It is assumed that these ideas and definitions are mostly in evidence in any culture that applies EC systems tools for use. The issue we must face as makers, users, inheritors and scholars of EC tools, however, is that the tool context and inherent in-built values on which this context is based, particularly relating to matters of effective use of EC tools in a B2C marketplace, may not be evident across all cultures. This would make the successful use of EC, in a global sense, a difficult and complex undertaking.

This chapter explains the ramifications of EC tools created within a particular context on global EC systems transfer and diffusion using electronic grocery shopping (EGS) systems as an example of a B2C tool. The problems and issues surrounding EGS transfer and diffusion in B2C relationships, on a global scale, are discussed and implications are highlighted. This chapter then suggests issues for further consideration by organizations considering the implementation of such systems.

INFORMATION TECHNOLOGY AND SYSTEMS TRANSFER AND DIFFUSION

The information technology and systems (ITSs) discipline and its more recent incarnation in various forms of electronic commerce (EC) tools and approaches is a predominantly Western phenomenon. From its earliest development to the personal computers (PCs) and supercomputers of the 1980s and '90s and the more recent Internet revolution, the ITS discipline has been dominated by and has dominated Western business approaches (Clark and Staunton, 1989; Amor, 2000; Philipson, 2001).

We know that ITSs are used by approximately 20% of the world's population (Elliot, 1999). As a percentage of the global population, this is not very high, but as the cost of ITS decreases and Internet infrastructure becomes more widely implemented, we are told that more people and diverse cultures will have access to ITS. We are also currently witnessing the rapid globalization of national economies and ITS is seen as a major driver of this process (Larsen and Levine, 1998). The Internet has grown very quickly from the early 1990s when there were 100,000 computers online. There were more than 150 million users online by 1999 and this almost doubled in 2000 to 275.54 million users. It is expected that this number will rise to 700 million by the end of 2001 (Denny, 1999; Nua Internet Surveys, 2000). Underpinning the uptake of ITS, especially in the West, is the assumption that the rest of the world sees the effectiveness and usefulness of the technology in the same light. It is clear that the Internet is now an online marketplace with the ability to facilitate the B2C transactions of a large and growing online population, at least in Western economies.

With the push for globalization, however, comes an increasing disparity between rich and poor nations so that ITSs on the most rudimentary level are still out of reach of many nations and cultures. In the U.S. a personal computer costs approximately one month's income whereas in Bangladesh it costs more that eight years' income (Elliot, 1999). In terms of basic telecommunications infrastructure, countries like Tanzania have only three telephone lines to every 1,000 people. Even with ITSs and telecommunications infrastructure in place, literacy and basic computing skills in poorer nations are considered to be a major factor in exclusion from the global economy (Denny, 1999). The new age of globalisation, where information is shared and ITSs has a significant impact in the world marketplace, would appear to be only taking place where there is a similar cultural, historical and economic context of development. It is the development context which facilitates the building of these ITS tools as well as their transfer and use within other contexts. The context of ITS tool creation, use, inheritance and knowledge may, therefore, be a limiting factor in its potential usefulness and applicability on a global scale.

The disciplinary model of Bunker and Dean (1997) deals with the creation, use, inheritance and study of tools within a given context and so would seem an appropriate starting point for the examination of these issues. The cultural context of tool creation encompasses the economic, historical, technical and social elements which all affect the way in which an ITS tool is created, transferred and diffused.

The tool Maker creates the tool. The tool User uses the tool for the advancement of practice and theory. The Scholar studies both the tool Maker and User and attempts to understand the domain of knowledge and skills that enhances both of these roles. The Inheritor learns from the creation, use and understanding of the tool and also understands the skills associated with the use of the tool. Each of these roles can be discrete in nature or combined in an individual. These four roles interact within a context that encompasses and reflects cultural factors that influence the way the tool is being built, used, studied or understood. The economic, historical, technical and social values within the culture are expressed in the required skill sets for tool making, use, inheritance and scholarly activities.

Figure 1: The disciplinary model (Bunker and Dean, 1997)

Cultural Context (economic, historical, technical and social – focussed in skill sets for tool-making, use, inheritance and scholarly activities)

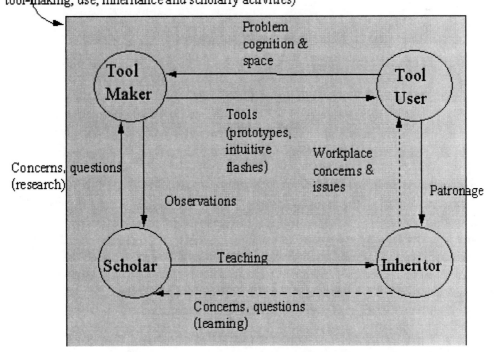

In focusing on the contextual elements of this model, a clear picture of Western contextual dominance of ITS tools emerges. Clark and Staunton (1989) also elaborate on the influence of Western context in the growth, transfer and diffusion of computing technology in the U.S., UK, Europe and Japan.

The Colonial Nature of Technology Transfer

It would thus seem essential to have a basic understanding of context that underpins technology transfer, diffusion and implementation. This is required in order to understand how the dominance of Western ideas in the creation and use of ITS (and more specifically EC systems) might affect its transfer and diffusion in non-Western business and cultures. Technology is defined by Robinson (1988) as being licensed or documented artefacts (equipment, software and conceptual models and tools), and the skills and ability to successfully use them, and is at the heart of the values and assumptions which underpin the context of ITS transfer and use. "Licensed and documented artefacts" are created within a specific context and which their creator can then transfer and diffuse (for a price) within new and sometimes radically different contexts. Resman and Zhao (1991) describe technology transfer as the shift or " tools, techniques, procedures and/or the legal titles" to accomplish a human purpose. These definitions assume a certain cultural context of technology transfer that encompasses Western ideas of technology licensing and copyright as well as the ability and right to "own" technology.

The literature, in general, is also characterized by a "colonial" attitude and use of language, towards the transfer and diffusion of various technologies. In McMaster's (2001) analysis of the diffusion literature, he summarizes these attitudes in a diffusion/colonization model. Those groups or individuals that innovate are described as exhibiting characteristics of: inventiveness; rationality; abstract thought; theoretical reasoning; mind; discipline; adulthood; sanity; science and progress. Those that are recipients of technology are described as exhibiting characteristics of: imitativeness; irrationality (emotion/instinct); concrete thought; empirical (practical) reasoning; spontaneity; childhood; insanity; sorcery and stagnation. It would seem that those groups or individuals who are technological innovators are seen in a more positive and enlightened way. The creators of the technology have a certain "moral" high ground which gives them an advantage in selling the benefits of the tool to the recipient. It is also obvious that the dominant mode of publication, scholarship and knowledge dissemination regarding ITS tools and approaches is by means of English language. For example, the International Conference on Information Systems (ICIS), the International Federation of Information Processing (IFIP) and other major IS journals such as *MIS Quarterly* are the major outlets for ITS ideas and innovations. The activity of technological innovation, transfer and diffusion is dominated by this cultural context which effectively forms a barrier to other cultural views and debate.

Headrick (1981) describes how technologies such as steamboats, guns and railroads facilitated European imperialism and colonialism through domination and conquest rather than technology transfer and diffusion. These technologies were sometimes modified at a local level, but the initial impact on the recipient societies was highly disruptive and necessitated wholesale changes to cultural values and standards of living, for example the North American Native, Middle Eastern and Chinese populations had their cultures radically impacted by these technologies. In understanding how these types of technologies impacted recipient populations, we can see potential impact of ITS which are under-pinned by Western cultural values and assumptions on non-Western cultures and societies.

The cultural context in which tools and artefacts are developed becomes an important factor for consideration as the tool, which is shaped by its culture, is not only used within that culture but also through the technology transfer process to other cultures. Culture as a way of seeing the world is expressed through various manifestations of structure (social and business), language, skills and behavior (Kluckhorn and Strodtbeck, 1976; Hofstede, 1980, 1998; Schein, 1984).

As ITSs fall into a general category of tools and artefacts, it is necessary for us to understand how ITSs are created, utilized, studied and inherited successfully (Bunker and Dean, 1997). An understanding of the process and role of tool creation and use within various cultural contexts, and whether it is possible (or desirable) in all cases to transfer or force the transfer of ITS from one culture to another, is also important. If we scrutinise World Bank-supported dam projects, the transfer and use of technology which stands to benefit millions of people by way of increased agricultural production and availability of clean and regular water and power supplies is soon revealed. This situation, however, also reveals disenfranchised and displaced local populations and the decimation of social systems that have been in place for centuries (World Bank Group, 2000; Whirled Bank Group, 2000). The transfer and implementation of this technology has been positive and beneficial but gives little understanding, satisfaction or comfort to the millions of people who have had their social, historical, economic and technical traditions irrevocably changed. So too, we can see the effect of ITS on the social, historical, economic and technical traditions of the cultures which have come into contact with them.

If we consider the problems associated with packaged software to be implemented in many different organizations and cultures, it is obvious that some of these problems emerge. Consider the current state of Enterprise Resource Planning (ERP) systems and the major problems of systems failures for many organizations. Are we dealing here with a simple business process problem or is the context in which the tool was created having a significant effect on the transfer and diffusion of the system (Bunker, 2000; Boyd and Connors, 2001)?

It is the contention of this chapter that the context of ITS tool creation, use, inheritance and knowledge (typically Western in nature) limits the effective transfer, diffusion and use of these tools (specifically electronic commerce electronic grocery systems) to more divergent cultural contexts.

The definitions within the technology transfer literature are an expression of cultural context and the underlying values and assumptions on which ITS tools and technologies are created, used, inherited and studied. This literature seems to be more concerned with technology business value rather than technology cultural values in the transfer process. This of course would limit any effective understanding, or true diffusion and adaptation of any technology under scrutiny.

ELECTRONIC COMMERCE (EC) TOOLS IN CONTEXT—THE ELECTRONIC GROCERY SHOPPING (EGS) EXAMPLE

The Internet has played a key role in the establishment of EC activities (especially in B2C relationships) and EGS systems have been dependent on the development of Internet technologies and their uptake speed and scale by potential consumers. Consumers in the West have begun to demand increases in the quality of service being offered by their grocery provider. Shoppers want a product selection adapted to their needs and the ability to shop at their convenience.

"The Internet allows 24-hour access from a PC..., consumers can visit their favorite stores whenever they want to." (Choudrie et al., 1998).

The introduction of the Internet and the development of EGS systems have allowed consumers to shop at their convenience rather than being bound to retail outlet trading times. The subsequent growth of the Internet and the increasing demand for value-added grocery shopping has created demand-pull for EGS services. Consumer demand for EGS services, combined with supplier demands for shopper profile information, has created a large uptake of EGS systems from a business and consumer perspective.

As discussed earlier in the chapter, however, we have also seen the need for contextual value or cultural compatibility between the creator and the recipient of a technology in order for the technology to be transferred and utilized successfully. A certain level of cultural homogeneity is necessary in order for the tools and artefacts of one culture to be successfully utilized within another (Bunker, 1998). EGS systems utilize the tools and artefacts of ITS which have been created from a predominantly Western and particularly North American cultural viewpoint (Simon and Doran, 1998). This viewpoint assumes that the shopping culture of the consumer accepts multiple distribution channels for consumer items, but it neglects resources and skills required by the consumer to best utilize these multiple channels, as well as any essential social activity associated with the shopping task and associated processes. These types of systems may be acceptable in a culture that has had a history and experience (and thus development of suitable associated technology and skills) of multiple purchase and distribution channels in B2C transactions such as the retail, catalogue and home-shopping B2C channels of the North America marketplace. We can see that EGS systems, in their current form, generally assume (Pereira, 1998; Heikkila et al 1998; Brandtweiner, 1998; Strader and Hendrickson, 1998):

- Computer ownership or access
- Internet access (Internet service providers as well as reliable and secure telecommunications infrastructure)

- Basic computing skills
- Product and outlet brand awareness (knowing exactly what you want and who you want it from)
- Product quality awareness (where it is manufactured and which company manufactures it)
- Basic purchasing strategies (little opportunity for special savings)
- Particular lifestyle benefits to consumers in terms of time savings, convenience and prestige of using EGS systems
- Acceptance of additional distribution costs to the purchase decision
- Population density for overall cost effectiveness of storage and distribution for the e-business
- A limited range of goods
- A "type" of customer behaviour (pattern buying, rational purchase decision and utility)
- A trust in the security and reliability of the system

A certain lifestyle, skill set and access to resources is assumed and the more 'social' element of the shopping experience is missing. Diverse cultural dimensions are not expressed within the definition of the tool.

In viewing EGS systems as tools or artefacts which have been created with in-built values and assumptions, then the cultural context of the user of an EGS system is important in understanding how these systems might be best implemented and utilized (Simon and Doran, 1998). Young (1971), in his "Introduction to the Study of Man," states that there are more than technical attributes of tools to consider when building, utilizing, transferring and diffusing technology. In fact many of the tool creator's values are represented by the technology. Johnson (1997) also discusses four types of value meanings in technology. These are: moral/metaphysical (past intended use of the technology), support (present intended use of the technology), material (in-built characteristics which influence the use of the technology) and expressive values (motivation for use of the technology), all of which contribute to the assumed skill sets required to utilize the technology. It is these expressive values that encapsulate the more diverse elements of the shopping experience within many non-Western cultural contexts. Value meanings link back to the definitions of tools as outlined by Young (1971). Tool making is not only technical in nature but is bound by cultural values and an understanding of how the tool has been created for use in an acceptable manner. This understanding reflects a certain level and mixture of skills, and Ayres (1978), in discussing his ideas on the theory of economic progress of civilization states, that the:

> "...*absolute mutual contingency of skills and tools is of supreme importance for an understanding of technology as a function of human behaviour.*"

Skills and technology are bound together as technology is created and used as a result of an assumed skill set which is heavily influenced by core assumptions and values (culture). It is evident that EGS systems (in their current state) assume limited technical and purchase decision skills within a culture and the B2C experience, while totally neglecting social skills and their importance.

EGS systems are engendered with the cultural attributes of Western society (Pargman, 1998). For non-Western cultures which may have different resource availability and different social marketplaces, these systems may not be as effective as more traditional means of transacting business. Many non-Western cultures, for instance, are considered "developing" economies, a value-ladened term to be sure, which is generally used to describe a local village-based economic structure. These economies are reliant on intricate social interactions and customs to ensure effective B2C trading relationships and the maintenance of a robust local economy. If you have ever visited a local marketplace in China or Egypt, (and elsewhere) you are able to see these relationships in action and their effect in a B2C transaction. The utility and logistical benefits associated with EGS systems may be of limited benefit to the types of economic structures where personal interaction is important, as they are a product of a different cultural context and therefore may be better suited to a Western mass-market-style of B2C transaction.

Cultural differences can be expressed in a number of ways. Research conducted by Kluckhorn and Strodtbeck (1976) and Hofstede (1980, 1998) are typical examples of the different assumptions and values on which various cultures are based. There are distinctly different philosophical positions in particular extremes of culture. The skills required to design, make, understand and use tools would also be significantly different from one type of culture to another, as well as the languages we use to define and represent them. An EGS system that lacks consideration and design for a diverse resource base and social attributes of a shopping experience may not necessarily fit within the shopping experience of other cultures and contexts. For instance, in many cultures in a B2C transaction, the process of bargaining over a particular price for a product is an important ceremonial and symbolic act that reflects on a vendor and a customer's perception of intent within the B2C transaction process. This affects the understanding by the customer of the product quality, integrity of the vendor, product range, etc., and also affects the vendor's understanding of his/her potential customers, marketing strategies and range of services or product to offer. The nature of information gathering and the transaction process takes on a significantly richer meaning in this context which may not be facilitated or captured by an EGS system.

EGS SYSTEMS IN CONTEXT

"A tool, like an utterance, only reveals its meaning to those who can infer it by reconstructing it in their own context" (Oakley, 1957; Bronkowski, 1977).

The context of EGS system development has important ramifications. All tools have technical, proprietary, social, historical and adaptive characteristics. All of these elements may affect the implementation and use of EGS systems that have been created by one culture for use within another.

The Technical and Proprietary Nature of Tools

While a particular EGS system may represent certain technical values and assumptions in one context, it may mean something completely different or be meaningless in another. For instance, we might consider the 80% of the global population who do not have the required access and infrastructure (both technical and logistical) to successfully implement an EGS system. This lack of infrastructure is an important consideration in many parts of the world, where building and maintaining infrastructure becomes cost prohibitive. Underlying assumptions in the form of various ways of viewing the world, and organizing technically can erect a barrier to how the technology can be utilized successfully. If the infrastructure does not exist, then the ability to utilize the technology successfully becomes limited.

Consider the local marketplace focus of a "developing" economy. This focus has its own inherent effective infrastructure for B2C transactions but may not have the technical base on which to operate effective EGS systems. Vendors and consumers may not have access to appropriate technology and there may not be adequate telecommunications or transportation infrastructure in place. Redevelopment or refocusing of such an economy to provide access to technology and infrastructure for effective EGS systems operation may disrupt or destroy the local economic context and its associated activities. This may lead to the destruction or disruption of the original effective B2C relationships.

The Social and Historical Nature of Tools

When we view various tools and their uses from a technical perspective, we can also see by the vast differences in cultural paradigms, that tools are not only technical in nature and function, but must also fulfill a social role by reinforcing relationships within cultures and between cultures.

EGS systems are also tools that have the capacity to change the way that consumers do business. They can change relationships and their social and business context (Ambrose and Johnson, 1988). Consider the nature of trust in the business-to-consumer relationship. How can an EGS system deal with this issue within a cultural context where trust is based on a more personal definition of dealing face-to-face with a representative of a company? Many cultures develop trusted relationships by investing considerable time and effort in getting to know potential customers (or from the customer side, potential vendors). A beverage may be offered while negotiating a deal, or a gift may be offered by both customer and vendor in order to offer good faith in finalizing a deal. It is also interesting to note that trust is one of the key issues cited in many studies, that forms a major barrier to EC tool uptake and use (Ambrose and Johnson, 1998).

The idea of the electronic "shop front" on the World Wide Web, on which most EGS systems are based, also assumes the use of electronic commerce technologies and systems that are common to all participants in and recipients of these technologies. How do countries that are rich social and complex consumer cultures (while being technically resource poor) utilize such systems when it is their physical marketplaces where people gather, that are important venues for trading and bargaining?

The Adaptive Nature of Tools (and Culture)

The technology transfer literature covers the issue of "indigenization" of technology by a recipient culture, a process, which it is stressed, that takes time. A culture may either elect to use, or may have a particular technology thrust upon them for use. Robinson (1988) discusses the fact that many cultures utilize these technologies by either changing them to suit their value sets or by changing certain values within their cultures to better utilize the technology. The one major factor in the success of this "indigenization" process is the longer the time taken, the more successful the adaptation of the technology or values will be.

Johnson (1997) also discusses the idea that all technology has intractable and flexible properties. The intractable properties of technology are those that assume skills and technology use and require certain patterns, social relationships and organization. More flexible technology properties are compatible with more diverse patterns of social behaviour. Technology that is more flexible in nature, however, may also result in misuse or unintended use of that technology. Ultimately, our 'view of the world' or cultural paradigm affects our perception on such matters. Johnson's (1997) discussion of the intractable and flexible properties of technology is also relevant, as the successful indigenization of technology may also be a result of the intractable or flexible nature of the technology itself. In fact, Pargman (1998) states that:

> "Once a technology has been created, it is an open question how it will be adapted in a social setting. This is the reason why it is so difficult to predict the effects of different kinds of technology beyond the apparent effects on efficiency and cost that are often decisive when it comes to the initial decision of whether to invest in a technology or not." (Pargman, 1988, from Sproull and Keisler,1991)

He goes on to say that the initial "bottom-line" gains are traditionally the major area of focus for systems implementations and that this focus has little predictive value about social and societal effects of systems (Pargman, 1998). The very nature of adaptation, whether it be within the tool, the culture or both, makes the success and failure of a tool a difficult thing to predict. At present we have EGS systems that are being pushed in terms of benefits to organizations and their supply chains, but what of the consumer and their needs? EGS systems have the ability to influence the way we make purchasing decisions as well as the way we socialize as individuals and groups, but how can we predict what these effects might be? In destroying or disrupting traditional marketplace arrangements, will we be creating a future that has little to offer in the way of social infrastructure for a B2C transaction? We only need to consider the effect that operations research and supply chain management theories have had on Western marketplaces. The "richer" social marketplace (the corner store, the small shopping village) has now been replaced by vast retail and outlet malls. These are an attempt at a more efficient and effective shopping experience which leaves us to ponder the resulting traffic snarls, pollution and social isolation.

THE IMPLICATIONS FOR GLOBAL ELECTRONIC COMMERCE

So what are the issues that we need to consider? Are EC systems tools (both physical and conceptual) a product of a particular context? If we are to have successful global EC systems transfer (like EGS systems), with the advancement of the global economy, is it necessary for countries and cultures to develop similar features and methods of operation? Is this feasible? Is there to be a true transfer and diffusion of EC systems, or must the acceptance of this technology necessitate change to the recipient's context and culture in order to use these technologies and systems in a successful manner?

Johnson (1997) discusses whether the global information infrastructure (GII) is a democratic technology and draws the conclusion that there is:

"...an inseparability, and unalterable link, between a technology and the institutions, policies and actors that produced it."

Thus, we see that the recipient needs time to make adequate and applicable changes to reflect the context in which the technology is to operate (indigenization). There needs to be a change of cultural paradigm by the technology recipient where this can take place. There may also be instances where the technology cannot be transferred due to the intractable properties of the technology itself (Johnson, 1997). Straub (1994) concluded that the benefits of the technological innovation may not exceed the problems and issues associated with cultural change and difficult and prolonged adaptation of those technologies. To this end Young (1971) has also stressed how critical language is in terms of cultural definition, tool creation and meaning and use. We only need to consider the very different use of the English language between North America and other English-speaking countries to understand how these differences might impact the implementation and use of EC systems throughout the globe, especially where there are significant linguistic differences. EGS systems developed within North America may be based on different customer data models (e.g., what data you are allowed to use legally and morally to define a customer). These data models may render these systems either difficult or impossible to use in a country like Australia where acceptable practice might dictate different definitions even though the language is essentially the same.

The example of EGS systems shows us that they have built-in assumptions and attributes that may not necessarily facilitate or enhance other commercial cultures. Is the tool necessarily appropriate for the context? Any recipient culture would seem to necessitate at least some "indigenization" of an EGS tool if it is to be used successfully and become widely diffused among those consumers.

Rosenberg and Frischtak (1985) stress that the types of organizations that do well at technology transfer are those with high levels of indigenous technology development and a history of technology accumulation, in other words, a certain "cultural" attitude to, and experience with, technology and its use. Heath (1998) states that:

"...epistemologies as measured by belief systems or mindscapes also play an important part in the acceptance of technology."

This would seem to augur well for more economically developed countries and cultures which see themselves as part of the global economy and are able to accommodate the fast pace of global technology transfer. What about the more developing countries and those countries that do not subscribe to global technology transfer at all costs? Will they be allowed or indeed be able to utilize these types of EC technologies and systems to suit their individual circumstances or will they be forced to conform to the accepted "norm" of EC systems use and utilization? This line of argument draws our attention to the colonial nature of IT & S (Headrick, 1981; Porra, 1999; McMaster, 2000) and its potential to be used for the express purpose of changing and dominating the cultures and countries who utilize it within the global information economy. This also has severe implications for less developed, non-English-speaking countries as well. As Amor (2000) states:

"Politics will have to focus on regional and transnational issues in order to survive. The existing national state will not have a very bright future, if they do not adapt to the changing environment."

We are currently witnessing this political fallout in the worldwide protest movement against globalisation. The effects of global homogeneity and the use of ITS as a catalyst for the world economy are being scrutinized. Robinson (1988) also outlines some of the special situations that influence technological innovation in less developed countries. These include:

"...macroeconomic characteristics, such as the economic system (market versus planned economics), factor resource endowment (hence different prices), stage of economic development, interest rate, inflation rate, unemployment rate, etc.; microeconomic characteristics, such as the availability of entrepreneurial talent and capital, supply, demand and competitive characteristics of industry, acceptable organizational forms, regional and local demand, etc.; social and cultural characteristics, such as educational levels, religious beliefs, national aspirations, caste and class structure and traditions; and the political environment and the stability of government policies on industrialization."

All of these situations point to the necessity for a common worldview that closely aligns with the technology creator in order for the technology transfer to be successful. Bauer (1995) also outlines an interesting argument put forward in the diffusion literature. The literature deals with indigenization of ITS in order to make it more useful for the recipient, however the diffusion model would have us believe that indigenization is delaying the use of new and better technology. This literature hides a fruitful paradox in that any delays to diffusion are considered to be negative, but it is these delays that make diffusion possible at all.

Thus, we see that a recipient needs time and a similar worldview to make adequate and applicable changes to reflect the context in which the technology is to operate (indigenization). There needs to be a change of cultural paradigm by the technology recipient and there may also be instances where the technology cannot be transferred due to its intractable properties (Johnson, 1997).

Organizations that are looking to implement and use B2C EC technologies like EGS would do well to consider and answer the following questions in order to ascertain their suitability to the business-to-consumer relationship:

- Does the system require a change in the way that the organization relates to its customers?
- Do these changes enhance the B2C relationship? In what way?
- Do these changes undermine the B2C relationship? In what way?
- How important is the face-to-face aspect of the relationship with your customers?
- Do existing or potential customers have the where-with-all (technical access and skills) to use the system?
- Are existing or potential customers likely to do business with your company in this way?
- How do you currently gather and interpret information about your customers. Will an EGS system enhance this process?
- Does the system limit your company's ability (in terms of sales dimensions or barriers) to sell to an existing or potential customer?

The pace of globalization of economies and the resultant 'push' to use IT and EC to facilitate this process may not allow sufficient time for true global technology transfer to take place. Organizations must consider what impact these systems might have on the way that they relate to and interact with existing and potential customers and the contextual changes to these relationships that must be considered for their effective use.

If global ITS transfer and the push to EC is to be fully understood and facilitated, then further research is necessary. We must better understand the cultural context in which information technology and systems are created as well as the cultural context of potential users of these systems. In focusing our attention on these contextual issues, we may have to admit that some EC systems and technologies may not be appropriate for transfer under certain circumstances, or may have to be radically redeveloped to accommodate differences in context. The cultural context of ITS development plays an important part in the successful transfer and diffusion of EC systems like EGS. This chapter has looked at EGS systems as an example, and their potential impact on the global B2C marketplace.

REFERENCES

Ambrose, P .J. and Johnson, G. J. (1998). A trust-based model of buying behaviour in electronic retailing. *Proceedings of the 4th Association of Information Systems Conference*, August 14-16, Baltimore, Maryland, USA.

Amor, D. (2000). *The E-Business ®evolution*. PTR/PH.

Ayres, C. E. (1978). *The Theory of Economic Progress*. New Issues Press, Western Michigan University, Kalamazoo, Michigan.

Bauer, M. (1995). Towards a functional analysis of resistance. In Bauer, M. (Ed.), *Resistance to New Technology*. Cambridge University Press.

Boyd, T. and Connors, E. (2001). Software hard sell that didn't deliver. *The Australian Financial Review*, March 29.

Brantweiner. R. (1998). Risks and challenges for retailers: The value chain transformation–A European perspective. *Proceedings of the 4th Association of Information Systems Conference*, August 14-16, Baltimore, Maryland, USA.

Bronowski, J. (1977). *A Sense of the Future*. MIT Press.

Bunker, D. J. and Dean, R. G. (1997). Information systems as tools: Towards an information systems paradigmatic framework. *Philosophical Traditions in Information Systems-Challenges of an Interdisciplinary View*. Faculty of Commerce, Workshop University of Wollongong, July 10-11.

Bunker, D. J. (1998). A Philosophy of Information Technology and Systems (IT & S) as Tools: Tool Development Context, Associated Skills and the Global Technical Transfer (GTT) Process.. MIS–shaped or misshaped? Emerging issues in the new global arena. *Proceedings of IFIP WG 8.7 Working Conference*, Helsinki, Finland, 199-214.

Bunker, D. J. (2000). Enterprise resource planning (ERP) system tools: The context of their creation and use within the technology transfer process. In Chung, H. M. (Ed.), *Proceedings of the Americas Conference on Information Systems AMCIS 2000*, August 10-13, Long Beach, California, 1533-1536

Choudrie, J., Hlupic, V. and O'Keefe, B. (1998). A framework for using information technology within the grocery retail sector. *Electronic Commerce in the Information Society, 11th Bled Electronic Commerce Conference*, Bled Slovenia, June 8-10.

Clark, P. and Staunton, N. (1989). *Innovation in Technology and Organization*. Routledge.

DeLisi, P. S. (1990). Lessons from the steel axe: Culture, technology and organizational change. *Sloan Management Review*, Fall.

Denny, C. (1999). In cyberspace, no-one can hear you if you're not connected. *Sydney Morning Herald Good Weekend Magazine*, September.

Elliot, L. (1999). A new world disorder. *Sydney Morning Herald Good Weekend Magazine*, September.

Headrick, D. R. (1981). *The Tools of Empire*. Oxford University Press.

Heath, J. (1998). Cultural attitudes and technology. In Ess, C. and Sudweeks, F. (Eds.), *Proceedings of Cultural Attitudes Towards Communication and Technology '98*, University of Sydney, Australia.

Heikkila, J., Kallio, J., Saarinen, T. and Tuunainen, V.K. (1998). Analysis of expectations on electronic grocery shopping for potential customer segments. *AJIS Special Edition–Electronic Commerce*, November.

Hofstede, G. (1980). *Culture's Consequences: International Differences in Work Related Values*. Sage Publications.

Hofstede, G. (1998). Attitudes, values and organizational culture: Disentangling the concepts. *Organization Studies*, March.

Hongladarom, S.(1998). Global culture, local cultures and the Internet. In Ess, C. and Sudweeks, F. (Eds.), *Proceedings of Cultural Attitudes Towards Communication and Technology '98*, University of Sydney, Australia.

Johnson, D. G. (1997). Is the global information technology infrastructure a democratic technology? *Computers and Society*, September.

Kluckhohn, F. R. and Strodtbeck, F. L. (1961). *Variations in Value Orientations*. Evaston, IL: Row, Peterson.

Larsen, T. J. and Levine, L. (1998). Information technology at the turn of the millenium: Past, present and future trends. *Proceedings of the IFIP WG 8.2 and 8.6 Joint Working Conference on Information Systems: Current Issues and Future Changes*. Helsinki, Finland, December 10-13.

Lien, L. (1994). Transferring technologies from developed to developing industrial and commercial environments, from IFIP transactions diffusion, transfer and implementation of information technologies. In Levine, L. (Ed.), *Proceedings of the IFIP TC8 Working Conference on Diffusion, Transfer and Implementation of Information Technology*. Pittsburgh, PA, USA, 11-13 October, 1993.

Maitland, K. (1998). Global diffusion of interactive networks–The impact of culture. In Ess, C. and Sudweeks, F. (Eds.), *Proceedings of Cultural Attitudes Towards Communication and Technology '98*. University of Sydney, Australia.

McMaster, T. (2001). The illusion of diffusion in information systems research. In *IFIP TC8 WG8.6 Fourth Working Conference on Diffusing Software Product and Process Innovations*, April 7-10, Banff, Canada.

Morieux, Y. V. H. and Sutherland, E. (1988). The interaction between the use of information technology and organizational culture. *Behaviour and Information Technology*, 7(2).

Nua Internet Surveys. (2000). *How Many Online?* Available on the World Wide Web at: http://www.nua.ie/surveys/how_many_online/index.html.

Oakley, K. P. (1975). *Man the Tool-Maker (6th ed)*. Trustees of the British Museum (Natural History), London.

Oakley, K. P. (1957). Tools makyth man. *Antiquity*, 31.

Pargman, D. (1998). Reflections on cultural bias and adaptation. In Ess, C. and Sudweeks, F. (Eds.), *Proceedings of Cultural Attitudes Towards Communication and Technology '98*. University of Sydney, Australia.

Periera, R. E. (1998). Factors influencing consumer purchasing behavior in electronic commerce. *Proceedings of the 4th Association of Information Systems Conference*, August 14-16, Baltimore, Maryland, USA.

Philipson, G. (2001). Australia's Bright Future, *Sydney Morning Herald*, Tuesday, June 19.

Porra, J. (1999). Colonial systems. *Information Systems Research*, March, 10, 1.

Resman, A. and Zhao, L. (1991). *Journal of Technology Transfer*, Spring.

Rey, L. (1998). Attitudes towards technology and communication across the multiple cultures of Switzerland. In Ess, C. and Sudweeks, F. (Eds.), *Proceedings of Cultural Attitudes Towards Communication and Technology '98*, University of Sydney, Australia

Robinson, R. (1988). *The International Transfer of Technology: Issues, Theory and Practice*. Ballinger Publishing Co. (Harper and Row, Publishers Inc., Cambridge).

Rosenburg, N. and Frischtak, C.(1985) *International Technology Transfer: Concepts Measures and Comparisons*. New York: Praeger Publishers (CBS Educational and Professional Publishing).

Schein, E. H. (1984). Coming to a new awareness of organizational culture. *Sloan Management Review*, Winter.

Simon, S. J. and Doran, P. M. (1998). Global Web page design: Issues of culture and gender. *Proceedings of the 4th Association of Information Systems Conference*, August 14-16, Baltimore, Maryland, USA.

Strader, T. J. and Hendrickson, A. R. (1998). A framework for the analysis of electronic market success. *Proceedings of the 4th Association of Information Systems Conference*, August 14-16, Baltimore, Maryland, USA.

Straub, D. W. (1994). The effect of culture on IT diffusion: E-mail and fax in Japan and the U.S. *Information Systems Research*, 5(1).

World Bank Group. (2000). *Water Supply and Sanitation*. Available on the World Wide Web at: http://www.worldbank.org/html/fpd/water/. Accessed July 18, 2000.

Whirled Bank Group. (2000). *Dams and the World Bank*. Available on the World Wide Web at: http://www.whirledbank.org/environment/dams.html. Accessed July 18, 2000.

Young, J. Z. (1971). *An Introduction to the Study of Man*. Oxford: Clarendon Press.

Chapter V

International User Interfaces

Barry Jackson
Massey University, New Zealand

INTRODUCTION

The developing global information infrastructure (GII), together with strongly supported initiatives promoted by the World Trade Organization (WTO), is making it possible for electronic commerce to become a truly international activity. Quite clearly, in order to realize the potential of the Internet as a conduit for the development of an international marketplace, there will need to be changes to the current business and economic paradigms that underpin the working of successful offline businesses. In almost every country worldwide, new models of commercial interaction are being developed to support businesses and consumers so that they can fully participate in, and benefit from, the expanded marketplace.

However, to make a success of such an activity requires more than enthusiasm by the international trading community, or an appreciation of new online business and economic paradigms, or access to modern computer-based communications technology; it also requires customers to be able to navigate and use the interface with success and understanding. This means that the developer and owner of the system, in addition to having a knowledge of online business, must have a keen understanding of the cultural and language attributes of their customers.

In this chapter, the focus will be concerned partly with issues relating to the cultural interaction of the customer with the system, partly with the development of an international user interface, and partly with examining some of the technical problems relating to the design and implementation of multilingual interfaces.

International Users

The use of the Internet is no longer limited to English-speaking peoples. In fact, the percentage of users accessing the Internet using the English language has fallen below 50% (Table 1). Global Reach (2000), after gaining feedback from a number of informed sources, has concluded that the percentage of English-language users will fall below 35% by the year 2002. This prediction is based on the phenomenal increase in online users using Asian languages such as Chinese, Japanese and Korean. The growth of Internet users in China is due, in part, to the surge in computer sales and a drop in telephone and Internet access fees. Furthermore the number of Chinese Internet users is likely to increase further if China, as expected, joins the World Trade Organization.

A comparison of the total language population of each group and the level of Gross Domestic Product (GDP) each population generates is shown in Table 1. If an expansion of e-commerce leads to a growth in trade and services worldwide, then the percentage of Asian language users is likely to increase even further. This in turn could see an increase in the level of GDP for many poorer, yet highly populated countries. However, there are many opponents of the initiatives of the World Trade Organization (WTO) who reject this scenario, as a quick visit to the Internet's numerous discussion fora on this subject would attest.

Growth of Internationalization

The Web is becoming a multicultural and multilingual environment where many sites are becoming available in the native language of the audience. Many

Table 1: Global Internet statistics (Global Reach, 2000)

	Internet access (M)	% of on-line world population	Internet access in 2003 (M)	% of on-line world population	Total population	GDP	% of Total GDP
English	189.6	49.6	225.0	32.2	322.0	11070.0	35.2
European languages	113.8	29.8	223.0	31.9	1089.0	10550.0	33.6
Asian languages	78.6	20.6	250.0	35.8	1441.0	9824.0	31.2
Total	382.0	100.0	698.0	100.0	2852.0	31444.0	100.0
(1) English							
(2) European (excludes English)							.
(3) Asian (includes Arabic, Chinese, Hebrew, Japanese, Korean, Malay, Thai)							

Note: The figures in the second column correspond to the number of people online in each language in millions. There is some overlap between English and non-English figures since many people access the Web in two languages. (The 1990 U.S. Census states that 32 million American people who are online do not speak English at home.) The total population column refers to the total number of people in each language family.

business enterprises, large and small, have seen the potential of trading in goods and services to international customers. There are opportunities for English-speaking companies already involved in the global market to port their Web sites to a local market to improve penetration of their business. At first sight this might be seen as an easy thing to do, simply translate the site into the local language. However, it is now acknowledged that it is not that simple. When creating a localized site, it is necessary to cater for cultural and social differences as well as the language and technical perspective of the users. Evidence from the marketplace would suggest that this interest in internationalization and localization has not been supported by an increased usability of the Web environment for international 'business-to-business' (B2B) or 'business-to-customer' (B2C) users.

Globalization, Internationalization, Localization and Usability

When discussing the use of the Internet for online business and communication, a number of key terms are used, for example, globalisation, internationalization, localization and usability. These terms are frequently used interchangeably and this has led to confusion and uncertainty. The following is a set of definitions or explanations that are used in this chapter and which will, it is hoped, gain universal acceptance.

Globalization

Globalisation has two related yet distinct definitions and meanings:
1. The process by which social institutions and practices are adopted on a global scale.
2. The process by which a business or company begins to operate at the international level.

These two definitions focus on the nature of internationalization and raise the question, "Does internationalization require participating countries to adopt a 'universal' set of social and cultural practices?" The loss of social and cultural identity, particularly among non-English-speaking countries, is one reason why there is such opposition to the WTO free-trade proposals, and one good reason why every effort should be made to ensure that products and services, including Web interfaces, should be localized.

International Users and Customers

International clients are assumed to be from countries other than where the Web site was initially designed. For example, a resident of Australia who visits a United Kingdom Web site, which was designed by a team in the UK, would be described as an international user or customer.

Internationalization

Internationalization refers to the process of making a Web site culture independent or culture neutral. Essentially this involves removing cultural icons or eliminating the use of metaphors that might have inappropriate references for some native users. There are several schools of thought as to how internationalization of a Web site should occur. The process appears to be directly associated with the level of resources the company can devote to the project. Small to medium-sized enterprises (SMEs) with little or no experience with e-commerce are likely to first develop a site to meet the needs of existing customers, perhaps later internationalizing the site for a wider audience, and then attempting to localize the site for the international user when they have consolidated their position. Larger international organizations, with experience of Web site development, would probably consider localization issues from the outset.

Localization

Localization refers to the adaptation of the contents to the audience's culture. The process of localization is much more than simply translating the language component, a process with which it is commonly confused. It includes the modification of text (date, time and currency formats), graphics (color and shapes), audio and video components. For example, much of the user interface might need to be reworked to accommodate the longer translations that some languages require in the limited text area in media objects such as buttons and labels. In summary, some of the basic requirements of localizations are:

- Translation of text from one language to another.
- Changing sort order and cultural conventions (flags, dates currency, symbols).
- Maintaining a consistent look and feel of the product from one language to another.

Usability

Usability, or more importantly, usability engineering is a process that can be followed, when developing a system, to ensure that it can be used effectively and understandably by the expected user.

Usability interface engineering involves a number of elements. Nielson (1994) suggested that usability engineering in a general sense involves a number of attributes. Applying these traditional attributes to the user interface:

- The interface should be easy to learn. It should contain visual and navigational features, symbols and metaphors that have value and meaning to the user.
- The interface should be efficient to use which could, in turn, lead to improved productivity for the user. In particular, speed and time need to be critically addressed in a well-designed interface and Web site.
- Having an interface that requires minimal re-learning for casual users as they move from one version of a Web site to another is another desirable property.
- A user-friendly Web page is essential if users are to remain satisfied and return to the site in the future.
- Finally, the interface should have no errors or misleading information. In particular, there should be no missing links or media objects that are unable to load for a variety of reasons.

BUILDING AN INTERNATIONAL USER INTERFACE

Interface Development Life Cycle

Developing a Web site or a set of interfaces has to be in keeping with the broader corporate product development environment. Considerable resources are used to establish corporate and product identity, and it is important during interface development that the benefits of these identities are not lost or dissipated. Of course, it is assumed that these high level identities are, at the very least, internationalized and are acceptable within the target international community. If not then they will need to be modified.

To produce a quality Web site requires frequent input from potential users and any development process should involve prototyping and interactive development as well as a set of guidelines and user profiles against which the usability of the system can be evaluated. The need to ensure consistency across the entire range of media, which form the total user interface, is also imperative, as are issues relating to compatibility with future versions of the interface. Figure 1 shows the stages of the interface development lifecycle. The model is partly based on the published work by Nielsen on the "Usability Engineering Life Cycle Model" (1999) and Holt's "Developing a Cultural Model" (1996).

A: Analysis

A1: Develop a statement of purpose

The statement of purpose provides the developers with a clear understanding of the purpose of the Web site or interface: what the Web site is attempting to achieve and who is the target audience.

A2: Understand the users

A user can be one of a number of people: installers, maintainers, support staff in addition to the customers accessing the Web site through the interface. The analysis process involves a logical stream of enquiry resulting in a determination of the core primary tasks expected of users of the system and a cultural stream of enquiry. These streams of enquiry lead to the construction of Logical and Cultural Models.

A2.1 Logical Model: Logical stream of enquiry

The logical stream of enquiry gathers factual and observational data about the user. This would include a determination of the users' knowledge, skills, abilities and experience. Relevant task analysis and functional analysis might be undertaken by observing the user performing roles similar to the ones proposed.

The reading and language skills of the users are of significance, as are the users' work environment and work practices. Such information can be gathered from questionnaires but undoubtedly direct observation by trained localization experts is much preferred.

Task analysis, where the customers are observed using a comparable system, is very useful in gaining an insight into the problem domain and can provide a source

Figure 1: Interface development lifecycle

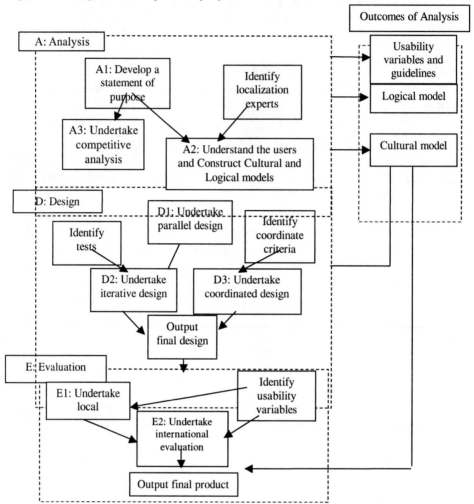

of metaphors and other hints on how improvements could be made to the system. Asking why and how questions of users is a feature of task analysis.

Carrying out a Functional Analysis could be very revealing for the analyst. For example, using a computer environment based on policies and procedures from another culture could cause the user to question the reasons why a particular set of tasks is carried out. However, there may be a justifiable reason why the local user needs to retain that function.

The logical stream of enquiry provides the developers with an understanding of the core needs of the user but are unlikely to address the wider cultural requirements. Nevertheless, much of what is learned about the user in this phase would be of considerable use in the evaluation phase of the development cycle.

Cultural Model: Cultural Stream of Enquiry

The cultural stream of enquiry examines the social and cultural issues that need to be addressed when designing interface to meet the localization requirements. A key outcome of this cultural enquiry is the cultural model. The cultural model is a comparison of two of more cultures using international variables. International variables are composed of categories of cultural data deemed to be relevant within the cultures under examination. The cultural data embedded in the international variables can be drawn from a wide spectrum of cultures: national cultures, corporate cultures, SMEs, work groups, gender and age groups.

On a more practical level, international variables can contain information about number systems, date systems, currency systems, writing and text systems. Less tangible data such as value systems, cultural systems, management and political systems will also be included.

The cultural model is a valuable resource for the systems developer. It:

- provides global information that can be used for developing the 'generic' international interface;
- identifies where cultural bias might be found in the user environment;
- suggests a set of possible cultural metaphors;
- indicates what localization factors need to be addressed;
- identifies possible criteria that could be used to measure the effectiveness of the Web site or interface.

Hoft (1996) suggests a series of steps that could be followed to create a cultural model. The following is a condensed version of her recommendations.

1. define the purpose of the model of culture;
2. gather data by applying an appropriate assessment method;
3. analyze the cultural data to identify international variables;
4. organize cultural data to develop cultural profiles of the user community;
5. Apply the cultural profiles or apply the cultural model to assess the product's design and usability.

The cultural stream of enquiry provides the developers with an understanding of the cultural needs of the users. The cultural model, cultural profiles and the associated international variables created in this phase would also be of considerable use in the evaluation phase of the development cycle.

Undertake Competitive Analysis

Analyzing existing sites of competitors is a form or prototyping. Users can learn how well competitors' sites function and interact with users. Such an analysis should provide an insight into possible usability characteristics and goals.

Outcomes of the Analysis Phase

The outcome of this stage would be:

- ◆ Cultural model of the customers
    - □ Identify effective cultural metaphors

- □ Determine the degree of localization that is necessary
- □ To provide measures for evaluating the effectiveness of the user interface
- ◆ Logical model
  - □ Understanding of the level of technology of the customer's Internet environment
    - Computer hardware/software
    - Communications
    - Good business practice
  - □ Criteria and Internet policy issues
    - Maintenance of the site
    - Security
    - Privacy
- ◆ Set of usability variables
  - □ Set of ad hoc guidelines for developing an effective interface

Design

Upon entry into the design phase, the design team has a user profile and a set of international variables that should help guide it through the design steps. The design team will also have a set of user requirements and goals that the Web site designer must address.

The initial step would be to identify from a set of alternative designs (parallel design), a design which has a sound foundation on which to build. Secondly, a participative approach is carried out, where successive prototypes are tested and modified, until an acceptable design is produced and implemented (iterative design). Testing during these stages is likely to involve a variety of methods, including empirical testing, heuristic evaluation, localization experts and real users. Reference to the 'total user interface' criteria representing the corporate perspective on media design is recommended during the iterative design phase (coordinating design). The final design would need to be signed off by the product Information Systems Consultant.

A prototyping strategy is adopted which in turn involves a number of interrelated design activities. A participatory approach is adopted where real users and localization experts have the opportunity to comment and provide feedback on each design version:

- ◆ Parallel design
  - Exploration of different design alternatives
  - Results in a single approach being adopted
- ◆ Iterative design
  - Each successive version is tested, possibly with real users and localized experts
  - Guidelines and results of heuristic analysis applied
- ◆ Coordinating design
  - Ensure consistency across the different media, which form the total user interface

Undertake Parallel Design

Most development teams would begin the design phase by producing a number of alternative designs. It is likely that individuals work independently to create alternative designs that are innovative and imaginative.

One of the preliminary designs is then chosen, or alternatively two or more designs are combined taking the best features from each. Of course, continued reference to the cultural profiles generated in the Cultural Model is made to ensure usability. Interfaces created by competitors identified during the analysis phase might also be compared with those created during the parallel design process.

Undertake Iterative Design

The iterative design phase is where the bulk of the development takes place. Each version of the design is tested for usability, perhaps drawing upon a variety of techniques. Perhaps only one or two aspects of the interface are examining if they are representative of others; and yet others are of concern in their own right.

In the first instance a heuristic evaluation technique might be adopted where the evaluator draws upon guidelines and knowledge gained from previous experience or research. Another inspection technique that could be used is the 'cognitive' walkthrough (Lewis, 1993). Alternatively, the evaluator might ask users to undertake an empirical test, where the users 'think aloud' or record their actions as they attempt to navigate the site or interface.

Undertake Coordinated Design

Consistency is one of the most important usability characteristics. The main purpose of this process is to ensure that there is consistency of design across the total user interface. This would include textual information relating to style, format, color and language. Symbols, logos, labels and copyright information must also be consistent. Consistency between earlier and later versions of the interface needs to be maintained if customers are to feel confident about the interface, and modifications must be seen by the user to be necessary and provide improved usability over earlier versions.

Large organizations, which have experience of marketing on an international basis, will have set in place product standards. These standards can be extended to cover issues relating to the Internet. Reference to these standards should be made during the iterative design phase and not at the end of the process.

Of course, during localization of the site, there may be conflicting requirements that need to be resolved.

Outcome of the Design Phase

The outcome of this stage is a site and associated interfaces, which is ready for detailed evaluation.

Evaluation

Nielson and Del Galdo (1996) suggest three levels of interface development that can be used as a basis of usability evaluation.

- At the first level, the interface should display the native language of the user. This would include the deployment of the appropriate native character set, mathematical and monetary notations and format of the related Web pages and documents.
- The importance of understandability and usability are the focus of level two.
- The third level addresses cultural characteristics of the target client group.

In general most businesses seeking to attract international customers have reached the first level of interface design and construct Web pages and supporting material using the customers' native language. There is an increasing awareness within the organization that to maintain competitive advantage, international businesses will need to comply with design issues at levels 2 and 3.

Undertake Local Evaluation

Upon completion of the iterative phase of development, and prior to fully implementing a Web site and all the associated user and product documentation, the developer would seek to evaluate the site for usability (Nielsen and Mack, 1994).

Heuristic Evaluation

Heuristic evaluation can be carried out by the developer. Molich and Nielsen (1990) suggested 20 usability principles that could be applied to interface designs. Most, if not all, can be applied to the design of Web interfaces:

- Simple with a natural wording
- Use the language of the user
- Be aware of the memory limits of the user
- Be consistent within and between pages on the site
- Provide feedback to the user to explain the actions being undertaken
- Ensure navigational points are clearly marked and understood
- Cater for the experienced and inexperienced user
- Clear error and help messages
- Prevent errors
- Provide user and help documentation

Ideally, heuristic evaluation should be performed using several evaluators. Molich and Nielsen in one of their studies found that on average a single evaluator found only 35% of the usability problems in the interface.

Pluralistic Walkthroughs

A modification of the Heuristic approach is the Pluralist Walkthrough (Bias, 1991). In this approach, representative users, product developers and usability specialists perform heuristic evaluation. Bias (1991) suggests that each page (screen) is evaluated individually one at a time. This is followed by a group discussion before moving onto the next page. Bias also proposes that the users present their views first before the usability and developers present their views. The presence of both users and designers allows for early input into the design phase in true prototyping fashion.

Undertake International Evaluation

Several methods are open to the developer to undertake international evaluation or inspection. Nielson (1996) suggests the following ways could be adopted to evaluate the interface:

- International inspection
- International user testing
- Usability laboratories

International Inspection

A close examination of the interface, drawing upon the expertise of specialists having knowledge of the culture and language of the target client group, is carried out. The developer provides the international inspector with access to the site and associated product and user documentation. Care has to be exercised to ensure security of the site to avoid misuse of information that might be gathered from the site from 'not so friendly' surfers of the Web.

Quite often it is possible that the development team might draw upon employees from several countries that might be prepared to offer an opinion on the usability of the site. Quite clearly, such employees might not have the desired objectivity.

International User Testing

This is, by far, the most detailed and effective way of evaluating the user interface. Such an approach involves real users who carry our real tasks rather than interface experts who conceptualize what the real user might do. Obviously, care must be taken to employ users who are likely to use the system when it is put in place. Payment for these services might need to be negotiated, and if cultural issues surface an employment agency with expertise in identifying reliable local users might need to be consulted.

Usability Laboratories

Usability laboratories are primarily used by large organizations, as the cost can be fairly high for the small developer. The laboratories are equipped with the appropriate hardware and software required by the international user and, in addition, camera and other recording equipment to monitor the actions and responses of the user. In some countries usability consultants have their own monitoring suites. On occasions they can be hired.

Outcome of the Evaluation Phase

The outcome of this stage is a Web site, which is ready to be operational.

Of course, the effectiveness of the site would be subject to ongoing review and evaluation.

ISSUES IN USER INTERFACE DESIGN

Introduction

Constructing well-designed Web pages can be a challenging activity. There are a number of excellent books on the subject that the discerning developer might seek to read and digest (del Galdo and Nielsen, 1996; Nielsen, 2000; Lynch and Horton, 1997; Doherty, 1999). Reference to the Web Content Accessibility Guidelines (WCAG) published by the World Wide Web Consortium (W3C) is recommended.

Symbols and Icons

Symbols and icons are key components of the Web page. Using such objects in a multicultural and multilingual environment can be problematic. For example, symbols such as the 'folder' and 'trash can' have been the subject of international debate. The need for some resolution to this type of problem has been so profound that the International Standards Organization (ISO) has set up a working group to consider international interface standards. Nevertheless, using symbols and icons can be very useful as part of visual language and contribute to making interfaces international and improve comprehension. If manufactures maintain a unified approach to the total interface, then the use of symbols and icons can be successfully transferred to other areas such as printed documentation, packaging and marketing literature. Symbols and icons can provide the international user with visual links that can support the understanding of new concepts and ideas that might be embedded in busy textual environment. Of course, there are times when textual information is superior. Creators of new symbols and icons might begin their work by researching international sign languages (Bliss, 1965; Marcus, Smilonich and Thompson, 1994).

Some languages, for example Chinese, carry special meaning within the character. For example, the symbol for immortality might draw upon the 'tortoise' character or the 'old man' character. This level of understanding might only be available from native speakers of the language.

Text (in Graphics)

A problem can occur during localization when graphic images contain embedded text. The solution is to provide the developer with a complete set of source files where the text and graphics are on separate layers. Of course, modifications, other than text, may be required to ensure culturally sensitive issues, such as color, are addressed.

Color

Color is an important part of design. Color is important not only as it enhances the attractiveness of the site but also because of the meanings it may convey. The message conveyed by a color depends on a number of factors such as culture, fashion, age and personal preferences. It is important to realize that the relationship between the site metaphor and the color can be very powerful.

Color symbolism varies significantly between cultures. Generally color has more positive associations than negative and quite often these associations are only triggered under specific circumstances. Table 2 lists some of the cultural associations.

Fashion

Color can also be an indicator of popularity and fashion and as such can indicate different periods of time and place. In western culture shades of grey can indicate a time before color movies, and if you want to take your site back to the 1950s, you could use bright yellow and turquoise.

Age

Sites designed to attract children are more likely to be successful using bright primary colors. Older people tend to prefer traditional cultural colors.

Personal

Of course, personal preferences can be difficult to overcome. Creators of Web sites, particularly international and localized sites, should put personal preferences aside and seek the views of the localization expert.

Fonts, Characters and Unicode

Creating and reading text in a different alphabet, say on a Web page, can be a major problem for many international users. Until quite recently, most computers used fonts that contained a maximum of 256 characters. Of these 256 characters the first 128 of these characters (ASCII set) include the numbers 0-9, lower case letters a-z, upper case letters A-Z and punctuation marks. This set supported the needs of the English-speaking community and many European languages. The second extended set of 128 characters contains accented letters, additional punctuation marks and currency symbols. The complete set of 256 characters is called the ANSI character set.

The growing international use of the electronic transfer of documents through the Internet requires a character set numbering thousands of elements. The 8-bit system which allows 256 characters has now been replaced by a 16-bit system that

Table 2: Cultural Associations

Color	Culture	Cultural association
Red	China	Symbol of celebration and good luck. Used in many ceremonies, weddings and New Year.
	India	Symbol of purity. Used at weddings.
	Western Cultures	Danger. Stop. Used for Christmas celebration with green.
	Eastern Cultures	Signifies joy when combined with white.
Yellow	Asia	Sacred, imperial.
	Western Cultures	Joy, happiness. Also jealousy and fear.
Blue*	China	Linked with immortality?
	Colombia	Linked with cleanliness, soap.
	Hindu Cultures	Color of Krishna.
	Jewish Cultures	Holiness.
	Middle East	Protective color.
Green	China	Not a good color—unfaithfulness.
	India	Colour of Islam.
	Ireland	National colour, religious significance.
	Western Cultures	Go. Environment associations. Friendly and safe.
White	China	White with black used at funerals.
	Eastern Cultures	Mourning and death.
	Japan	White carnations signify death.
	Western Cultures	Purity. Important at weddings.
Black	Western Cultures	Associated with death and funerals.

* Blue is considered to be the "safest" international color.

can theoretically identify 65,536 characters. This system is called Unicode. It covers almost all known languages including Chinese, Korean and Japanese. Unicode is supported by the latest operating systems for the Macintosh and Windows environments.

Current versions of Internet Explorer and Netscape Communicator accept the Unicode standard and can display 38,887 characters. Both browsers allow the user to specify the preferred language of incoming documents. At a higher level of sophistication, some Web sites can be configured to handle language negotiation, so that when a browser requests a file, the preferred language version of the file is sent to the browser.

The key operating systems' developers, Microsoft and Macintosh, provide resources for developing multilingual documents. Further information can be obtained from published sources (Kano, 1995; Nielson, 2000; Bishop, 1998; Rockwell, 1998; Stiff, 1995; Dicherty, 1999). A visit to Alan Wood's Web page would be well worthwhile for the novice developer (Wood, 2000).

Example Sites

There are a number of excellent sites on the Internet, which exhibit good localization characteristics. The following three are of interest and quite informative. Examine them and one or two of their localized versions, and judge for yourself whether or not they comply with your usability measures:

Sun Microsystems
http://www.sun.com

The Sun Microsystems site is of particular interest for the interface developer, as Nielsen, arguably the most respected researcher of usability engineering, led the development team that created Sun's Web site. There are almost 50 localized versions of the site throughout the world.

Yahoo
http://www.yahoo.com

Owner of possibly the most used Internet search engine, the site is available in a number of languages.

Microsoft
http://www.microsoft.com

Microsoft Corporation is the largest software company in the world. It displays its entire site in over 25 languages. Its development team adopts the design strategy outlined in this chapter, and is able to update its international site almost concurrently.

REFERENCES

Bias, R. (1991). Walkthroughs: Efficient collaborative testing. *IEEE Software*, September, 8(5), 94-95.

Bishop, M. (1998). *How to Build A Successful International Web Site*. Scottsdale, AZ: Coriolis Group.

Bliss, C. K. (1965). *Semantography*. Sydney, Australia: Semantography Publications.

Doherty, W. (1999). Creating multilingual Web sites. *Multilingual Computing and Technology*, 10(3), 34-37.

Global Reach. (2000). *Global Internet Statistics (by language)*. Available on the World Wide Web at: http://www.glreach.com/globalstats/index.php3/. Accessed December 20, 2000.

Holt, N. L (1996). Developing a cultural model. In del Galdo, E. M and Nielsen, J. (Eds.), *International User Interfaces*. New York, Ny: John Wiley and Sons, Inc.

Kano, N. (1995). *Developing International Software for Windows 95 and Windows NT*. Redmond, WA: Microsoft Press.

Marcus, A., Smilonich, N. and Thompson, L. (1994). *The Cross-GUI Handbook for Multi-platform User Interface Design*. Reading, UK: Addison-Wesley, Reading.

Molich, R. and Nielsen, J. (1996). Improving a human-computer dialogue. *Communications of the ACM*, March, 33(3), 338-348.

Nielsen, J. (2000). *Designing Web Usability: The Practice of Simplicity*. Indianapolis, IN: New Riders Publishing.

Nielsen, J. (1994). *User Interface Design for Sun's WWW Site*. Available on the World Wide Web at: http://www.sun.com/sun-on-net/uidesign/.

Nielsen, J. and Mack, R.L. (Eds.). (1994). *Usability Inspection Methods*. New York, NY: John Wiley and Sons.

Rockwell Browning. (1998). *Using the Web to Compete in a Global Marketplace*. New York, NY: John Wiley & Sons.

Technical Aspects of Web Translation. (1999). *AvantPage*. Available on the World Wide Web at: http://www.avantpage.com/Web-technical.html. Accessed August 3, 1999.

Wood, A. (2000). *Alan Wood's Web Page*. Available on the World Wide Web at: http://www.hclrss.demon.co.uk/.

Section II

e-Commerce, e-Business, Internet, Strategic and Management Issues

Chapter VI

Electronic Business Strategic Orientation

Eric Deakins
University of Waikato, New Zealand

INTRODUCTION

This chapter addresses the current lack of empirical research into the organizational impacts of electronic business (e-Business). Any organization that delivers, or intends to deliver, Internet products or services can only be successful if its realized business process goals are operationally aligned with a set of (credible) top-level strategy goals. By introducing the concept of Aware and Enlightened organizations, this chapter posits that alignment of the organization's (e-Business) information systems, quality, and learning strategies with the top-level e-Business strategy is a catalyst for superior e-Business outcomes. It recognizes that most organizations still attempt to achieve a fit between a financially focused business strategy and an organization structure that matches the environment and helps to meet expected performance. Hence, some traditional approaches for achieving sound strategy-process linkages are reviewed and a strategy alignment model is proposed that is judged capable of delivering superior firm performance to Internet-enabled organizations. A set of (pre-tested) instruments is then described that can be used to assess changes in alignment between the firm's top-level e-Business strategy and its information systems, quality, and learning strategies that occur as a result of the e-Business initiative. Because it is important that the goals of the project team are also properly aligned with the top-level e-Business strategy, a project-level alignment model is also described that assesses the degree of alignment between the project deliverables and the firm's e-Business strategy.

This chapter has relevance for practitioners and academics who wish to understand how e-Business initiatives impact the alignment of key business processes with strategic business objectives.

BACKGROUND

Electronic commerce (e-Commerce) has been variously defined as "the use of electronic transmission mediums (telecommunications) to engage in the exchange, including buying and selling, of products and services requiring transportation, either physically or digitally, from location to location" (Greenstein and Feinman, 2000). This chapter is not confined to e-Commerce, and its findings are equally applicable to electronic business (e-Business), this being a superset of e-Commerce that encompasses the many other types of business information exchanges not directly related to the buying and selling of goods and services.

There is no doubt that the Internet provides tremendous opportunities to companies that can leverage it, and there has been large growth as a result. For example, between 1998 and 1999, total Internet revenue increased by 62% from US$322,530 million to US$523,923 million, a trend that continued into 2000 with a 40% increase in revenue recorded between Quarter 1 in 1999 and 2000. Of the 1999 growth, Internet commerce saw an increase of 72% from US$99,813 million to US$171,473 million. Interestingly, over the same period revenue per (e-Commerce) employee also increased dramatically, by 37% (Anon., 2000).

While the Internet undoubtedly offers opportunities to those companies that are able to excel at delivering innovative (and relevant) products or services, its landscape is littered with the remains of those that believed a good idea was a sufficient precursor for success. By early in 2001 a major shakeout that had begun in mid-2000, of (predominantly) larger Dot.com companies, was almost complete. At the time of writing, indications are that smaller (up to 10 employees) brick-and-mortar companies are realizing modest, though steady profits from realigning their business processes to take advantage of the Internet, while simultaneously paying close attention to 'good old-fashioned' business fundamentals (Weintraub, 2001). It is interesting that, in an era when the number of companies implementing e-Business initiatives is accelerating, there has been little published research into the ability of e-Business initiatives to align business processes with the business strategy direction.

The Strategy-Process Linkage

Often the first major challenge that faces a would-be Internet organization is the creation of a sound Internet business model that demonstrates solid rates of dollar (or other significant strategic) return. Interestingly, even while the quest for this 'silver bullet' continued through the late 1990s, some authors were questioning the wisdom of financial targets as the goal of business strategy in an era of unpredictable and discontinuous change, claiming that the only sustainable strategy is one focused on achieving corporate adaptability (e.g., Haeckel, 1999). However, most organizations in the information age continue to adhere to the long-recognized business principles of Porter (1980) that attempt to achieve a fit between financially focused business strategy and organization structure, and processes that matches the environment and helps to meet expected performance.

Once the e-Business model has been determined, the next key challenge is to operationalize (virtualize) the product or service offering in a manner that ensures business processes are operationally aligned with the top-level e-Business strategy. Such a fit is typically achieved not through a grand plan but through a series of decisions and projects that are constrained by short-term objectives and practicalities (e.g., Bhattacharya and Gibbons, 1996).

Organizational Transformation

Prahalad and Hamel (1990) proposed that sustainable competitive advantage could only be achieved through developing and leveraging certain competencies held within the organization; thus, strategy was recognized to be a function of core competencies as well as of the external environment. Accompanying this early work on competencies was the realization that, to develop and leverage competencies to gain competitive advantage, company processes must work across functional boundaries (Hammer and Champy, 1993). Later, dissatisfaction with Business Process Change (BPC) techniques (Davenport, 1995) and a dearth of empirical research (Deakins and Makgill, 1997) was to lead authors to predict a new '2nd generation' of BPC that would create an environment supportive of change through learning and knowledge sharing (e.g., Kettinger and Grover, 1995). Such features would go far beyond traditional BPC methods, -being more characteristic of contemporary Learning Organization principles (e.g., Senge, 1990). Innovation studies stress the importance of organizational memory and knowledge-acquisition processes (e.g., Van de Ven and Polley, 1992), hence a well-developed organizational Learning Organization Philosophy (LOP) facilitates knowledge sharing and application and establishes committed, yet motivated, relationships, enabling movement toward a vision embodied in BPC (Kettinger et al., 1995).

Enlightened and Aware Organizations

While information technology is acknowledged to be the chief enabler of e-Business processes, studies have shown that organizations that invest in IT do not automatically enjoy stronger performance (e.g., Weill, 1992). However, other studies have demonstrated that business performance is generally improved when the organization's Information Systems Philosophy (ISP) is aligned with its business strategy (Chan, Huff, Barclay and Copeland, 1997). Other studies have shown that organizations able to leverage off their strong Quality Philosophy (QP) also experience a more successful BPC outcome (e.g., Berry, 1991; Bounds, York, Adams and Ranney, 1994).

In a recent paper by the author, an Aware Organization was idealized as one that has, through its implementation of e-Business, completely aligned three philosophies: information systems, quality, and learning (hence the associated strategies) with the business strategy (Deakins, 2000). In contrast, an Enlightened Organization was defined as one that has not completely aligned all three philosophies (strategies) with the business strategy (this was expected to be the general case).

In summary, the 'Competencies' in Prahalad's (1990) strategy-linkage model are leveraged by the organization's knowledge and understanding of three key philosophies that comprise the organization's Enlightenment State. An earlier position paper posited that such a Competencies/Enlightenment State coupling would inform the process of strategy making, leading to superior firm performance (Deakins and Makgill, 1998) (see Figure 1).

Enlightened Project Teams

Figure 2 indicates that the organization's Enlightenment State is achieved through the actions of its Learning Organization Philosophy (LOP) aligning the Information Systems Philosophy and Quality Philosophy with the business strategy. To achieve maximum benefit for the organization, the e-Business project team must adopt a project strategy that has its goals fully aligned with the goals of the business strategy (e.g., Grover, Jeong, Kettinger and Teng, 1995).

Such project team activities are represented in Figure 2 using an earlier process alignment model (Earl, Sampler and Short, 1995). This comprises four lenses of enquiry that provide grounding into planning integration: process, strategy, information systems, and change management and control. One of the assumptions of the study was that effective change initiatives require the domains be aligned to some degree. Thus, it is possible to determine how an organization's Enlightenment State, prior to the e-Business initiative, aligned the project goals and otherwise informed the management of change (see Figure 2).

Figure 1: Enlightened organization model (Deakins and Makgill, 1998)

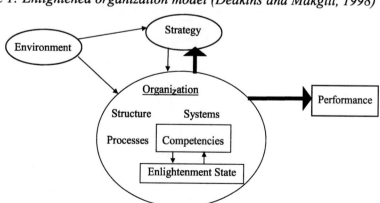

Figure 2: Business strategy and philosophies inform BPC project strategy and control

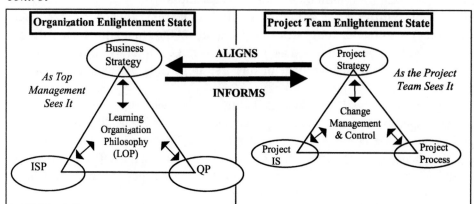

The Conceptual Model and Research Questions

Traditional companies that have chosen not to follow a pure separation strategy face the additional challenge of how best to integrate Internet-enabled processes with their legacy operations (Gulati and Garino, 2000). To determine the nature and extent of changes in the organization's Enlightenment State that are directly attributable to the e-Business initiative, it is necessary to determine the extent that the domains of information systems (IS), quality, and learning are aligned with the business strategy orientation, both before and after the e-Business initiative. A recent IS-strategy alignment model, by Chan et al. (1997), was extended by the author for this purpose, by the addition of quality and learning elements (see Figure 3).

Thus the primary research objective is to determine the nature and extent of changes in the Organization's Enlightenment State that are directly attributable to the e-Business initiative.

Figure 3: Strategic alignments with business strategy (modified from Chan et al., 1997)

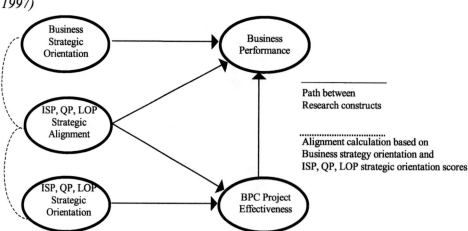

Organization-to-group aspects of learning will influence the goals of the project team, impacting change outputs and project effectiveness. While there is no consensus on what organization learning is, or how it occurs, e.g. (Fiol and Lyles, 1985), some tentative learning measures have been proposed by Crossan et al. (1995) that are based on a synthesis of frameworks by Senge (1990) and Huber (1991). These measures were utilized to determine the extent that organization-to-group aspects of learning informed the e-Business project team. The matrix in Figure 4 describes how learning occurs at and between the 3 levels: individual, group, and organization and captures the tensions between them. As well as the pure learning processes along the diagonal, concerned with how well the organization manages the discreet process of learning, the feed forward measure provides evidence of how well the organization builds on individual learning to integrate it at the group level and how well it institutionalizes the learning process in its systems, structures, and procedures. Conversely, the feedback measure provides an idea of how well the organization uses the learning embedded in its systems, structures, and procedures, to facilitate learning at the individual and group levels. Thus, in principle it is possible to determine the overall nature of organizational learning both before and after the e-Business initiative.

To determine the nature and extent of changes in the Organization's Enlightenment State that are directly attributable to an e-Business initiative, the following research questions are posed:

Question 1–What was the degree of alignment between the quality, learning, and information systems strategies prior to the e-Business initiative?
Organisational knowledge of the domains of quality, learning, and IS, and their strategic alignments with the business strategy, are likely to be relevant to the success of any significant process change (Earl et al., 1995). Combining these measures of domain alignment yields an overall measure of organization alertness (State of Enlightenment) prior to the change.

Question 2–What was the degree of alignment between the quality, learning, and information systems strategies following the e-Business initiative?

Figure 4: Organisation learning matrix (Crossan et al., 1995)

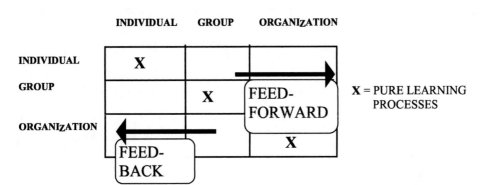

Similar to question 1 above, the aim is to ascertain the organization's State of Enlightenment following the e-Business project, to detect any changes as the result of the project initiative.

Question 3–What was the degree of alignment between the organization's strategic goals and the goals of the project team?

Project-team knowledge of the domains of IS, quality, and learning, and their alignment with the business strategy, are particularly relevant to BPC (Earl et al., 1995). This question aims to determine whether the organization's knowledge management before the change impacted the values held by the project team. In a more enlightened organization, it is expected that visioning, commitment and enabling from the top management team (in the guise of an exceptional business strategy) will generate planning team commitment, urgency and the pursuit of change in an involvement-oriented climate (e.g., Kotter, 1995).

Question 4–What organizational learning occurred ahead of the e-Business initiative?

Organization-to-group aspects of learning will influence the goals of the project team, thereby impacting change outputs and project effectiveness. The association between the research questions is shown in Figure 5.

Survey Design

The need to identify an organization that has undergone an e-Business initiative involving significant business process change determines that a method of non-probability purposive sampling be used by the researcher. This research also adheres to the principle that an instrument should never be developed from scratch when a well-developed, or fairly well developed, instrument that fits the level of analysis and level of detail required by a particular research model already exists (Zmud and Boynton, 1989). Consequently, a number of extant measurement instruments were considered and a corresponding measurement model developed, based on the research model.

Instrument Development

An instrument developed by Venkatraman (1989a), which was subsequently refined by Chan et al. (1997), was used to measure the strategic orientation realized by the business. Table 1 outlines the eight dimensions of the resulting STROBE instrument that is to be completed by the Chief Executive Officer. A second instrument, also based on one by Chan et al. (1997), was used to explicitly parallel

Figure 5: The effect of organizational enlightenment on project effectiveness

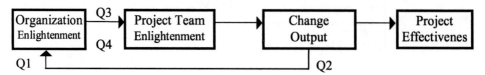

the dimensions used in STROBE to assess realized strategic orientation of the organization's information systems. Table 1 outlines the resulting STROIS instrument that is to be completed by the Chief Information Officer. Two further parallel instruments were developed to assess the realized strategic orientation of the organization's learning organization strategy and its quality strategy. A fifth instrument to assess (e-Business) project effectiveness, also based on the work of Chan et al. (1997), is to be completed by the Chief Officer of mission-critical departments. Table 1 outlines the dimensions of the resulting PE instrument. A sixth instrument to assess aspects of organizational learning was based on the work of Crossan and Hulland (1995); Table 2 provides some example measures. All instruments and procedures were further developed to allow corresponding responses by the e-Business project team.

Table 1: Dimensions of higher order constructs (modified from Chan et al., 1997)

STROBE: Strategic Orientation of Business Enterprise (Realized Strategies)	
Company Aggressiveness	Push to dominate (increase mkt. share) even if this means reduced prices and cash flow
Company Analysis	Reliance on detailed, numerically oriented studies prior to action
Company Internal Defensiveness	Emphasis on cost cutting and efficiency; internally 'lean and mean'
Company External Defensiveness	Forming tight marketplace alliances (i.e., with customers, suppliers and distributors)
Company Futurity	Having forward-looking, long-term focus
Company Proactiveness	First to introduce new products and services; a step ahead of the competition
Company Risk Aversion	Reluctance to embark on risky projects
Company Innovativeness	Creativity and experimentation are strengths
STROIS: Strategic Orientation of e-Business Information Systems (Realized Strategies)	
Aggressive	Deployments used by the business unit when pursuing aggressive marketplace action
Analytical	Deployments used by the business unit when conducting analysis of business situations
Internally Defensive	Deployments used by the business unit to improve the efficiency of business situations
Externally Defensive	Deployments used by the business unit to strengthen marketplace links
Future Oriented	Deployments used by the business unit for forecasting and anticipation purposes
Proactive	Deployments used by the business unit to expedite the intro of products and services
Risk Averse	Deployments used by the business unit to make business risk assessments
Innovative	Deployments used by the business unit to facilitate creativity and exploration
PE: Project Effectiveness (Value and Business Contribution of e-Business Project)	
Operational Efficiency	e.g., improvement in the efficiency of internal company operation attributed to project implementation
Management Effectiveness	e.g., improvement in management decision making, planning and span of control attributed to project implementation
Establishment of Market Linkages	e.g., the creation of electronic ties to customers, suppliers and distributors
Enhancement of Products/ Services	e.g., via changing the content of existing products and services

Table 2: Example measures of organizational learning (Crossan and Hulland, 1995)

Measures relating to Organization-to-Project Team Learning
It is easy to access information from previous studies. The organizational structure facilitates the sharing of ideas.
Measures relating to Project Team-to-Organization Learning
We are rewarded for sharing our ideas with others. We share new insights throughout our organization. New ideas spread rapidly throughout our organization.

Determination of Strategic Alignment Using Profile Similarity Indices

Following the return of the completed instruments, dimensions of strategic alignment can be calculated using Profile Similarity Indices (PSIs) (Edwards, 1993). These will be described via consideration of Information Systems alignment as quality and learning alignments are similarly treated.

IS strategic alignment is the alignment between business unit (or organization) strategic orientation and IS strategic orientation. Chan et al. (1997) conceptualized business unit strategic orientation as assessing the 'personality' of the organization whereas IS strategic orientation examines the existence of company systems that could 'support' various personalities. Matching and moderation measurement approaches are employed for the purpose of assessing strategic alignment, meaning support for the company personality (Chan et al., 1997; Venkatraman, 1989b).

Matching approaches use the difference in the scores recorded between STROBE and STROIS. Based on the work by Edwards (1993), matching is determined by an alignment index (D), where: $D = \sqrt{((\sum_i^n (X_i - Y_i)^2)/n)}$, i=1...n and X_i and Y_i are individual measures within a dimension. In practice, the five-point Likert scales used in the survey instruments generate matching scores between 0 (i.e., 5 – 5) and 4 (5 – 1) where 0 indicates perfect alignment and 4 the worst possible alignment.

Moderation approaches use the interaction terms to determine a measure of performance (Z), where: $Z = (\sum_i^n (X_i * Y_i))/n$, i=1...n and X_i = strategy, and Y_i = the contextual variable that fits with strategy for performance improvement. In its formal representation Y is a moderator if the relationship between the variables is a function of the level of Y (Venkatraman, 1989b). Here X * Y reflects the joint effect of X and Y. In practice, moderation values vary from 1 (i.e., 1 * 1) to 25 (5 * 5), with implications for business performance as outlined in Table 3.

A business unit values each of the dimensions of its strategy differently. Thus, for example, if the strategy dimension called Analysis has the largest value (average of the individual measures within the dimension), it is considered to be of highest

Table 3: Matching and moderation implications for business performance

Dimension of Strategy	Dimension of IS	Matching	Moderation	Implication
Low	Low	High	Low	Low performance and minimal potential for IS leverage
Low	High	Low	Medium	Low performance and wasted IS effort
High	Low	Low	Medium	Low performance and high potential for IS leverage
High	High	High	High	High performance and low potential for IS leverage

strategic value to the organization. Weighted average values are obtained by summing the individual (dimension) matching/moderation scores weighted according to their strategy dimension value.

Limitations of Profile Similarity Indices

According to Edwards (1993) there are numerous methodological problems in using Profile Similarity Indices in congruence research. He claims that:

- They combine measures of conceptually distinct constructs and entities into a single score that is conceptually ambiguous.
- They disregard information at the absolute level of both entities with regard to the direction of difference.
- They do not reflect which elements are responsible for the differences between two entities.
- They impose a restricted set of constraints on the coefficients relating the measures of the Profile Similarity Indices to the outcomes.

Other researchers have concluded that the criticisms levelled at difference scores that have arisen in education and developmental research do not translate directly into management research (Tisak and Smith, 1994).

Pre-Test Characteristics

The developed instruments were piloted in a conventional business process change environment that did not involve any elements of e-Business (Deakins et al., 1998). The unit of analysis for the pilot was the IS Business Unit of a large telecommunications company. The project, which involved a degree of process change, was intended to deliver a system to record, monitor and report on internal IS Help requests and the effectiveness of the IS group. The Total Design Method (TDM) approach to survey administration was used to guide the design process, to gather data and to test the measurements and models (Dillman, 1978). In the pilot a total of 36 questionnaires were used to capture the views of the various parties to the project, comprising members of the Senior Management Team, the Project Team and other key stakeholders impacted by the project. An internal company co-ordinator was appointed to identify and liase with the appropriate respondents. While Chan et al. (1997) demonstrated positive aspects of instrument validity and reliability, such assessments were not assumed for the pilot study and remain to be tested in any full study.

Representative Pilot Study Results

Assessing Realized IS Strategic Alignment

Due to space limitations, only results for Information Systems alignment are presented here; both quality and learning elements were treated in a similar manner.

Pre-project alignment of the realized IS strategy with the realized business unit strategy is shown in Table 4. This table shows that, overall, the alignment of realized IS strategy orientation with realized business strategy orientation scored 1.80

(weighted average) using the matching technique (perfect match = 0, perfect mismatch = 4). The individual dimension scores reflect this overall lack of IS/ Business Strategy alignment (lack of IS support for the business unit personality). The corresponding value, using the moderation technique, was a performance score of 8.26 that indicates average performance with some potential for future IS leverage. The dimension Externally Defensive is noteworthy. While it does not exhibit the largest mismatch, its weighting reflects special strategic significance for the business unit. It may be concluded that this important dimension is not being supported by IS to the extent required.

The corresponding post-project alignment in Table 5 shows that the STROBE instrument detected no change in strategic orientation following the project. While there has been an improvement in IS alignment across all dimension scores, this progress may, in part, be due to other factors. Indeed, several of the dimensions of IS support for the business unit personality have scores that exceed the values required for perfect strategic alignment.

Alignment of the Project Strategy with the Business Unit Strategy

Table 6 shows the degree of alignment between the pre-project (team) goals and pre-project business unit strategy orientation. An overall matching score of *1.19*

Table 4: Analysis of pre-project realized IS strategic alignment

DIMENSION	Strategy	Weighting	IS	Matching D	Moderation Z
Aggressive	3.71	0.14	2.43	1.67	9.80
Analysis	2.40	0.09	2.40	1.41	5.60
Externally Defensive	4.14	0.16	2.14	2.07	8.86
Futurity	2.67	0.10	2.67	1.49	7.22
Internally Defensive	3.71	0.14	3.14	2.27	10.71
Innovativeness	2.83	0.11	2.50	1.53	6.83
Proactiveness	3.33	0.13	2.17	1.96	6.83
Risk Aversion	3.17	0.12	2.71	0.91	8.50
Weighted Average:				**1.80**	**8.26**

Table 5: Analysis of post-project realized IS strategic alignment

DIMENSION	Strategy	Weighting	IS	Matching D	Moderation Z
Aggressive	3.71	0.14	3.38	1.26	12.60
Analysis	2.40	0.09	3.20	1.26	8.00
Externally Defensive	4.14	0.16	3.86	0.53	16.00
Futurity	2.67	0.10	3.22	1.53	8.67
Internally Defensive	3.71	0.14	4.00	1.51	14.86
Innovativeness	2.83	0.11	3.50	1.15	10.33
Proactiveness	3.33	0.13	3.33	1.63	11.00
Risk Aversion	3.17	0.12	3.29	0.91	10.50
Weighted Average:				**1.20**	**11.49**

indicates a degree of agreement (0 = perfect alignment). Table 7 indicates that no change in overall alignment was detected between the post-project outcomes and post-project business unit strategy, due to the cancelling effect of changes in the Innovativeness and Risk Aversion dimension scores.

Assessing Organizational Learning

To help explain the learning processes behind the above results, the tentative framework proposed by Crossan et al. (1995) was used to measure organizational learning. The pure learning process, Figure 6, was calculated by averaging the Likert scores along the diagonal. Averaging the scores of the cells above the diagonal derived the feed-forward measure. Averaging the scores in the cells below the diagonal derived the feedback measure. Finally, averaging of the scores within each of the three cells that focus on the pure learning processes–individual, group and organization–derives the measures. It can be seen that all the measures of organiza-

Table 6: Alignment of pre-project goals with business unit strategy

DIMENSION	Strategy	Weighting	Project Strat.	Matching D
Aggressive	3.71	0.14	3.38	1.08
Analysis	2.40	0.09	4.50	1.58
Externally Defensive	4.14	0.16	3.43	1.00
Futurity	2.67	0.10	3.33	1.53
Internally Defensive	3.71	0.14	4.00	1.08
Innovativeness	2.83	0.11	3.50	1.53
Proactiveness	3.33	0.13	3.75	0.71
Risk Aversion	3.17	0.12	2.67	1.34
Weighted Average:				**1.19**

Table 7: Alignment of post-project outcomes with business unit strategy

DIMENSION	Strategy	Weighting	Project Strat.	Matching D
Aggressive	3.71	0.14	3.38	1.08
Analysis	2.40	0.09	4.50	1.58
Externally Defensive	4.14	0.16	3.43	1.00
Futurity	2.67	0.10	3.33	1.53
Internally Defensive	3.71	0.14	4.00	1.08
Innovativeness	2.83	0.11	3.50	2.33
Proactiveness	3.33	0.13	3.75	0.71
Risk Aversion	3.17	0.12	3.50	0.63
Weighted Average:				**1.19**

tional learning fall predominantly in the middle of the range, on a seven-point Likert scale, demonstrating only average learning abilities.

Assessing Project Effectiveness

Four dimensions were used to describe the impact of the project on the business unit's effectiveness. On a five-point Likert scale, operational efficiency (2.89), management effectiveness (3.81), market linkages (3.31) and products/services (3.52) combined to give an overall score of 3.38 (where 1 = strongly disagree that the project has led to improvement and 5 = strongly agree that the project has led to improvement).

CONCLUSION

Any organization that delivers, or intends to deliver, Internet products or services can only be successful if its realized business process goals are operationally aligned with a set of (credible) top-level strategy goals. In an era when the number of companies implementing e-Business initiatives is accelerating, there has been little published research into the ability of e-Business initiatives to align business processes with the business strategy direction.

This chapter addresses the deficiency of empirical research into e-Business and describes results of preliminary research that has the potential to empirically explore the nature of e-Business implementation, based on theories as well as field experiences of process change specialists. Specifically, it:
- links an organization-level process alignment model (Deakins, 2000) to a corresponding project-level model by Earl et al. (1995), in order to determine the degree of congruence between the firm's business strategy and the e-Business project implementation strategy;
- proposes that good alignment of the organization's information systems, quality, and learning philosophies (hence strategies) at the organization level with those at the project level are a catalyst for superior e-Business project outcomes;

Figure 6: Organization learning matrix

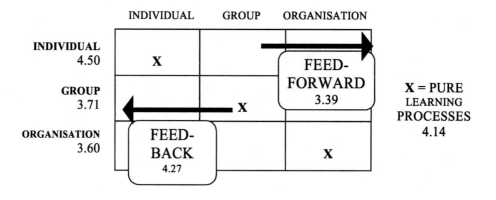

- determines the degree of congruence between the firm's business strategy and the e-Business project implementation strategy;
- investigates the nature and extent of organizational learning that aligns and informs the activities of the project team;
- describes and illustrates the use of pre-tested instruments that are suitable for measuring the degree of alignment between the firm's information systems, quality, and learning strategies and the business strategy, both before and following an e-Business initiative.

All of the instruments have been pre-tested in a commercial (although non e-Business) environment. Although subject to confirmation of their reliability and validity, the author judges that the instruments are capable of providing superior performance to Internet organizations via an ability to diagnose specific dimensions of e-Business–organizational misalignment. Such diagnoses help identify specific leverage points for remedial action.

This chapter has relevance for practitioners and academics who wish to understand how e-Business initiatives impact the alignment of key business processes with strategic business objectives. Future work will involve investigation of a range of e-Business initiatives to test the overarching hypothesis that the alignment of information systems, quality, and learning (strategies) with the business strategy is a catalyst for superior e-Business outcomes. It is expected that the results of such a study will be of interest to managers, consultants and researchers in the e-Business arena.

REFERENCES

Anon. (2000). *The Internet Economy Indicators™: Internet Indicators Key Findings*. Available on the World Wide Web at: http://www.internetindicators.com. Accessed December 20, 2000.

Berry, T. H. (1991). *Managing the Total Quality Transformation*. New York: McGraw-Hill, Inc.

Bhattacharya, A. K. and Gibbons A. M. (1996). Strategy formulation: Focusing on core competencies and processes. *Business Change and Reengineering*, 3(1).

Bounds, G., York, L., Adams, M. and Ranney, G. (1994). *Beyond Total Quality Management*. New York: McGraw-Hill, Inc.

Chan, Y., Huff, S. L., Barclay, D. W. and Copeland, D. G. (1997). Business strategic orientation, information systems strategic orientation, and strategic alignment. *Information Systems Research*, 8(2).

Crossan, M. and Hulland, J. (1995). Measuring organiaztional learning. *Working Paper Series No. 95-29*, Western Business School, London, Canada.

Davenport, T. H. (1995). The fad that people forgot. *Fast Company*, (1).

Deakins, E. (2000). Electronic business strategic orientation and organizational alignment. *Department of Management Systems Working Paper Series, No.2000-07*, October.

Deakins, E. and Makgill, H. H. (1998). The importance of alignment in business process change projects. *Proceedings of the Ninth Australasian Conference on Information Systems (ACIS98)*, Sydney, NSW Australia, September, 148-160.

Deakins, E. and Makgill, H. H. (1997). What killed BPR? Some evidence from the literature. *Business Process Management Journal*, 3(1).

Dillman, D. A. (1978). *Mail and Telephone Surveys: Total Design Method*. New York: John Wiley and Sons.

Earl, M. J., Sampler, J. L. and Short, J. E. (1995). Strategies for business process reengineering: Evidence from field studies. *Journal of Management Information Systems*, 12(1), 31-56.

Edwards, J. R. (1993). Problems with profile similarity indices in the study of congruence in organization research. *Personnel Psychology*, 46, 641-665.

Fiol, C. M. and Lyles, M. A. (1985). Organizational learning. *Academy of Management Review*, 10(4), 803-813.

Greenstein, M, and Feinman T. M. (2000). *Electronic Commerce: Security, Risk Management and Control*. New York: McGraw-Hill.

Grover, V., Jeong, S. R., Kettinger, W. J. and Teng, J. T. C. (1995). The implementation of business process reengineering. *Journal of Management Information Systems*, 12(1), 109-144.

Gulati, R. and Garino, J. (2000). Get the right mix of bricks and clicks. *Harvard Business Review*, May-June, 107-114.

Haeckel, S. H. (1999). *Adaptive Enterprise: Creating and Leading Sense and Respond Organizations*.Boston, MA: Harvard Business School Press.

Hammer, M. and Champy, J. (1993). *Reengineering the Corporation A Manifesto for Business Revolution*. New York: Harper Business.

Huber, G. P. (1991). Organizational learning: The contributing processes and the literatures. *Organization Science*, 2(1), 88-115.

Kettinger, W. J. and Grover, V. (1995). Toward a theory of business process change management. *Journal of Management Information Systems*, 12(1), 9-30.

Kotter, J. P. (1995) Leading change: Why transformation efforts fail, *Harvard Business Review*, March-April, 59-67.

Porter, M. E. (1980). *Competitive Strategy: Techniques for Analyzing Industries and Competitors*. New York: The Free Press.

Prahalad, C. K. and Hamel, G. (1990). The core competence of the corporation. *Harvard Business Review*, May-June.

Senge, P. M. (1990). *The Fifth Discipline: The Art and Practice of the Learning Organization*. New York: Doubleday Currency.

Tisak, J. and Smith, C. S. (1994). Defending and extending difference score methods. *Journal of Management*, 20(3), 675-682.

Van de Ven, A. and Polley, D. (1992). Learning while innovating. *Organizational Science*, 3, 92-116.

Venkatraman, N. (1989a). Strategic orientation of business enterprises. *Management Science*, 35(8), 942-962.

Venkatraman, N. (1989b). The concept of 'fit' in strategic research. *Academy of Management Review*, 14(3), 423-444.

Weill, P. (1992). The relationship between investment in information technology and firm performance: A study of the valve-manufacturing sector. *Information Systems Research*, 3(4).

Weintraub, A. (2001). The mighty mini-dots. *Business Week*, March, EB21-EB24.

Zmud, R. W. and Boynton, A. C. (1989) Survey measures and instruments in MIS-inventory and appraisal. In Kraemer, K. L. (Ed.), *Harvard Business School Research Colloquium: Vol. 3*. The Information Systems Research Challenge: Survey Research Methods, Harvard Business School, 149-186.

Chapter VII

Human Factors and e-Commerce

Catherine Wallace
Massey University, New Zealand

INTRODUCTION

This chapter addresses the lack of attention paid to what is commonly referred to as an organization's greatest asset, its people, in an increasingly Internet-connected business environment. The literature suggests that Internet usage is growing exponentially and is likely to have a huge impact on the way businesses are run and how they interact with their customers, their suppliers and their business partners.

While there has been a range of research done on the profile of online users, types of sites, number of hits and income generated from Internet sales, there is a distinct lack of research about the impact of the Internet on the functioning of organizations and the impact on their systems and processes. Lack of in-depth information about the effect an integrated Internet presence has on an organization has a number of important implications. We are not yet fully aware of the best processes and practices to implement to ensure effective and efficient online organizations.

This chapter has relevance for business operators and academics who wish to understand how business principles transfer into an online environment, and what new strategies and techniques are required to realize the potential opportunities and benefits of this medium. Special emphasis is placed on the human factors and communication issues involved.

e-Business

e-Business is the complex fusion of business processes, enterprise applications and organizational structure necessary to create a high-performance business model (Kalakota and Robinson, 2001). Boddy and Boonstra (2000) define e-Business as the integration, through the Internet, of an organization's processes from its suppliers through to its customers, commonly referred to as B2B. These authors make the point that without an organization adopting an e-Business foundation, e-Commerce cannot be executed effectively.

The Internet is increasingly being used for commercial purposes by companies that are attracted by the low costs of making information available, the possibilities of reaching a global audience, the opportunity to use the medium's interactivity to have a direct dialogue with the customer, to use the technology available for automating some customer service functions, to integrate various office systems, for public relations and selling products and services.

Kalakota and Robinson (2001) say that the first phase of e-Commerce (1994-1997) was about presence: making sure that everyone had a Web site and had something on it; often referred to as brochureware. Not all companies knew why they were doing it, but they knew they needed an online presence. Kalakota and Robinson say the second phase (1997-2000) of e-Commerce was about transactions–buying and selling over digital media with the focus on order flow and gross revenue. The third phase of e-Commerce (2000) has a focus on how the Internet can impact profitability by increasing gross margins, and Kalakota and Robinson refer to this phase as e-Business. It includes all the applications and processes enabling a company to service a business transaction. In addition to encompassing e-Commerce, e-Business includes both front- and back-office applications that form the core engine for modern business. Therefore, e-Business is not just about e-Commerce transactions or about buying and selling over the Web; it's the overall strategy of redefining old business models, with the aid of technology, to maximize customer value and profits.

Hartman, Sifonis and Kador (2000) say companies they have studied go through a series of predictable phases: brochureware, customer interactivity, transaction enabler, one-to-one relationships, real-time organizations and communities of interest (COINs). At the beginning of what they refer to as the Net Readiness era, organizations use the Internet as a bulletin board for brochures, employee telephone directories, and over time, for more critical documents such as catalogues and price lists. For these companies, the Net was a publishing medium and it ensured an online presence but it didn't exploit interactivity. In the second phase of customer interactivity, companies create a dialogue with customers by empowering the customer to enter, ask, demand and dictate the kind of value that needs to be delivered. The term customer could refer to consumer, end-customer, employee and so on. In the third phase, companies begin to use the Net as a transaction enabler to expand transaction-oriented processes such as selling product, procuring supplies and enabling internal processes such as human resources activities, etc.

Hartman, Sifonis and Kador's (2000) fourth phase focuses on one-to-one relationships with the Internet being used to create "customized silos of interactivity." Web technology allows companies to deal with customers on a one-to-one basis, meaning product pricing becomes fluid, dictated by individual customers, often in an auction process. In the fifth phase, real-time organizations, where "zero latency organizations" are able to plan, execute and aggregate buyers and sellers in a virtual arena. These companies understand needs and deliver value in real time. The final phase refers to COINs that the Internet enables companies to create in terms of content, community and commerce that closely link various partners in a value chain.

The second of Raisch's four phases is Value-Added E-Marketplaces that provide value-added services to support their customers with transaction support services, as well as enabling the customer-driven creation of customized products and services. This type of new value creation through a combination of digital and physical value delivery systems is now more possible than in the pre-Internet economy. Raisch (2001) talks of the three Cs of e-Business: content, community and commerce. He refers to two types of communities and the first, communities of interest, is similar to Hartman, Sifonis and Kador's (2000) sixth phase (COINs). He defines this as communities of people that gather around an organization's content because they are truly interested in the subject matter such as music, sports, news, specialty products, etc. These may be as small as two people discussing content or as large as millions discussing news issues on Yahoo.com. Raisch's other community type is communities of commerce that are groups of people that gather around a company and its content and are economically tied to the company because of a business relationship.

Growth in e-Commerce

Few commentators on e-Commerce disagree that we are experiencing the start of a true paradigm shift though many disagree on just how big it is going to be. Forecasts on the impact of Internet commerce on business range widely. Huff, Wade, Parent, Schneberger and Newson, (1999, p. 1) say that in estimating the increase of business-to-consumer electronic commerce from 1997 to 2000, forecasters varied from a "low" estimate of a seven-fold increase to a high estimate of 180-fold increase.

Hartman, Sifonis and Kador (2000) cite International Data Corp that worldwide Internet commerce will top $1 trillion by 2003. The research firm estimates that most of that growth is accounted for by more consumers buying online, by larger dollar amounts per transaction and by increased business-to-business purchases on the Web. The company also estimates that by 2003 United States-based users should account for less than half of all Internet commerce, compared with 74% in 1999. Raisch (2001) cites current estimates from Forrester Research on the future of e-Commerce, predicting that by 2004 in the United States alone, total online trade will reach almost $2.7 trillion, with roughly $1.4 trillion coming from online marketplace transactions.

Business-to-business (B2B) is the fastest growth area in the Internet economy and its potential is just starting to be realized in some quarters. Forrester Research (December 1998, cited in Raisch, 2001) estimates that Internet-based electronic business relationships will account for $1.3 trillion in sales by 2003. A Boston Consulting Group report (December, 1999, cited in Raisch, 2001) places this figure higher at $2.8 trillion. Deloitte's e-Business leader in New Zealand, Alasdair MacLeod, has said that currently over 97% of e-Commerce in New Zealand is business-to-business (MacLeod, 2001).

The number of Web sites and content providers has also increased in the last decade. The increased quantity and quality of content attracts new users, and the growth in consumers online has in turn attracted new content providers and business-based sites. With the increased amount of traffic over the Internet, businesses need to be concerned about whether their sites effectively promote business, manage delivery and attract and hold the attention of online customers.

Organizational Benefits of E-Commerce

Rasmussen (1996) believes that the benefits a customer gets from using the Internet mirror those of firms. Individuals, teams and organizations can all gain a competitive advantage if people can access the Internet whenever they want, whether it is for communications, research, placing orders, support or service, provided the information is relevant, accurate, timely, clear and often, concise. As speed and access to information continue to improve, individuals and organizations need to have both the research skills to locate, decipher and interpret information and the opportunities to use this.

Factors associated with e-Commerce 'false starts' by John Brennan, Andersen Consulting (cited in Bell, 1999) are: early over-ambition; lack of integration with the organization's strategy and infrastructure; failure to adapt strategy, infrastructure and mission; focus on the Internet to the exclusion of existing channels (risking large investment for low returns); unfamiliarity with customer needs; rapidly changing customer behavior; lack of sustained executive commitment, inadequate resourcing and maintenance planning, implementation shortfalls; public confidence issues, privacy and consumer rights concerns and public concern over lack of privacy of their personal data, destroying the organization's credibility.

Lee Neubecker, senior product marketing manager for online community products at Lycos, breaks e-Commerce models into the three Cs: communities, content and commerce. "Most e-businesses fall short on at least one of these three Cs," she says, noting that traditional businesses tend to have the hardest time with the idea of community (cited in Emigh, 1999). Message boards and chat sessions are ways to build community. Content refers to information conveyed over the Web. News stories and stock quotes are two examples. Commerce is where consumers or businesses pay money to purchase physical goods, information or services that are posted or advertised online.

Oliver (2000) gives seven laws of e-Commerce for strategic planners operating in an Internet business world. He says there is no such thing as a sustainable advantage with everything moving at Internet speed so it is necessary to constantly plan and react and rethink a whole business strategy at a moment's notice. No longer is the business master of their customers; they are the master of the business. Another area of change is the need for businesses to share information rather than keeping it secret to gain an advantage. With much of the information about businesses being open and available, it is necessary to offer some added value to the transaction to win and keep customers.

Oliver (2000) says businesses need to ensure their strategic thinking is global, both in breadth with how to sell globally and in inspiration of what works best in different global situations. As companies move from the "not-com" where they are very much grounded in time and place, to "dot com" where they are situated within the electro-mechanical spectrum of the Internet and other wired and wireless networks, nothing changes more than how companies must deal with customers. In the traditional marketplace, success is often characterized by making it easy for customers to come to the business with location being an essential element. In the Internet marketplace, the business must go to the customer with what happens to customers once they are on the Web site of immense importance. The customer now has a say in determining the relationship, the product or service offered, delivery criteria and often price. Success in "space" as opposed to "place" means that the company needs to make the customer a true player rather than a spectator.

Oliver (2000, p. 10) says today's successful leaders are building flexible organizations designed around customers. Rather than dictating strategy from above, they are letting strategy flow from the organization. Fast-growing companies tend to share a common trait: they demonstrate an amazing ability to fine-tune their strategies reflexively, nimbly moving to where their customers want them to be.

Organizational Culture Responsive to Change

"An organization's culture reflects assumptions about clients, employees, mission, products, activities and assumptions that have worked well in the past and which get translated into norms of behavior, expectations about what is legitimate, desirable ways of thinking and acting. These are the locus of its capacity for evolution and change" (Laurent cited in Evans, 1990).

e-Commerce is changing the way companies and their customers interact with each other. Established ways of doing business and traditional distribution channels, especially in the business-to-business sector, are being challenged. The Internet allows manufacturers to sell directly to their end-users. Buyers and sellers who used to rely on brokers, dealers, wholesalers and field salespeople now deal directly with each other. Companies can communicate quickly and cheaply regardless of distance enabling business to be done with people and organizations that were previously beyond reach. The challenge for managers is to make profitable use of these possibilities. Boddy and Boonstra (2000, p. 19) conclude that as managers use the Internet to support more of their companies' core activities, they also need to make progressively more significant organizational changes.

Success with the Internet requires continual changes in organizational culture, structures and personnel (Boddy and Boonstra, 2000). While the technical and design aspects receive a lot of focus, doing business on the Internet also depends on making coherent changes to other aspects of the organization. As organizations become increasingly flatter and deal with knowledge-based products, successful managers of Internet organizations need to be able to control and understand their organizations' cultures. Those managers who anticipate, plan for and adjust their business processes in the face of changes brought by the Internet have gained some benefits. Those who have seen technology as a magic bullet with which to solve their problems have made things worse (Markus and Benjamin, 1997).

Boddy and Boonstra (2000) found that the majority of issues management face when doing business on the Internet are organizational rather than technological. Successful implementation appears to have required constant adjustments to the organizational infrastructure, including changes in culture, people and structures. If the prevailing culture supports the Internet proposal, then people are more likely to accept it with enthusiasm and commitment. A culture that is supportive and endorses Internet initiatives is essential to organizational survival and success in an environment where organizations are competing on service rather than price margins. If there is a mismatch between the culture and the Internet use envisaged, there will be resistance, resentment and a lack of commitment.

Managers must identify and communicate the need for any changes in behaviors related to putting a business on the Internet. It is also essential that the message be disseminated throughout the organization accurately, in a timely fashion and with sufficient detail. Accurate messages reduce misunderstandings and uncertainty. Timeliness provides urgency and currency, and detail provides the proper context for employees to evaluate business and skills requirements. These three aspects are especially important for businesses shifting to e-Business rather than those that begin as an e-Business or a 'pure play.' Organizations undergoing change may face several types of resistance: resistance based on the need for additional information, resistance based on lack of understanding and uncertainty, and resistance based on deep mistrust (Deise, Nowikow, King and Wright, 2000). The need for more information is a common type of resistance that can be alleviated through use of active communication by strong leadership and employee involvement in the change.

The entire workforce needs to understand the changes involved in moving from a traditional environment to one that operates online and has electronic partnering with other organizations. The new business case or model and the vision for change should clearly define the organization's refocused strategy and the anticipated changes. Frequent and open communication is required to reinforce new patterns of behavior as the company changes its business operations and makes increased use of the Internet throughout the business. Communications need to clarify what has changed, what may change and what has not changed.

In order to accelerate change, management needs to drive communication and demonstrate commitment through overt actions. Networks are likely to need redesigning to support change and continuous improvement around process and culture, increasingly so as the business is involved with supply chain and demand chain partners. During the development cycle for example, customers and suppliers must actively participate in establishing a collaborative environment for the development of services. Company employees need to learn to work directly with their partner company colleagues. To create value-added relationships, networked companies must engage in an open exchange of information and ideas. It is necessary to manage tacit and explicit, formal and informal forms of communication in order to support the organizational change strategies and new business environment. Communications patterns will change with greater use of Internet technology in the organization. Deise, Nowikow, King and Wright (2000) say that for this reason an explicit communications and knowledge-management program should be an integrated component of the transition to e-Business and employees encouraged to provide key content for these organization-wide programs.

Hartman, Sifonis and Kador (2000) say the Internet redefines every assumption about dealing with customers. They claim the "E-conomy" throws the well-intentioned but unworkable management discipline of customer relationship management on its ears. Internet customers have so many options to choose from in any product or service category that it is not the customer who's being managed, as that system is far too passive. Instead, it is the customer who manages the relationship, requiring organizations to let go of the arrogance that customers and clients can be managed. The authors say that in the E-conomy, customers can only be served, listened to and valued and then, if the company does everything right, the customer may agree to be served.

An organization needs to research customers to find out what they expect from its Web site and if they will use it. They could be asked what they think of other online services they use–what they don't like and what they do, the things they find useful and the sort of information they'd like to see included. This will ensure a good starting point for the content to include on the site and may save the organization from some pitfalls. Another aspect to consider is the other audiences that an organization may attract by being online. The site isn't constrained by business hours or geography, so the organization's systems need to have the capacity to cope with an international audience.

Development of an Integrated Internet Presence

Research indicates that New Zealand's smaller businesses have not been as quick as larger firms to take advantage of the Internet and e-Commerce (Ministry of Economic Development, 2000, p. 4). The survey from the Information Technology Policy Group of the Ministry of Economic Development (2000, p. 1) indicates that although New Zealand businesses are well prepared, they have yet to come to grips with the implications of e-Commerce. While two-thirds of businesses claim to be engaged in some type of e-Commerce with other organizations already, only about one in 10 have integrated this activity with their internal business systems.

Companies that create an effective Web presence can streamline operations, shorten response time to customer requests, gather more market data, increase their reach, offer richer information on their products and services and ideally sell greater quantities. Application integration is the key to e-Business (Kalakota and Robinson, 2001). Successful process integration requires a major application overhaul in order to develop an integrated front-end/back-end infrastructure to overcome process inefficiencies, inaccuracies and application inflexibility. This view is also stated by Deise, Nowikow, King and Wright (2000), who say that if an organization's adoption of e-Commerce is successful, it can literally take over the business and have a huge organizational impact. Increased activity through the Internet can fragment a company by placing great pressure on the sales force and then on the company's back-end processes and those who carry out those activities. Even if a company doesn't intend to disintermediate its distribution network of internal sales people or outside distributors, an Internet sales channel that ties directly to the customer can undermine all of the relationships that have been built throughout the offline sales and distribution system. The company may need to mediate channel conflicts in its own organization and within its network of business partners.

e-Procurement can have a large impact on most members of an organization. The technological change can be quite small, but the resulting change in culture significant. In complying with the new buying arrangements, employees will not use the fax or phone to order, but will use the intranet accessed through their desktop computer. For individuals there is some loss of choice in the buy; that control shifts to the organization's head office. Local buying arrangements also change as can any informal arrangements that have historically cemented many of these relationships. Buying decisions become less political, more directly based on price and increasingly based on service level.

Regardless of whether an organization is selling to multinational companies or a handful of local customers, a strong commitment is necessary to become equipped for Internet business. If the Internet is to be an integral part of the way a company operates, the effort to gear up for e-Commerce and an Internet-enabled value chain must be understood and accepted by key functional areas within the organization as well as management. This commitment and understanding is necessary because each step down the path towards full integration has deep implications for business processes and organizational culture. Company leadership must be willing to commit the resources in people, money and focus necessary to carry e-Commerce deployment through to fulfillment. Managers and employees must embrace new tools and processes for internal communication, sales processing and customer fulfillment. Regardless of what stage of its Web development and involvement a company is at, the organization is being asked to transform itself, adapt to new ways of working and deliver customer value.

Businesses need to consider how the Web site will combine with other business activities and what changes are required as a result. Electronic commerce may lead to the realignment of current business procedures to maximize the long-term benefits for the company. Integrating existing databases and legacy applications with Web-based new applications is not a trivial task. It is essential to have senior management involvement as the potential impact of the integration on the functional areas of the business as well as the technical sophistication of the new systems can be quite disruptive.

One of the barriers to success named by Hartman, Sifonis and Kador (2000) is "putting lipstick on a bulldog." Companies "Webbify" old business practices or models by sticking on a Web front-end without regard to underlying process issues. They end up with a broken and inefficient process that has a pretty user interface (a good-looking bulldog). The authors say another barrier to success is "islands of Webbification" where companies engage in the creation of discontinuous and nonsynergistic applications or pockets of e-Business that are often redundant, without driving towards an overall direction. Hartman, Sifonis and Kador (2000) say this characteristic is endemic to most companies of any reasonable size. Consultation with employees affected by proposed changes is essential. In addition to anticipating customers' needs, viewing customer information as a strategic asset for both parties and treating each customer as a unique entity with unique needs and desires, it also means providing a single corporate or company face to the customer. It is essential to do this wherever the customer may interface with the company through different departments, in different locations and at different times. Customers increasingly expect integrated, seamless and multichannel customer service. Deise, Nowikow, King and Wright (2000) write of e-enabled companies that have information systems allowing them to be customer-centric and engineered around customer information touch points. These companies can provide simplified, effortless ordering, personalized Web pages and significant customer service.

Web Site Part of Overall Communications Strategy

The growth of Web sites for businesses, institutions and individuals has led to a huge amount of advice about how to develop and maintain a successful site. More often than not, this advice is atheoretical, prescriptive, based on conventions rather than evidence or focused primarily on technical and commercial aspects of a site rather than its ability to engage with the site's visitors, according to Durham (2000, p. 1). Some of the major communication faults of Web sites are not paying enough attention to the aims of the site and the audience's needs, leaving major communication choices to the technical experts, an overly strong focus on the visual communication elements and lack of analysis about the communication effectiveness of the site.

Some organizations do undertake research on their own and other organizations' Web sites. This may involve keeping a watching brief on what competitors are doing, or usability studies to find out more specifically how well the site's information and structures align with the users' needs and interests. Some of this information may come directly from site visitors who may be required to register in order to get access to a site or download information, or they may be encouraged to provide information in return for prizes or free gifts. Other ways organizations measure the use of their Web site is by gathering navigational information. Visitors' paths can be tracked through the site, recording the number of clicks made by the visitor, the time spent at different parts of the site as well as the level of 'drill down' or movement into the site from the home or first page of the site.

Organizations are considering the level of interactivity available on their site and moving from email links, a search function and downloadable files to subscription services, voter surveys, order facilities and in some cases bulletin boards and chat rooms. More research needs to be done about audience involvement on organizational Web sites and the cost-benefit analysis of interactivity from an e-Business perspective.

Communication and collaboration are the critical success factors when building a successful knowledge enterprise (Raisch, 2001). Building an open communication climate between employees, customers and partners is critical. An essential component of this is a customer-focused, value-added Web site integrated with the organization's back-office systems.

Site-Related Communication

The large volume of incoming email received by companies often surprises them. The growth of email as a form of customer interaction often outstrips companies' ability to handle it. Email is an important, low-cost customer service tool. It is ideally deployed in three ways: by conveying complex information to customers who require detailed answers to product or service queries, by updating order status and by generating leads by informing customers that their products they are interested in are now available through the company's Web site.

e-Business technology eliminates the need for a customer service representative (CSR) to be available by phone every time a customer has a simple question or requests a simple answer. In some situations, CSRs may respond to emails for customers who could not be serviced directly from the Web site. It is crucial that customer emails are acknowledged at least as promptly and efficiently as fax or physical mail: failure to do so results in dissatisfied customers and poor perception in the marketplace. Several early major corporate Web sites with customer response email capability, such as American Airlines, found they were swamped with messages and were completely unprepared to deal with the flood of inquiries—a potentially great opportunity became a marketing disaster. Responding to email is critical for organizations of all sizes; perhaps more so for small and medium-sized enterprises. Satisfied email queries may lead to order placement and a deepening of the customer-business relationship.

If an organization's online presence supports a virtual community, typical communication activities of an online community can include chat rooms, threaded discussions, bulletin boards, email, e-zines, newsletters, bulletins and general Web postings. The various forms of communication cover synchronous and asynchronous communication and may be one:one, one:some or one:many. To ensure prompt feedback and effective communication occurs, organizational resources need to be deployed to ensure each form of communication is adequately catered for.

Whether virtual or not, communities generally share the three Is: interest, incentive and interaction ability (Raisch, 2001). Internet communities often form for the purposes of exchanging information and knowledge and to facilitate commerce. Members of a community must have the ability to interact with each other, and the easier it is for a potential community to interact, the more likely it will interact and the stronger it will grow. Providing services to users can contribute to providing a vibrant online community, especially those services that facilitate communication among community members and between community members and the organization. Raisch (2001) suggests these services could include free email, chat rooms, threaded discussions, search engines, maps or directions, yellow pages, bookmarks, free downloads and news clipping services.

Identifying and serving the needs of community participants is essential for building and maintaining a strong community. The greater the relevant content and functionality, the stronger the relationship with the community member or participant. Communicating with the community during the community-building process may be through focus groups, advisory boards and researching the content and format of both online and offline media addressing the target audience or segment. Ongoing market research should include both monitoring and active involvement in community activities.

Involving community members in site activities, and integrating the site into the regular routine of the community member and where appropriate their organization, can build loyalty and value. Building a feeling of investment in the community by providing opportunities for input can also be useful for determining the evolution of the site. While online involvement can take many forms, those entailing person-to-person communication tend to build the strongest loyalties (Raisch, 2001). Strong community building minimizes the need for the visitor to go elsewhere for function or content by maximizing the number and duration of visits by making the environment as rich and compelling as possible. Jupiter Communications (cited in Raisch, 2001) reports that online customers can sustain only 10 significant relationships with Web sites at any one time.

Customers who send email expect instant results, and companies must respond that way. They need to send instant messages saying they've received the email and will have an answer in 24 hours. Companies also shouldn't have messages sent to a general address for a huge range of issues. Instead, it needs to be clear to whom messages are sent and who can act on them (Ohlson, 1999c).

Marketing

Kotler (1991) says marketing communication consists of advertising, sales promotion, public relations and personal selling. The communications mix depends on communications objectives, target audience, nature of the message, available communications channels and communications budget. A number of writers (Hoffman and Novak, 1995; Kalakota and Winston, 1996; Vassos, 1996) have considered how the different nature of the Internet is changing marketing communication.

Hoffman and Novak (1995) state the Internet enables marketing communications to become more interactive, available on demand, targeted through micro-marketing, individualized through one:one marketing and enables differentiation that helps to reduce price competition. In most studies business-to-consumer interaction has been addressed, rather than business-to-business. As yet a model for business-to-business electronic marketing communications does not yet seem to exist that provides an integrated approach to deal with several possible marketing communications channels, including the Internet (channel coherence) and also takes into account the characteristics of Internet-enabled industrial markets (Timmers, 2000).

A key marketing concept that is often discussed in the context of Internet commerce is one-to-one marketing which is enabled by the Internet and technologies like databases, customer profiling and data mining. Peppers and Rogers (1997) define one- to-one marketing as using customer databases and interactive communications to sell to one customer at a time as many products and services as possible over the entire lifetime of that customer's patronage (instead of selling one product at a time to as many customers as possible in a particular sales period). One-to-one marketing is based on the knowledge of the customers and company flexibility to deliver customized products and services. This necessitates knowledge of the individual customer, assessment of the lifetime value of customers rather than their one-off value, increasing the level of interactive communications with the customers, keeping customer records and development of the customer needs in addition to the development of the internal flexibility to respond to a potentially wide variety of customer needs by customized development, production and delivery of products and services (Timmers, 2000, p. 159).

"Internet companies are based on low margins and high volumes and it is critical to attract customers quickly to achieve profitability. Marketers must balance their expenditure on attracting, retaining and servicing customers with the revenue stream generated by customers" (McNaughton, 2000). "Basic marketing principles are a sound foundation for Internet marketing. It is the context in which the principles are applied that is changing. Internet businesses have relatively few tangible assets, yet the Internet can offer significant cost advantages for technology-based companies over traditional businesses."

Growth in Internet advertising (or Web advertising) in the U.S. has been extremely rapid since its introduction in 1994. The Web is likely to remain a secondary advertising medium for advertisers in the short term because of its low reach, limited intrusiveness, low bandwidth and lack of standardized measurability. Web advertising is also unlikely to have a negative impact on the amount of money spent by companies on more traditional advertising media. Current revenue from Internet advertising in New Zealand is minimal and it appears that New Zealand is well behind the United States in its use of the Internet as an advertising medium (Vosper, 1999). Vosper in her 1999 study of New Zealand SMEs and Internet advertising found that the lack of coherent and reliable information about visitors, effectiveness and impact of Web advertising are major deterrents to Internet advertising. SMEs want to understand more about how to use the Web to better effect and recognize that the potential of the medium as an advertising vehicle lies in the immediacy of its delivery, the ability to create relationships with customers and its cost-effective nature.

In the United States, email marketing is being considered as the ultimate commercial application of online advertising–the so-called "killer app" (Jayne, 2001). Email can be a very powerful cheap direct marketing tool–providing one-to-one, interactive communication with willing customers, and able to generate quick real-time response to specific offers. It can be used to reinforce branding, drive customer loyalty, generate new customers or offer new products to an existing customer base.

Seth Godin (www.permission.com) sees permission marketing as the only solution to the 3,000-a-day message attack on people's time and attention span. Traditional "interruptive" advertising has to be quirkier or more controversial, and to hit harder or more often to break through this communications clutter. Godin sees permission marketing as based on getting a customer to "opt-in" to your marketing communications and "it's what will unlock the power of the Internet." Unlike traditional marketing channels, what the Internet offers is the capability of personalizing communications to each customer's needs and wants. Permission marketing is increasingly being seen as an effective alternative to banner advertising and it represents a growing share of total online marketing spending. In 1999, U.S. businesses spent US$97 million on it and that figure is expected to reach US$7.3 billion by 2005 (Jayne, 2001).

One reason for a slower uptake of email e-marketing techniques appears to be the adverse publicity given to failed B2C initiatives. People are also adverse to spam and unless email offerings are well tailored and targeted, they can be perceived as an irritation. On the other hand, sending customized messages to people who actually want them generates the sort of response rate that is a vast improvement on traditional direct marketing rates. As a result, marketing departments within a business must figure out the appropriate promotion and advertising campaigns for their target segments. Web technology allows these marketing campaigns to be delivered, analyzed and modified in real time, gaining a significant advantage over conventional marketing methods. As an example, organizations can analyze buyer data to determine the correct point-of-sale promotions including cross-selling and up-selling offers. All of these considerations have a significant impact on the new processes that must be developed in the organization's marketing area.

Channel enhancement provides a drastic change to the way companies perform sales and order management activities. Those employees who formerly took sales orders over the telephone are now free to perform troubleshooting on orders or to perform other value-added activities, including maintaining sales data on the Web site, such as pricing and product descriptions. Another advantage of Web-based marketing is that the effects of price changes can be assessed by quickly measuring the change in sales volume that results from a temporary change in price. In addition, sales representatives are now able to obtain up-to-date information in real time on products, markets, customers and competitors. This capability allows the employees to concentrate on increasing revenues and sales (Deise, Nowikow, King and Wright, 2000).

Over the past few years, the advent of customer-information systems has allowed a company to capture data about customers in the hopes of identifying unique buying attributes or trends (Deise, Nowikow, King and Wright, 2000). It was not until the application of the Web that businesses operating in a mass production world have been able to truly to personalize relationships with customers. This ability has led to new competition from businesses to put strategic plans in place to go after lifetime value from new customers and in new markets. With e-Business, companies have the opportunity to replicate the personal customer relationship that existed prior to mass markets. Companies are able to use knowledge of the customer to personalize customer service while continuing to sell standard products.

Communication with Employees

A study conducted by *InformationWeek* with 988 responding managers (Chabrow, 1998) found that information most frequently included in intranets consists of corporate policies and procedures, document sharing, corporate phone directories, human resource forms, training programs, customer databases, product catalogues and manuals, data warehouse and decision support access, image archives, purchase orders, enterprise suits and travel reservation services. This range of information can be used via intranets for electronic commerce, customer services, reduced time to market, enhanced knowledge sharing, enhanced group decision and business process, empowerment, virtual organizations, software distribution, document management, project management, training, facilitating transaction processing, eliminating paper-based information delivery and administrative process support (Robinson, 1996).

Intranets are a cost-efficient method for communicating with internal customers and stakeholders. Internal documentation, business forms, announcements, product specifications and so on are served from Web servers onto the network, either with or without linking them to the outside world. Brooks (1998) says when employees are empowered to go online and change their own demographic or financial data, it helps to ensure the data is accurate. Employees may also perceive that their company is making an investment in them through the development of an intranet, giving them the information and tools they need to make intelligent informed decisions.

The negative aspects of intranets don't receive as much coverage as the benefits. One of these is the ease of posting documents online that may mean a proliferation of ill-organized material. Another issue can be that the presentation and content doesn't conform to any particular style guidelines, meaning that the quality and tone can be uneven with some pages not checked for accuracy. Deise, Nowikow, King and Wright (2000) see e-Business as a disruptive technology and the use of it has serious implications for the ways that companies manage their day-to-day operations. Channel enhancement requires fundamental changes in the way existing processes are executed. While these new processes may not be completely different from previous systems, they do represent a new way of doing things. Some processes may be eliminated through channel enhancement, freeing up resources to focus on more value-added activities. In addition to existing processes, channel enhancement also requires businesses to develop processes in new areas.

Meeting Customer Demand

Established companies moving towards the Internet have three broad types of customers: those who insist on doing business the traditional way, those who are willing to move gradually to the Internet and those who want to use the Internet immediately. Each company needs to decide how to interact with each group during their move to the Internet. Many established businesses use the Internet to complement conventional channels by recognizing existing strengths such as a trusted brand, established customer base and their distribution and payment infrastructure. An advantage of a new dot.com or pure play business is that all their customers, of necessity, are online already so efforts do not need to be made to migrate existing non-Internet customers.

When customers buy through a Web site, the roles of employees change. If effective systems are in place, staff can spend less time handling the routine aspects of the transaction such as payment and delivery requirements. More time can be spent on tasks that build the business such as understanding customer needs and being proactive towards them. "These changes in staff responsibilities mean that different types of skills are needed and rewarded. There is more need for creative qualities and a tendency to define staff roles less, resulting in a fundamental change to a company's culture" (*Financial Times*, 1999, p. 9).

When doing business internationally over the Web, the target market needs examining. Some items are the legal requirements, delivery costs, tax charges and account costs for such localized operations such as after-sales service and customer help lines. Marketing is far more effective in the target market's native language. Web sites can be centrally managed and standardized, but product pricing and backup services are better localized. Vendors will be asked to deliver 24-hour uptime, additional language and currency capabilities for electronic commerce, and to convert more visitors to buyers through the use of personalized, targeted offerings. One recent IDC survey showed that sites that have pitches and pages targeted to specific individuals have conversion rates that are much higher than other sites, Gens said (cited by Sykes, 1999).

CONCLUSION

Customer Service

The Web can be used to provide personalized and responsive service specific to a particular customer—an individual, a family or a company. Internet technology provides online support and service that enhances the "faster, better, cheaper" model of Internet buying. The Internet medium allows the approach to customers to be highly individual and responsive, developing trust and a personalized response with the customer during the sale and afterwards.

The self-service channel model offers companies the opportunity for relatively low-variable transaction costs. Some organizations give customers access to databases that only company employees could previously use. Customers need to get better, more timely and more precise information about products and suppliers. Internet technology can provide a way for customers to get real-time data about products, availability and pricing. Internet technology allows a high degree of interactivity so the customer can easily create, edit, send, confirm and track orders through systems that are highly effective, responsive and flexible.

Deise, Nowikow, King and Wright, (2000) claim that research has shown that only delighted customers are truly loyal customers. Customer delight provides a level of customer satisfaction that keeps customers coming back. Providing a relationship that is merely "satisfying" as opposed to "delightful" leaves a company vulnerable to others seeking to take customers away because they are easier for the customer to do business with. Creating new or added value can be accomplished through strengthening customer relationships by integrating sales, configuration, planning and design processes with customers through new and existing channels.

Overall customer satisfaction with buying products online is high, in spite of customer service and delivery problems, according to a study issued by Dataquest, a unit of Gartner Group Inc. Five-hundred and five households were surveyed and 88% said that they were satisfied with their online purchasing experience, particularly the ease of placing orders and making reservations (cited in Ohlson, 1999a).

According to Dataquest, merchants haven't implemented effective links to back-office systems or given much attention to online customer support. As a result, retailers are offering 24-hour shopping but not 24-hour support, which may make it difficult to win customer loyalty (Ohlson, 1999b).

As the Internet evolves, companies will lose control as customers become empowered. Customers won't care about business matters; they'll care about their own needs—and expect them to be met, according to Horowitz (cited in Ohlson, 1999a). Businesses will have to personalize content to satisfy those customers. That will lead to difficult obstacles for businesses to overcome.

REFERENCES

Bell, C, (1999). Gamble or goldmine? *MIS New Zealand*, August, 37-45.

Boddy, D. and Boonstra, A. (2000). Doing business on the Internet: Managing the organizational issues. *Journal of General Management*, 26(1), 18-35.

Brooks, M. K. (1998). HR intranets: An ROI strategy. *HRFocus*, August, 13-14.

Chabrow, E. (1998). Instruments of growth. *InformationWeek*, October 5.

Deise, M.V., Nowikow, C., King, P. and Wright, A. (2000). *Executive's Guide to e-Business from Tactics to Strategy*. New York: John Wiley & Sons Ltd.

Durham, M. (2000). Organizational Web sites: How and how well do they communicate? *Australian Journal of Communication*, 27(3), 1-14.

Ernst and Young, (1999). *eCommerce in New Zealand: First Annual Study Results*, April.

Emigh, J. (1999). e-Commerce strategies. *Computerworld Online*, August. Available on the World Wide Web at: http://www.computerworld.com/home/print.nsf/CWFlash/990816BBFE.

Evans, P. (Ed.). (1990). *Human Resource Management in International Firms*. London: Macmillan.

Financial Times. (1999). *IT Review*, September, 9.

Hartman, A., Sifonis, J. and Kador, J. (2000). *Net Ready: Strategies for Success in the E-Conomy*. New York, NY: McGraw-Hill.

Hoffman, D. and Novak, T. (1995). *Marketing in Hypermedia Computer-Mediated Environments: Conceptual Foundations*, July. Available on the World Wide Web at: http://www2000.ogsm.vanderbilt.edu and http://www.permission.com. Accessed May 17, 2000.

Huff, S.L., Wade, M., Parent, M., Schneberger, S. and Newson, P. (1999). *Cases in Electronic Commerce*. New York, NY: McGraw-Hill.

Information Technology Policy Group, Ministry of Economic Development (2000). *Electronic Commerce in New Zealand: A Survey of Business Use of the Internet*. Wellington. Available on the World Wide Web at: http://www.med.govt.nz/consumer/elcom/survey/survey.pdf.

Jayne, V. (2001). Netting better custom. *Tuanz Topics*, 11(1), 5-8.

Kalakota, R. and Winston, A. (1996). *Frontiers of Electronic Commerce*. Reading, MA: Addison-Wesley Longman, Inc.

Kalakota, R. and Robinson, M. (2001). *E-Business 2.0: Roadmap for Success*. Reading, Massachusetts: Addison Wesley Longman, Inc.

Kotler, P. (1991). *Marketing Management, Analysis, Planning, Implementation and Control*. Englewood Cliffs, NJ: Prentice-Hall.

MacLeod, A. (2000). *E-Marketing Presentation to MBA Marketing Elective Students*, January, Institute House, Palmerston North.

Markus, L. and Benjamin, R.I. (1997). The magic bullet theory in IT-enabled transformation. *Sloan Management Review*, Winter, 55-68.

McNaughton, R. (2000). *Naked Business Models Help Internet Firms*. Available on the World Wide Web at: http://www.otago.ac.nz/news/press_releases/200002-08-00_press_release.html. Accessed November 18, 2000.

Ministry of Economic Development. (2000). *E-Commerce: A Guide for New Zealand Business*. Wellington: Author.

Ohlson, K. (1999a). Net ads growing quickly. *Online News*, April. Available on the World Wide Web at: http://www.computerworld.com/home/news.nsf/CWFlash/9905042iab.

Ohlson, K. (1999b) Companies must cater to e-customers. *Computerworld Online*, May. Available on the World Wide Web at: http://www.computerworld.com/home/news.nsf/CWFlash/9904283horowitzspeech.

Ohlson, K. (1999c). Brace for more customer email. *Online News*, June. Available on the World Wide Web at: http://www.computerworld.com/home/news.nsf/all/9906093email2.

Oliver, R.W. (2000). The seven laws of e-Commerce strategy. *Journal of Business Strategy*, September-October, 8-10.

Peppers, D. and Rogers, M. (1997). *Enterprise One-to-One: Tools for Competing in the Interactive Age*. New York: Bantam Doubleday Dell.

Raisch, W.D. (2001). *The e-marketplace: Strategies for success in B2B ecommerce*. New York: McGraw-Hill.

Rasmussen, J. (1996). The Internet. *CMA Magazine*, March, 70, 11.

Robinson, J. (1996). Intranet 100: The revolution is here. *InformationWeek*, November, 106-108.

Sykes, R. (1999). IDC: Vendors must change to greet new Net. *Online News*, March. Available on the World Wide Web at: http://www.computerworld.com/home/news.nsf/CWFlash/9903103direct.

Timmers, P. (2000). *Electronic Commerce: Strategies and Models for Business-to-Business Trading*. England: John Wiley & Sons Ltd.

Vassos, T. (1996). *Strategic Internet Marketing*. Indianapolis, IN: Que Corporation.

Vosper, G. (1999). Towards an Internet advertising strategy for small and medium New Zealand businesses. *MBA Research Report*, July.

Chapter VIII

Virtual Absenteeism

William H. Friedman
University of Central Arkansas, USA

INTRODUCTION

This chapter will discuss problems arising from employee use of the Internet for personal pursuits during paid working hours. Since there are both financial and non-financial consequences of such behavior (Friedman, 2000), it is worthwhile to evaluate existing attempts to deal with this problem and suggest some new ones. Nevertheless, virtual absenteeism is not a totally negative phenomenon; hence, one needs to give a fair hearing to the claims of the employees engaged in this activity. It is not necessarily an economic loss to the employer when employees take care of private matters or even play on the Internet, if it is within reason and results in a refreshed approach to the job at hand.

Still, if the employee is excessively occupied with non-business Internet activity, there is no doubt a corresponding decrease in the amount of conscious attention given to the processing of organizational concerns. Moreover, ethical issues emerge concerning the misuse of time, avoidance of responsibility and violation of employee-employer contracts, implicit or explicit. Since the employer is defraying the cost of both the hardware and software involved, Internet misuse results in expenses far exceeding losses from such minor trespasses as personal telephone calls and company stationery misappropriated for personal reasons. Further, diversionary materials such as magazines and games brought to the workplace by employees which were paid out of their own pockets, while clearly resulting in lost time for the employer, at least did not require highly sophisticated and expensive technology to support the diversions. Finally, it is necessary to show that the sheer scale of modern slacking requires very special measures that consider not only financial, but legal, social, moral and psychological ramifications as well.

Terminology for Preciseness

We should be clear at the outset about certain terms:

Stealing is defined as "To take (the property of another) without right or permission" (American Heritage Electronic Dictionary, 1992).

Virtual absenteeism or *cyberslacking* involves visiting pornographic sites and news sites, shopping, stock trading, vacation planning, gaming, chatting, in other words, engaging in Internet activities unrelated to the job on company time and using company resources.

Infantilization involves treating people as if they were still young children or condescension towards them.

Addiction implies psychological dependence on something (perhaps involving compulsive behavior) despite its (potentially) harmful effects.

Satisficing is choosing an option that is suboptimal, but which seems justified because of the cost of finding or acting on the absolute maximal option.

Rationalization is the act of proposing reasons to justify one's behavior to satisfy oneself or an audience, however incorrect the reasons may be.

THE ISSUES

Extent of the Problem

Excessive cyberslacking in and of itself should be cause for managerial concern because of its possible deleterious effects on productivity, but there are serious side effects as well, which receive treatment in other sections of this chapter. The Internet presents a vast array of time-consuming and tempting diversions from business work—more than businesses have ever had to face previously. Of all these opportunities to engage in pursuits not directly furthering the company's interests, it is probably most galling to employers, when their employees use company time and bandwidth to seek other jobs. However, if an organization is made aware of this tendency in certain individuals, it perhaps would be an occasion for a heart-to-heart talk with the disaffected employee. If job seeking were pervasive in an entire department (Drinkwater, 2000) then, possibly, it would constitute an early warning signal of mass defections or poor management in that department. The company would be wise to draw the relevant conclusions and institute corrective managerial action in that department or with respect to the employees involved. Clearly, to become aware of cyberslacking, an employer would normally engage in monitoring Internet usage with all the costs and risks implied in doing so, such as employee resentment and expensive monitoring technology.

There may be unforeseen benefits stemming from the freedom to cyberslack and, consequently, reason not to curtail it totally, provided that the company is aware of its causes and contexts as well as the nature of the activity. In the final analysis, the company must decide where harmless use (which might conceivably benefit the company) ends and harmful abuse begins.

Two recent surveys (SurfCONTROL Web site 2, 2000) give these results: "56% openly admitted to using the Internet for personal reasons while at work" (JSB's SurfCONTROL and QuickTake.Com(SM)), and "Americans spent on the average 21 hours last month [February, 2000] (more than one hour per day) conducting personal Web surfing at work" (Nielsen-NetRatings). Thirty-two percent acknowledged their job-hunting activities on the Web.

Additionally, the level of abuse is growing in severity: "Employees spent about one-third of their online time in recreation, a 1999 report from JSB's SurfCONTROL shows. That was double the amount of online goofing off in 1998" (Griggs, 2000).

The problem is not, of course, confined to the United States. Britain's third largest mobile phone company, Orange, determined that it must dismiss a sizable number (30 to 40) of key employees who allegedly abused their Internet privileges. The official Sydney Olympics Web site alone had 840, 000 hits on its opening day (SurfCONTROL Web site 4).

Still one might think that surfing the Internet is no different from gazing out the window while on the job. Caplan (2000) writes: "It [slacking] was going on before there ever was a computer on anyone's desk." In a forthcoming article Block similarly argues that cyberslacking is not a new problem in concept, hence calls for no new managerial strategies. Block argues that in pretechnological times there was chess and now we have computer gaming; before there was surreptitious reading of magazines on the job, now we have surfing for porn, and so on in this manner. It should be obvious, however, that the expenses to the employer are so much greater with the misuse of technology and that the temptations immediately available to the employee are so numerous and so readily available on the employee's own desk, that we have a case of a quantitative difference that causes a vast difference in quality and, therefore, a much graver danger to the business. Moreover, the very power and cost of providing Internet service, as well as the magnitude and cost of the risks involved, put Web surfing into a much different category. Slacking, in terms of time wasted, is not the only concern.

Economic Effects

There are indirect costs as well: increased Internet use, beyond what is necessary for the business, requires purchase of additional bandwidth and consumption of unneeded resources. Increased Internet usage brings security problems as well. It is clear that the more Web sites visited unnecessarily (or even legitimately, of course), the greater the exposure to viruses in the form of a malicious JavaScript and the like. Corporate intelligence is also at risk from unnoticed applets transmitting proprietary information and being more susceptible to being hacked. This exposure can rapidly escalate as employees exchange suspect URLs with one another, thus however causing additional logons:

- A realistic estimate of the cost of cyberslacking (based on research conducted by the Saratoga Institute of Human Resources) for just one hour per day of Web surfing by 1,000 Internet users in a company is $35 million each year. For the

Fortune 1000 companies as a group, this cumulative 'one hour' could sum to $35 billion (SurfCONTROL Web site 1, 2000).

- Internet abuse costs British businesses £1.4 million per week (Corbelli, 2000). The official Olympic Web site alone had 840,000 hits on its opening day. (SurfCONTROL Web site 4).
- The additional burden of dealing with downloaded images and movies can crash a company's network: in the case of Xerox, so many employees downloaded porn videos that it choked Xerox's vast computer network, to the extent of preventing other workers from opening or sending email. "There were people spending all solid day doing nothing but clicking the mouse and downloading pictures," reported Xerox cybercop Mike Gerdes, who runs the company's eight-member SWAT team on computer abuse (Naughton, 1999).
- Software downloaded from suspect Web sites could contain viruses or might represent copyright violations, the possibility that company secrets had been sent out over the Internet and some unexpected company information, for example, employee files being made available over the company's own Web site (Casser, 1996).
- Ironically, cyberslacking creates yet an additional expense by causing the employer to purchase software to deal with the problem.

Moral Issues

There is no reason that the notion of stealing should apply only to physical property and not time. For instance, certainly intellectual property is also subject to theft. Arguably, to misappropriate anything whatsoever that is of value to an individual or organization is to pilfer. The time employees misuse, but for which they are compensated, as well as the monetary value of Internet access privileges via company equipment, may properly be considered objects of thievery. Something of economic value is obviously being stolen. Despite its being a moral trespass, cyberslacking is, in actual practice, not the sort of theft that ends up being prosecuted in court. Other related activities discussed elsewhere in this article (like exposing company secrets) are, however, precisely the sort of activity that is and should be prosecuted.

Ralph Waldo Emerson discussed the type of theft relevant to cyberslacking in his essay, Compensation: "In labor as in life there can be no cheating. The thief steals from himself. The swindler swindles himself" (Emerson, 1947). Without a doubt, obsessed virtual absentees are depriving their company of the value of their services, and as the company's revenues decline, so do the chances of a decent bonus for themselves. Moreover, they might have to be laid off. Even worse, however—since Emerson tells only part of the story in order to appeal to the would-be thief's self-interest—the cyberslacker's actions also affect other workers and, of course, any shareholders negatively. Emerson's statement needs to be expanded: the thief swindles himself and innocent others.

If, however, the apparent Internet addict somehow still renders value to the company, perhaps even as a result of the cyberactivity, which might foster subconscious problem solving or provide a necessary break from drudgery or intense creative endeavor, there is obviously then no loss to others and thus no swindle. Naturally, this somewhat exceptional case would have to be demonstrated to the employer. The employer ought then to make it known to everyone that this is an exceptional case and not necessarily the norm, so as not to create a precedent for all other workers not in this category. Here the employer would have to be both deft and fair in extending such privileges to all employees on a merit basis. Certain jobs, like producing a routine report on time or being readily available to customers, simply call for straightforward, consistent work, and not necessarily creative work. Hence, there is an important distinction to be made about how time is spent in an environment of routine tasks or where the employee is expected to be constantly occupied versus an environment where work can be made up, say, in a final spurt just before the deadline. Time diverted to Web surfing would be much harder to justify morally and practically, where routine tasks are not the norm and lost time cannot be made up. As a caution, one should note that nothing in this paragraph ought to be considered as reason to disregard the other problems engendered by cyberslacking.

Psychological Issues

Rationalization: A worker once said: "I'm not cheating anyone. I'm a multitasker." "After all," she continued, "everyone shirks at work sometimes. Besides, what's more beneficial? Talking on the phone to a friend or maybe becoming more computer literate because you're using the computer?" (Naughton, 1999). Her points may be substantially correct, but the behavior is nevertheless unjustified. What would she say if no one shirked at work? Another worker contends that "'cyberslacking' can also be called catching up on personal business [which] a long workday denies." As a general rule, one must simply try to schedule the affairs of personal life on personal time. In the hierarchy of obligations, such employees claim (conveniently for themselves) that their lower level duties can reasonably supersede those at an obviously higher level. At a different time or place when other obligations did not trump their convenience, their explanations would be credible.

Infantilizing: Employee monitoring systems are fraught with difficulties for both those doing the monitoring and those being monitored. Here is the reaction of a person who was "chastised" by a monitoring system about shopping on the Internet. She complained that the 'strongly worded' company email warned ... she could be fired from work for cruising the Internet. "I felt like I was back in first grade and the teacher thought I was cheating" (Naughton, 1999). It has to be conceded that warning employees in a certain tone or punishing adults for cyberslacking may be regarded by them as more appropriate to young children. In fact there is a danger is that cyberslackers may come to regard themselves as still in the child mode of trying to get away with something until caught. Some solutions below deal with these problems.

Guilt: Cyberslacking can be the cause of guilt feelings, if the employee at some level really believes that what he or she is doing is wrong. Furtive activity breeds further guilt and often leads to a feeling of "I can get away with things (e.g., other misappropriations)."

Guilt is compounded when virtual absentees are engaged in job seeking at the office. While everyone is free to seek alternate employment, most people would concede that it is particularly disloyal to use the resources of one's present employer to do so. Both the disloyalty and the surreptitious nature of the activity lead to increased guilt.

Stress: Internet activities may be a welcome relief from stress, and for that reason, companies may wish to foster such activity, perhaps in the manner described above and also below in the remedies. On the other hand, excessive cyberslacking could in and of itself be the cause of stress, for instance, as one gets further and further behind in one's work. Then again, the ensuing guilt could bring on yet more stress.

Addiction: An ever-present danger to the employee who spends an inordinate amount of time Web surfing is that he/she may become too habituated and dependent. Perhaps this is due to social incompetence away from the computer, there being no alternative source of satisfaction from the job, and the like.

With inordinate involvement in cyberslacking, the possibility of recovering and making up for lost time vanishes almost totally. If the Internet addiction also feeds on say another addiction like gambling on the Web or pornography, there is a serious personnel issue, one that is costly to both the company and the employee. The problem is one for the economy at large: "Virtual absenteeism caused by uncontrolled addictive Web entertainment is costing UK businesses millions of pounds in lost profit every year" (SurfCONTROL Web site 4).

Legal Implications

Employees are often under the impression that they have privacy rights protected by the law when they engage in Internet activity. However, the courts have consistently decided that companies may be held liable for the email messages and Internet activities of their employees (Rosenberg, 1999). Examples causing liability are misuse of copyrighted materials, leaking company or private information, and the like. Also, if an internal passerby sees objectionable material on a co-worker's computer screen, that too, could lead to lawsuits, perhaps based on charges of creating a hostile environment.

The actions of employers to detect cyberslacking appear to be fully within the law and even legally protected. No corresponding safeguard exists for the employee. "With no general legal protection of workers' privacy, no actual protection exists. The courts have found little reason to challenge the determination, and actual activities, of management to employ every means at its disposal to monitor the work, stationary and otherwise, of its workforce" (Rosenberg, 1999).

Recently, U.S. federal officials have initiated an investigation of some of the major players in e-Commerce, such as Amazon.com, eBay and eToys on account of their Internet advertising, which simultaneously collects consumer information (Wolverton and Sandoval, 2000).

Conceivably, they could share this information with employers, if the vendors could be sure the employee/customer would never learn about it. DoubleClick has also acknowledged a probe by the Federal Trade Commission into its practice of collecting customer information (Rosenberg, 1999).

Proposed Solutions

An approach that appeals to the employee's sense of responsibility such as the one used by Texas Instruments (McManus, 1999) would go a long way to preventing feelings of being infantilized, while still exerting some moral influence. Their policy asks the employees to consider the legality of their computer activity, how it conforms to the company's values, if it seems wrong to the employee himself or herself and how it would feel if the act were widely publicized. The strategy here is not only to have the employees police themselves, but also to enlist their prior moral training and natural moral sensibilities. As a further back up, the employees are asked to imagine what the consequences of inappropriate behavior would probably be to themselves.

A correlative adjunct to showing faith and trust in the employees would be to have them form committees to formulate policies pertaining to Internet usage. McManus (1999, p. 646) suggests forming committees to balance privacy concerns and company security. However, other committees might be concerned with balancing respect for employee freedom to work as seems most natural to the employee and the economic interests of the employer in light of the widespread tendency to use the Web for healthy relaxation or occasional personal business, yes, even for moderate cyberslacking. Productivity might actually increase with such a corporate culture.

If the situation in a given organization seems to warrant it, the employer could choose to treat the problem as a moral or legal issue. First, the employer would provide workshops involving an explanation of the moral issues of cyberslacking. The end result would then be to establish clear-cut company policies designed to avoid legal liability.

Another option open to the employer is to treat the problem of cyberslacking as a psychological disorder. Naturally, this would make sense only if there were excesses or evidence of compulsive behavior. Should the problem be compounded by feelings of self-reproach, remorse and stress caused by either running short of time or fear of being caught, there are various treatment protocols for addiction, guilt and tension. The employee could be referred or apply on his or her own to an appropriate counselor.

If there is no pressing psychological problem, the best approach might be some form of social redirection. A remedy for cyberslacking as an employee's substitute social activity might be to organize social functions where the cyberslacker is made to feel especially comfortable. This may even take the form of arranging social activities around the Internet itself. An innovative human resources department could attempt to co-opt the tendency of the employees to surf while on the job by redirecting this propensity to "worthwhile" or edifying sites (areas that might inform or train the employees). Employees seem to agree that this would be a good thing, as one has said: "To be business savvy means understanding the Internet and you can't really do that unless you're online" (Fletcher, 2000).

This philosophy can be further encouraged by providing special equipment at the job site and even lend such equipment to the employees so they can surf the Web at home. In this manner surfing can become a type of fringe benefit that both enhances the employee's knowledge or skill while simultaneously increasing morale as well as engendering loyalty to the organization—not to mention avoiding many of the ill effects of cyberslacking.

Implementation of the Philosophy of Co-Option

- Announce that this activity, as long as it does not create problems for the company, will be countenanced if productivity does not decline.
- Confine surfing to lunch hours or personal time.
- Award bonuses for bringing ideas to the organization from the Web and learning new skills.
- Provide specific or random time slots (recesses) between 9 and 5 for personal surfing to relieve the dissonance and guilt, thereby removing the felt need to surf on designated company time.
- Create an "Acceptable Use Policy." For instance, an employee should agree to make up lost time due to surfing. If so, surfing would be permitted, provided individual performance is not lessened. The freedom to take such breaks might even lift both morale and productivity. A special contract would be drawn up specifying both the employee's rights and responsibilities with regard to computer usage.

The policy would contain understandable rules governing Internet access along with definite criteria to determine whether a requested connection would be allowed or not. For example, the policy might stipulate that:

1. only designated persons, groups, workstations or specific areas would be allowed non-business access;
2. time of access will be regulated;
3. duration of access will be limited;
4. types of sites, both encouraged and prohibited, would be described; and
5. how much simultaneous access would be permitted in accordance with available bandwidth resources.

As a contributor to *Newsweek* (Messick, 1999) wrote, "Progressive companies that allow employees the occasional Web-surfing opportunity will be rewarded with lower absenteeism, higher morale and greater productivity." Here the operative word is "occasional"; perhaps one should add or even substitute the word, "reasonable."

Control and Punishment

A restrictive, theory X type of management might be deemed necessary in certain circumstances, say, if the lenient policies suggested below have failed. In such cases there would have to be increased supervision by managers or, better, by employees governing themselves. These are the suggested policies:

- Co-worker or group reinforcement of company policy would be instituted to prevent cyberslacking, i.e., peer policing. Some companies even require that employees snitch on coworkers involved in cyberslacking.
- Designate one employee to monitor the Web usage of several others. This involves certain controlling behaviors, which are usually distasteful to managers and their designated subordinates, such as disciplining employees, encouraging snitching and spying on employees.
- Making an example of those who are caught, e.g., negative raises, firing. Companies expend a great deal "of money to train workers, and it's more efficient to keep an experienced employee than having to find and train a replacement" (Griggs, 2000). Thus, the success of such tactics should be carefully examined. There are also economic drawbacks to be considered: "if the value of…Web access control isn't significantly greater than the cost of the control mechanism, control doesn't make sense' (Gibbs, 1999).
- Remove the ability of employees to access the Web either altogether or only in tightly controlled situations.

Filtering

Ashley J. Phillips noted that filtering could offer businesses certain advantages over monitoring. For one thing, less labor is involved, and filtering can prevent an employee from logging onto objectionable sites. No personal supervision is required when a company installs site-blocking software for corporate networks, in particular, if it uses artificial intelligence to identify and control which Web addresses can be accessed. Such software utilizes "virtual control lists," employing "pattern matching to dynamically determine the context of a Web site and restrict access to it." There are also programs that not only allow employers to find out what sites their employees access but the amount of time involved (Griggs, 2000). This can help shape future policy on Internet access.

"Expert Filtering is a unique technology that combines three distinct filtering techniques: Positive Filtering, General Filtering and Negative Filtering" (SurfCONTROL Web site 3, 1999). These will be discussed directly.

Positive Filtering

There is a program, namely, SuperScout 2.5, that sorts "over 500,000 business URLs by their Standard Industrial Classification (SIC) code and then rate[s] their business relevance. Access is permitted or denied based on individual organizational policy and the Web site's relevance to the company's business" (SurfCONTROL Web site 3, 1999). A company might even reward employees who bring ideas to the company as a result of their accessing the approved sites.

General Filtering

This type of filtering takes into account those companies that might allow some recreational surfing at work, so surfing is permitted to URLs listed on a database of acceptable sites, such as those offering news, financial services, shopping, sports and entertainment. A company can turn this type of access on and off during certain periods of the workday. "What's needed is a system that creates an acceptable Internet universe, letting employees know what Web sites they CAN go to, rather than where they CANNOT go," according to Steve Purdham (SurfCONTROL Web site 3, 1999).

Negative Filtering

There are Web sites that organizations might definitely want to prohibit their employees from visiting while on the job. Such offensive sites are those that are sexually graphic, cater to or foster prejudice, or are otherwise de-moralizing, which if visited on company equipment and during company hours can detrimentally impact corporate morale and reputation. Moreover, it would not be a stretch to say that other employees might complain to various governmental agencies that might subsequently levy fines, institute lawsuits or impose unwelcome strictures on the company.

Philosophical Options

It may very well be that some "moral" battles are not worth fighting, in particular those involving the policing of employees. Here "worth fighting" does not pertain to economics or even management practices, but to the question of whether the principle involved is important enough to justify the effort. Whether such a choice is morally justified or not is still a matter of philosophical debate. Swanton (1993), for one, defends the thesis that "It is sometimes rationally preferable, perhaps even required to satisfice." Acting according to the virtue of providing a friendly environment for workers can be more rational than the absolute, act-oriented maximizing of immediate profits.

One could also argue that emphasis on a relatively minor peccadillo might divert attention from prevention of greater moral abuses, such as harassment or peculation. However, it should be recalled that embezzlement, revelation of company secrets, harassment and neglect of security are also issues connected with cyberslacking. Still, there is reason to believe that if an organization is careful about even minor moral issues, the employee would soon understand that breaches of higher obligations are going to be taken particularly seriously.

Extension of the Research

Some research topics related to organizational Internet use and abuse that could be treated in this same vein would be:
- Dealing with hacking from the employer's computer.
- Establishing an organizational email policy with respect to privacy use for personal matters, harassment, etc.

- Being lax on security with regard to exposing the company to penetration or viruses.
- The issues surrounding employees operating a private business on the employer's computer.
- Video surveillance of work and restroom areas.
- The non-business matter of the control of children's Internet activities.
- The role of government (if any) in privacy issues within an organization, much like OSHA.
- Proposals for protecting privacy in computer matters.
- Collecting consumer information, with or without the knowledge and consent of the consumer.

REFERENCES

American Heritage Electronic Dictionary. (1992). Houghton-Mifflin, version 3.0A.

Block, W. (forthcoming). Cyberslacking, business ethics and managerial economics. *Journal of Business Ethics*.

Caplan, S. (1999). Why blame the Internet for slacking? *Letters, Newsweek*. December.

Corbelli, M. (2000). Orange draft 3 0800. *Personal Email*, October.

Drinkwater, D. (2000). *Personal Communication in my Class on March 15*.

Emerson, R. E. (1947). *Compensation in the World's Great Thinkers, Man and Man: The Social Philosophers*, 439. Cummins, S. and Linscott, R. N. (Eds.). New York: Random House.

Fletcher, L. (2000). PC benefit enhances skills, communication. *Business Insurance*, Chicago, February, 34(9).

Friedman, W. (2000). Is the answer the Internet addiction Internet interdiction? Young, H. M. (Ed), *Proceedings of the Association for Information Systems*, August, 1562-1567.

Gibbs, M. (1999-2000). *Counter Points Network World*, December-January, 17(1), 99.

Griggs, T. (2000). Web monitoring: Companies watching what workers watch. *The Baton Rouge Advocate*, January, 8-I.

McManus, Y. (1999). Ethics and technology in the workplace. *AMCIS 1999: Proceedings of the Fifth Americas Conference on Information Systems*, 644-646.

Messick, T. (1999). Clicking at work. *Letters, Newsweek*. December.

Naughton, K. (1999). Cyberslacking. *Newsweek*. November, 62-65.

Rosenberg, R. S. (1999). The workplace on the verge of the 21st century. *Journal of Business Ethics*. October, 3-14.

SurfCONTROL. (2000a). March. Available on the World Wide Web at: http://news.excite.com/news/bw/000306/ca-jsb-surfcontrol?printstory=1.

SurfCONTROL. (2000b). *Cyberslacking at Work Continues to Threaten Productivity Survey Zeroes in on Newest Internet Distractions*. Available on the World Wide Web at: http://www.surfcontrol.com/news/in_the_press/ pressreports/introweek021700.html/. Accessed March 15, 2000.

SurfCONTROL. (2000c). *Internet Market Press Release: "JSB 'Raises the Stakes' In Corporate Internet Filtering Marketplace."* Available on the World Wide Web at: http://www.surfcontrol.com/news/press_releases/15-03-1999_2.html. Accessed March 15, 2000.

SurfCONTROL. (2000d). *Virtual Absenteeism Soars as Olympic Web Mania Sets*. Available on the World Wide Web at: http://www.surfcontrol.com/news/ press_releases/content/09_26_2000b.html. Accessed September 26, 2000.

Swanton, C. (1993). Satisficing and virtue. *The Journal of Philosophy*, January, 90(1), 35.

Wolverton, T. and Sandoval, G. (2000). Probes are latest headache in e-commerce. *CNET News.com*, February. Available on the World Wide Web at: http:// news.cnet.com/news/0-1007-200-1551662.html. Accessed March 15, 2000.

Chapter IX

Systems Thinking and the Internet: New Thinking for a New Era

Kambiz E. Maani
University of Auckland, New Zealand

"The unleashed power of the atom has changed everything save our modes of thinking, and we thus drift toward unparalleled catastrophes."
Albert Einstein

INTRODUCTION

In the past decade two movements have had a profound influence on the way we think and communicate–Systems Thinking and the Internet. Both are grounded in sciences and technology and complement each other in principle and practice. But the similarities almost end here. While one has become a household name, the other still remains a mystery. The Internet was born in the elite military and academic quarters, but has rapidly moved to public neighborhoods and has already become a mass movement. Systems Thinking also originated from scientific circles and is only now beginning to make a public appearance.

Despite their benign appearances, both Systems Thinking and the Internet challenge mankind's age-old ways to think and disseminate information. At a fundamental level, they challenge the hierarchy and authority, and power and leadership. Through technology, the Internet has, in essence, brought down the boundaries that define business, trade and even nationhood. Through equally powerful scientific principles, Systems Thinking has broken the superficial dichotomies of the whole vs. the part, the individual vs. the community, integration and autonomy, and business and society.

In business and management, the last 20 years have seen concepts and paradigms that have dramatically challenged the prevailing workplace assumptions and practices. Among these are Just-in-Time production philosophy, total quality management, and more recently supply chain and enterprise resource planning (ERP). Each one of these paradigms has progressively removed the conventional boundaries between the organization, the customer, the supplier and the competition. Collectively, and now assisted by the power of the Internet, they have pushed our thinking and practice closer to a systemic integration of the enterprise.

Why New Thinking?

For well over a century, we have subscribed to a way of thinking known as analysis. In analysis, in order to understand something, a concept, a product, a law, an organization, the human body, we break it apart into pieces and study the pieces separately. This 'divide and conquer' approach has served us well. It has enabled efficient mass production of goods and services. It has brought a new social and economic order, which has produced unprecedented wealth and standard of living in the industrialized world.

Now in the dawn of the 21st century, this way of thinking is showing its age. The signs of divisions and fracture are increasing daily, begging for fresh approaches to stubborn and chronic problems. In the business and management field, this thinking has resulted in fragmentation of functions and has created complexity and cross-purposes within organizations. Today, the accelerated interconnectedness and interdependence of businesses, organizations, industries, economies and nations facilitated by the Internet is evident and inevitable. This sense of 'globalization' has resulted in a growing number of unions, alliances and joint ventures in recent years. At the political and trade levels, we see the emergence of EU and APEC and strengthening of UN, NATO and GATT. At the industry level, we observe the increasing convergence of airlines such as Star Alliance and One World as well as numerous partnerships and shared activities. In the health sector, integrated care, uniting the disjointed primary, secondary and tertiary segments, is becoming an international trend. In business and commerce the fast emergence of cross boundary and integrative models of management such as TQM, BPR, supply chain management, enterprise resource planning (ERP) and e-Commerce are manifestations of this growing interdependence.

Systems Thinking offers a new way of thinking based on the primacy of the 'whole' and relationships. It deals with hidden complexity, ambiguity and mental models. It provides tools and techniques to leverage change and to create lasting interventions.

Like computers, which used to be the domain of specialists, 'systems science' was considered a technical subject requiring proficiency in mathematics and computer modeling. Recent books have attempted to demystify (the field of) Systems Thinking and make it accessible to a wider range of audiences (Maani and Cavana, 2000).

Summary: Why Systems Thinking?

- Increasing complexity in our lives
- Growing interdependence of the world
- Revolutions in management theories and practice
- Increasing global consciousness and yet 'local' decision making
- Increasing recognition of learning as a key organizational capability

In this chapter we introduce the Systems Thinking paradigm and discuss its relevance and necessity for business and management practice in the Internet era. Before that, in order to better understand our position today, we will take a quick tour of management thought developments in the last century.

Management Thought

Despite our most impressive advances in sciences and technology, our prevailing worldview and the way we work at the dawn of the 21st century, is deeply rooted by the thinking that originated in the 17th century! This thinking is influenced by the sciences of that era, and in particular by Newtonian physics. Newton viewed the world as a machine that was created to serve its master–God (Ackoff, 1993). The machine metaphor has persisted since then and still today occupies our thinking and vocabulary. "Cog in the wheel," "the wheels of government," "the machinery of state" (Zohar, 1994, p. 25) are but a few examples. This mechanistic view of the world was developed during the Renaissance and was based on three fundamental beliefs that (Ackoff, 1993):

- Complete understanding of the universe was possible.
- The world could be understood through analysis (breaking wholes into parts).
- All relationships can be described through simple cause-and-effect relationships.

Oxford physicist Danah Zohar observes in this regard, "The power and simplicity of Newton's...mechanical laws of motion, and the force of the new empirical method, drew nearly every influential social, political and economic thinker of the seventeenth, eighteenth and nineteenth centuries to use them as model" (Zohar and Marshal, 1994, p. 24). These laws have served us well in the past and will continue to be valid in the future. They helped man to walk on the moon and reach planetary stars. They have made our daily physical chores much simpler and somewhat trivial.

However, beyond scientific and mechanical devices, the philosophical extension of the mechanical laws to social and political domains have outlived their useful purpose. As futurist Alvin Toffler described, "the Age of the Machine is screeching to a halt" (Zohar and Marshal, 1994, p. 28). Zohar explains the nature and implications of these laws to the society. "The basic building blocks of Newton's physical world were isolated atoms that bounce around in space and collide with one another like billiard balls...Political thinkers of the time compared these colliding atoms and their interacting forces to the behavior and interactions of individuals in society as they confront each other in pursuit of their self-interest...Still today, economists and sociologists who follow 'Rational Choice' theory argue that individuals will always choose to act in pursuit of their own self interest," (Zohar and Marshal, 1994, p. 25). Zohar thoughtfully demonstrates how the atomistic/ mechanistic view stresses (Zohar and Marshal, 1994, p. 26-28):

- The hierarchy
- The stability, certainty and the absolute
- Isolated, separate and interchangeable parts
- Relationships based on conflict and confrontation
- A single point of view
- The specialist expertise

The major industrial breakthroughs that followed and became the bedrock of our modern society, including division of labor, free-market economics, mass production, and scientific management, all underlie the above characteristics. The mechanistic view of the enterprise became less tenable in the 20th century partly due to the emergence of the corporation and increasing prominence of human relation issues at the workplace. At the turn of the 20th century, as the need for growth capital increased, major companies became publicly owned (corporatized). The human relation movements of between 1940s and 1970s–in particular, the Hierarchy of Needs Model, the Two-Factor Model, Theory X-Theory Y and Theory Z [1]–made organizations more benevolent.

But it was not until the 1980s that the management practices of the West came under serious scrutiny. This was precipitated by the oil crisis of the early seventies that awakened the mighty U.S. auto industry to its problems. This crisis shifted the focus of attention from the West to the East–the rising star of Japan. Underlying this shift was a new management paradigm that became known as total quality management (TQM). TQM became the single most important "thought revolution" (Shiba, Walden and Graham, 1994) of the eighties. The basic tenants of Total Quality Management, namely, customer focus, continuous improvement and total participation, challenged the 'Fordism' and 'Taylorism'[2] concepts of the time. These tenants have now permeated business and management practices of many organizations.

The late eighties saw another breakthrough in management thinking known as Business Process Re-engineering (BPR). Although not new fundamentally, it added another dimension to TQM by focusing the attention to radical process-oriented changes in work and organizational design. Today, the Internet plays a key and significant role in the business process redesign, notably in B2C (business-to-customer businesses known as dot.coms) and B2B (business-to-business) e-Commerce models.

In the early 1990s, the work of MIT's systems dynamics group became known internationally through the seminal book of Peter Senge, *The Fifth Discipline–The Art and Practice of Learning Organization*. That made learning organization a buzzword that still persists today. According to Senge, Systems Thinking is the fifth (and final) disciple or core capability of learning organizations. Senge describes a learning organization as one "which is continually expanding its ability to create its future" (Senge, 1992, pp. 1-8.). He identifies five core capabilities of the Learning Organization, namely, Personal Mastery, Shared Vision, Mental Models, Dialogue and Systems Thinking. These capabilities are dynamically interrelated, and collectively they lead to organizational learning.

Both Deming[3] and Senge agree that quality management and organizational learning have much in common. Senge identifies three stages or 'waves' of quality management: (1) workers' learning through problem solving and decision making, (2) middle management's learning to empower (sharing of power and decision making), and (3) institutionalized learning where learning permeates the entire enterprise and becomes an organizational asset (Senge, 1992). He asserts that Western management is going through the first and second waves of the quality movement and it will be some time before they reach the third wave.

Origins of Systems Thinking

In the early part of the 20th century, quantum physicists began to challenge Newtonian precepts. Foremost amongst these was Werner Heisenberg, whose questioning of the Newtonian "truth" led to his Uncertainty Principle in 1923. Later, in 1947, Norbert Weiner developed Cybernetics, which is the science of man-machine relationships. Another milestone was Von Bertalanffy's seminal book *General Systems Theory*, in 1954. Later in 1958, Jay Forrester of the Massachusetts Institute of Technology introduced and demonstrated the applications of feedback control theory in simulation models of organizations (Forrester, 1958, pp. 37-66). Forrester's seminal work marks the birth of the professional field known as System Dynamics, which is the application of systems theory to economics, environment and organizations.

In the early eighties, a different approach to systems thinking was developed in the UK. The hallmark of this approach is known as soft systems methodology (SSM) developed by Peter Checkland (1984). This approach, sometimes referred to as the 'British' approach or soft OR (Operations Research), is mainly qualitative, in contrast to the MIT's mathematically based systems dynamics approach. Nevertheless both approaches are complementary and can be used together. SSM is particularly powerful in the problem definition and identification stage.

System Defined

The word system is used in a variety of ways in our daily language. It often evokes different images in our minds, perhaps something that is a collection of other (and smaller) things that form a group or entity. Words such as 'whole' and 'interconnected' often come to mind in relation to systems. Daily we use, influence and are influenced by systems. These systems are biological, social, mechanical and natural. In the morning, our biological clock tells us it is time to get up. A host of mechanical systems, e.g., shower, toaster, refrigerator, garage door opener and car, enable us to perform our functions. Our work itself is a system comprising many subsystems: human, technical, legal and social. The weather system influences our daily life plans and lifestyle. Our lifestyles, in turn, influence the weather system.

So, what do these systems have in common? A system is a collection of parts that interact with each other to function as a whole. However, a system is not the sum of its parts—it is the product of their interactions (Ackoff, 1993). A system subsumes its parts and can itself be part of a larger system.

Examples of Systems (Kauffman, 1980, pp. 11-12)

- Mechanical Systems (thermostat, cruise control, float valve, guided missle, etc.)
- Biological Systems (body temperature, thirst/hunger, balance, etc.)
- Ecological Systems (population/food, predator/prey, etc.)
- Social-Economic Systems (judicial, political, production, inflation, etc.)

Systems Thinking in Daily Language

A number of expressions that we use in daily language reflect Systems Thinking. Some of these are shown below. Many other expressions and idioms can be found in other languages and cultures.

- What goes around comes around
- We're in this together
- Vicious/virtuous cycle
- He is on a roll
- Chronic behaviour
- Cyclical pattern
- Fluctuating pattern
- Ripple effect
- Spiral effect
- Snowballing
- Cycle of poverty
- Self-destruction
- Counteracting forces
- Domino effect

Systems Thinking Dimensions

Systems Thinking (ST) is a discipline for understanding complexity. This complexity underlies business, economic, scientific and social systems. ST has three dimensions: paradigm, language and methodology. These dimensions are described below:

Paradigm: Systems Thinking is a way of thinking about the world and relationships. This paradigm describes the dynamic relationships that influence the behaviour of systems (wholes). This consists of three types of thinking:[4]

- *Dynamic Thinking*—recognizing that the world is not static and things change constantly.
- *Operational Thinking*—understanding the 'physics' of operations and how things really work and interact.

- *Closed-Loop Thinking*–recognizing that cause and effect are not linear and often the end (effect) can influence the means (cause).

Language: As a language Systems Thinking provides a tool for understanding complexity and dynamic decision making. Systems Thinking language (Anderson and Johnson, 1997):
- is visual and diagrammatic.
- has a set of precise rules.
- translates perceptions into explicit pictures.
- emphasizes closed interdependencies (it is a 'circular' language).

Methodology: Systems Thinking has a set of modeling and learning technologies. These tools can be used to understand, measure and predict the behaviour of systems, as well as to facilitate and accelerate group learning. These tools include Stock and Flow Modeling, Microworlds (Computer Simulation) and Learning Laboratory.

Principles of Systems Thinking

Systems Thinking embodies a number of principles that collectively provide a framework for its theory and practice. These principles are explained below (Anderson and Johnson, 1997, pp. 18-20):
- *The Big Picture*–This principle teaches the art of seeing the forest and trees (Senge, 1990), that whatever situation or problem we are in can be related to other phenomena or systems.
- *Time and Space*–This principle teaches that cause and effect are often not close in time and space and that time delays and the chain effects of actions mask the connection between cause and effect. By extension, many of today's problems are related to and often the consequence of yesterday's solutions (Senge, 1990).
- *Short and Long Term*–This principle states that while chronic short-term 'solutions' can impede long-term outcomes, one cannot ignore short-term measures. A child who is facing a dangerous situation must be saved, even if doing so calls for an immediate harsh action that may hurt the child in the process. Here the aim is survival. Many organizations face potentially 'life-threatening' situations. A drastic short-term intervention may well be justified in these circumstances. However, if such 'crisis management' interventions persist and become the dominant mode of operation, the side effects can jeopardize the very life of the organization in the long term. In fact, a significant number of organizations 'die' every year. The average life span of a Western organization is just over half that of the human species (De Geus, 1995).
- *Soft Indicators*–This principle indicates that there is more to a problem than what we can 'see.' The popular performance indicators, including the widely known key performance indicators (KPI), critical success factors (CSF) and even the balanced score card, can only reveal part of the story. Invariably, a

host of other, more subtle, 'invisible' and potentially more powerful factors are at play that influence the behaviour and performance of organizations. We call these 'soft' measures. They include such things as morale, burnout, commitment, loyalty, confidence, care for customers, learning capacity and more. These can be regarded as the 'early' measures of the internal health and vitality of an organization and can determine the 'pulse' of the organization well before the outwardly hard measures do.

- *System as Cause*–This principle states that we contribute to our own problems not only through unintended consequences of our decisions and actions but because of our mental models (assumptions, beliefs, values, etc.). In contrast many individuals as well as organizations view themselves as 'victims' rather than the cause of their problems.
- *System vs. Symptom*–This principle states that a problem cannot be solved without understanding the system that generates that problem. This principle underlies the continuous improvement philosophy of quality management where root causes of a 'problem' should be identified (i.e., Cause and Effect, Ishikawa or Fishbone Diagram) before a lasting solution can be found.
- *'And' vs. 'Or'*–This principle states that there are often several causes for a given problem or situation (multiple causality). This is in contrast to the 'single-cause' thinking that is prevalent in today's society and in management practice.

Linear vs. Systems Thinking

On a sheet of paper write your answer to this question: What makes organizations successful?[5] Now examine your answer. *How* did you write your answer? Chances are that you wrote a list of items or factors. Not surprising! This is the way we are conditioned to think. This is known as linear thinking. Implicit in linear thinking are the following assumptions:

1) That factors are independent.
2) That causality runs one way (from cause to effect).
3) That factors are equally important.

This highlights the weakness of performance indicators such as Critical Success Factors that implicitly assume the above. By contrast, Systems Thinking maintains that factors are not independent, and that causality is 'circular' (e.g., if A affects B and C, then B and C can most likely affect A as well as each other and so on). For example, if one of your success factors was "investment in training," then this will surely affect the organization's human capacity and, down the line, its financial position. In turn, the firm's financial strength will increase its ability for further training and so on. This creates a reinforcing process.

Four Levels of Thinking

Daily, we are exposed to information from a multitude of sources–the news media, papers, radio, television and the Internet. Generally this kind of information reports events–what happened, where, when, who, how, etc. This is a snapshot view of the world. This level of information is very shallow and only touches the surface. For example, the stock market information that is reported daily reflects the snapshot of the day's activities. It tells us whether the stocks went up or down (often both up and down within the day) and by how much. We also get the volume of shares traded, dollar value of stocks traded (capital turnover) and much more. All of this information is event level.

Sometimes there is a commentary about a news item or an issue where one looks back and examines the trends and patterns of events and data. This provides a richer picture of reality and gives more insight into the 'story.' In the stock market example this could mean looking at trends of past months or years, observing the fluctuations and trying to explain what caused 'pulses' into the system, such as news of a merger, a quarterly economic report or a political scandal.

Yet, it is rare to see a study of how the trends and patterns relate and affect each other. This is a much deeper level of thinking that can show how different factors play out to bring to bear the outcomes that we observe. In stock markets, for example, this would mean trying to relate a host of factors that systemically cause the fluctuating patterns. These factors could be economic, social, political or structural. The critical thing is to understand how these factors influence each other to bring the observed results.

And yet, there is another much deeper level of thinking that hardly ever comes to surface. These represent the thinking or 'mental models' of individuals and organizations that influence why things work in certain ways. These mental models are based on the deep-seated beliefs, values and assumptions that we (privately) hold, and yet underlie why we do things the way we do. Harvard educationalist Chris Argris calls these the "undiscussables" (Argris, 1990, pp. 25-27).

The four levels of thinking described above are depicted in Figure 1.[6] This figure can be imagined as an iceberg, where event level is only the tip and yet most of us tend to operate at this level.

Leverage and Management of Change

Most often change requires quick and drastic actions. Invariably, such actions lead to resentment and alienation and ultimately higher staff turnover in organizations. This is because when management takes decisive actions, chances are that they react to events. Over time, these actions backfire because what is commonly perceived to be the problem is only the symptom of it.

In Systems Thinking leverage refers to actions or interventions, which have the greatest impact on the system in terms of arresting a trend or breaking a vicious cycle. Leverage has much deeper implications than 'solving a problem,' as it often requires fundamental and systemic changes, as opposed to removing the symptoms of a problem. In healthcare for example, we may attempt to 'solve' the surgical waiting list in public hospitals by applying the sophisticated queuing theory and create computer models to minimize waiting times. However, the cause of a growing waiting list could be partly rooted in the lack of cooperation and coordination

Figure 1: Four levels of thinking

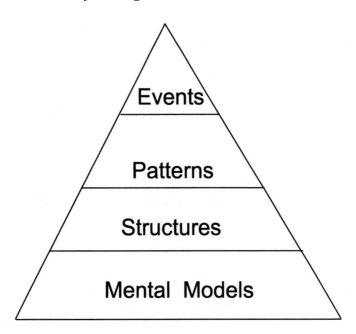

amongst health providers, which leads to poor capacity management and resource utilization across the system. The latter requires systemic thinking and consideration of multifaceted structural factors.

Systems Thinking facilitates seeing these leverage points and creating lasting intervention strategies. Figure 1 highlights the notion of leverage in Systems Thinking. As we move down from the tip to the base, the impact of 'change' increases drastically as the focus of intervention moves to deeper and more fundamental levels, namely, to systemic structures and mental models.

Systems Modeling

Systems modeling can be viewed as a language for thinking. Like any other language, systems language is not an end by itself, rather it is a means to convey a message, articulate an insight and express a feeling. Systems language is visual and intuitive and like other languages it has certain rules and syntax (Maani and Cavana, 2000).

An Example

Let's consider as an example the effects of time pressure on productivity and quality–a common dilemma in today's fast-paced business life. First, let's imagine what else (other variables) could be affected by these 'variables.' Can you think of some? How about customer satisfaction, demand for the service (or product) and volume of work done to name just a few. Now let's use the systems language, known as Causal Loop Diagram (CLD), to describe possible relationships among these variables. On one hand, one can imagine the direct and positive effect of time pressure on productivity, which then leads to greater volume of work done. In turn, more work done relieves the time pressure, hence reducing productivity and the amount of work done, counteracting the initial effect. On the other hand, time pressure undermines quality, as incidents of errors tend to increase. Lower quality, in turn, reduces customer demand, which, in due course, relieves time pressure as customer demand would decline. These effects are shown in Figure 2 as B1 and B2 Loops (B stands for "Balancing"–a counteracting effect which brings stability and control over time).

What else could possibly happen here? Imagine yourself in this situation, working long hours week after week. What happens to your morale, motivation and energy level? Perhaps the word is burnout. What is then the effect of burnout on productivity? Yes, negative! This effect is shown in the CLD as R1 loop (R stands for "Reinforcing"–a self-feeding or self-perpetuating effect that leads to steady growth or decline). This loop (R1) captures the dynamics of time pressure, burnout, productivity and the amount of work done. The overall (or systemic) effect of these 'loops' depends on the dynamic interplay of these variables and relative strength of the loops over time. What systems modeling can tell us is that these forces dynamically interact towards either a state of stability (business as usual) or ultimate decline (out of business), depending on the 'loop dominance' over time.

The qualitative systems modeling example illustrated above can be extended to quantitative or dynamic systems modeling. However this topic is beyond the scope of this Chapter.[7] With dynamic modeling, 'live' simulations of real-life situations can be developed, different scenarios can be tested under a variety of assumptions and the results can be quantitatively assessed. Dynamics modeling takes into account the inherent uncertainty of the real world and allows for different scenarios to be considered concurrently. Situation-based models (known as Management Flight Simulators) are often used in a 'learning laboratory' environment where management teams 'practice' hypothesized game plans and learn from experimentation and error.

Figure 2: Time pressure dynamics

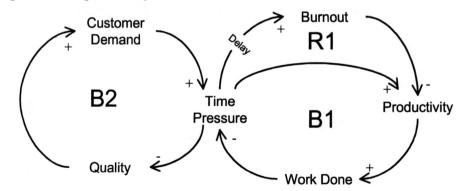

The Challenge for the Internet

The extraordinary power and appeal of the Internet poses both an opportunity and a threat. A threat if it is viewed as an end by itself–a fascinating technological artifact, tool or toy that connects every one to everyone else and provides unlimited information at the keystroke. This threat and fascination goes beyond the Internet. It permeates in our media, entertainment press and even in academic institutions. It is rooted in a preoccupation with information. If the Internet remains an 'information tool,' it will fall short of its potential.

Referring to Figure 1, information provides, by and large, an event view of the world. It is a snapshot of reality, which captures the most recent, the latest thing–the latest GDP, CPI, stock price, fashion, hero, villain, idea, etc. This faddish behaviour is in itself rooted in a predominant focus on the short term and the transient.

The power of the Internet revolution lies in the 'communalization' of information. The same way that the invention of the printed press spread the 'knowledge' to the common person and eroded the power of the clergy and the aristocracy, the Internet has created an 'information common' for masses. It has been said that information is power. That is, those with access to (privileged) information could hold an advantage over those without. However, the more enlightened concepts of leadership and organization maintain that information becomes more useful and hence powerful when it is shared. This empowers the workforce and spreads the leadership to all levels of the organization. Information sharing also helps break down the traditional barriers between functional silos and facilitates horizontal and vertical integration in the organization.

But the true potential of the Internet is as yet untapped and hardly debated in public fora. Ackoff (1995) defines a progression from data to information, to knowledge, to understanding and to wisdom. Understanding is "evaluated knowledge," the difference between "doing things right and doing the right things." Understanding is the answer to the why rather than the 'what' and the 'how,' which information and knowledge respectively provide. No amount of information and knowledge will, on their own, rid us of prejudice, poverty, aggression and war. The Internet is essentially a 'shell' and a tool and therefore not capable of providing the answer. How this tool is used will determine whether its potential is reached. The challenge for the Internet is to transcend itself as an information tool and to become a channel to enhance understanding.

The more urgent and fundamental dilemmas that we face today in the organization and in the society at large require a collective will that comes from a deeper understanding of our place in history and our collective destiny towards an organic unity. System theory provides a way of thinking about the world and relationships. It offers the art and the science of seeing the tree and the forest. The core principles of systems theory, discussed earlier, collectively provide a paradigm and a language for deeper understanding of the chronic issues besting our times. Used appropriately and with care, they can challenge our age-old views and assumptions and move us towards a shared understanding. The synergy between the Internet and Systems Thinking occurs at this intersection–their complementarity. Together they provide a symbiotic relationship akin to the body and the soul.

CONCLUSION

At the turn of the 21st century, we are embarking on an era characterized by constant change, complexity, interdependence, and speed in business and economics as well as social and political life on the planet. In order to succeed (or even survive) collectively, we need new tools and paradigms. The Internet has provided us with such a tool, a mechanism of instant and global communication transcending conventional barriers of the past.

Coupled with this advance, there is a compelling need for managers, leaders, policy makers and knowledge workers to make sense of the ever-increasing complexity of today's world, and to understand what causes this complexity in business, political, community and social systems. Systems thinking and modeling provide a paradigm, a language and a technology for understanding the dynamics that underlie change and complexity. Using systems thinking and modeling makes it possible to:

- examine and foresee the consequences of policy and strategic decisions;
- implement fundamental solutions to chronic problems;
- avoid mistakenly interpreting symptoms as causes;
- test assumptions, hypotheses and scenarios;
- find long-term solutions and avoid 'fire-fighting' behaviour;
- boost employee morale and improve productivity;
- implement change management without adverse side-effects.

Together, Systems Thinking and the Internet provide the body and the soul for a new era.

ENDNOTES

1 These models are attributed to Maslow, Herzberg, McGregor and Ouchi respectively.

2 This refers to Henry Ford's concept of mass production and Fredrick Taylor's scientific management.

3 Edward W. Deming, American statistician known as the father of modern quality management.

4 Barry Richmond, *The Next Step*, High Performance Systems, Inc. 1997.

5 This exercise is adapted from one presented at a High Performance Systems workshop.

6 The original author is unknown.

7 This subject is treated in detail in *Systems Thinking and Modeling–Understanding Change and Complexity* by K. Maani and R. Cavana, Prentice Hall, 2000.

REFERENCES

Ackoff, R. (1993). *Systems Thinking and Thinking Systems*, June. Interact.

Ackoff, R. (1995). *Systems Thinking in Action Conference*. Boston.

Anderson, V. and Johnson, L. (1997). *Systems Thinking Basics*, Pegasus Communications, Inc.

Argris, C. (1990). *Overcoming Organizational Defences-Facilitating Organizational Learning*. Boston, MA: Allyn and Bacon.

Checkland, P. (1981). *Systems Thinking, Systems Practice*. John Wiley.

De Geus, A. (1995). *Systems Thinking in Action Conference*. Boston, MA.

Forrester, J. (1958). Industrial dynamics–A major breakthrough for decision makers. *Harvard Business Review*, 36(4).

Kauffman, D. L., Jr. (1980). *Systems One, An Introduction to Systems Thinking*. The Innovative Learning Series, Future Systems, Inc.

Maani, K. and Cavana, R. (2000). *Systems Thinking and Modeling–Understanding Change and Complexity*. Prentice Hall.

Senge, P. (1992). Building learning organizations. *Journal for Quality and Participation*, March.

Shiba, S., Walden, D. and Graham, A. (1994). *A New American TQM*. Productivity Press.

Zohar, D. and Marshal, I. (1994). *The Quantum Society*. Morrow Press.

Section III

Internet Management, Sustainability and Philosophical Issues

Chapter X

The Internet, Sustainable Development and Ecosystems Management

James F. Courtney
University of Central Florida, USA

Sandra M. Richardson
Texas Tech University, USA

David Paradice
Florida State University, USA

INTRODUCTION

Sustainable development promotes the idea that development should be capable of meeting the needs of today without sacrificing the resources needed by future generations. This notion has evolved from recognition of the current problems faced when development occurs without regard for its impact on the surrounding ecosystem. The problems that occur are legion and the solutions complex. They involve many stakeholders with often significantly different perspectives and vastly different goals. New approaches to defining problems, approaches that incorporate multiple perspectives and support communication among multiple stakeholders, are needed to structure the complexity of modern decision-making situations and achieve sustainable development.

A recent study, sponsored jointly by the United Nations Development Program, the UN Environment Program, the World Bank and the World Resources Institute, identifies the problems at hand. The study assesses the global status of five types of ecosystems: agricultural, coastal, forest, freshwater and grassland. The resulting report, issued in September of 2000, states that "the current rate of decline in the long-term productive capacity of ecosystems could have devastating implications for human development and the welfare of all species" (United Nations, et al., 2000, p. 6). The 197 scientists who conducted this study found, among other things, that:

- Half of the world's wetlands were lost in the last century.
- Logging and conversion have shrunk the world's forests by as much as half.
- Some 9% of the world's tree species are at risk of extinction.
- Fishing fleets are 40% larger than the ocean can sustain.
- Nearly 70% of the world's major marine fish stocks are over-fished.
- Soil degradation affects two-thirds of the world's agricultural lands.
- Some 30% of the world's original forests have been converted to agriculture.
- Twenty percent of the world's freshwater fish are extinct, threatened or endangered.

The current state of the world's ecosystems is alarming. When one considers that the global economy has tripled in size since 1980 and the population has grown by 30% to six billion people, how this state came to be is understandable. However, continued growth is expected in both the global economy and the world's populations (United Nations et al., 2000). These trends will continue to put pressure on our current troubled ecosystems. Without some type of change in how these ecosystems are managed, their condition will only worsen.

To address the problems pointed out by this report, and to turn the current trend around, the report calls for an "ecosystems approach" to manage the world's resources. This is an integrated approach that recognizes the "system" in ecosystem, manages systems holistically rather than sectorally and realizes that ecosystems span jurisdictional boundaries. People are viewed as part of the system and "…social and economic information is integrated with environmental information, …thus explicitly linking human needs to the biological capacity to fulfill those needs" (p. 21). The ecosystems approach involves local communities and the public in general, and integrates urban planning into ecosystems management and decision making, as "urbanization and urban consumers are among the most significant pressures on ecosystems today" (p. 22).

Information and decision-making are key issues in the ecosystems approach. Information is assembled to allow for analysis of trade-offs among ecosystem goods and services, and environmental, political, social and economic goals. The report addresses an "information gap" (p. 21) and calls for assembling, organizing and distributing knowledge and information about ecosystems and the political, social, cultural and economic environment in which they exist.

The report goes on to say that "we can continue blindly altering Earth's ecosystems, or we can learn to use them more sustainably" (prologue). The UN's so-called Brundtland Report (1987) suggests that development is sustainable if it "meets the needs of the present without compromising the ability of future generations to meet their own needs." Some believe that "…sustainability is one of the most important issues in the history of mankind–indeed in the history of life on the planet" (Nieto, Neotropian and Durbin, 1995).

Sustainability also has ethical dimensions, as described by C. West Churchman in his "Ethics and Sustainability Online Forum" (haas.berkeley.edu/~gem/gift.html). Churchman celebrates the new millennium in "A Gift to Future Generations," saying that:

"Since it's about the whole of humanity, this celebration is global. Since it's about the good things and the bad things in human life, the celebration is ethical. And since the overall condition of humanity is a result of our decisions, the celebration is management. The acronym is gEm [Global Ethical Management], a jewel with plenty of sparkle and a lot of flaws."

Clearly ecosystem management (ESM), sustainability and global ethical management raise broad-ranging, complex and vexing issues. They are linked, in that they embrace a long-term view of development, one that considers the needs of our progeny, as well as ourselves. They are "messes" (Ackoff, 1999) in the sense that each element of the mess is itself a complex problem that strongly interacts with every other element of the mess. They are "wicked" problems (Rittel and Weber, 1973) in that they have no definitive formulation, and no clear-cut solution, except perhaps from the perspective of a single group of stakeholders. Problems that are this complicated and ill-structured require thinking that recognizes their complexity and attempts to deal with that complexity in a holistic way, rather than via reductionism, which tends to rob such problems of their richness and leads to simplistic solutions that only make the problems worse. Churchman's (1971) Singerian inquiring system, and Mitroff and Linstone's (1993) Unbounded Systems Thinking provide a framework for dealing with problems of this ilk. Dealing with such problems requires sharing of data, information, knowledge and wisdom on a grand scale, a task for which the Internet is ideally suited. The question is where to begin to deal with problems of such complexity. We suggest that Singerian inquiry, discussed next, provides a framework in which we may begin to discuss how the Internet may be utilized to help deal with ecosystem management problems.

Singerian Inquiring Systems and the Multiple Perspective Approach to Ecosystems Management

In a widely celebrated treatise, Churchman (1971) applies systems theory to the philosophies of Leibniz, Locke, Kant, Hegel and Singer to develop the notion of "inquiring systems," the objective of which is to create knowledge. The Singerian inquirer is named after Churchman's mentor, Edgar A. Singer, who was a disciple of the pragmatic school of philosophy, founded by the highly regarded American philosopher, Charles S. Peirce (http://www.pragmatism.org/default.htm). Peirce believed that philosophical inquiry should produce pragmatic knowledge, that is, knowledge useful in solving real problems. He contributed to a wide variety of areas, including metrology, semiotics and mathematics. Other well-known philosophers in the pragmatic tradition include William James, John Dewey, and Singer and Churchman, themselves. While Churchman chose to honor his mentor in naming the Singerian inquirer, it actually incorporates the ideas of many in the pragmatic field, including those listed above.

Singerian inquiry provides an approach that is well suited to dealing with wicked, messy, highly ill-structured problems (Mitroff and Linstone, 1993; Courtney et al., 1998: Richardson et al., 1999, 2001; Courtney, 2001) such as those of ecosystems management. In describing the Singerian inquirer, Churchman says it, "…is above all teleological, a grand teleology with an ethical base" (1971, p. 200). Singerian inquirers seek a highly idealistic purpose, the creation of "exoteric" knowledge, or knowledge for "every man," as opposed to scientific, esoteric knowledge that, as it matures, becomes relevant to an increasingly smaller audience. It seeks this knowledge in such a way as to take human and environmental considerations into account. In other words, the Singerian inquirer seeks the ability to choose the right means for ethical purposes for a broad spectrum of society; it seeks goals consistent with global, ethical ecosystem management and sustainable development.

The Singerian inquirer views the world as a holistic system in which everything is connected to everything else. From the Singerian perspective, problems and knowledge domains (disciplines) are highly non-separable. Complex social and managerial problems must be analyzed as wholes (Mitroff and Linstone, 1993). The artificial division of knowledge into disciplines and the reduction of complex problems into simple components inhibit the solution to social and management problems. Solving complex problems may require knowledge from any source and those knowledgeable in any discipline or profession.

Linstone's Multiple Perspectives Approach (Linstone, 1984) and Mitroff and Linstone's Unbounded Systems Thinking (UST) are based on the Singerian model and promote heterogeneous views of organizational decision making. A synthesis of broad worldviews is developed, rather than adopting the limited view of a single perspective. The Singerian style and UST also recognize the connectedness of things in the universe, especially of complex social problems. They realize the non-separability and irreducibility of elements in complex problems and issues. The development of multiple perspectives is the very core of UST. A critical aspect of developing multiple perspectives is open, honest, effective dialogue among all relevant stakeholders in the problem involved. Managers in such an environment must be careful to respect the rights and viewpoints of the parties involved, and be open and honest themselves in order to gain the trust of those who will be affected by the decision.

The Singerian approach and UST develop multiple perspectives in several ways. First, as Singer (1956), Churchman (1971), and Mitroff and Linstone (1993) put it, the system "sweeps in" other problem-solving styles, which means it uses any or all of them where appropriate in decision-making processes, and may include any knowledge as needed from any discipline or profession to assist in understanding the problem. Mitroff and Linstone (1993) refer to the four non-Singerian (Leibnizian, Lockean, Kantian and Hegelian) models as reflecting a technical perspective. All of these approaches are mechanistic and analytical in nature. None is preferred, although one may be more suited to a particular decision or problem than others. Each is based on an industrial-age machine metaphor, and even view man from a mechanistic viewpoint. That is, man is viewed as a rational, objective, thinking machine.

To overcome the limitations of the technical perspective, UST sweeps in what Mitroff and Linstone call organizational and social, and personal and individual perspectives. These perspectives "bring to the forefront human beings collectively and individually in all their complexity" (p. 99). They go on to say that:

"All complex problems–especially social ones–involve a multiplicity of actors, various scientific technical disciplines, and various organizations and diverse individuals. In principle, each sees a problem differently and thus generates a distinct perspective on it" (p. 99).

Thus, Singerian inquiry and UST, consistent with the needs of ecosystem management and sustainable development, integrate knowledge and information from a variety of domains, including both social and "hard" sciences, politics and from the public in general.

Information and Technology in Singerian ESM

Ecosystems management problems are complex and wicked. The Singerian inquirer provides a framework to help organize our thinking about ecosystems and their sustainability. The Internet can support a Singerian approach to ecosystem management and can contribute to dealing with ecosystems management issues in numerous ways: by serving as a medium for capturing ecosystems data; by facilitating creation, organization, storage and sharing of ecosystems information and knowledge; by fostering a global dialogue among those interested in ecosystem issues; by helping to develop common goals and objectives among those affected by ecosystem problems, thereby fostering a more holistic view of ecosystem problems and issues; and by providing access to models that analyze ecosystems data and help in making policy decisions.

Data Collection and Ecosystems Information Management via the Internet

The UN report emphasizes the need for accurate information to assist in ecosystems management. The report stresses the need for data at all levels–local, regional and global. This data, and models to analyze the data, will provide the basis for policy decisions and for measuring progress, in a Singerian sense, in restoring and maintaining ecosystems' health. Indeed, the UN Environment Programme provides a satellite telecommunications system known as Mercure (http://www.centre.unep.net/), which provides full Internet connectivity and various types of data and other services, including:

- publishing national environmental information such as State of the Environment reports and practical best-practices advice;
- investigating urgent environmental matters, whether natural or manmade, such as forest fires, floods, earthquakes, volcanic eruptions, tropical storms, chemical spills and the effects of war;

- providing a number of telecommunication and conference services;
- conducting research on environmental issues and accessing scientific data needed for environmental assessment;
- publicizing environmental activities, events and issues;
- supporting development of environmental legislation by providing environmental reference services, such as legislation relating to the many international conventions;
- facilitating searches made by all users requiring environmental information by maintaining clear, targeted directories to such information.

The UNEPnet Mercure system is based on a philosophy of "thinking globally, but acting locally." Information created and updated in different nodes is automatically and regularly distributed to the other nodes in the network. This allows Mercure users, particularly those in developing countries, to more easily and quickly access important and useful information on their local networks. UNEPnet supports a variety of information exchanges, including environmental assessment and impact analysis, such as the thematic earth resources data sets mediated by UNEP's Global Resource Information Database (GRID), and policy and legislative development regarding environmental and ecosystem issues. GRID (http://www.grida.no/) provides an array of ecosystem data via geographic information systems (GISs) and global positioning systems (GPSs).

Using the Net to Move Toward Ecosystems Knowledge Management

Information is particulate in nature. Facts and data, bits and pieces of thought about a variety of ecosystem concepts are stored in countless media and places throughout the globe. The Internet provides a technical infrastructure for bringing the data together and doing more with it. The Singerian approach suggests that understanding and knowledge are created when data is interpreted in context and that interpretation is shared with others (Nonaka and Takeuchi, 1995). When considering solutions or approaches to the current problems in ecosystems management, the use of the Internet is a perfect fit. Discussion and news groups can enter into a dialogue concerning the interpretation of data under any number of contexts. Questions may be asked by anyone with Internet access. Thus, the Net serves as a catalyst for increasing ecosystem knowledge.

The UNEPnet system exemplifies the Singerian model of ecosystems management by embracing a holistic approach to solving problems. The use of the Internet reinforces this approach by providing the means for data to be collected in many places and to reach all of the parties involved. Inclusion of the public, all who are interested or affected by the decisions made by those in power, is emphasized in Singerian ecosystems management. Ecosystems management encourages the integration of economic and social information with technical and scientific information to bridge the current information gaps between these perspectives. The Internet provides the means for the public to easily access all data. It provides the means for anyone to combine and store what they believe to be current, relevant and meaningful data from any perspective. In this manner, users may fill any information gaps they have in their perspective of ecosystems management.

Measuring Progress Towards Sustainable Development

The Singerian ESM model emphasizes measurement. Financial statements are an ubiquitous form of measure in the organizational world. The idea of including corporate responsibility into financial reports has been around for over a decade and does not seem to be going away anytime soon. The introduction of corporate actions to financial reporting was first seen in the 1980s when the green movement motivated companies to account for their impact on the world's natural resources. Many organizations, including the World Commission on Environment and Development (WCED), the World Business Council on Sustainable Development (http://www.wbcsd.ch), the Global Reporting Initiative (http://www.globalreporting.org), the Institute of Social and Ethical Accountability (http://www.accountability.org.uk) and SustainAbility (http://www.sustainability.org.uk), are continuing work on standards and reporting requirements for businesses that would encourage much broader considerations, including ecosystems concerns, in corporate reporting, and are using the Internet to distribute information about their work.

Today, with an estimated $2 trillion flowing into socially responsible investment funds (Learner, 2000), it is evident that the demand for corporate responsibility is more than a fad. More and more companies are starting to produce these reports as evidenced by the fact that emphasis is being placed on reporting standards. Nowhere is this more evident than in the Dow Jones Sustainability Group Index (DJSGI), a group of more than 200 global companies demonstrating superior economic, environmental and social performance (Learner, 2000). This type of reporting accomplishes more than just providing appearances for the investing audience. In order for this reporting to be meaningful, there must be standards. Anytime there is a yardstick for measuring performance, such as accounting standards, opportunities evolve for corporations. Standards provide enterprises with the tools to look inside the organization and focus on its performance, in other words environmental reporting allows an organization to judge the quality of its management. Deloitte Touche Tohmatsu's Robert Jornardi states that "Corporate growth which destroys our environment is worse than useless" (Learner, 2000, p. 63). Clearly, the need for sustainable development is being recognized widely, along with the need to measure progress in attaining sustainability.

The World Business Council for Sustainable Development (WBCSD), a global alliance of 150 firms, has developed "eco-efficiency" measures and reporting standards which have been published on the Internet (http://www.wbcsd.ch). As the WBCSD Web site indicates, eco-efficiency means "…the delivery of competitively priced goods and services that satisfy human needs and bring quality of life, while progressively reducing ecological impacts and resource intensity throughout the life cycle, to a level in line with the earth's estimated carrying capacity." Guidelines for calculating a firm's eco-efficiency index (EEI) have been developed, and currently 23 companies are pilot testing the approach. The WBCSD and the companies piloting the EEI are working with the Global Reporting Initiative (http://www.globalreporting.org/) to develop standards for reporting eco-efficiency studies and progress towards sustainable development. The WBCSD and the Global Reporting Initiative encourage their members to use the Internet as a means of communicating with stakeholders worldwide.

Shell International is a member of the WBCSD and has been a leader in using the Internet as a means of distributing information about its sustainability efforts. Its Web site (http://www.shell.com/royal-en/0,6091,,00.html) describes Shell's values and nine principles for Shell companies, including those relating to employees, shareholders, local communities, business partners and society. Principles relating to health, safety and the environment are emphasized, along with the need to communicate with numerous stakeholders. The Web site also addresses "issues and dilemmas," including global warming, human rights issues, sustainable development, biodiversity, alternative energy sources, water use and industrial legacies. Forums are provided on all these issues, and postings are frequent by people scattered across the globe. The site also describes strategies and training programs for getting managers and operations personnel to consider a broad range of factors in planning and executing company activities.

Global Dialog and Perspective Building on the Internet

The application of the Singerian and UST models through online debates and forums, such as those of International Shell described above, can elevate the ecosystems approach to a more meaningful level. The emphasis of these models on the connectivity of all things, a teleological approach, consideration of ethical issues, non-reductionist views, the significance of erasing the lines between disciplines and the sweeping in of new ideas, when combined with the use of the Internet are what convert data shared via the Internet to information, and information into effective action. It is the context, consideration and contemplation, under the weight of a problem or question, that give the use of the Internet value.

When Internet technology is placed in balance with the overall system, an information culture (Davenport, 1997) can develop. The ability to think about and employ information and the act of sharing information across boundaries are what will give the Internet its value and its place in a Singerian ecosystems management perspective.

Internet-Based Ecosystem Model Management

Problems in ecosystems data management can often be traced to one of several sources. In some cases the data simply is not available; the technology cannot be reliably deployed to a location in order to collect the data. In some cases data is collected, but it is not collected in a form amenable to scientific study. For example, the data collected may be measured in the wrong units: daily data being collected rather than hourly. In some cases the data is collected in a sufficient manner, but difficulty exists in transferring the data in a timely manner to the location where analysis can occur. For example, meters in remote locations must be accessed (i.e., read) manually and only then can the data be transferred to the analysis site.

Even in cases where data is of high quality and accessible, one must always be concerned that the models of analysis are adequate. Models can fail in at least three ways. First, the model may be under-specified, with critical elements omitted. Second, elements within a model may be combined inappropriately. Third, in dynamic environments models can often become obsolete due to the changing conditions of the reality the models are intended to represent.

The Internet and other current technologies provide a framework for overcoming all of these problems, and for doing so in a manner consistent with Singerian inquiry and the UST method. Each location where data is needed can be defined as an Internet node. While establishing and maintaining a server in a corporate environment is not a trivial task, establishing a single point server with a single data-collection task should be a relatively less complicated proposition. As microchip technology continues to reduce the physical size of computing equipment, a server-on-a-chip is now feasible, along with the resultant ability to locate that server in places here-to-fore inaccessible or incapable of supporting computing equipment. GPS and wireless technologies provide the technical infrastructure for "connecting" even the most remote location to the Internet. Since the Internet is continuously available, timely access of any node is feasible. Remote administration of these "servers" also provides an opportunity to re-program them in ways to ensure that the data collected meets the needs of the analysis. More (or less) frequent data collections could be programmed and (assuming the measuring equipment can be so calibrated) different unit measures may be specified.

Each node may be considered a component of a larger model. As such, each node may be combined (or eliminated) from analytical models as needed. As the environment of analysis changes, some components may be removed. As understanding of a particular situation becomes greater, new components, perhaps components never before imagined as being part of the analysis, may be added. In a Singerian sense, new components may be swept into the model. In a UST sense, new perspectives may be added.

An advantage of this approach is that a wide range of models may be constructed. One can envision a hierarchy (or network?) of models ranging from relatively simple, single-perspective models to quite complex, multi-perspective models. The more complex models would be built by combining the less complex models. Such an approach allows for problems to be represented in ways that support the translation of problem formulations from general, qualitative terms to specific, analytical terms (Paradice, 1992). This approach allows "local" decision makers at any place in the network to construct models of sufficient complexity to meet their specific needs.

Implementing this approach would require each component to be "known" to the system in two ways. First, how the component is described and used needs to be made known. West and Hess (2001) provide an interesting example of how geographic information systems software can be used to integrate ecosystems data with regulatory data relating to those ecosystems. They use metadata as a knowledge management tool to store declarative data regarding relationships, integrity and the presentation of geographic data used in the GIS they describe. One would need similar categories of metadata in this instance. In more general terms, we can identify a similar need for relationship data describing how a component model relates to the larger scheme of models defined by the five ecosystems of the World Resources report. How the component is used–its inputs, functioning and outputs– could be specified in metadata. Assumptions embedded in the component function could also be described in the metadata. Metadata could also maintain the relationships of the users and the developers of the component, providing a history of its development and use.

McFadden et al. (1999) describe the need to maintain operational, enterprise and data mart metadata when describing an enterprise data model. We expect an ecosystem model to be at least as complex as any enterprise model. Following this taxonomy, one would need operational metadata to specify how the component functions, enterprise metadata to describe how to reconcile the data of the component with the data in the larger system of components (i.e., across the Internet) and data mart metadata to describe any derived data and rules for reconciling derived data with the enterprise data. McFadden et al. note that these reconciliations must also accommodate historical data. Ideally, the network itself would contain enough intelligence to utilize the declarative knowledge embedded in the metadata to implement integrity checks regarding model use.

Second, the component needs to be known (i.e., identified) to the Internet. This could be accomplished by adopting a JINI technology approach. JINI is essentially a "plug-and-play" approach defined for adding hardware components to a network. This "plug-and-play" philosophy should be extended to the network-based model components. We note that computer-based systems are the only man-made systems in common use in which the user interface appliance must perform an inordinate amount of work in order for the system to be useful. Sinks and toilets can be connected to water systems and they will work. Lamps and televisions can be connected to electrical and cable systems and they will operate. Telephones can be connected to a very complex telephone system and they will function flawlessly. Only computer systems require major reconfiguration of the user interface appliance in order to be useful. In implementing the JINI approach, "intelligence" for the model construction and maintenance can move more to the network, instead of residing in the model applications themselves. In the long run, this infrastructure along with the metadata approach described above will allow model builders to focus more effort on building effective decision support models and less effort on the nuances of getting the model to execute properly.

Moving these activities to the network also mitigates most model builders' biases toward utilizing more powerful computers when facing increasingly complex environments. In the past, solving more complicated and complex problems required use of more powerful computers because more powerful models required more powerful computers. This is analogous to growing a bigger ox each time a larger field needs to be plowed. A better and more timely solution is to tie two oxen together (Hopper, undated). Similarly, a better solution to attacking more complicated problems may be to combine existing models and computing resources, not "grow" larger ones.

SUMMARY

Ecosystems management problems are complex and wicked. The Singerian inquirer provides a framework to help organize thinking about ecosystems and their sustainability. The Internet can support a Singerian approach to ecosystem management and can contribute to dealing with ecosystems management issues in numerous ways.

The Internet provides a mechanism for capturing ecosystems data. Technologies exist to locate Internet nodes literally anywhere in the world: from the most arid desert landscape to the most tropical rainforest to the murkiest wetland. "Server-on-a-chip" technology brings heretofore unheard of computing power to these environments. GIS and GPS technology provide a means for data transfer from these environments to any analysis center in the world.

The Internet can facilitate the creation, organization, storage and sharing of ecosystems information and knowledge. Researchers, scientists, politicians and citizens alike can now have access to data and existing analyses located anywhere in the world. Adoption of a common modeling language would greatly encourage the development of multi-level models perhaps capable of providing solutions to local ecosystems issues while simultaneously addressing a component of a more global ecosystem issue. Even in the absence of a common modeling language, the mere availability of existing models to those attacking ecosystems problems facilitates analysis of ecosystems data in a way unattainable just a decade ago. This model access can only help those making policy decisions.

As Shell's Web site illustrates, Internet use can foster a global dialogue among those interested in ecosystems issues and helps to develop common goals and objectives among those affected by ecosystems problems. As such it fosters a more holistic view of ecosystems problems and issues.

The Internet, however, provides a solution only on a technical perspective. Complex problems require social, cultural and organizational perspective integration as well as the technical perspective. The Singerian philosophy, when combined with the technical tools provided by the Internet, provides a more complete problem formulation tool kit to decision makers confronting sustainability.

The Internet is, by nature, somewhat disorganized and unwieldy. It will surely be difficult to achieve complete coordination and consolidation of ecosystems information in the foreseeable future. However, the UN has taken the lead in promoting the concept of ecosystems management, and will likely serve as a coordinating organization in what might otherwise be a chaotic situation. The increasing interest in ESM and sustainable development are also likely to lead to more organizations like the WBCSD, the Global Reporting Initiative and Sustainability, all of whom cooperate and share information via Web sites. Cooperation among the players in this arena is expected to continue and lead to better consolidation of information sources.

Sustainable development, and its companion, ecosystems management, are among the most important issues facing humankind today. We must do a more effective job of managing the planet's resources so our children and theirs may live comfortably and safely. The Singerian model of ecosystems management provides a framework for us to think of how this lofty goal may be achieved. The Internet provides the technological foundation for sharing ecosystems data and information and for the creation of knowledge related to effective ecosystems management policies. Global sharing of data, information and knowledge, and the encouragement of dialog concerning ecosystems issues should lead to sounder policies and a brighter future for our progeny. The fate of the planet depends upon it.

REFERENCES

Ackoff, R. L. (1999). *Re-Creating the Corporation: A Design of Organizations for the 21st Century*. Oxford University Press.

Churchman, C. W. (1996). A gift to future generations. *Ethics and Sustainability Online Forum*, The University of California at Berkeley. Available on the World Wide Web at: http://haas.berkeley.edu/~gem/gift.html.

Churchman, C. W. (1971). *The Design of Inquiring Systems: Basic Concepts of Systems and Organizations*. New York, NY: Basic Books, Inc.

Courtney, J. F. (2001). Decision making and knowledge management in inquiring organizations: A new decision-making paradigm for DSS. *Special Issue of Decision Support Systems on Knowledge Management and Decision Support Systems*, 31(1), 17-38.

Courtney, J. F., Croasdell, D. and Paradice, D. B. (1998). Inquiring organizations. *Australian Journal of Information Systems*, 6(1), 3-15, and reprinted in *Foundations of Information Systems: Towards a Philosophy of Information Technology*. Available on the World Wide Web at: http://www.cba.uh.edu/~parks/fis/fis.htm.

Davenport, T. H. (1997). *Information Ecology*. New York, NY: Oxford University Press.

Hopper, G. (undated). This analogy was spoken by Commodore Hopper in an undated video tape obtained by one of the authors.

Learner, N. (2000). Green approach. *Continental*, December, 4(12), 61-63.

Mansell, R. and Wehn, U. (Eds). (1998). *Knowledge Societies: Information Technology for Sustainable Development*. New York, NY: Oxford University Press.

McFadden, F. R., Hoffer, J. A. and Prescott, M.B. (1999). *Modern Database Management*, fifth edition. Boston, MA: Addison-Wesley.

Mitroff, I. I. and Linstone H. A. (1993). *The Unbounded Mind: Breaking the Chains of Traditional Business Thinking*. New York, NY: Oxford University Press.

Nieto, C. C., Neotropica, F. and Durbin, P. T. (1995). Sustainable development and philosophies of technology, Techne. *Journal for the Society for Philosophy and Technology*, 1(1). Available on the World Wide Web at http://scholar.lib.vt.edu/ejournals/SPT/. Accessed on December 17, 2000.

Nonaka, I. and Takeuchi, H. (1995). *The Knowledge Creating Company*. New York, NY: Oxford University Press.

Paradice, D. B. (1992). SIMON: An intelligent, object-oriented information system for coordinating strategies and operations. *IEEE Transactions on Systems, Man and Cybernetics*, 22(3), 513-525.

Richardson, S. M. and Courtney, J. F. (1999). An electric utility learns to adapt: A Singerian organization approach. *Proceedings of the 1999 Meeting of the America's Conference on Information Systems*.

Richardson, S. M., Courtney, J. F. and Paradice, D. B. (2001). An assessment of the Singerian approach to organizational learning: Case from academia and the utility industry. *Information Systems Frontiers Special Issue on Philosophical Reasoning in Information Systems Research*, 3(1), 49-62.

Rittel, H. W. J. and Webber, M. M. (1973). Dilemmas in a general theory of planning. *Policy Sciences*, 4, 155-169.

United Nations Development Programme, United Nations Environment Programme, World Bank, World Resources Institute. (2000). *Summary: A Guide to World Resources 2000–2001, People and Ecosystems: The Fraying Web of Life*. Available on the World Wide Web at: http://www.wri.org/wri/wrr2000/.

United Nations World Commission on Environment and Development. (1987). *Our Common Future*. New York, NY: Oxford University Press. (Commonly referred to as the Brundtland Report.)

West, L. A. and Hess, T. J. (forthcoming). Metadata as a knowledge management tool: Supporting intelligent agent and end-user access to spatial data. *Decision Support Systems*.

Chapter XI

The Internet: Intercultural Communication and the Idea of Sustainability

Peter Raine
International Honours Program, USA

Hopefully, the spirit of "Respect for Nature, Concern for People" will gradually be fostered, so that technology will not overburden nature during this time of development.

Shui-Bien Chen, President, Republic of China

INTRODUCTION

The relationship between a complex technological process and an emerging intellectual concept may, at first sight, seem tenuous. However, we may discover a connection if we consider that they are both global issues. Sustainability in relation to environmental issues involves all peoples in all places; it cannot be separated into a concept applicable for individual nation states, or specific bio-regions. Moreover, the concept of sustainability is directly related to communities and their social and economic fabric. We cannot act and do things in isolation: communication is essential. The Internet is a global communication system capable of influencing attitudes in many important areas, not least environmental concerns. This global communication system is currently fostering a special kind of 'virtual' community where discussion and transfer of information takes place on a wide variety of issues. Whether such a 'digital' community is a suitable focus for the promotion of the concept of environmental sustainability is the theme of this chapter.

In the first instance, we need to consider the nature of technological tools and how such tools may affect human relationships, not only with each other, but also with the natural environment. Secondly the question of universalism inherent within the modern rational and technological worldview needs to be considered in relation to emerging cultural pluralism. This discussion then leads to the question of whether the Internet is becoming confined by dominant universalistic trends that may limit intercultural exchange on environmental issues. Thirdly, it is important to consider what sustainability actually refers to in terms of its connection with authentic communities in actual places. The idea of sustainability is still in the process of definition. However, the focus of sustainability is not just conservation or preservation, it is fundamentally connected with dwelling, caring and saving (Heidegger, 1977b). As there are a plethora of interpretations, dialogue between different cultures and worldviews is necessary to bring the concept into the realm of global consciousness. Sustainability requires a multicultural approach if it is to become a truly reforming idea in the twenty-first century. The question here is: can the Internet facilitate an open dialogue on environmental sustainability? This leads us to ask whether the Internet will remain an open and ever-expanding horizon capable of crossing worldview boundaries and linking diverse communities, or whether it is fated to become ensnared by the predilection for Western-generated utopian visions. A 'digital utopia' is unlikely to produce outcomes capable of facilitating interdependent and pluralistic communities which will be necessary to guide the evolution of an environmentally sustainable civilization.

The Science of Technology

In the modern era a relationship with technology is inescapable: it is a defining condition of our times. While it is all to easy to see technology as a form of advanced tool-making, the effect of technology on social systems belies simplistic explanations. Technology is not just the business of making machines as a means to an end, but it is a cultural force because it is a significant human activity from which meaning is derived. Martin Heidegger (1977a, p. 4) comments:

"...the essence of technology is by no means anything technological. Thus we shall never experience our relationship to the essence of technology so long as we merely conceive and push forward the technological, put up with it or evade it. Everywhere we remain unfree and chained to technology, whether we passionately affirm or deny it. But we are delivered over to it in the worst possible way when we regard it as neutral; for this conception of it, to which today we particularly like to do homage, makes us utterly blind to the essence of technology."

The danger here is not technology itself, but the failure to recognize that the ordering capacity of technological reality is not a truly human order. Technological reality is not a truly human order because there are no subjective qualities involved: no love, no beauty, no poetics, no art and no intrinsic value.

Peoples' relationship to each other and their natural surroundings should not–
and cannot–be confined exclusively within technological ordering. Raimon
Panikkar (1984, p. 246) explains:

"Technology claimed, in its self-justification, that it would free Man from
the terror and shackles of nature–after it had blasphemed and desecrated
her, of course. We are not only inundated with technological gadgets, but
entangled in the technological universe. It entraps us in a purely techno-
cratic world which is neither divine, nor human, nor cosmic. It creates an
artificial empire from which there is no exit...The power that the
megamachine puts in human hands is a superhuman power that Man
cannot handle."

While the Internet is, in effect, a tool to facilitate human communication, it
remains a form of technological ordering. It is not the same as face-to-face, or
person-to-person communication because the technological aspect creates a significant distortion in terms of identity. The idea that computerized communication
networks have the potential to free us from hierarchical structures and allow for
individual expression has significant limitations (Pearce, 1995). Foremost is the
dislocation engendered by information technology which results in the fracturing of
any sense of local community. The means of communication are not universally
available and frequently involve an isolated focus that concentrates on only one
aspect of communication, i.e., the display and exchange of words and selected
images that have been–or can be–carefully edited to present a person or idea in its
best light. We end up with a society which legitimizes itself through the formation
of specialist interest-based relationships (Saul, 1997). These interest groups often
only relate with other disconnected groups or individuals who may have little, if any,
association with the wider community of people and the environment where they
actually reside. While this may have positive implications for the formation of
a global 'society,' the local community rarely benefits. A second important
issue arises when such dislocated activities are considered to be a source of
meaning in terms of what makes us essentially human. By elevating such
technological revealing as a means of measuring meaning and truth sets a
dangerous precedent. Dangerous because such attitudes can draw proponents of
technological systems into defensive economic (profit-driven) positions, thereby
increasing the possibility of increasing limitations and control of electronic
communication. This would lead to an ever-shrinking horizon of inquiry and
effectively reduce the Internet to the same state as many other modern global
communication systems where a few powerful sectors that benefit from universalistic approaches determine and control a specific form of communication.

Such limitation and control would eventually weaken the potential of the
Internet to act as a cross-cultural tool. Yet a retreat from technological communication systems or negation of their possible value will not suffice. Rather we
need to search for a more fundamental solution. Panikkar (2001, p.138) suggests
that a radical change in attitude is required to overcome these limitations:

"It is not therefore a question of just reforming the technocracy, or of returning to a pre-technological lifestyle, or of finding a convenient escape hatch. Neither is it any longer merely a question of wresting the reins of the historical process from the powers that be and taking them into our own hands, but rather of attuning ourselves once again to the rhythms of reality, of relearning to cooperate with the entire universe in and around us for the very survival of Being."

The survival of nature and all beings now depends on human choices that recognize our fundamental interconnectedness. It is no longer just a matter for one people, nation or civilization to address the environmental crises of our time–we are all involved in the search for sustainability. This is not merely the sustainable use of resources, or just a matter of sustainable management of nature, it also concerns cultural sustainability and the survival of local communities in places. The current process of globalization is pushing many societies from a state of autonomy to a new understanding of interdependence. Intercultural interdependence is crucial to the realization of the goal of sustainable living for all peoples and all life.

The first step towards affirming this interdependence requires cross-cultural communication which in turn implies the need to embrace cultural pluralism. One of the most important barriers to the realization of pluralism is the widely accepted universalistic ideology upheld and promoted by the Western worldview. Cross-cultural approaches are currently limited by the dominance of the Western urge to universalize everything.

Universalism Versus Cultural Pluralism

The history of the West reveals a strong preference for grand master narratives that provide a secure and distinct basis for stability in its worldview (Tarnas, 1991). Because of this tendency, the West has traditionally been sharply critical of, and resistant to, other worldviews, especially those who have embraced a plurality of explanations for reality. Pluralism is therefore not a concept that rests easily in the minds of Western thinkers. Information technology is a product of a civilization which depends upon rationality as a basis for its worldview. Rationalism–the desire to produce clear and distinct outcomes–arises from the compulsion to enclose mysterious aspects of reality within a 'safe' framework. Such enclosure demands exclusion of contradictory approaches to reality, especially any systems that challenge the foundations of rationality and reason. The modern worldview tends to exclude religious descriptions of reality and it is dogmatically resistant to worldviews that choose to embrace plural truth claims. Technological communication systems are consequently limited to a predetermined set of culturally restricted symbolic presentations. This alone suggests that such communication systems suffer inherent limitations that ultimately fail to include those cultures that find themselves outside the modern worldview boundary.

Universalism is a way in which some human communities establish their collective identity, and articulate their basic common convictions about what is real, meaningful and of value. Universalism as a form of cultural orientation is common to many worldviews. However, in the Western worldview it is the fundamental form of expression, and when applied apologetically, universalism leads to the exclusion of others who may approach truth from a different horizon of intelligibility. Kreiger (1991, p. 4) describes apologetic universalism as:

"... that form of encompassing worldview constituted by the presupposition of its own absolute totality and the denial of the validity and truth of other worldviews. It is based on the principle of exclusion and inclusion which nurtures the hope that eventually all opposition will be overcome."

The results of Western apologetic universalism can be clearly seen in the modern era. The evolution of democracy as a favored form of governance, the dominance of economic ideology, the elevation of scientific objectivity as the only reliable truth discerning method and the technological hierarchy of nation states are some obvious examples. Others include: the notion of 'universal' human rights, the so-called 'free' press, the hegemony of property rights and the elevation of Western cultural norms as the underlying principle of 'development.' Pluralism, on the other hand, challenges the assumption that modern reason is the ultimate ground from which our awareness of reality springs.

Pluralism is both a problem for thinking and an ideal to be attained. Evolving pluralistic attitudes do not suffer from any compelling obsession to reduce everything to absolute unity, nor do they subscribe to any ultimate duality. Panikkar (1996, p. 172) comments:

"The pluralistic attitude accepts the stance that reality may be of such a nature that nobody, and no single human group can coherently claim to exhaust the universal range of the human experience. Reality is not totally objectifiable because we, the subjects, are also part of it."

Pluralism precludes blank condemnation, absolute verdicts, total breaks in communication and the demand for total surrender to dominant ideologies. Pluralism in its most positive sense is the nemesis of orthodoxy and universalism. It denies power and control as a means to coerce divergent groups into dialogue based solely on the Western precepts of argumentation and dialectics. Pluralism is an emerging paradigm, in part created by the meeting of diverse cultures and the new climate of tolerance towards different descriptions of reality. In the current era a multi-perspectival and cross-cultural approach to conflicts may be better suited to finding solutions to environmental problems which often manifest on a global scale.

In order for the proponents of differing worldviews to enter into meaningful dialogue with each other on complex issues such as the concept of sustainability, they must accept one another's intrinsic viability. In modern times, as in no other previous period, acceptance of the reality of global pluralism is promoting the value of differing cultural perspectives about shared concerns. This kind of acceptance means that no single group will be able to dominate others at all levels, and as population pressure increases, the need to share rather than secure resources will become of paramount importance to the survival of all people, whether rich or poor, 'developed' or 'under-developed.'

It is interesting to note at this point that the increasing use of electronic mail services (e-mail) has contributed positively to encouraging pluralism. In the past migrants usually had to make a significant break from their original culture when they emigrated to other countries (particularly those who emigrated to Western countries). This was largely because communication systems and financial restrictions did not allow them to keep close contact with their own people and culture. The result was the evolution of 'expatriate' communities where traditions were slowly eroded due to the influence of the dominant culture they had joined. As generations passed, ties to the homeland weakened and migrant groups ended up with a mix of cultural influences which essentially favored their host countries. The advent of high-speed e-mail has facilitated closer ties with original traditions and strengthened cultural diversity. People who are secure in their own traditions and cultural values are in a better position to argue for pluralistic societies and values that recognize the importance of multicultural approaches. The idea of 'placeless' and disconnected minority underclasses is rapidly becoming outdated as migrants strengthen their identity through the use of modern communication systems. For example, a person from a small village community in India migrating to London or Los Angeles can now keep in regular contact with his or her extended family, traditions and religious practices. There is no longer a need for total assimilation. This has important implications for the evolution of a cross-cultural dialogue on sustainability.

The Concept of Sustainability

Environmental issues are at the center of the pluralistic debate as the so-called 'global' techno-economic forces try to secure ever-increasing access to 'resources' which they deem necessary for production of consumable materials. It is precisely these demands which have led to the emergence of the idea of sustainable management of natural resources. The difficulty is that those who are now seeking solutions are, for the most part, representatives of the worldview that caused the problem in the first instance. Those peoples who are suffering the most from global environmental degradation often do not have a voice in the decision-making processes. Ironically, many traditional indigenous societies had as part of their everyday cultural practices what is now called the 'new' concept of environmental sustainability. Clearly there is a need for dialogue between diverse worldviews to enter into a meaningful dialogue on the issue of what sustainability is, and more importantly, whom it is for.

Sustainability as a modern concept has a relatively short history. Brought to international attention by the Report of the World Commission on Environment and Development (WCED) in 1987, sustainable development was formally endorsed by political leaders from more than 170 countries at the Rio Earth Summit in 1992. The Report (WCED, p. 43) explained that sustainable development was:

"Development that meets the needs of the present without compromising the ability of future generations to meet their own needs. It contains within it two key concepts: the concepts of 'needs,' in particular, the essential needs of the world's poor, to which overriding priority should be given, and the limitations imposed by the state of technology and social organization in the environment's ability to meet present and future needs."

However subsequent debate has spawned a number of interpretations. We now have debate on whether we are referring to sustainable 'management,' sustainable 'development' or sustainable 'societies.' The idea of sustainable economics is an oxymoron in the sense that modern economic theory precludes the idea of sustainability simply because the fundamental measure of economic health is unlimited growth. Yet no living being or system, such as the earth's biosphere, can sustain permanent or unlimited growth. Cultural sustainability is rarely considered in relation to global debates on sustainability. Yet for groups such as the Australian Aboriginal peoples, New Zealand Maori, and the first peoples of the Americas, cultural sustainability is of paramount importance in terms of their visions of the future and traditional connections to natural environments. The concept of sustainability, irrespective of its application, remains largely undefined. Yet in many respects sustainability with reference to 'development' is a moral or normative guiding principle. It is not so much about what is but what should be. It has to do with value choices. Sustainability confronts us with a situation where facts are uncertain, values are in dispute, the stakes are high and a decision is urgent (Viederman, 1995).

There are, however, many interesting interpretations. For example, New Zealand's Resource Management Act 1991 (RMA) introduced one of the world's first legally binding sustainable laws. The RMA (1991, p. 24) defines sustainable management as:

"The use, development and protection of natural and physical resources in a way, or at a rate, which enables people and communities to provide for their social, economic and cultural well-being and for their health and safety while sustaining the potential of natural and physical resources to meet the reasonably foreseeable needs of future generations."

The RMA (1991, p. 25) goes on to include cultural values. In Section 6– Matters of National Importance–authorities are required to recognize and provide for:

"The relationship of Maori and their culture and traditions with their ancestral lands, water, sites, waahi tapu (sacred places) and other toanga (spiritual treasures)."

The linking of environmental issues with the spiritual and cultural well-being of people who hold a different worldview to the currently dominant one is in many ways unique. However, after nearly 10 years of application, the RMA has failed to engender any meaningful dialogue between Maori and non-Maori New Zealanders on the vexed question of Maori spiritual links to the natural environment. The reason for this is complex, yet directly related to the fact that Maori are "forced to come to the Western table where reason, dialectics and argumentation are the dominant modes of communication" (Panikkar, 1995, p. 102). The focus is one of presentation of evidence. Maori must prove, in Western terms, what their sacred world means. The essential problem here is one of validity. Western thought will not–and perhaps cannot–validate truth claims which are not 'rational' or 'reasonable.' Communication across their respective worldview boundaries is effectively halted by Western universalistic principles. Herein lies the essence of the problem of communication between diverse human groups. We need to discover and empower a new form of dialogue which facilitates genuine communication in order to approach the complexities of modern problems. This is particularly relevant to environmental problems and the emerging concept of sustainability. It is also the point where the Internet, as a global communication system, has important possibilities and potential. But first we need to examine a possible process to facilitate a meaningful dialogue which can reach beyond the limitations of argumentation and dialectics.

Dialectical and Dialogical Dialogue

The current model of dialogue, commonly referred to as conflict resolution or conflict mediation, is essentially a dialectical dialogue. Dialectical dialogue is based on the fundamental assessment that we are all rational beings and that the nature of reality is logical and objective. Dialectical dialogue is a 'reasonable' dialogue which assumes that thought takes priority over being, and that cultural universals preclude un-reason. It is a dialogue concerned with objects, opinions and doctrines welded together by ideas and definitions; the product of knowing subjects (Vachon, 1995). The horizon of intelligibility in a dialectical dialogue is firmly grounded in the logos of a particular culture and usually ignores the mythic core of other worldviews. The dialectic dialogue is currently used as an instrument of power in so-called conflict resolution. It does so because argumentation and dialectics cannot reach the level of dialogue required to overcome the radical distance that separates different worldviews from one another. For this we need a dialogical dialogue.

Panikkar, in his lifelong attempt to outline a method for inter- and intra-religious dialogue evolved what he termed diatopical (dia–across, or, between, the topoi–place) hermeneutics Panikkar (1979, p. 9) notes:

"Diatopical hermeneutics stands for the thematic consideration of understanding the 'other' without assuming that the 'other has the basic self-understanding that I have."

Panikkar's three-step interpretative process is specifically designed to overcome the limitations of argumentation and dialectics by allowing participants in dialogue to move into the realm of symbolic discourse where commonality may be discovered.

The first of the three levels of discourse is that which takes place within the culture, tradition and religion which make up a worldview. It involves the explanation of components of that worldview and its traditions as experienced by an interpreter within its own boundaries. It is an expression of how a particular worldview 'looks,' how it 'feels' to live within that particular view. This step consists in elucidating a faithful and critical understanding of one's own tradition so that explanation of the set of taken-for-granted truths about the reality which constitutes our 'world' can be described. This is a matter of verification; 'how' we do things, 'what' we do and 'why' it is important that we do them. This is also the beginning of a discourse of enclosure in that it sets the limits of our understanding of a particular issue. Dialectics and argumentation are not necessarily a hindrance to this level of dialogue because we are expressing reality as we see it in everyday terms. This kind of interpretation is morphological; that is, it gives us the form of a worldview and mediates communication within the boundaries of a particular worldview horizon (Panikkar, 1979).

The second interpretative step involves the process of defining the boundaries of a worldview. These boundaries are defined by the relationship between the core aspects of a worldview which are embedded in its founding texts and events. Panikkar called this step a diachronical (dia–across, chronos–time) interpretation in reference to the changing contours of the context over time (Panikkar, 1979). This means that we need to understand what was meant by those who present the founding texts and stories in the context that they themselves experienced at that time. To understand the essential nature of another's worldview, one must know where the 'other' is coming from; that is: the 'how' and 'why' of their founding texts. The knowledge of those founding texts also allows each worldview representative to enclose their worldview within a definable boundary. For meaningful dialogue to achieve its stated aim, each party needs to know where a worldview begins and ends, what its mythic expression is and how far intelligible cognition extends. This interpretation brings a particular way of 'seeing' and 'knowing' the world to life by revealing its beauty, wisdom and intrinsic coherence to those of differing worldviews. Here spokespeople are encouraged to recount their creation stories and express myths which tell their people how reality unfolds for them. A worldview, in this sense, is like all living things: it has an origin, and emerges in the same manner as a tree from a seed to expand to the limits of its teleological necessity. This second level of discourse establishes the boundaries of a worldview by setting the criteria for meaning and validity in that worldview. Diachronical interpretation leads to a discourse of disclosure, which is the third level of dialogue.

This is the diatopical hermeneutic which is the search for, and interpretation of, symbols which may be common and intelligible to divergent worldview. Because symbols present the myth, a symbolic interpretation does not pierce the mythos and so avoids the demythicisation associated with dialectics and argumentation involved in the first two levels. It is these authentic symbols which grant our beliefs their unity, continuity and power to legitimize and sustain a 'world' of meaning and values. The task is to carefully interpret the symbols which are capable of carrying meaning across worldview boundaries. Clearly comparison will not suffice because there is no superior standpoint from which to make such comparisons which, by their very nature, deny the belief of the believer and turn symbols into signs (Panikkar, 1979). Rather we must learn to "think in, and with, the symbols of another tradition as with our own" (Krieger, 1991, p.70). The third level of discourse operates within the space of encounter between different worldview boundaries.

Situated beyond argumentation and dialectics, it is a discussion of how truth, values, beliefs and faith are presented in symbolic form. Panikkar (1980, pp. 205-206) explains:

"By diatopical hermeneutics I understand a hermeneutic which is more than the purely morphological (drawing from the already known deposit of a particular tradition) and the merely diachronical one (when we have to bridge a temporal gap in order to arrive at a legitimate interpretation). It is a hermeneutic dealing with understanding the contents of diverse cultures which do not have cultural or direct historical links with one another. They belong to different loci, topoi, so that before anything else we have to forge the tools of understanding in the encounter itself, for we cannot–should not–assume a priori a common language."

This type of dialogue requires a peculiar kind of conversion. Such a conversion is not merely an act of 'jumping across' from one worldview boundary to become included within another. It requires the realization that another's truth is equally as valid as one's own. Participants cannot be asked to sacrifice their own worldview for another, but rather, to expect theirs to be enriched by additional revelations of truth. This is the essential result of active and positive pluralism–a direct contrast to the current model of fragmentation, where one universalistic worldview tries to dominate others to affirm its own being. By disregarding the collective wisdom of a multitude of diverse perceptions of reality, universalistic worldviews isolate themselves by retreating to a defensive position. The defensive position engendered by modern universalism not only attempts to enclose emerging pluralistic paradigms, but also limits communications about important global issues such as sustainability.

Information, Knowledge and Communication

Information is the term most closely associated with Internet science. The 'information' superhighway, 'information' technology and 'information' systems are common phrases used in everyday speech. Information dissemination, however, is an entirely different concept to dialogue. Information is derived from the Latin informare, meaning to give shape to, to fashion or describe. Dialogue on the other hand is from the Greek dia, across or through and logos, reason. Hence technological communication is founded on fashioning, describing and shaping reality, whereas human communication is based on conversation reaching across or beyond the boundaries set by reason. Dialogue is a more open system in the sense that it allows for a much wider range of possibilities. Information is a self-limiting concept because it encloses reality within the limits of certain truth claims. Information is correct or incorrect, believed or disbelieved, accepted or rejected depending upon which truth criteria is accepted. Dialogue, and particularly the dialogical dialogue outlined above, is a system of communication which seeks to expand the truth criteria to include other ways of knowing (Broomfield, 1997).

The Internet, as a technological ordering of reality, has largely become an information dissemination system. Information is usually presented in relation to authority or authenticity. Web sites become authoritative foci for knowledge about 'things,' 'events' and 'activities.' Interpretation of information is decidedly channeled through rational exegesis. Moreover, information is primarily focused on Western or modern forms of knowledge, using Western symbols and Western truth claims as the basic structural unit. Intercultural interpretation is rare and symbolic interpretation virtually non-existent because the nature of the communication system belongs primarily to one worldview.

A secondary, but important consideration, is the hierarchical nature of information systems. Knowledge and information is ordered according to certain criteria in terms of its verifiability. Priority is given to scientifically provable and rational explanations for phenomenon. Hence a geological or geographical description of a certain landscape is awarded merit in terms of intelligibility where a spiritual or sacred description is usually regarded as quaint, interesting or mythological. Yet for many peoples, a sacred description is wholly intelligible and awarded the highest priority in terms of 'knowledge.'

An example of two radically different descriptions of reality can be seen when considering scientific and Maori versions of the origin of landforms. In the center of the North Island of New Zealand, a volcanic plateau has been awarded World Heritage status. This region and its volcanoes are defined in scientific terms as a series of andesitic cones formed by the movement of Indo-Australian and Pacific tectonic plates. A scientific description goes on to give the origins, age and reasoned explanation for their composition. In short, this presents an intelligible and accessible explanation based on many years of research. Tuwharetoa people who originally gifted the volcanic peaks to the government of New Zealand in 1887 describe the mountains as their matua (or parent of the land), the center of their mana (spiritual power) and the peaks are identified with their tupuna (or divine ancestors). This sacred relationship of the people with their land is not confined to some past relationship. It is very much alive today, as a spokesperson for the tribe relates (cited by Potton, 1987, p. 164):

"We look upon the mountains with deep respect and reverence and a tinge of many other complementary emotions, pride certainly being one of them. Proud that they are ours–Te Hao Taku Manawa. The breath of the mountain is my heart. Our reverence for the mountains goes deeper in that in time with the essence of our genealogies, all life originated from the same parents Papa-tu-a-nuku, the earth mother and Rangi, the sky father, so that man and all other life forms are in harmony with one another in the bonds of kinship."

Tuwharetoa also have numerous accounts of the origin and placement of the volcanic peaks or Warrior Mountains who battled for supremacy on the plateau. For Maori this is sacred knowledge, a special kind of 'information' that makes their landscape intelligible to people from other regions. Both the scientific and Tuwharetoa descriptions are valid if viewed from within their own traditions. While both peoples are talking about the same 'thing,' they are saying different things about it. A dialogue on sustainability approached from a scientific view would include geological and ecological aspects but not necessarily sacred consideration. In terms of the Maori perspective, this would be a scientific monologue where people who presented different parts of the same worldview would debate various values for conservation or preservation. Sustainable management of the World Heritage area in Maori terms would establish sacrality as the primary consideration. Sacred knowledge would be at the apex of their 'information' hierarchy. It is notable that all current literature (including the Web site) on the topic of the Tongariro National Park begins with physical and ecological descriptions followed by an historical analysis beginning with European contact. Maori 'mythology' is relegated to the latter parts or sometimes introduced in the form of introductory chapter quotes.

A meaningful dialogue on sustainable management or 'development' of the region would need to begin from a different standpoint if it was to include the cultural and spiritual concerns of Maori people. Herein lies the importance of the interpretative process outlined above. If we (i.e., those who hold a modern worldview) genuinely wish to understand and speak with Maori on the question of sustainability, then we need to begin by listening to their account of how reality unfolds for them. To validate their truth claims, we must understand how their worldview evolved in a historical sense, how their perceptions arose and what their founding myths were. We would also need to explain how it is to 'be' in our own worldview and what our founding myths are–particularly our myth of scientific rationality.

The Internet has the potential to advance these two stages of Panikkar's dialogical system, either through the Web site process or e-mail. However, it is only possible if those who would be party to such discussions entered in the spirit of genuine inquiry and with an open and honest attitude; and the foundation of any understanding must be firmly rooted in a relationship. Such relationships would, of necessity, be founded prior to any subsequent 'digital' communication. In this example, sustainable management of Tongariro National Park is not just a matter for academicians, park managers or tourists. It is of paramount importance to seek knowledge, wisdom and form relationships with people who live in the region, especially Tuwharetoa who have a long history of close association with the mountains as their place. This is, of course, only one example. There are numerous others throughout the world where indigenous people, local folk, as well as poor people are often not consulted on how their places will be developed, managed or exploited. Often those who hold a radically different worldview to the currently dominant one are not included in any discussions about their views on such matters.

The Potential of the Internet to Facilitate Dialogue on Sustainability

The Internet has definitely raised awareness of environmental issues through-out the world and encouraged debate about sustainability. This has been beneficial in the sense that it has sped up the dissemination of information and knowledge about global environmental crises, including the links between human rights abuses and environmental devastation. It has also been useful to authenticate and communicate the concept of sustainability, albeit in modern terms. However, most of the Web sites are firmly grounded in the Western hierarchical and universalistic tradition of information presentation. There have been only limited attempts to present such information in a way that allows for other ways of knowing. And many of those sites which have attempted to present other worldviews according to different symbols and structures are rarely legitimated by mainstream thinkers. The problem remains within the hegemony of rationalistic searches for 'clear and distinct' solutions and descriptions. This is not to suggest that the potential of the Internet as a means for intercultural dialogue is by any means exhausted. What is required is a change in the way communication is approached.

It is possible to divide Internet use into at least four broad categories: information sites, business and e-Commerce, entertainment and personal communication modes (such as e-mail and specific interest 'chat' groups). Debate and meaningful dialogue on sustainability, business, e-Commerce, and entertainment sites lie outside our area of interest. Information sites and personal communication systems offer the greatest potential for intercultural and pluralistic exchange. As we have seen above, the idea of presenting information in a hierarchical structure effectively excludes many potential contributors. Another important consideration and attitude change involves overcoming the current desire to perceive the Internet as a wholly global system existing as a 'virtual' community. It is a system which allows people from all parts of the globe to communicate with each other, yet the concept of a 'virtual' community is essentially illusory. People who use the Internet exist in real time in a physical world. They live in places where 'real' issues occur. A dialogue on sustainability is based on 'actual' issues, not 'virtual' ones.

Increasingly people in rural and remote areas are connected to the Internet. It is no longer the realm of a privileged minority of city dwellers. For many peoples, sense of place and community are inseparable. Many of the previously voiceless and isolated communities can now contribute if they wish. Yet many remote indigenous communities and tribal groups connected to the Internet often find themselves alienated from modern communication systems because they are unable to express their views in a way which is meaningful to them (Rassmussen, 2000). They cannot describe themselves, their values or issues important to them through a system which does not yet recognize their way of knowing. This is not a real or absolute barrier. In a sense it is a 'virtual' barrier created by the dominance of symbols and images arising from the Western worldview. There is a need for a new approach to the creation and management of modes of communication currently accepted as the norm.

New 'dialogical' Web sites could be created where people or groups of people could begin by explaining what their view of reality is like for them, using their own symbols and expression not necessarily formatted in common Internet style. This would open the door for others to reply by asking questions and offering their own views. This builds understanding. It is not simply fostering information exchange or seeking conversion from one view of reality to another. It is, as Panikkar insists, an interpretation of the form of one's worldview. The second stage is an explanation of how each worldview arose in historical terms. This can be presented in a form which details appropriate histories from the point of view of that particular group of people. Such histories can be entirely independent of modern historical concepts, which means that they do not have to be verifiable in accordance with commonly accepted versions. The purpose is not to argue an alternative version of history but to explain the inherent intelligibility of that worldview.

Current use of the Internet, in terms of Web site formatting, suffers from limitations set by the type of software operating systems available. It appears that a new generation of software development is likely to make Internet use not only more interactive, but also more diverse. With the advent of increasingly sophisticated digital imaging, video links, Web cameras and person-to-person interactive audio connections, communication will no longer be limited to set styles. For those peoples who prefer to communicate through dance, music, poetry or spoken words, the Internet will be able to provide an avenue which does not limit communication to information dissemination in the form of written words, static images or documentary-style visual productions. This is a truly revolutionary development because it allows for forms of expression not commonly accessible in the past. People will now be able to make themselves known to a global audience using their own mode of expression and medium of communication. It is this aspect of the Internet that, if connected with the understanding gained through 'real' relationships, could facilitate a symbolic discourse–the third stage of Panikkar's dialogue. The potential is effectively unlimited. The limitation on Internet usage currently rests on the supposed inability of participants to encourage and bring into practice such pluralistic and intercultural modes of communication.

If we can understand and validate other people's worldviews, then we may be able to address their concerns about the dominant paradigms and ideologies that impose modernism upon them. We can also begin a dialogue with people who hold different values about their relationship with the natural world. A starting point may be discovered whereby we can all contribute to the evolution of a sustainable world.

CONCLUSION

The Internet has the potential to become a positive pathway for dialogue on sustainability, not only across cultures, but also within any particular worldview. The practical application of successful sustainable management and development of natural resources is dependent upon the evolution of sustainable communities and sustainable cultures. The goal of a sustainable civilization can only be fulfilled if people can actively participate in decision-making processes. There is a tendency today to offer monocultural solutions to environmental problems. The choices are set up in opposition where only two possible solutions are offered, either those derived from the modern worldview, or from traditional viewpoints, i.e., anthropocentrism, or cosmocentrism. Answers are sought from either the rational ecological approach or from indigenous shamanic spirituality. Rarely is a truly cross-cultural encounter attempted where those who hold what appear to be incommensurable worldviews share their respective wisdoms through dialogue (Raine, 2001).

The Internet provides us with a unique opportunity to investigate an alternative path. If we can begin to set up sites to facilitate dialogue on the vexed question of sustainable environments, cultures and societies, we may be able to move from a 'virtual' community endlessly expressing opinions on the possibility of 'digital' utopias to actualizing and empowering real communities in actual places. A realizable vision of an earthly 'paradise' is a far more admirable quest than that of a retreat into a new defensive universalism which closes down the possibility of a pluralistic future. Sustainability must be applicable for all peoples. It must make sense to all of us; otherwise it will fail to curb incremental environmental degradation now occurring on a global scale. This is not a viable alternative in the long term. Humans may find themselves rejected by the Earth's living system because our current rate of resource depletion and ecological disturbance fails to contribute to the long-term well-being of the planet. Sustainability in the relationship between human beings and our natural environment is of crucial importance to future generations. The Internet can be part of this evolution if people so choose. If they do not take advantage of this unique opportunity, the Internet is likely to become increasingly confined to trivialities and suffer the same fate as television and other current mass media systems that support the status quo.

The task ahead is to actualize the untapped potential of the Internet, as a global communication system, by opening up a horizon of expression which will allow for all people to participate in meaningful dialogue. Meaningful dialogue is aimed at mutual understanding between people who hold dissimilar worldviews, but along the way each participant may give the other important insights into their own traditions (Panikkar, 1981). This in turn could facilitate further exchange and so the dialogue can build on itself. What is crucial though is that we accept the call to dialogue in the first instance. We may have to be prepared to sacrifice something, to be drawn into the unknown, and be prepared for the changes in our understanding which may result. The criteria for meaningful dialogue on sustainability requires that we as participants understand the nature of communication technologies (and the nature of communication) as cultural forces and reject the hierarchical structure which currently dominate them. We also need to embrace cultural pluralism and give up any urge to universalize everything through our own particular cultural lens.

We do not need a 'virtual' utopia, or indeed, any kind of utopia. We need real communities in real places communicating and relating with each other about what is important to us all–the long-term sustainability of our Earth and all its diverse ways of being. If technology is not to overburden nature in the coming decades, we need to adjust our attitude to communication technology and turn it into a force for intercultural understanding. The problem lies not in the complex nature of the Internet, nor indeed the ordering nature of technology itself, but rather in our ideas of what it is for. It could become a tool which can enable a shared vision of a sustainable Earth to emerge. The choice is ours.

REFERENCES

Broomfield, J. (1997). *Other Ways of Knowing: Recharting our Future with Ageless Wisdom*. Vermont: Inner Traditions.

Chen, S. B. (2000). Address to *The World Congress on Information Technology*, Taipei.

Heidegger, M. (1977a). *The Question Concerning Technology in the Question Concerning Technology and Other Essays* (W. Lovitt, trans). New York: Garland Publishing, Inc.

Heidegger, M. (1977b). *The Turning in the Question Concerning Technology and Other Essays* (W. Lovitt, trans). New York, NY: Garland Publishing, Inc.

Kreiger, D. (1991). *The New Universalism: Foundations for a Global Theology*. New York, NY: Orbis Books.

Panikkar, R. (2001). *The Rhythm of Being–The Radical Trinity*. New York, NY: Orbis Books.

Panikkar, R. (1996). The defiance of pluralism. *Soundings*, 79, 1-2.

Panikkar, R. (1995). *Cultural Disarmament: The Way to Peace*. Louisville, KY: John Knox Press.

Panikkar, R. (1984). The destiny of technological civilization: An ancient Buddhist legend. *Alternatives X*, Fall.

Panikkar, R. (1979). *Myth, Faith and Hermeneutics: Cross-Cultural Studies*. New York, NY: Paulist Press.

Panikkar, R. (1980). The dialogical dialogue. In Wahling, F. (Ed.), *The World's Religious Traditions: Current Perspectives in Religious Studies*, Edinburg: T & T Clark.

Panikkar, R. (1981). *The Unknown Christ of Hinduism*. New York: Orbis Books.

Pearce, M. (1995) From urb to bit. *Architectural Design Profile No 118: Architects in Cyberspace*, 7. London: Academy Edition.

Potton, C. (1987). *Tongariro: A Sacred Gift*. Auckland: Landsdowne Press.

Raine, P. A. (2001). Beyond universalism, the shaman and the ecologist: An ever open horizon. *INTERculture*, (140), 1-64.

Rassmussen, D. (2000). Dissolving Inuit society through education and money. *INTERculture*, (139).

Resource Management Act. (1991). Wellington: New Zealand Government Print.

Saul, J. R. (1997). *The Unconscious Civilization*. Ringwood: Penguin Books.

Tarnas, R (1991). *The Passion of the Western Mind*. New York, NY: Ballantine Books.

Vachon, R. (1995). Guswenta, or the intercultural imperative. *INTERculture*, 27.

Viederman, S. (1995) Knowledge for sustainable development: What do we need to know? In Trzyna, T. C. (Ed.), *A Sustainable World: Defining and Measuring Sustainable Development*, Sacramento, CA: IUCN and California Institute of Public Affairs.

World Commission on Environment and Development. (1987). *Our Common Future*. Oxford: Oxford University Press.

Chapter XII

Only Connect? The Impact of the Internet on Lived Experience

Neil Turnbull
Nottingham Trent University, UK

INTRODUCTION: TECHNOLOGY AS PROBLEM FOR EVERYDAY LIFE

Those of us who live in the 'late-modern' developed world live in a world that is increasingly technological in character. This is not a new insight by any means; and it is usual to begin discussions of the likely personal, social or cultural impacts of new technologies with some acknowledgment of this fact. However, the commonplace nature of this observation should not be allowed to disguise its significance; and a mere cursory examination of the recent history of our involvement with some of the most significant and broadly used technologies reveals a truly startling state of affairs.

Since the 1950s at least, those living in the developed world have witnessed the arrival of a glut of new technological devices, many of which had only previously existed in the fertile imaginations of modern science fiction writers. Imagine describing the significance of these inventions to a person from the pre-modern past. It might go something like this: at the beginning of the twentieth century, the majority of people have motorized chariots–cars–to take them to and from their places of work. They have 'far-seeing' and 'far-speaking' devices–respectively televisions and telephones–that enable people to see and speak to absent things and people. Once only the gods lived this way and framing the problems surrounding the nature and significance of technology in this historical way, makes our technological world appear as a modern nirvana in comparison to the world inhabited by those of the pre-modern past.

Clearly then, technology is one of the dimensions along which we can differentiate our ideas of the modern and the pre-modern. The devices referred to above have, without doubt, been one the key factors involved in modernizing many aspects of everyday life, a change that can only be described as a 'great technological transformation' of the everyday world. Many of these technologies[1] –especially those sanitation, culinary and cleansing technologies that have transformed the 'domestic' sphere–have seemingly been designed for 'emancipatory' social ends, liberating us from the dull and compulsive chores of home and workplace.

However, not all recent technological innovations can be seen as 'socially progressive.' Other innovations, especially those that have been designed to take us beyond and beneath the terrestrial world, pose challenges–and in some cases direct threats- to some of our most cherished and deeply held conceptions of the world. Space, nuclear and biotechnologies are species of this genus of technology. Other modern technologies fall somewhere between these two extremes and hence from a moral and political view seem deeply ambiguous (Feenberg, 1990). They offer both profound threats and opportunities. The Internet is an example of this third type of technology and it is a technology whose wider social and cultural significance remains unclear (see Jones, 1997). The Internet–as a synthesis of existing televisual and telecommunications and computing technologies–can be seen as a new total communication and information environment that has the potential–if used in certain ways–to radically transform what we mean by communication, consumption and entertainment. But it can also be seen–especially from an everyday point of view–as a disruptive, perhaps even destructive force.

The question of the nature and significance of everyday life has come to occupy a prominent position in recent discussion in moral and social philosophy. According to the philosopher Charles Taylor (see Taylor, 1989), it is only within the context of everyday world–the world of productive work and the family–that the old classical philosophical questions about the nature of 'the good' make sense. As he puts it:

"[t]his sense of the importance of the everyday in human life...colors our whole understanding of what it is truly to respect human life and integrity. Along with the central place given to autonomy, it defines a version of this demand which is peculiar to our civilization, the modern West." (Taylor, 1989, 14)

If technology has transformed everyday life, then technology has helped change our definitions of what it means to be in and of the 'modern West.' But it would be a mistake–as Taylor does–to see everyday life as something entirely divorced from the technological realm (and only subject to 'technological impacts'). As phenomenologist of technology, Albert Borgmann has argued, technologies are now both a characteristic of, and a constraining pattern to, the entire fabric of our everyday lives, to such an extent that everyday existence can now almost be defined by the manner in which technology increasingly orders and sustains the ebbs and flows of everyday living. For Borgmann, everyday life in our late-modern times has a characteristic pattern and:

> "[t]his pattern is visible first and foremost in the countless inconspicuous objects and procedures of daily life in a technological society. It is concrete in its manifestations, closest to our existence, and pervasive in its extent. The rise and rule of this pattern I consider the most consequential event of the modern period. Once the pattern is explicated and seen, it sheds light on the hopes that have shaped our times, on the confusions and frustrations that we have suffered in the attempt to realize those hopes, and on the possibilities of clarifying our deepest aspirations and of acting constructively on our best insights." (Borgmann, 1984, p. 3)

When conceived from such everyday vantage points, the problem of the Internet has a twofold character. Firstly: "To what extent is the Internet being 'taken-up' as an everyday technology?" And secondly: 'once 'taken-up,' how is the Internet likely to change and/or conserve the rules that pattern everyday interactions?' As the Internet is–when viewed historically–relatively still a technological infant, it is the first question that is currently the most pressing one. Hence, in the following discussion, I focus on the first aspect of the problem, especially the question of the everyday pre-conditions that might make for a successful up-take and those that might make up-take more problematic. Not all technologies heralded as having likely revolutionary impacts are actually taken-up as everyday technologies (especially in their original form and functionality). For example, the modern form of the safety bicycle only emerged after a historically protracted series of negotiations between different interested social groups (Pinch and Bijker, 1987). There is no guarantee that the current fashionability of the Internet will lead to its wholesale take-up as a broadly used everyday technology, and some recent research has suggested that the Internet might not be being taken-up to the extent predicted by early predictions at all (Uhlig, 2000).

However, the question of the everyday significance of new technologies like the Internet has not yet been on the agendas of philosophers, social and management scientists and policy makers (Lie and Sørensen, 2000). Typically, the Internet is simply assumed to have a likely significant and determining effect on everyday life by forcing a new information highway 'though our own backyard' (Jones, 1997, p. 12). However, such assumptions can lead to stereotypical and oversimplified understandings. Many are dazzled by the newness of the Internet and its ability to take us 'beyond' the mundane realities of everyday living. As Jones puts it:

> "[w]e marvel at the sights and sounds brought into our homes and places of work and sometimes are dismayed at their intrusion into our lives, but we think less about the Internet's non-spatial features. We think more about the ability to take us places and less about its insertion into the mundane practices of everyday life." (Jones, 1997, p. 12).

There is some acknowledgment in the academic literature that the Internet is likely to make ordinary social life very different, probably much busier (see Gergen, 1991), but much of this work–as I explain below–has also been dazzled by the very newness of the Internet as a technological object. In particular, what is lacking in many of these accounts is a clear definition of how the Internet differs from other late-modern information and communication technologies (and in what ways it is similar). The Internet is simply assumed to be radically new. The problem with this way of conceiving the Internet is that, when seen from an everyday point of view, no technology is ever radically new. Each technology is always assimilated into an existing set of patterns–one might say traditions–of technology usage. There is a hermeneutics to everyday technology use, and, in the case of the Internet, this still remains theoretically and philosophically opaque. What still remains unclear is in what ways is the Internet taken-up and used as a relaxing from of escape like the television? Or is it used more seriously and socially like the telephone? In what ways is it understood in everyday terms as different from both the former? The important point to draw out here is that it is only once the nature of the connection between the Internet and current well-embedded everyday technologies is made clear that the broad significance of the Internet will become apparent.

Technology, Wisdom and the Problem of Technology Management in Everyday Contexts

Unless the Internet is validated as a potentially significant and usable device by everyday users,[2] it will not be significantly taken-up. How then do we understand what factors may enhance and which may inhibit its take-up? This can only be understood via an analysis of demand for technology in the everyday world. Answers to this type of question involve a moral and political demand for a deep and comprehensive insight into the nature and significance of the use of our technologies. For the question 'what makes a technology significant in an everyday sense?' is ultimately a philosophical question that asks for an examination of the relationship between technology and the everyday world as the repository of goodness and justice. The everyday world demands technologies that promise a more edifying set of qualities to everyday life. Hence to understand what is at stake in the everyday consumption of technology, we need to examine how modern technology has become deeply implicated in our modern conceptions of 'the good' and 'the just.' It is a demand for what might be termed technological wisdom. This is a kind of wisdom that would allow us to make wise choices in what technologies to take-up and how to use them.

This is the central question that provides the main focus for this chapter: how might the Internet be seen as an 'everyday good'? It is important to point out that this philosophical question amounts to an appeal for an understanding of the best form of everyday management of technology, for in order to be taken-up, any technology need to be seen as fitting into existing routines in some way. It is easy to forget that good management requires wisdom. It is also easy to forget that management is not the sole prerogative of professional managers. The problem of management is more general than is generally conceived: it emerges whenever there is some uncertainty involved in how to navigate a particular problem space, and thus management is first and foremost about a certain kind of non-specialized 'know-how' that is not easy to articulate in formal terms (Dreyfus and Dreyfus, 1986). What kind of philosophical understanding does the Internet require in order to be used wisely? To answer this question requires a philosophical reflection on how best to use the Internet given some of the basic–and in the end ethical–constraints that make everyday life as we know it possible.

However, as far as contemporary technology users are concerned, the 'revolutionary' technologies of the past–such as telephones and televisions–no longer transform the everyday realm but are very much a piece of it. They are themselves part of the familiar and routine furniture of the everyday world. They stand in a passive–one might say 'regulative'–relationship to everyday activities, and their transforming effects on everyday routines have since passed into history. The Internet's relationship to the everyday–as it is still relatively unfamiliar–is, however, potentially more active and disruptive.

The idea that the Internet is likely to be disruptive of some of the basic dimensions of everyday life is also not new. According to recent commentators, the Internet is seen as the likely harbinger of a new and radically transformed society (Rheingold, 1993; Leadbeater, 1999). These commentators discuss the Internet in terms of its likely 'impact' on both workplace settings and wider sets of institutional arrangements. In so doing they not only conceive of the Internet in overly abstract and global terms–divorced from the concrete everyday situations within which the Internet is currently used–but also view it as equivalent to a 'sociological meteor from outer space' with its own inherent momentum and inevitable moral, social and political 'impacts.' They tend to forget that everyday users have choices over whether and how to use particular technologies and it is in this sense that technologies are ultimately defined by how they are taken-up at the point of use (Grint andWoolgar, 1997). To counter the rhetorical and exaggerated nature of many of these claims requires a more micro-level focus that focuses upon everyday 'experience' of the Internet, especially the tension between actual and potential experience of the Internet.

To frame the question in this way is to frame the question phenomenologically. For phenomenological philosophers such as Martin Heidegger and Maurice Merleau-Ponty, experience, *Erlebnis*, gives the quality of the world its 'vital value, grasping it first in its meaning for us' (Merleau-Ponty, 1962). My aim here is to assess how everyday users negotiate the meaning of the Internet in everyday settings and especially how they might maximize its utility given the moral constraints of the everyday world. I attempt this via a discussion of possible scenarios for significant Internet take-up, scenarios that explore the everyday conditions of possibility for the emergence of the Internet as a significant everyday technology. One particular advantage of this approach is that it allows us to move beyond the somewhat 'technologically determinist' conceptions of the relationship between technology and everyday life implicit in both the recent theoretical accounts and common-sense impressions of the likely significance of the Internet. Once seen as a problem for ordinary lived experience, it becomes possible to ask different kinds of questions, such as: 'What factors and forces are likely to support particular 'positive' experiences of the Internet that expand the range of possibilities available in the everyday world? Is the Internet being used to its full potential or is it being used to shore-up existing everyday routines? Do everyday routines need to adapt in order to make sure that the technology in question is used to full effect, that is, 'used well' (and not as a toy)?

The parallels with the telephone are significant here. When it first emerged in 1878, the telephone at first appeared to be nothing more than a toy. Its significance as a communication device was masked behind certain fixed and rigid perception that stemmed from the institutional status of the telegraph as the primary medium of mass telecommunication. In order to overcome these fixed and rigid patterns of perception–that were supported by certain routines in the everyday use of telecommunications technologies at the time–the fledgling telecommunications industry had to take the initiative and give advice on how best to use the new technology. The everyday significance of the telephone was not obvious at first; potential users had to be shown how to speak with it. As Aronson has noted:

> "It may be obvious now when the telephone seems to be an appendage of mouth and ear how many different uses (and misuses) it has, but those living in the telegraph age had to learn them. To convince Americans that they needed the telephone, they first had to be taught how to use the telephone and what to use it for." (Aronson, 1977, p. 25)

In order guarantee that any technology is significantly taken up, its everyday practical utility needs to be clear and demonstrable. Hence if the Internet is to be significantly taken up, the question of how it is to be managed–that is, wisely incorporated into everyday strategies for living–needs to be directly addressed.[3]

In our late-modern technologically accelerated culture–where the birth of each new technology antedates the conception of another–the problem of the everyday management of new technologies becomes an acute one at best, at worst an impossibility. The pace of technological change breeds uncertainty (and its psychological correlate anxiety). Uncertainty, as has been well documented by economists, creates disincentives to invest time and effort in making sure that any new technological innovation is used optimally. Uncertainty generally forces the everyday user to fall back on conservative strategies for dealing with novel situations. In times of uncertainty, individuals fall back on the perceived certainties contained in custom and tradition, and this may force them to wrongly reject useful technologies; or at least view them in overly circumscribed functional terms. Thus given that the context that surrounds any possible technological up-take is clouded by uncertainties, everyday users of new technological applications have first to decide which are the most significant technological innovations–the innovations that are likely to 'survive' for at least a workable and economically sustainable length of time–and which are not. As many technological innovations have historically not survived for any significant length of time, the problem of 'faddism' and 'gadgetry'[4] loom large in the mind of everyday technology users.

The problem of Internet management is the problem of how to walk a tightrope in order to achieve a 'golden mean' in our understanding of technology, a tightrope stretched between the everyday moral constraints that surround the use of technology and that technology's set of ideal functional possibilities. Phrased in this way, it becomes possible to see how any technology might become associated with the 'good' and thus be put to good uses. And it is the search for good uses of the technology that gives the best definition of the expression 'technological wisdom' referred to above.

In making this link between knowledge of the good and wisdom, I am following in the tradition of classical philosophy, especially the Aristotelian tradition in philosophy. The idea here is to understand how to conceive of the Internet in its best form and function–its 'final cause'–given the moral constraints of everyday living. At the moment the final form and function of the Internet remains unclear and it is for this reason that–as philosopher of technology, Emmanuel Mesthene stated–that technologies such as the Internet require the input of wisdom if they are to 'add to more freedom and thus more humanity' (Mesthene, 1983, p. 112).

Beyond Faddism and Gadgetry

One of the problems involved in developing an adequate philosophy account of any new technology is that the users of any new technology are always in danger of being seduced by the apparent novelty, power and sophisticatedness of the functionality of the technology. The Internet is a good example of this kind of seductive technology; and with the Internet there is always the problem that those taking-up the technology are being taken-in–with the subsequent risk of being disappointed by the technology–by some of its less philosophically and functionally significant features. There are two possible modes of seduction involved here, each symptomatically associated with two very different ways in which any technology can be misperceived. Firstly, one can be seduced by the cleverness and complexity of the surface or interface of any new technology. It is in this way that technologies become aesthetisized objects of fascination with which to amuse and enchant. In effect they become misperceived as super-sophisticated toys. Once misperceived in this way, the new technology suffers a certain functional 'downgrading'; it is reduced to the status of a mere 'gadget' and the user reduced to the pathological status of a mere 'gadget lover' (see McCluhan, 1964).[5] Understanding technologies as gadgets is currently a widespread feature of everyday understandings of technology. It explains, perhaps, why certain technologies heralded as innovative quickly suffer a quick and brutal obsolescence. For once the period of enchantment wanes; disenchantment tends to set in.

The second way that technologies seduce is when users are taken-in by media and industry rhetorics, especially those claiming that any technology is an avatar for a new social and historical era. Here, the seduction can give rise to certain grandiose technological misperceptions of the new technology as the possessor of world-historical powers of social, psychological and/or cultural transformation. As a consequence, the user's self-perception becomes inflated. The users see him/herself as at the progressive 'cutting edge' of history and culture; he/she, like the technology itself, is 'of the future.' Many everyday users, theorists and journalistic commentators on the Internet have clearly already been seduced in this way by emergence of the Internet. For them, unless a person or group is 'connected,' 'wired' or 'online,' then that person or group is not only unfashionable, but a 'cultural laggard.' Many academics (see Toffler, 1970, for a good example of this kind of work) commentating upon the alleged significance of recent technological innovations in information and communication technologies, have been prone to this kind of misperception. In this case users, theorists and commentators become what can only be described as 'intoxicated' with the very idea of the new technology itself. There is little concern with specifics of function, and ungrounded and somewhat fantastic views of technology are proposed. For Leadbeater for example–following Toffler– the Internet is likely to bring about a new electronic democracy where people vote on a variety of social and political issues from the comfort of their own homes. In fact for many writing about the Internet at in 1990s, the Internet was perceived to be the embodiment of 'democracy itself, the golden promise of interactivity descended unto earth to help usher us into a populist utopia' (Frank 2000, p. 2).

However, when new technologies are misperceived in this way, they run the risk of becoming short-lived 'fads,' 'fetishises'[6] of real technologies with real actual and potential functions. By fetishising the new technology, these commentators treat the new technology in question as a 'thing apart' from self and society; something with its own inherent and inevitable logic and likely social and cultural trajectory. They forget that any new technology–in order to work in the optimal way required to make their utopian speculations even remotely plausible–requires attitudes of acceptance (up-take) and a willingness to incorporate it within everyday strategies for living (management) by those mundane users who see in the Internet the prospect for an enhanced form of everyday living. Hence it is a mistake to view technologies like the Internet as 'wonder devices'; the Internet is more fruitfully understood as posing a series of deep dilemmas from everyday living. In order to use this technology wisely, we must first take account of the dilemmas that surround the Internet if we are learn how to make good choices regarding how best to put it to use.

It would be easy to dismiss these misperceptions if both faddist and gadgetist conceptions of technology had not helped frame both the academic and popular perceptions of the Internet. The Internet, in fact, has been the object of some particularly blatant 'faddist' and 'gadgetist' analyses of its likely significance. A good example of 'gadetism' in studies of the Internet can be found in the work of American anthropologist Sherry Turkle (see Turkle, 1996). Turkle's work is interesting because it attempts to understand the significance of the Internet from the perspective of certain non-technical and non-commercial–in some sense then 'everyday'–users. Turkle's concern is with the nature of the psychological, social and cultural changes that are likely to emerge on the back of the Internet given the internet's functional potential to link disparate individuals into a real-time multi-user communication system. The conclusion that Turkle draws from her Internet ethnographies is that the Internet, in everyday terms at least, is a paradoxical technology in that it is both social and antisocial, simultaneously creating an expanded sense of community and greater possibilities for personal anonymity.

However, the most important everyday consequence of the Internet, according to Turkle, is much more fundamental. For her, the Internet is likely to have a profound impact on the nature of the psyche of its users by making possible a new psychological space for self-exploration and discovery. In Turkle's account, the Internet is best conceived as 'a psycho-social laboratory' that allows individual users to experiment with their identities. It is this latter aspect of the Internet–its ability to allow the playful and risk-free presentation of a version of the self other than the one normally presented during more routine everyday interactions–that Turkle thinks makes it an instrument for a new kind of subjectivity in advanced western societies, the 'postmodern, multiple and fragmented view of the self' (Turkle, 1996, p. 22).

It is exactly this kind of focus on hobbyists and other technological obsessives that, I believe, needs to be avoided if we wish to make any serious analyses and prescriptions concerning the everyday significance of the Internet. Turkle's Internet users -most of whom are late adolescent, bohemian(ish) and, by and large, well-educated Americans–tell us nothing about what kind of significance that the Internet is likely to have outside of contexts that can only be viewed as marginal– 'subaltern'–as far as most everyday users are concerned. Most people simply don't 'fall in love' with the Internet in the way Turkle's hobbyists clearly have. Further-more, everyday lives are structured according to very different rhythms and routines from those in Turkle's bohemian technological sub-cultures. Moreover, it is the members of such hobbyist groups that are the most susceptible to the kind of technological seductions referred to above. Thus what we see in Turkle's Internet ethnographies is not a depiction of the everyday use of this technology at all, but a depiction of the Internet from the vantage point of those seduced by it.

The Potential of the Internet as an Everyday Technology

Certain strands of social philosophy (see Feenberg, 1995, for a discussion) have viewed technology, especially modern 'industrial technology,' as one of the principle agents of contemporary social change. This kind of literature technology is celebrated as an agent of progress that has made possible liberation of humanity from its entanglement in the dark forces of nature. For this type of philosopher of technology, we 'late-moderns' are the first age to witness the arrival of total technological environment that gives our world a feeling of 'technological 'com-pleteness' such that 'we are the first age who can aspire to be free of the tyranny of physical nature' (Mesthene, 1983, p. 109).

To view matters this way however, is to overlook that the most significant technological innovations of recent times have been radically different from the industrial technologies that the social philosophers–the most famous of which was Karl Marx–defined as their remit. In particular the agendas underlying new information and communication technologies like the Internet are far removed from the old industrialist technological agenda to 'transcend the tyranny of physical nature.' The appeal of the Internet is that it precisely does not stand in the same 'dominating' relationship to both nature and culture as do productive technologies that defined the industrial age. The Internet has clearly been designed for other, more clearly social and communicative purposes; and thus the Internet must be seen as a radically different kind of technology in comparison to its industrial ancestors.

What the Internet represents, when seen from the vantage point of the contemporary social philosopher, is a radically new kind of technology, a new dominant force of communication rather than an industrial force of production (see Poster, 1997). It is a technology that, given the right institutional framework[7] supporting a particular kind of everyday living, could radically enlarge the space of communication possibilities of any individual or group by enhancing the range, speed and clarity of communicative interactions. The biggest social and political problem, as far as the Internet is concerned, is that the requisite institutional framework that might allow its full communicative potential to emerge is not yet in place.

What kind of social relations and patterns of everyday life can we realistically envisage when–and if–the Internet is used to its full communicative potential? If the steam engine gave the world the industrial era with the social relations of the market, what kind of social configuration do network technologies such as the Internet support? Social theorists such as Manuel Castells have recently begun to address the question at length, and his work is useful in bringing out how to conceive of the everyday potential of the Internet (see Castells 1999). For Castells, the convergence of print and broadcasting technologies that has given rise to innovations in ICT such as the Internet herald the arrival of a new 'networked society' whose basic values center around non-material social and cognitive concerns. For Castells, the era of networked society is organized by a new ideology that he terms 'informationalism' where information no longer is conceived as a 'public good'–resource held in common–but becomes something capable of being 'exchanged' (and thus a commodity). The importance of the Internet, for Castells, is that it is a technology that is shepherding into existence the new informationalist network age; an age–in contrast to those of the past–when humans must perform their activities in a new 'technological paradigm' constituted around micro-electronics-based information and communication technologies (Castells, 2000).

Castells' main point is that the networked society is likely to produce a variety of quite profound changes at the level of social relations and especially in the nature and quality of everyday experience. According to Castells, with the advent of the networked society, social relations become 'looser,' more driven by questions of interest than moral or social obligation. As a consequence, they also become more fleeting and ephemeral; losing their previously constitutive orderliness, solidity and solidartaristic qualities. For Castells, this shift in the nature of contemporary social relations is due to the fact that the Internet supports a new form of social interaction, a form of interaction that is based on the relations of what he terms *connectivity* between actors mediated by electronic networks. In networked societies, so the argument goes, each individual has become an actor in technological network with other actors.

Although there is clearly something of a fetishistic conception of technology at work here–leading Castells to make some rather reckless claims concerning the degree of reality that can be ascribed to his vision of a new informational order–his main contention, that examples of new technologies such as the Internet can be seen as a new communicative force making possible new more 'connected' yet transient forms of social relation, is interesting, powerful and theoretically useful. However his work represents only an ideal-typical account of what the Internet could be ceterus paribus. At present, most forms of Internet connectivity are weak. People surf, or browse or socialize in chat rooms and in the latter case it easy to think that a strong connection has been made between chat room members. However, chat room discussants don't experience a sense of social connection to each other in the way that they might experience a sense of connection to a partner in a telephone conversation. This is the truth in Turkle's claim that the Internet is a psychosocial laboratory; at present the Internet is still a ludic space rather than a fully social and communicative one. This involves only a kind of modest form of connectivity; what Jones calls 'aimless connectedness' (Jones, 1997, p. 17). Even those aspects of the Internet that seem the most fully communicative–like e-mail for example–are not social in the way telephone communication is social. With telephones it is possible to identify the 'person on the other end' (Schegloff, 1977), whereas with e-mail and the Internet it is not as yet possible to do this (giving rise to the moral problem of 'gate-keeping' with Internet and e-mail communications). On the telephone there is, after all, talk, whereas on e-mail there is only messaging.

Thus e-mail communication to date suffers from a certain 'instrumentalism.' In this way e-mail communications differ radically from everyday conversations. The latter are constrained by moral rules of conversation. These are not just matters of etiquette–rules about interruption and turn taking and so on–as they function to protect individual identities and statuses (preventing, perhaps semi-literally, a 'loss of face'). Internet interaction–especially e-mail–by way of example, tends to be extremely perfunctory and is less concerned with the identities and statuses of the sender and receiver of the message. There are, as yet, no clear rules for Internet communication–although various chat room communities have attempted to define them for their own needs–and this can give rise to a real sense of moral uncertainty about how to 'go on' in cyberspace. This gives some everyday users the perception that the Internet is still an 'uncivilized space,' a space of danger, especially for children.

Thus conversation, in the strict sense of interpersonal dialogue, is not the goal of the e-mail user. E-mail communication is not fully dialogical but has–to date at least–the restricted aim of 'passing on' or 'passing round' specific information that is deemed useful to the parties concerned. In the restricted context of e-communication, each conversant tends to view each other pretty much as a letter writer views his/her co-correspondent. The sense of social connection is weak, as much imagined as real. The Internet 'only connects' individuals in a functional or playful ways and does not socialize them into new communities of communicative technology users. But this is not to deny that the Internet's ability to enhance connectivity carries with it at least the possibility of a freer and more open system of social communication. Hence Castells' theory gives us a picture what the Internet could be given an appropriate institutional context that would allow the Internet to be used in an optimum way as an everyday technology.

CONCLUSION: THE INTERNET AND THE CONSTRAINTS OF EVERYDAY LIFE

For a phenomenologist of technology like Heidegger, such eulogies to the emancipatory potential of the Internet ignore its more worrying dimensions. In particular, a phenomenological analysis of the Internet would point out that the Internet is, like all new information and communication technologies, likely to radically later our ordinary lived ways of experiencing both space and time (see Simpson, 1995). Castells himself is aware of this problem and he notes that the Internet is likely to radically reduce the gap between conception, execution and reception of any idea (see Castells, 2000). In this case information is likely to be experienced as 'instantaneous'–on 'tap'–giving rise to a new sense of time: what he terms 'timeless time' when all events–both past, distant and future–become instantaneously present at the flick of a switch. Castells understands this as simply a new technology-induced sociological fact of late-modern living. But for phenomenologists this is a real moral concern (and thus something to be contested). For them, with the emergence of the Internet, our sense of time–our basic temporality–may become distorted. According to writers such as Jones, this is exactly what is happening with the Internet. For him:

> "the Internet's insertion into modern life represents a further displacement, or divergence between our sense of 'lived' time...and our sense of 'social' or 'functional' time (the time that we sense as form of obligation, as a time for doing)." (Jones, 1997, p. 13)

If the widespread use of the Internet is splitting our basic sense of temporality, then this raises profound questions for both the everyday and organizational management of the Internet. In both contexts, we still assume that a single, uniform and linear temporality is in place. If the Internet disrupts this basic sense of everyday temporality, it disrupts one of the basic axes along which life can be seen as 'routine.' Our sense of 'the routine' becomes more and more defined by an idea of functional or playful as opposed to ordinary lived time. When this happens we are left with the problem first raised by Heidegger: "What is left of a time for thinking, for reflecting and for engaging in face-to-face, conversation? What is left of what we once knew of our ordinary and everyday 'common life together'? Is not the everyday world as we know it in danger of being 'crowded out' by a new 'technological world' of permanent action and instrumental performance?" (See Zimmerman, 1990, for a discussion).

At this juncture we are all faced with what seems a deep and startling choice: a choice between two worlds, each with its own characteristic phenomenology. One cultural, rooted, temporal and social, centered around the moral and psychological importance the human face. The other more functional and timeless, centered around the traditional technological values of speed, efficiency and the new Internet value of connectedness. These are the two poles around which the philosophical problem of the Internet currently orbits. What is needed is to steer a wise course between them in order that the potential of the Internet can become actual at the everyday level but without basic disruption to the everyday world; the only world through which it can be perceived as significant. This will mean that Internet evangelists will have to note of the conservative force that bears down on each new technology from its everyday contexts. Unless those involved in the Internet industry take heed of everyday factors, and show how the Internet ought to be used, then it is likely that the Internet will remain a gadget or, at best, become a mere extension to more familiar everyday technologies such as the telephone and the television.

ENDNOTES

1 One of the key problems involved in any philosophical excursus onto the shores of technology is the problematic nature of the semantics of the term technology (see Leo Marx, 1997). Here the term will be used broadly to cover all those devices that have emerged from intensive research and development activity in large corporations. In this scheme, cars, toasters, telephones and computers are technologies, but craft-made tables, chairs, cutlery, etc., are not. The advantage of defining this, this way, is that it allows technology to take up an historic position of association with science, and not be viewed as a 'mere tool.'

2 An everyday user of a technology is a user who wishes to use any technology to allow the everyday world of production and the family to flourish. The everyday user needs to be contrasted with the specialized esoteric user who uses technologies to transcend the strictures and structures of everyday living.

3 It is important not to confuse the meaning of 'management' when applied to the everyday realm with the philosophy, theory or science of management (that is, with *managerialism*. Here, the term 'management' will be defined with the problem of everyday usage in mind: as "the effort to mitigate the deleterious psychological, social and cultural effects of the everyday changes wrought by any particular new device, whilst at the same time ensuring that the technology in question is used to its optimum psychological, social and cultural potential." In the case of the Internet, the management problem becomes: "How ought the Internet to be used so that the everyday psychological, social and cultural costs do not outweigh its everyday benefits?"

4 A gadget is an object taken up because of its appearance of cleverness and sophistication. A fad technology is an object taken-up because of its appearance of originality or 'newness.'

5 For McCluhan, 'the gadget lover' sees a technology as narcissistic extension of him/herself. In this way, the person externalizes some aspect of him/herself, a process McCluhan terms 'self-amputation.' This process, for him, results in a certain state of 'psychic numbness' that approximates to a state of 'being in love' with the technology (see McCluhan, 1964, pp. 41-47).

6 The term fetish in social philosophy has a particular meaning (see Freud, 1927). In this literature to make fetish out of something means taking part of an object for its whole significance. In the case of the Internet, those who fetishise it pursue a narrow focus and ignore the contexts of Internet uptake and use.

7 It is still unclear exactly what kind of institutional framework would best support broad and progressive uses of the Internet. Clearly much of the current institutional frameworks–especially those surrounding questions of property, knowledge, education and the nature of work–are woefully inadequate when faced with the challenges posed by the Internet.

REFERENCES

Aronson, S. (1977). Bell's electrical toy: What's the use? The sociology of early telephone usage. In de Sola Pool, I. (Ed.), *The Social Impact of the Telephone*, Cambridge, MA: MIT Press.

Bijker, W. E. (1997). King of the road: The social construction of the safety bicycle. In Bijker, W. E. (Ed.), *Of Bicycles, Bakelites and Bulbs: Toward a Theory of Sociotechnical Change*, 19-100. Cambridge, MA: MIT Press.

Borgmann, A. (1984). *Technology and the Character of Everyday Life: A Philosophical Inquiry*. Chicago, IL: University of Chicago Press.

Castells, M. (1999). *The Information Age: Economy, Society and Culture*. Oxford: Blackwell.

Dreyfus, H. and Dreyfus, S. (1986). *Mind Over Machine: The Power of Human Intuition and Expertise in the Era of the Computer*. New York, NY: The Free Press.

Feenberg, A. (1995). *Alternative Modernity: The Technical Turn in Philosophy and Social Theory*. Berkeley, CA: University of California Press.

Frank, T. (2001). The big con. *The Guardian' Review*, January, 1-2.

Freud, S. (1927). Fetishism. Republished *Pelican Freud Library*, 'On Sexuality' (1977), 7, 351-57.

Gergen, K. (1991). *The Saturated Self: Dilemmas of Identity in Contemporary Life*. New York, NY: Basic Books.

Grint, K. and Woolgar, S. (1997). *The Machine at Work: Technology, Work and Organisation*. Cambridge, MA: Polity.

Jones, S. (1997). The Internet and the social landscape. In Jones, S. (Ed.), *Virtual Culture: Identity and Communication in Cyber Society*. London: Sage.

Leadbeater, C. (1999). *Living on Thin Air: The New Economy*. London: Viking.

Lie, M. and Sørenson, K. H. (1996). Making technology our own: Domesticating technology into everyday life. In Lie, M. and Sørensen, K. H. (Eds.), *Making Technology Our Own*. Oslo: Scandinavian University Press.

Marx, L. (1997). Technology: The emergence of a hazardous concept. In *Social Research*, 64(3), Fall.

Materials for an explanatory theory of the networked society. (2000). *Sociology*, January-March, (51), 3-24.

McCluhan, M. (1964). *Understanding Media: The Extensions of Man*. Cambridge, MA: MIT Press.

Mesthene, E. (1983). Technology and wisdom. In Mitcham, C. and Mackey, R. (Eds.), *Philosophy and Technology: Readings in the Philosophical Problem of Technology*. New York, NY: The Free Press.

Merleau-Ponty, M. (1962). *Phenomenology of Perception*. London: Routledge.

Poster, M. (1997). *The Second Media Age*. Cambridge, MA: Polity.

Rheingold, H. (1993). *The Virtual Community: Homesteading in the Electronic Frontier*. Reading, MA: Addison Wesley.

Schegloff, E. A. (1977). Identification and recognition in interactional openings. In de Sola Pool, I. (Ed.), *The Social Impact of the Telephone*. Cambridge MA: MIT Press.

Simpson, L. C. (1995). *Technology, Time and the Conversations of Modernity*. London: Routledge.

Smith, A. (1996). *Software for the Self: Culture and Technology*. London: Faber and Faber.

Toffler, A. (1970). *Future Shock*. London: Pan Books.

Turkle, S. (1996). *Life on the Screen: Identity in the Age of the Internet*, London: Wiedenfield and Nicholson.

Uhlig, R. (2000). Millions log off the Internet to join the real world. *The Daily Telegraph*, December.

Zimmerman, M.E. (1990). *Heidegger's Confrontation with Modernity; Technology, Politics, Art*. Indianapolis, IN: Indiana University Press.

Chapter XIII

The Internet: An End to Classical Decision Modeling?

Ray J. Paul
Brunel University, UK

INTRODUCTION: DECISION MODELING—
CAN IT NOT BE?

Problem formulation, data collection, modeling, testing running, analyzing and results–these are the pre-Internet staged approaches to decision aiding, when the modeling time allowed to the analyst was to some extent determined by the fact there were few alternative approaches that were either better and/or faster. It is possible that the Internet now facilitates "cut-and-paste" modeling, the development of an acceptable approximate model, suitable for the immediate decision, constructed from bits of programs from anywhere on the Web. It is this possibility that is examined in this chapter. First we look at classical decision modeling, then at a hypothesized Internet alternative approach and lastly mention some dangers of the Internet approach, which is, what might happen to the benefits of mental activity?

CLASSICAL DECISION MODELING:
CAN IT BE?

Classical decision modeling can be exemplified by discrete event simulation modeling. Giaglis et al. (1996) make the case for using simulation modeling as follows, first by defining the decision modeling objectives, and then showing how simulation matches these objectives.

Decision Modeling Objectives

It has been argued (Willcocks and Smith, 1995; Galliers, 1993) that businesses and business processes are complex systems, and therefore carefully developed models are necessary to understand their behaviour in order to be able to design new systems or improve the operation of existing ones. As businesses are essentially 'socio-technical' systems, we can distinguish the basic requirements of the decision makers regarding the modeling process into two separate areas: 'technical' requirements which refer to those needs that call for the application of engineering principles in process analysis and design, and 'social' requirements which refer to the needs that emerge from the social nature of business systems. These requirements include:

Technical Requirements

Formal Modeling. Formal engineering principles should be adopted during the modeling process in order to enable the development of models that can be readily understood and agreed upon by all parties, thus providing a common basis for decision making.

Quantitative Modeling. Managers need to have quantitative information that will allow for informed decision making (e.g., cost-benefit analysis) and for direct comparison between alternative system designs.

Stochastic Modeling. Modeling should take into account the stochastic nature of business processes, especially the way in which they are triggered by external factors and should allow for representation of and experimentation with situations where a great degree of uncertainty exists. Sensitivity analysis of business models becomes a significant issue in this case.

Model Documentation. Models should be easy to document for exchanging information between modelers, analysts and decision makers. Model documentation can also be used as a reference in subsequent modeling exercises and/or if the model development teams change.

Model Adaptability/Reusability. Models should be easily updateable to follow changes in actual processes. Thus, they can be continuously used for future modeling exercises. Reusable models could assist in reducing the cost of model building and can provide an additional means of justifying the initial investment.

Objective-Driven Modeling. Decision modeling is usually performed having in mind specific business goals to be achieved through the modeling exercise. The evaluation of alternative configurations is therefore highly dependent on the objectives of the particular study. Business models should reflect this requirement of decision makers and allow for output analysis that can be configured according to objectives so as to provide alternative views of measuring business performance.

Social Requirements

Feasibility of Alternative Designs. Modeling and decision making in business contexts should take into account such factors as legislation restrictions, user acceptance of changes, etc. It is not sufficient to simply derive a particular system configuration that seems to optimize business performance, if the changes required in business processes cannot be practically implemented for this configuration.

Communication of Models. Business models are often used in brainstorming sessions of business management in order to assist in deciding changes. The models should therefore allow for easy communication of results between different parties. Moreover, generating alternatives and modifying the model during the decision-making process is another very important aspect of business modeling, as managers clearly need to be able to interact with the models as new information or ideas emerge during brainstorming sessions.

User Friendliness. Modeling tools should be easy to use to allow users of the processes to be personally involved in the modeling exercise. The personal involvement of users should increase the confidence of the whole enterprise in the change initiative, thus enabling a greater degree of acceptability of the derived results.

Modeling approaches should combine the requirements identified above if they are to be proven useful tools for business decision making. In the next section we assess the potential of simulation modeling as a suitable decision modeling technique.

Simulation as a Tool for Decision Modeling

Simulation incorporates characteristics and capabilities that can accommodate all the requirements identified above.

Formal Modeling: Simulation is a formal and robust technique. It does not rely heavily on mathematical abstraction, therefore it is suitable for modeling even complicated management systems (Pidd, 1998).

Quantitative Modeling: Simulation is basically a numerical technique, therefore it can be used to generate quantitative output data on various parameters that influence a business system performance. Output Data Analysis, Experimental Design and other techniques can be employed to ensure a significant degree of mathematical robustness at every stage of a simulation project.

Stochastic Modeling: Statistical representation of real-world uncertainty is an integral part of simulation models. Indeed, simulation is perhaps the most suitable modeling technique regarding its ability to capture the dynamic and stochastic behaviour of real systems. Sensitivity Analysis for example can be employed to assess a simulation model's validity with respect to variations in the values of (unknown) system parameters.

Model Documentation: The development of a simulation model requires certain assumptions about the real system, which can be documented as the model is being developed. Therefore, documentation of simulation models can be a relatively easy task. However, users in practice do not always pay enough attention to the documentation process. Simulation packages, which allow for automatic documentation of models, can prove particularly useful for this purpose, although they cannot entirely replace the modeler's role.

Model Adaptability/Reusability: Simulation models can easily be updated to reflect changes in real-world processes. With respect to BPM, a great opportunity exists to integrate workflow capabilities in simulation environments to support not only the modeling and redesigning exercise, but also the actual carrying out of business tasks, thus resulting in highly flexible and continuously reusable models.

Objective-Driven Modeling: Due to their flexibility, simulation models can be customized to serve multiple purposes of management. Modelers can specify alternative output measures and apply different output data analysis techniques to simulation models, thus allowing for multiple uses of a single business model according to management requirements.

Feasibility of Alternative Designs: Simulation as a process is meant to help with identifying appropriate solutions to complex decision problems. The feasibility of alternative designs in a business context is essentially a step that has to be built into the assumptions made during model development. If certain managerial, legislative or other restrictions occur, they should be taken into account during the experimentation phase by adhering to these assumptions. In this way, 'social' requirements can be addressed.

Communication of Models: Simulation models, especially when combined with graphical, animation and/or interactive characteristics, are probably the best means of communicating the essence of a model to managers and decision makers.

User Friendliness: Simulation models for business process analysis can be as friendly as their developers choose them to be. In general, simulation allows for a great degree of user friendliness (e.g., through graphical user interfaces), which is supported by the majority of existing simulation packages.

In the next section we will concentrate on an assessment of simulation when described in the context of the process of decision aiding.

THE CLASSICAL PROCESS OF DECISION MODELING: NOT TO BE?

In many textbooks on operational research and in some textbooks on simulation modeling, the simulation process is described as follows, and as shown in Figure 1. There is a real-world problem. This problem is formulated as a logical model. Logical models can be activity cycle diagrams, flow charts, block diagrams, etc. There are a variety of ways to represent the logic of a formulated problem. The next step is to convert the logical model into a computer model; sometimes it is a computer program, sometimes it is a data-driven generic simulation system. This computer model is verified, tested to see if it is doing what the analyst wants it to do. The model is used as an operational model to produce some results, or some conclusions or for implementation after the operational model has been validated against the real-world. An implicit assumption is that the product of the modeling process is a set of results, usually numerical, which lead decision makers and/or analysts to some conclusions, from which some decisions are implemented. Many textbook expositions point out that the process is not quite as linear as has just been described. There are many iterations or feedbacks in the process as understanding of the real-world problem changes.

In many real-world situations, however, the above description of the simulation process is inadequate. Real-world problems are owned by interest groups. The definition of the problem is influenced by the owners of the problem, especially for complex strategic decision-making. Such problems are usually owned by many interest groups, some of whom may be in conflict. Because the problem is complex, formulation is a very difficult task. The construction of a logical model representing the formulation of the problem is, in many instances, the most difficult aspect of the problem. In fact, understanding what the problem is may be the object of the whole exercise. The analyst should be prepared to constantly undertake problem reformulation to obtain a common understanding of the problem as part of the modeling process.

A dynamic (changing) logical model needs to be turned into a computer model with relative ease. Otherwise, if this part of the process takes a long time, contact with the real-world problem starts to diminish. If the analyst discusses the computer model with the decision makers infrequently, then the chance that the computer model represents the real-world problem is small. In many instances, the function that the computer model serves is to perform a medium of communication for the structuring of the problem for all participants in the decision-making process.

It is obviously necessary to verify that the computer model does what one thinks it should. But it is questionable as to how much emphasis should be placed on producing the operational model which is going to be used for experimentation purposes. In many cases, the production of a computer model which secures problem definition agreement among the decision makers may be sufficient to satisfy all participants. It may not be necessary to actually pursue the modeling process to the point of getting statistically valid results. In the event that the latter should be required, it is usually a minor part of the whole modeling process. It is curious that so many textbooks concentrate on the theoretical aspects of this part of the modeling process.

In summary then, the problems associated with decision modeling, as exemplified by simulation, are as follows. First of all, most problems to which one applies simulation are poorly defined. In fact one might go further, and claim that if the problem is not poorly defined, there are probably better and more reliable methods of solving the problem than the rather crude technique of simulation modeling. Secondly, any problem of any complexity, which is important, will probably involve conflicting interests and understanding. One must anticipate that if the modeling process is going to lead to change in the organization, then it is unlikely that all decision makers will see these changes as favorable to them. The analyst must anticipate negative attitudes and spoiling tactics. As much as possible, the modeling process is used in a neutral way to help the participants in the decision-making process understand their problem, and come to a resolution among themselves. The third problem associated with simulation modeling is that there never exists a static

Figure 1: The process of simulation

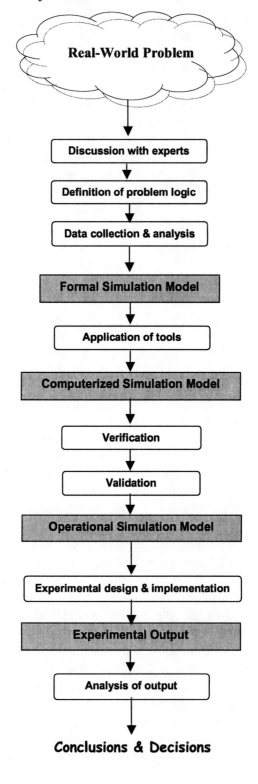

specification of the problem; it is always dynamic. Even if one succeeds in satisfying the conflicting views of the decision makers, it is probable that for complex problems the specification still undergoes change. The real-world is dynamic and therefore the perceived problem will be dynamic as well. The fourth problem with simulation modeling is the question of 'model confidence,' which is better terminology than the commonly used description of verification and validation. No computer program of any size can possibly be verified. No model of any size can possibly be validated against the real-world, especially given that the real-world is not static. The model cannot be proved to be correct. The aim should be to use methods that demonstrate confidence in what the model is doing and the way it is doing it.

The last feature associated with simulation modeling, which is a desirable characteristic, is that it involves decision aiding. Discrete event simulation modeling is a quantitative technique. The outputs are numerical, and numerical values tend to indicate that one course of action might be better than another. However, such a numerical technique cannot represent all possible factors in the problem scenario. It can crudely represent most or some of them in a quantitative way, but it cannot represent subjective factors. It must be remembered that the simulation-modeling process is not designed to find the answer or answers. It is there to help decision makers make decisions, or to help decision makers gain an understanding of their problem. The numerical output of the simulation model in itself may often be of no particular intrinsic value. Learning about the processes of the interactions that go on within a complex environment, the relationships between the variables, is probably the dominating characteristic of interest in simulation modeling.

WEB-BASED MODELING: TO BE?

So why might the Internet bring about changes to decision modeling in the future? A large proportion of the current generation of students entering higher education in the developed countries are already familiar with the pastime of browsing the Web and playing computer games. Both of these activities might loosely be depicted as approaches based on "suck it and see." Browsing and adventure games encourage the participant to try out alternatives with rapid feedback, avoiding the need to analyze a problem with a view to deriving the result.

Such Web users, in order to use simulation, might need and desire development tools that allow for fast model building and quick and easy experimentation. Furthermore, such Web users should have a natural affinity to the use of simulation models as a problem understanding approach (Paul and Balmer, 1993; Paul and Hlupic, 1994).

Web-enabled simulation analysts will be opposed to classical software engineering approaches and methodologies. They will be seeking tools that will enable them to assemble rather than build a model. Some feel the change of "culture" that we can expect from future generations of computer users can be gauged from a recent experience of mine on a visit to Taipei (Taiwan). A class of school children were using the local university's multi-media lab. A 10-year-old schoolboy was typing in HTML codes faster than I can and dynamically checking it by running a rather impressive text/video/sound demonstration system. The boy could not speak, read or write any English; everything was symbolic to him.

So how might this work? Figure 2 represents a possible future scenario, where the webber-analyst grabs and glues bits of model that might be deemed sufficiently appropriate. Running the model thus assembled enables its fitness-for-purpose to be tested. If satisfactory, problem understanding is attained, and in the postulated fast-moving world, the problem participants move on to other matters. If the assembled model is unsatisfactory, it is rejected and 'grab-and-glue' is retried. This retry might be made up of entirely new bits, so it is not necessarily modification. The webber-analyst then follows this GGrrr approach (Grab-and-Glue, run, reject, retry) at a fast rate, getting insights during the GGrrr process and satisfying the stakeholders of the problem in a time acceptable to them.

Of course, a GGrrr model would not have to mimic the real-world problem necessarily, in the same way that Neural Networks are not a model of the brain. The GGrrr model would only need to give appropriate outputs to some inputs to fulfill its purpose.

Page et al. (2000) discuss these issues at more length, and unusually for a top refereed academic journal, with some emotion. Quality as ever is an issue raised, but of course no software can be 'proved' correct in these circumstances. When it takes so long to get an answer(s), it is a bit limp to also admit that the model may be indeterminately wrong! However, if it becomes possible to "glue" bits together fast and experimentally, then maybe the emphasis will shift dramatically from "is the model correct?" to "is the analysis, albeit with unproven software, acceptable given the large experimentation that swift modeling has enabled us to carry out in a short space of time?" In other words, the search space might be dramatically reduced not by accuracy (the old way), but by massive and rapid search conducted by an empowered webber-analyst (the new way).

We are in a period of rapid technical change (though some authors claim this will come to an end and life will settle down again–see Fernandez-Armesto, 1995). Every attempt we make to use these technological advances adds to the opening up of new opportunities to make change. This is particularly noticeable in business, where new companies are emerging fast, old ones sinking daily, mergers, acquisitions, takeovers, etc. are prevalent. Even in the military sphere, the nature of the task to be faced changes quickly (war, peace-keeping, policing, training allies, reassessing threat as the world moves on, etc.). Analysis needs to be fast, else the problem has moved on anyway. Methods that can produce ballpark estimates quickly, enhanced with more accurate methods if time allows, might well become the order of the day. Principles based on output analysis, rather than modeling analysis, will then be more appropriate. If the traditional analytical and academic communities try to maintain their current principles, they will become historians, worthy of a footnote about Luddite neanthanderals in the next millennium history.

Figure 2: Internet modeling

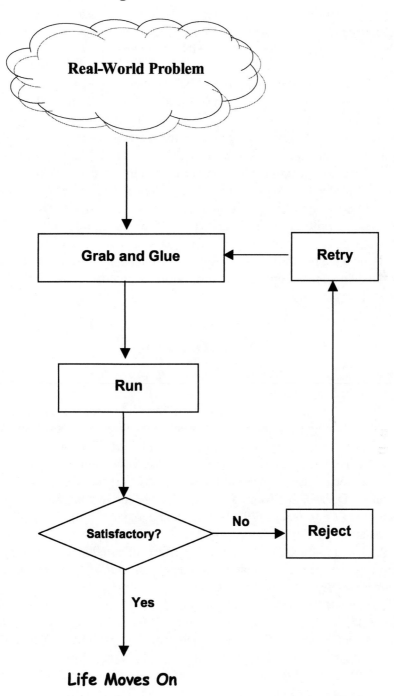

CONCLUSION: TO BE OR NOT TO BE?

Are there any problems associated with a Web-based GGrrr approach (if it can ever be reached in practice)? Many probably, but the one that springs to mind in this chapter is encapsulated in the anagram SINSFIT (simulation is no substitute for intelligent thinking, said by Kiviat in his keynote address in 1990). Most thinking tools can replace the word simulation in SINSFIT, since the benefit of a thinking tool is that it can facilitate thinking. Would GGrrr also facilitate thinking? In classical decision modeling, it is recognized that the modeling process brings unexpected benefits and insights. Would these be lost with GGrrr or speeded up?

Simulation systems described by Crookes et al. (1986) have been used in a number of military applications; these are described by Holder and Gittins (1989), Williams et al. (1989) and Stapley and Holder (1992). The interesting characteristic of the use of the simulation systems by these groups is that they partially replaced previous systems quite successfully and very effectively. The models described in the first two papers were eventually joined together in a reasonably short space of time. So the claimed flexibility and effectiveness of these systems has actually been demonstrated in a real application. Innovators using these approaches could introduce GGrrr systems.

REFERENCES

Fernandez-Armesto, F. (1995). *Millennium: A History of the Last Thousand Years*. New York: Touchstone.

Galliers, R. D. (1993). Towards a flexible information architecture: Integrating business strategies, information systems strategies and business process redesign. *Journal of Information Systems*, 3(3), 199-213.

Giaglis, G. M., Paul, R. J. and Doukidis, G. I. (1996). Simulation for intra- and inter-organizational business process modeling. In Charnes, J. M., Morrice, D. J., Brunner, D. T. and Swain, J. J. (Eds.), *Proceedings of the 1996 Winter Simulation Conference*, 1297-1304. San Diego, California. Baltimore, MD: Association for Computing Machinery.

Holder, R. D. and Gittins, R. P. (1989). The effects of warship and replenishment ship attrition on war arsenal requirements. *Journal of the Operational Research Society*, 40, 167-175.

Kiviat, P. J. (1990). Simulation, technology and the decision process. In Balci, O, Sadowski, R. P. and Nance, R. E. (Eds.), *Proceedings of the 1990 Winter Simulation Conference*, San Diego: Society for Computer Simulation, 243-249.

Page, E. H., Buss, A., Fishwick, P. A., Healy, K. J., Nance, R. E. and Paul, R. J. (2000). Web-based simulation: Revolution or evolution? *ACM Transactions on Modeling and Computer Simulation*, 10(1), 3-17.

Paul, R. J. and Balmer, D. W. (1993). *Simulation Modeling*. Lund, Sweden: Chartwell-Bratt Student-Text Series.

Paul, R. J. and Hlupic, V. (1994). The CASM environment revisited. In Tew, J. D., Manivannan, S., Sadowski, D. A. and Seila, A. F. (Eds.), *Proceedings of the 1994 Winter Simulation Conference*, 641-648. Orlando, Florida, New York: Association for Computing Machinery.

Pidd, M. (1998). *Computer Simulation In Management Science*, 4th Ed. Chichester: John Wiley & Sons, Inc.

Stapley N. R. and Holder, R. D. (1992). The development of an amphibious landing model. *Journal N.S.*, 18(3), 193-202.

Willcocks, L. and Smith, G. (1995). IT-enabled business process reengineering: From theory to practice. *Proceedings of the 3rd European Conference on Information Systems*, 471-485. Athens, Greece.

Williams, T. M., Gittins, R. P. and Burke, D. M. (1989). Replenishment at sea. *Journal of the Operational Research Society*, 40, 881-887.

Chapter XIV

The Question Concerning Information Technology: Thinking with Heidegger on the Essence of Information Technology

Lucas D. Introna
Lancaster University, UK

"The essence of technology is by no means anything technological. Technology is a way of revealing."

(Heidegger)

INTRODUCTION

The purpose of this chapter is to explore the essence of information technology using the work of Martin Heidegger. In particular I will refer to his well-known 1954 essay, "The Question Concerning Technology" (Heidegger, 1977d). It is hoped that the ideas put forward by Heidegger in this work can be extended to include also information technology—which may help us say something about the Internet. Since his essay appeared, machine technology—the emphasis in his essay—has been overtaken by a much more pervasive technology—information technology. The question then becomes: can the notions of technology developed by Heidegger be extended to include information technology? If this can be done, what is the implication of this for our understanding of information technology today? In particular how can it help us reflect on the management of the Internet?

One may well ask why this is necessary. Do we not understand information technology? We engage with it every day in so many ways. Surely, we have a very good grasp of its potential and its failings. Yes, this is true. Nevertheless, when speaking about information technology in this manner, we tend to speak about information technology in its artifactual sense. We tend to refer to the things we use, whether this be word processors, e-mail or the screen of 'departing flights' in the airport terminal building. Viewing technology as mere artifacts is like viewing a person as a photograph or a mere body. Technology is never mere artifact. Technology 'is' what it is when it functions in the world as 'possibilities for' doing something. If we want to understand technology, we must understand the world it makes possible—and also the potential worlds it hides. Heidegger urges us to understand technology as a phenomenon. That means we must understand technology in the way it 'plays itself out' in everyday life. To understand the phenomenon of aircraft technology, we must not only study aircrafts. We must also understand air travel and the way in which air travel has transformed our world. The technology of aircrafts 'is' what it is as part of a system of national and international air travel. Only when considering the world of air travel—and the other worlds it relates to— do we begin to understand the meaning of aircraft technology. Technology as a phenomenon, its meaning, is the way it functions in a world of everyday going on. And it is this meaning that we draw upon when thinking and acting in the world of technology. Thus, the purpose of this chapter is to use the work of Heidegger to help us reveal the meaning of information technology. It is only through the 'opening up' of this meaning that we can begin to make sense of the way in which information technology is changing and transforming our world—its meaning for us. It is only through such an understanding that we can begin to grasp the possibilities and cost of information technology. It seems that this is important in a world in which information technology has become a self-evident necessity with almost automatic legitimacy.

The chapter will be structured as follows: first, I will discuss the Heidegger's essay on technology as the basic frame to be extended; second, I will discuss information and information technology, applying the notions developed in the first section, and finally draw some conclusions and implications of such a view— especially for the information society. In the discussion I will often refer to philosophical concepts that may be unfamiliar to the reader. They are included for the sake of completeness and for compatibility with the literature I refer to. In most cases one could follow the argument without having a detailed understanding of these concepts as such. I would encourage the reader to push ahead and take the chapter as a 'whole' before trying to understand the more subtle details and philosophical references. If the reader then wishes to pursue the topic in more depth, this chapter will help as a bridge to the philosophical literature it draws upon.

Understanding Technology: From *Technē* to *Gestell*

Heidegger's view of technology is part of his general project of the history of *being*. For Heidegger *being* is not a substance, a Platonic idea or a Leibnizian monad, but rather a temporal event, an unfolding of *being* itself—*being* as a verb. According to Heidegger we understand the world not by looking at its elements from the 'outside' but rather by our active involvement in the unfolding happening of the world. I know a keyboard not by staring at it, but rather by using it to type this text. However, this is not enough. I do not merely type texts as such. I am typing this text because I am writing a chapter in order to publish it. I want to publish the chapter in order to be an academic, and so on. This is the referential whole, the world, of computer keyboards in which it refers to other things and activities and they refer to it. Thus, a keyboard is a 'keyboard' as part of its functioning in the world of typing, writing, publishing and so forth. In using it in this world of writing, I understand the meaning of keyboards—its *being* in Heidegger's terminology. Things have their *being* in, and only in, their referential whole—their world. Therefore, for Heidegger the question of technology is not merely another ontic field of human endeavor or enquiry. It is rather at the very center of his ontological project. Heidegger uses the ontic/ontological distinction to indicate the difference between a collection of empirical things (ontic view) and their meaning as phenomenon (ontological view) as described above. As such he argues for a radical ontological questioning into the essence(ing) of technology. In such an ontological enquiry, there will not be any recourse to quick and simple definitions. He urges us not to impose *being*-ness (thing-ness) onto *being* (is-ness); we must allow *being* to be revealed as it shows itself in the world—in its own terms, in its own happening, as it were.

To understand Heidegger's particular phenomenological view of technology, we need to step back and explore some of the things that lead him to this view. As a heuristic starting point, we could say that the key to this understanding is the notion of 'revealing.' For Heidegger to understand technology, as a phenomenon, is to understand that the essence of technology is its revealing of the world to us in particular ways and not in others. The meaning of every technology is the possibilities it reveals to us in the world of everyday going about. For example, once the stone-age humans discovered the techniques to extract iron from rocks, some rocks were no longer 'just rocks' they became seen as possibilities for making iron tools. Thus, we always look at technology, not as mere objects, but as possibilities for A, B and C. As such technology always and immediately 'reveals' its essential meaning for us. For Heidegger, this view of technology, as revealing, is intimately tied to the Greek notion of 'truth' as revealing. The connection between technology and truth, in the phenomenon of revealing, can be traced back to their common ancestry in Greek culture. That is therefore where we will have to start our journey.

Revealing the World: Truth as *Alēthia*

In his essay "On the Essence of Truth," Heidegger argues that the correspondence theory of truth is dependent on a more originary concept of truth, namely that of revealing or revealing as self-revealing (Heidegger, 1977c). The correspondence theory of truth holds that propositions are 'true' if they correspond to the 'object' they refer to. Thus, the statement 'it is raining' is true if it is in fact raining. However, Heidegger argues, that this sense of truth—which natural sciences depend on for their ontic science practice—relies on a more primitive sense of the world in which we already understand what it means to rain—itself irreducible to propositions. For example we may propose that it rains when it is 'wet.' However, 'wetness' or any other attribute of 'raining' we may bring into play in our propositions ultimately refer to a tacit understanding already present before propositions are constructed. It is to this sense of truth that Heidegger wants to point us to, as a clue to understand technology as revealing. Heidegger argues that the essence of truth can best be understood in relation to freedom—or a free relation. Not freedom as unlimited or unrestricted choice, but freedom as a relation of mutual revealing, a mutual letting be, a mutual disclosure;

> *Freedom, understood as letting beings be, is the fulfillment and consummation of the essence of truth in the sense of the disclosure of beings. "Truth" is not a feature of correct propositions which are asserted of an "object" by a human "subject" and then "are valid" somewhere, in a sphere we know not; rather, truth is the disclosure of beings through which an openness essentially unfolds. To let be—that is, to let beings be as the beings they are—means to engage oneself with the open region and its openness into which every being comes to stand, bringing that openness, as it were, along with itself.*

(Heidegger, 1977c, p. 127)

This "letting be," or truth as the disclosure of *being*, can literally be translated as the Greek word *alēthia* (or unconcealment in English). It is unconcealment as an ongoing event that reveals, that brings into the open that which beings 'is' in themselves. Truth is the revealing of the world to us from itself, by itself. It is a primitive and subtle understanding we have of the world because we are always already busy 'in' it—we are never removed from the world. As such the world of our everyday life makes immediate sense and is meaningful for us as those that dwell in it.

Caputo (1988) argues that Heidegger uses the word *alēthia* in two senses. In the first sense, the phenomenal sense, "*alēthia* means the phenomenality of the being, its self-showing, prior to its reduction to an object of an assertion, or later on, to an object for a thinking subject." Thus, we already know the world, phenomenologically, before we make assertions about it because we already live and have our *being* in that world. The world already 'showed itself to us'—as embodied, engaged and involved human beings going about in the world of everyday life. The world is not 'hidden' and strange to us. It is mostly familiar. So when somebody claims "it is raining" we already have a rich and lived sense of what that means. In the second sense, *alēthia* (or a-lēthia) means the opening up of the realm of the unconcealed itself, the very granting of the presence of the present. A-lēthia makes truth possible. But to the heart of a-lēthia belongs lethia (hiddenness) which is not only concealment but also self-sheltering. In unconcealing, in creating the clearing, a-lēthia conceals itself. Truth is not only that which phenomenally is, but also presupposes a granting of presence, a clearing that makes phenomenality possible. This means that the particular openness to the world of 'our time' is itself already a particular relation with truth. This openness to the world is made possible by an ongoing historical consciousness in which the world reveals possibilities for *being* in a particular way. For example the things that we now 'see' as possibilities were not possible for the Greeks—however, we never notice this openness itself. We hardly notice the profound possibility of affecting the behavior of another thousands of miles away—by our e-mail or telephone conversation. Yet in and through telecommunication, possibilities of *being* have revealed itself that were simply unavailable to those living in the ancient Greek world. At this level of reflection, 'revealing' becomes epochal. 'Epoch' is here understood as a specific age or period in which the world was or is conceived in a particular way (such as the Victorian age or epoch for example). In the manifold epochs of a-lēthia, a manifold of senses of *being* and truth emerges. In this regard Heidegger views modern technology as a particular epoch of *being* as opposed to the ancient Greek world. Likewise I want to argue, and show, that information technology, especially in its networked form, represents a new epoch of *being*. Nevertheless, the essence of technology remains revealing. In every epoch this revealing manifests itself differently. In order to understand the essence of modern technology, we must first turn to the way technology was understood in the ancient Greek epoch, i.e., the way it revealed the world to them.

Technology as Revealing: *Alēthia* and *Technē*

For Heidegger the ancient Greek notions of *technē* and *alēthia* are closely linked. *Technē* is also a revealing of the world. It is a making that is also already a revealing. In ancient Greece the word *technē* was not only reserved for the work of the craftsman. It was also used in relation to the work of the artist and the poet. Thus, for the Greeks *technē* was poetic—closely linked with the notion of *poiesis*. *Poiesis* is the bursting forth of what 'is.' It is the same notion at the root of our modern word 'poetry.' Thus *technē* was, for the Greeks, the facilitation of *poiesis*, very much in the way we understand poetry today as the revealing of the world to us through the words of the poet. To understand this Heidegger refers to the work of the artisan in Greece—and pre-modern—society. The artisan did not make or manufacture 'things' as such. The relationship between the skills of the artisan and the material being transformed was one in which the artisan drew on his tacit understanding of the world—the referential whole—of the 'thing' being made. In the poetic (*poiesis*) activity of *technē*, the artisan remained open to the possibilities of the material, his skills and the world of use. These possibilities were felt rather than thought. Through a process of poetic production, the artisan allowed the possibilities to emerge rather than to 'impose' it from the outside. Thus, *technē* in the hands of the skilled artisan becomes a revealing of the world through useful and meaningful things that are revealed in and through the artisan—useful and meaningful because they already refer to the world and flow from an understanding of the world already present in them. The artisan's tacit openness to the world becomes sedimented into every element of the works being produced.

Obviously, this is a rather romantic, almost nostalgic, picture of the work of the artisan in Greek society. However, we must not allow this to prevent us from grasping the essential point. In a poetic work—such as a work of art—there is a dialectical play between the artist and the subject. The artist must 'wrestle' with it in such a way as not to impose but to allow it to reveal itself (in its own terms as it were). Heidegger (1977d) argues that our modern-day view of *techne* as "making or manufacturing" is a correct but non-essential view of what *techne* is:

> *Thus what is decisive in* techne *does not lie at all in making and manipulating nor in the using of means, but rather in the revealing...*
> *It is as revealing, and not as manufacturing, that* techne *is a bringing-forth.* (p. 295)

The work undertaken by the artisan may succeed or it may fail. But even at its best the accomplishing can be only provisional, "because humanity cannot master *being*, and the pull of self-concealing (lēthia) is forever taking place even as *being* is brought to happen as unconcealing" (Lovitt, 1980). How does this concept of *techne* as poetic revealing in Greek culture relate to modern technology?

Modern Technology and the Forgetting of *Being*

What happened to the Greek concept of *techne*—*techne*, as the participation in the bringing-forth (*poiesis*) of *being*? Heidegger argues that *being* in its manifold epochs (the history of *being*) is progressively concealing (withdrawing). Take careful note of the fact that we are now referring to the epochal element of *alēthia*—the revealing that progressively 'hides' itself. This self-concealing is outlined in Heidegger's history of *being* or "the forgetting of *being*." I will only be highlighting a few elements of this history of the forgetting of *being* (what 'is') here. For more detail, refer to Farland (1978), Schurmann (1986) and especially Zimmerman (1990).

The forgetting of *being* starts with Plato who reduces the uniqueness and situatedness of *being* to form (*eidos* or idea). The general essence (*eidos*) shines forth in the particular. No longer can humanity gather-forth in a unique and spontaneous manner. Everything emanates from the *eidos*—*being* is form. *Techne* is no longer a creative participation in the self-revelation of *being*, it is now conformance to the one absolute and eternal *eidos*. It is now a correct perceiving, a correct knowing. Plato moves away from *alēthia* as unconcealment to *alēthia* as conformance to *eidos*. This shift is the starting point of the forgetting of *being*, the emergence of the correspondence view of truth, the 'correct' (orthotes) seeing.

With the translation of Greek into Latin, many essential insights were lost, so Heidegger argues. For the Romans, 'work' becomes that which is affected in working and accomplished in action—thus the emergence of causality. *Being* is that which makes present. *Being* is that which causes to "be." In the Christian theology of the Middle Ages, God is the highest cause. Plato's *eidos* is now located in God's mind. Truth is now correspondence to the mind of God. Humanity must mirror God's mind in nature then it will discover *being*. Truth becomes divine.

With Descartes *being* becomes subjective. Humanity seeks the certainty of existence in itself, its own self-consciousness. What is true is what is knowable, and what is knowable is what humanity can posit before its own consciousness ('observe' with its senses), that which humanity can re-present (*vor-stellen*). *Being* is now "that which stands as object over and against humanity, within its consciousness as knowing subject" (Lovitt, 1980, p. 67). The 'real' *being* is once again equated with correspondence. This time the correspondence is between the assertion and the representation (in the subject). In this epoch *being* is accurately 'captured' by those assertions (by the subject) that correspond with *being* (object). *Being* is that which is objectified in the consciousness of humanity. This 'objectification' by re-presentation becomes the foundation of the logical and mathematical description of the world—the advent of modern science. With *being* as re-presentation the foundation for modern technology is laid. The technological conception of the world comes into full play. Nothing can escape the representation as object by the subject. *Being* is commanded to appear as 'object' before a 'subject.' The leading-forth becomes a commanding-forth. *Being* as 'object' is subjected (brought under control) by the 'subject.' It is from this epoch that our modern view of technology flows.

The Essence of Modern Technology as *Gestell*

For Heidegger modern technology is still a mode of *alēthia*. Yet, it is a particular way of revealing the world. Its revealing is not poetic, it is rather a commanding-forth that commands, sets-up (stellen) beings as objects of manipulation. The urge of Modern society to conquest nature, and its urge to know and to control, places it in a particular relationship with the world. The forces of nature must be harnessed for the benefit of all humankind. Nature, for humanity, becomes a set of means—a set of inputs. It is revealed as a collection of forces to be commanded-forth. Nature is on stand-by for humans to call upon. A resource that can be unlocked, transformed, stored and distributed in chains of activities, all linked into a big network of stores, all on immediate stand-by (standing-reserve) for humanity to command-forth. All beings are mere "means" or chains of means commanded-forth toward a material and artificial end—the glorification of humanity as controller—as sole commander and constituter of *being*. The irony of this revealing is that humanity, in this commanding-forth, ultimately also becomes a mere input, a resource, on stand-by. As such, humans also become another link in the chain that is commanded-forth as a means (this is clearly demonstrated by the use of the term 'human resources' in contemporary management theory).

When the ancient artisan created a pair of shoes, the artisan gathered the elements together to create a unique work—a unique shining forth of a particular presencing. Every pair of shoes was a poetic work of *technē*, a unique revelation, a shining-forth of *being*. The bringing-forth of the work was an end in itself. Not just any end in a vague, undefined sort of way. In the work the artisan became constituted as a 'location' of truth. Through their work their existence becomes authenticated—

the artisan is brought-forth, revealed, as an authentic 'clearing' of *being*. In modern society the employees in rhythm with the machines mass produce shoes in standardized shapes and sizes. People buy shoes to get to work, to run athletics, to jog in the park. Shoes is a purpose in itself—even if the purpose is to make a fashion statement and nothing more. They have become products or means, manufactured for consumers—themselves being consumed. The factory, the laboratory and the schools have all become manufacturers of products. They are revealed as products—resources/means—standing-by, standing-reserve—to be commanded-forth. This revealing, that is standing-reserve to be commanded-forth, is for Heidegger (1977d, p. 305) the essence of modern technology, it is Gestell (the enframing, the setting-up):

> *Enframing means the gathering together of that setting-upon that sets upon man, i.e., challenges him forth to reveal the real, in the mode of ordering, as standing-reserve.*

However, the revealing of Gestell is also a concealing. Thus, "above all, enframing conceals that revealing which, in the sense of *poiesis*, lets what presences come forth into appearance" (Heidegger, 1997d, p. 309). It is not only a concealing of *being*, but also a concealing of humanities possibility of *being*. As humanity is that which is itself enframed, enframing is not the 'doing' of humanity. It is an epoch of *being*. It is part of the unfolding history of *being*. The essence of technology emanates from the ongoing withdrawal of *being*, the progressive concealment (lēthia) of *being*. Thus, "the Gestell is the way that presence currently has of filling up the clearing [a-lēthia], a way it is granted in, and by the withdrawal of the clearing. Technology is what issues from the invisibility of the clearing; it is not what *being* is, but the way it pretends to be, one more way of making present, but not the granting of presence itself" (Caputo, 1988, p. 543).

How can we now use these thoughts to reflect on information technology? Is information technology also a mode of *Gestell*? Is information technology the next epoch in the history of the concealment of *being*—a more profound mode of *Gestell*? These will be the questions that need to be reflected upon in the next section.

Information Technology in the mode of *Gestell*

In order to reflect on information technology, I will start by thinking about information. In thinking about 'information' one could try and trace (as Heidegger did for example) the notion of information in early Greek thought and language. This would make a lot of sense since Heidegger believed—as argued by Lovitt (1977)—that "the reciprocal relationship between *being* and man is fulfilled through language. Hence to seek out what language is, through discovering what was spoken in it when it first arose, and what has been and can be heard in it thereafter, is in fact to seek out that relationship. It is to endeavor to place oneself where the utterance of *being* may be heard and expressed." However, one will search in vain in the classical Greek writings for the term (concept or notion) of information. It, or something like it, does not exist. In the absence of a classical Greek notion of information, maybe the etymology of the modern English word of 'information' will shed some light on a possible interpretation of "what was spoken in it when it first arose." In the next section I will argue that we can indeed make sense of information as a mode of *technē*. This interpretation will then be contrasted with the interpretation, in the modern epoch, of information as a mode of *Gestell*—information as *Gebild*, as I will argue.

Information as *Techne*

The word 'information' is a noun derived from the verb 'inform.' Inform (in English and in French) has its origin from the Latin verb *informare* which literally means "to put into shape, to form, to mould" (in=into and formare=form or shape) (Partridge, 1966; Klein, 1966). The word 'inform' was originally used as a verb to describe the process of instruction (Skeat, 1879). In some old English dictionaries the noun 'information' is not listed, however, the verb 'inform' is listed as denoting the notion 'to instruct' or 'to impart knowledge.'

To *informare* is not to 'tell' something or to 'give' some facts. To inform is to 'mould,' to patiently shape. The shaping and moulding is not to get 'a' shape or 'a' mould as such—it is not a making. It is merely to create a clearing for *being* to reveal itself. As such it is a struggle, with the student—not as an imposing—but as guiding and as participating in the coming into *being* of insight—truth to be more precise. The teacher does not impart knowledge 'in little packets' for the student to consume. The real teacher "let nothing else be learned than—learning. His conduct, therefore often produces the impression that we really learn nothing from him, if by 'learning' we now automatically understand merely the procurement of useful information. The teacher is ahead of his apprentices in this alone, that he has still far more to learn than they—he has to learn to let them learn" (Heidegger, 1977b, p. 356). The teacher and the student participates in the *poiesis*, the bringing-forth of *being* from that which is confusing (lēthia). The teacher skillfully and knowingly wrestles with the lethia, the confused reality, to create a clearing, to allow the *being* to burst forth in unconcealment, in *alēthia*. Now the student's understanding is disposed anew. The teacher (with the student) gathers-forth all the elements, applying the skill of *informare* in bringing together the teaching elements in a unique and meaningful way. From this gathering together emerges understanding and insight as the work. Hence, to paraphrase Heidegger, what is decisive in information as *techne* does not lie in the making and manipulating of facts nor in the using of these facts as means of instrumental knowledge, but rather in the revealing (*alēthia*). To inform is to reveal, to unconceal, as truth, that which is concealed. This is the essence of inform-mation. However, in the modern epoch inform-ation (*informare*) becomes information (*Gebild*) technology—it becomes a mode of *Gestell*.

Information Technology as *Gebild*

Information in the modern epoch is a mode of revealing that has it *being* in *Gestell* as such. Information 'informs' somebody about something or some state of affairs. It 'tells' about some thing, or some one. It is a picture (Bild), a representation.

It points to something and says something about that which it is pointing to. As a pointer, a picture, it can be called up or be called forth. As a picture, it is a fixedness of facts about that which it represents. Once it is fixated it can be called forth as a means for defined ends, such as decision making (as sales figures in a management report) or for pleasure (as a film in the cinema). Hence, the development of information technology has its birth in the forgetting of *being* that constitutes *being* in that which humanity can represent (*vor-stellen*). Information technology is the technology (*Gestell*) that enframes *being* as represented and enables humanity to manipulate the representations (programs, models, objects, entities, attributes). It is Descartes—in his constitution of *being* as represented—and not Babbage or Von Neuman or Boole, who is the real father of information technology. From the outset, in the heart of the enlightenment epoch was the seed that would come to fullness in the information society.

Information is the fixation, the picture, of that which 'is.' The picture represents the 'facts.' As a fixated picture, it can become standing-reserve for consumption. In the age of information [technology], as a picture, that which can be represented can be manipulated—can be controlled—is. Hence Heidegger (1977a, p. 34) argues: "The fundamental event of the modern age is the conquest of the world as picture. The word 'picture' [Bild] now means the structured image [Gibild] that is the creature of man's producing which represents and sets before. In such producing, man contends for the position in which he can be that particular *being* who gives the measure and draws up the guidelines for everything that is" (My emphasis). As such, information, as *Gebild*, is a distinctly modern (and technological) mode of revealing. It flows from *Gestell* itself.

Gebild is the setting before, a representing, that objectifies whatever 'is,' each particular *being*, in "such a way that man who calculates can be sure, and that means be certain, of that *being*" (Heidegger, 1977a, p. 127) This certainty in the object— as set up before, as created by the fixated, the information—reciprocally sets up the certain subject. As Heidegger explains: "This is the fundamental equation of all reckoning belonging to the representing that is itself making itself secure. In this fundamental certainty man is sure that, as the repersenter of all representing, and therewith as the realm of all representedness, and hence all certainty and truth, he is made safe and secure, i.e., is" (Heidegger, 1977a, p. 150). In *Gebild* Descartes' "I think therefore I am" becomes 'I have a representation (information, a pointer, a fixation, a picture), therefore I am.' Herein lies the mystery of the modern explosion of information—the birth of the information society. It is the desperate anxiety of the modern humanity to fixate itself, to be certain of itself as 'is.' The irony, of course, is that instead of becoming a 'location for *being*,' humanity becomes enframed—fixated in *Gebild*.

The work of Baudrillard is the most elaborate expression of this. The real, for Baudrillard (1983), is dead; it is not merely dead, it never existed. The assumed relationship between the real and the representation was itself an image. There is no sense in the distinction between the map and the territory, the copy and the original, the fictional and the factual, the simulation and the real. Baudrillard (1983, p. 2) argues: "Abstraction today is no longer that of the map, the double, the mirror or the concept. Simulation is no longer that of a territory, a referential *being* or a substance. It is the generation by models of a real without origin or reality: a hyper real. The territory no longer precedes the map. Nor survives it. Henceforth, it is the map that precedes the territory–PRECESSION OF SIMULACRA–it is the map that engenders the territory...." There are no foundations, no ultimate referent, everything is always already interpretation, always already simulation. Without a foundation that can act as the guiding principle–the judge as it were–of what is real or imitation, true or false, genuine or counterfeit, all distinctions become arbitrary. Baudrillard (1983, p. 5) confirms: "Strictly speaking, nothing remains for us to base anything on. All that remains for us is theoretical violence–speculation to the death, whose only method is the radicalization of hypotheses." Distinctions now become the outcome of the microphysics of power, local language games, regimes of truth, intersubjective agreements and at the end of this spectrum Baudrillard's total anarchism. All distinctions must be made plastic by self-referentiality. This is the "logic of simulation which has nothing to do with a logic of facts and an order of reasons. Simulation is characterised by a precession of the model, of all models around the merest fact—the models come first, and their orbital circulation constitutes the genuine magnetic field of events" (Baudrillard, 1983, p. 31). All are simulations; the models 'create' the facts. Facts have no sense of their own; they circulate the models in an infinite regression.

Baudrillard argues that the real is fabricated by staging its negative. For example, he explains that Disneyland is staged so that we can say Disneyland is 'make believe' (imaginary) and the world that surrounds Disneyland (Los Angeles and the rest of America) is real. In a similar manner we stage criminality so that we can fabricate a system of justice that is seen as legitimate. In staging the negative we fabricate (or make sensible) distinctions such as real and imaginary, true and false, right and wrong. As Baudrillard (1983, p. 25) argues: "The Disneyland imaginary is neither true nor false; it is a deterrence machine set up in order to rejuvenate in reverse the fiction of the real" (no emphasis). In the face of the postmodern nihilism, the modern society is becoming desperate in its efforts to preserve the real. This is seen in the proliferation of the staging of the negative. The proving of the real by staging the imaginary is now exploding the proving of the truth through scandal, the proving of the law by transgression, proving work by strike, etc.

In the final phase of the image, any pretence to the real is lost as the system becomes self-referential and a law onto itself. This is the stage of the hyperreal: "the collapse of reality into hyperrealism, the meticulous reduplication of the real, preferably through another reproductive medium such as advertising or photography [or cyberspace and virtual reality]. Through reproduction from one medium into another the real becomes volatile, it becomes the allegory of death, but it also draws strength from its own destruction, becoming the real for its own sake, a fetishism of the lost object which is no longer the object of representation, but the ecstasy of denigration and its own ritual extermination: the hyperreal" (Baudrillard, 1993, p. 72). In the hyperreal the crisis of representation that has occupied the modern mind for so long is overcome with the real sealed off in an infinite circle of pure repetition.

In the epoch of the hyperreal, the real is now "that which it is possible to provide an equivalent reproduction (in other words *Gebild*). At the end of the process of reproducibility, the real is not only that which can be reproduced, but that which is always already reproduced: the hyperreal" (Baudrillard, 1993, p.73). It is clear from the above brief analysis that there is an infinite regress in the logic of Baudrillard. We stage the imaginary to fabricate (simulate) the real. The simulation becomes a simulation of a simulation that accelerates us into the dimension of the hyperreal. In the hyperreal everything is already simulation; everything is always already reproduction. In hyperreality humanity is sure that, as the repersenters of all representing, and therewith as the realm of all representedness, and hence all certainty and truth, they made safe and secure is. However, that which was secured with representation (the secure subject before which, and for which the setting up was secured), now too becomes set up, commanded forth as a mode of *Gestell*. The position of humanity as the representor now becomes the represented. The world becomes concealed in *Gebild*.

If this interpretation of information technology makes sense then what are the implications of this for our post-modern information society?. Before considering this one needs to acknowledge that there are many aspects of this analysis that need further development. Nevertheless, the above analysis does seem to give us enough hints to reveal the essence of information technology. In the next section, I will attempt to outline some of the implications of this essence.

The Phenomenon of the Information Society

There are many aspects of the phenomenon the information society that we can concentrate on, such as the way in which education has become objectified as the exchange of 'information packets.' Presumed to be meaningful in themselves. However, in this last section I want to focus on that which is particularly troublesome about the world revealed as 'pictured,' as *Gebild*—namely the way in which information technology reveals our fellow human beings as 'images.' In my discussion, I want to focus especially on the implication of this revealing for the moral dimension that is at the heart of our social *being*. I want to focus on the concealing of our fellow human *being* as 'significant others' that seems to be happening in and through the revealing of information technology as *Gebild*.

In order to help me make this clear, I want to turn to the work of Emmanuel Levinas (1961, 1974, 1996), for Levinas ethics is not some 'code of conduct.' Rather ethics happens—or not—when the self-certain ego becomes disturbed (shaken or questioned) by the proximity, before 'me,' of the absolute 'other'—the absolute singular, the face before me 'here and now.' This other, who is always wholly 'other' that takes me by surprise, overturns and overflows my categories, themes and concepts. I cannot encounter the 'other' in terms of my categories, ideas or concepts. For Levinas the claim of conventional ethics that we can know, the right thing to do, is to claim that the absolute singular can become absorbed into, domesticated by, the categories of my consciousness. Once the 'other,' this singular face before me, has become an instance in my categories or themes, it (the face) can no longer disturb the self-evidentness of those categories. Nothing is more self-evident than my categories, and likewise with the singular now absorbed as an instance of them. As jew, nigger, rich, poor, homeless, rapist, criminal, capitalist, idealist (and every other category we care to name) the singular disturbing face disappears in the economy of the category. In the category, we can reason about rights, obligations, laws and principles, and yet ethics may never happen—actual faces starve, die, are humiliated, scorned as they circulate in the economy of our categories. They fall through the cracks of our debates, arguments and counter-arguments, and yet we feel justified— we have our reasons; it was the right thing to do after all.

In *Gebild* a profound distance (not merely a physical distance) is introduced between the 'other' and I. In this distance, it becomes difficult to 'see' the 'otherness' of the other. As such the 'other' becomes categorized and thematised as something—as an image, to be consumed as I wish. We even talk of the 'image' we have of the other. In our appropriation of the other as an image, we remain unchallenged, undisturbed, confirmed in the self-certainty and the self-evidence of the image. It is my contention that this transformation from poetic revealing to image introduces a substantially increased potential for profound social distance to emerge. The very source of the ethical relation, the face of the 'other,' that disturbs, that calls me into question, becomes faded and could totally disappear, in the age of the image.

To make the discussion a bit more concrete, I will reflect on a personal experience of mine. In South Africa we used to live in a house where the front door was very close to the pavement, providing easy access to the front door. We often had needy persons knock on the door asking for help. When opening the door one is confronted with a face, 'here and now.' The person pleads for help. After allowing the person to explain their circumstances and maybe after asking some questions, one may feel compelled to help because in their speaking, their face disturbed you—calls your self-certainty into question with its raw passivity and nudity. "Maybe I am responsible, have I not also taken the 'place' of this singular face before me?" Allowing them to speak to me—face me—creates the possibility for them to reveal themselves, to disturb the self-evidence of my images of them. Sometimes it happened and sometimes it did not. The face does not have force, it merely calls into question. Some time later we bought a new house with a high wall around it. It had an intercom system connecting the front gate with the front door. Now the person must press a call button. The call is answered and the persons must attempt to make their claim through the mediation of the intercom system. Upon reflection, I noticed a change in my response to these solicitations. Somehow, it just became easier to deny assistance. The voice became a potential for *Gebild*. It became easy to impose an image on the naked voice and it was so easy to categorize. More importantly, in the distance produced by the mediation, my categorisation remained undisturbed, unchallenged. The potential for self-revealing diminished; the ethical relation between the 'other' and me became transformed—not in an explicit and obvious way, but in a subtle yet very fundamental way.

I want to close this chapter by posing the following questions. Do we understand the essence of information technology? If my interpretation of the essence of information technology is correct, even in a limited way, what is the implication for the information society? I seems to me that we need to reflect on these issues with some great care and attention. Maybe the Internet will bring substantial possibilities to all of us, but what if we simultaneously erode the most essential dimension of our social *being*: our moral and ethical openness to each other? Maybe there is a huge overhead cost, yet to be discovered? In my view this is the real challenge in managing the future of the Internet. It is not really an ontic issue, it is rather a fundamentally ontological issue which is at stake here.

REFERENCES

Baudrillard, J. (1983). *Simulations* (Paul Foss, Paul Patton, Philip Beitchman, Trans.). New York: Semiotext(e).

Baudrillard, J. (1993). *Symbolic Exchange and Death* (Iain Grant, Trans.). London: Sage Publications.

Caputo, J. D. (1988). Demythologizing Heidegger. *Review of Metaphysics*, 14 March 14, 519-546.

Erickson, T. (1996). The World Wide Web as social hypertext. *Communications of the ACM*, 39(1), 15-17.

Farland, J. M. (1978). Contemporary critiques of technology. *Unpublished PhD Thesis*, University Microfilms International, Ann Arbor, Michigan, Boston.

Heidegger, M. (1977a). The age of the world picture. In Lovitt, W. (Ed.), *The Question Concerning Technology and Other Essays*, 115-154. New York London: Harper and Row.

Heidegger, M. (1977b). Martin Heidegger: Basic Writings (David Farrell Krell, Trans.). San Francisco: HarperCollins Publishers.

Heidegger, M. (1977c). On the essence of truth. In Krell, D. F. (Ed.), *Martin Heidegger: Basic Writings*, 113-141. San Francisco: HarperCollins Publishers.

Heidegger, M. (1977d). The question concerning technology. In Krell, D. F. (Ed.), *Martin Heidegger: Basic Writings*, 283-317. San Francisco: HarperCollins Publishers.

Klein, E. (1966). *A Comprehensive Etymological Dictionary of the English Language*. Amsterdam: Elsevier Pub.

Levinas, E. (1969(1961)). *Totality and Infinity*. (Alphonso Lingis, Trans.). Pittsburgh: Duquesne University Press.

Levinas, E. (1991(1974)). *Otherwise Than Being or Beyond Essence*. (Alphonso Lingis, Trans.). Dordrecht: Kluwer Academic Publishers.

Levinas, E. (1996). Ethics as first philosophy. In S. Hand, S. (Ed.), *The Levinas Reader*, 75-87. London: Blackwell.

Lovitt, W. (1973). A gespraech with Heidegger on technology. *Man and World*, Fall, (6), 44-59.

Lovitt, W. (1977). Introduction. In Lovitt, W. (Ed.), *The Question Concerning Technology and Other Essays*, 13-39). New York and London: Harper and Row.

Lovitt, W. (1980). Techne and technology. *Philosophy Today*, Spring, 62-72.

Partridge, E. (1966). *Origins: An Etymological Dictionary of Modern English*. (4th ed.). London: Routledge and Kegan Paul.

Schurmann, R. (1986). *Heidegger on Being and Acting: From Principles to Anarchy*. Bloomington, IN: Indiana University Press.

Skeat, W. W. (1879). *An Etymological Dictionary of the English Language*. Oxford: Clarendon Press.

Zimmerman, M. E. (1990). *Heidegger's Confrontation with Modernity: Technology, Politics and Art*. Bloomington, IN: Indiana University Press.

Section IV

Internet Online
Data Issues

Chapter XV

Internet Data Mining

Kuldeep Kumar
Bond University, Australia

John Baker
Universal College of Learning, New Zealand

Gold mining is a process for sifting through lots of ore to find valuable nuggets. Data mining is a process for discovering patterns and trends in large data sets to find useful decision-making information.

SPSS

INTRODUCTION

Data mining has emerged as one of the hottest topics in recent years. It is an extraordinarily broad area and is growing in several directions. With the advancement of the Internet and cheap availability of powerful computers, data is flooding the market at a tremendous pace. However, the technology for navigating, exploring, visualizing and summarizing large databases are still in their infancy.

The quantity and diversity of data available to make decisions has increased dramatically during the past decade. Large databases are being built to hold and deliver these data. Data mining is defined as the process of seeking interesting or valuable information within large data sets. Some examples of data mining applications in the area of management science are analysis of direct-mailing strategies, sales data analysis for customer segmentation, credit card fraud detection, mass customization, etc. With the advancement of the Internet and World Wide Web, both management scientists and interested end-users can get large data sets for their research from this source. The Web not only contains a vast amount of useful information, but also provides a powerful infrastructure for communication and information sharing. For example, Ma, Liu and Wong (2000) have developed a system called DS-Web that uses the Web to help data mining. A recent survey on Web mining research can be seen in the paper by Kosala and Blockeel (2000).

Both statistics and data mining are concerned with drawing inferences from data. The aim of inference may be to understand the patterns of correlation and causal links among the data values (explanation) or making predications for the future data values (generalization). At present data mining practitioners and statisticians seem to have different approaches to solving problems of a similar nature. It appears that statisticians and data miners can profit by studying each other's methods and using a judiciously chosen combination of them.

Data mining techniques can be broadly classified in three areas:

Exploratory Data Analysis (EDA): As opposed to traditional hypothesis testing designed to verify a priori hypothesis about relations between variables, EDA is used to identify systemic relationships between variables when there are no a priori expectations as to the nature of those relations. Computational EDA includes both simple and basic statistics and more advanced, multivariate exploratory techniques designed to identify patterns in multivariate data sets.

Sampling Techniques: Where an incomplete data set is available, sampling techniques are used to make generalizations about the data. Various considerations need to be accounted for when drawing a sample, not the least of which is any a priori knowledge about the nature of the population.

Neural Networks: Neural networks are analytical techniques modeled after the process of learning in the cognitive system and the neurological functions of the brain. These techniques are capable of predicting new observations from other observations after executing a process of so-called learning from data. One of the major advantages of neural networks is that they are capable of approximating any continuous function, and the researcher does not need to have any hypothesis about the underlying model, or even to some extent which variables matter.

EXPLORATORY DATA ANALYSIS AND DATA MINING TECHNIQUES

Graphical Representation of the Data

When a large number of observations (discrete or continuous) is available, it becomes necessary to condense the data without losing any information. The condensed data can be put in a tabular form, known as frequency distribution, or in graphical form. There are quite a few techniques available to represent data in a graphical form such as bar diagram, histogram, frequency polygon, stem and leaf plot and box-cox plot. The graphical representation can give us a lot of information about data, for example, whether it is symmetric or skewed, and also if there is any outlier or influential observation present in the data. Some of these techniques are described briefly in the following paragraphs.

Histogram: In drawing the histogram of a given continuous frequency distribution, we first mark off along the x-axis all the class intervals on a suitable scale. After that on each class interval erect rectangles with the height proportional to the frequency of the corresponding class interval so that the area of the rectangle is proportional to the frequency of the class.

Stem and Leaf Plot: A stem and leaf display is a method of presenting data so that gaps or concentration in the data become visible.

Box-Cox Plot: A box plot is an exploratory data analysis tool that describes the central 50% of a data set, its skewness, its range and any outlying observations. Box plots are particularly useful for comparing data sets. The ends of the box in a box diagram are two horizontal lines marking the lower hinge (first quartile) and the upper hinge (third quartile). It also marks the lowest and highest observation and the outlier.

Descriptive Statistics

Descriptive statistics consists of measures of central tendency, dispersion, skewness and kurtosis. This is a very important tool in data mining and it gives a lot of information about the nature of the database. Any basic package like EXCEL or SPSS can be used to find these descriptive statistics, as the example of the Australian Gold Index in Figure 1 shows. Some of these descriptive statistics are described briefly below:

Measures of Central Tendency: These measures give us an idea about the concentration of the values in the central part of the distribution; the most commonly used measures of central tendency are mean, median (with the mode not being found useful in this context). The mean of a set of observations is their sum divided by the number of observations. It is affected by extreme values, and in the presence of outliers or extreme values, it gives a distorted picture of the distribution. Median of a distribution is the value of the variable, which divides it into two equal parts. Median is not affected by extreme values but as compared to mean it is affected much by fluctuation of sampling. It is also becoming common practice to display a running average as a way of identifying trends. For example, in Figure 1, we show the 5-day, 10-day, 25-day and 200-day moving average to demonstrate how gold prices vary over time and where the highs and lows are relative to short-term or longer term trends.

Measures of Dispersion: These measures basically describe the spread or variability of the data. The variability of a distribution can be an important issue. For example in finance or economics variability is considered as risk. Similarly in quality control high variability is considered bad. The simplest measure of variability is range, which is the difference between the lowest and highest observation in a data set. The standard deviation is a numerical measure of the average variability of a data set around its mean. Variance is the square of the standard deviation and is the averaged square deviation between the observation and the mean. The coefficient of variation is the ratio of standard deviation and mean, and is used to compare relative variability across population.

Figure 1: Australian Gold Stock Index showing 'high-low' daily data and 5-day, 10-day, 25-day and 200-day moving averages (Source: www.the-privateer.com)

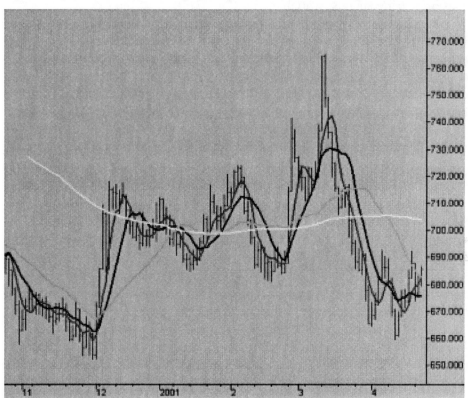

Skewness: The coefficient of skewness measures the degree of departure from symmetry. The distribution may be symmetric, positively skewed or negatively skewed. For positively skewed distribution, mode is to the left of the mean and tail is to the right. For negatively skewed distribution, mode is to the right of the mean and tail is to the left. For skewness near zero, the distribution is symmetric.

Kurtosis: The coefficient of Kurtosis (k) measures the flatness or peakedness of a distribution. For a normal distribution the value of k=3. However, for a flat distribution the value will be less than 3 and for a peaked distribution it will be greater than 3.

Data Driven Modeling

Correlation: The coefficient of correlation (r) is a measure of the strength of the linear relationship between two variables x and y. The value of r is always between -1 and +1, regardless of the units of measurements used for the two variables. A value of r near or equal to zero implies little or no linear relationship between two variables. In contrast, if r is close to 1, it shows a strong positive relationship between two variables, and if r is close to -1 it shows a strong negative relationship between two variables. It may be mentioned that high correlation does not imply causality, and so high value of r does not indicate that one variable is causing a change in other variable.

Regression: Regression analysis is one of the most widely used techniques in many fields of study. It can be applied to such problems as forecasting or estimating. In regression analysis we try to find a relationship between a dependent variable, which we want to forecast or estimate, with other independent variables, which are also called explanatory variables. The relationship between the dependent variable and other independent variables may be linear or non-linear. The estimated equation showing the relationship between these variables can be used for prediction or estimation of the dependent variables. We can also tell by doing statistical tests which variables are significant in explaining the dependent variables and how much variation in the dependent variable can be explained by this model. The coefficient of the regression model can have meaningful interpretation showing if one explanatory variable increases by one unit what would be the impact on the dependent variables. There are few sophisticated methods like stepwise regression, which take care of various problems encountered in the regression modeling. The details of the regression modeling, including various steps for building the regression model, can be seen in the book by Mendenhall and Sincich (1999, 5th edition).

Data-Reduction Techniques

Principal Components Analysis

When a large number of measurements are available, it is natural to enquire whether they could be replaced by a fewer number of measurements or of their functions, without loss of much information for convenience in the analysis and in the interpretation of the data.

Principal components, which are linear functions of the measurements, are suggested for this purpose. It is therefore relevant to examine in what sense the principal components provide a reduction of the data without loss of much information we are seeking from the data. Any standard textbook on multivariate analysis will give more details about this elegant technique; one in particular worth mentioning is by Flury (1997).

Factor Analysis

A statistical procedure, which gives both qualitative and quantitative distinctions, can be quite useful. Similar to the PC analysis considered earlier, the factor analysis also possesses this dual quality, and the aim is to summarize the interrelationships among the variables in a concise but accurate manner as an aid in conceptualization. This is often achieved by including the maximum amount of information from the original variables in as few derived variables, or factors, as possible to keep the solution understandable. Factor analysis can be used to search data for the possible qualitative and quantitative distinctions, and is particularly useful when the sheer amount of available data exceeds comprehensibility. Out of this exploratory work can arise new constructs and hypotheses for future theory and research. Through factor analytic techniques, the number of variables for further research can be minimized while also maximizing the amount of information in the analysis. The original set of variables is reduced to a much smaller set, which accounts for most of the variance of the initial variable pool. The smaller set of variables can be used as operational representatives of the constructs underlying the complete set of variables. This index could be used to identify the future behavior of the finance companies. The traditional common factor model is given by for i = 1... p, (p - dimension):

$$X_i = a_{i1}F_1 + a_{i2}F_2 + ...a_{ik}F_{pk} + E_i$$

Here the model specifies that each of the original variables X_i can be represented as a linear combination of a set of variables $F_1, F_2, ...F_k$ (k = p) called common factor, plus a variable. E_i called the specific factors, which represent a component unique to that particular Xi and not shared by the other Xs.

We notice here immediately one difference between factor analysis and principal components analysis. In PCA the number of components or "factors" is by virtue of the model, always p; whether or not some are discarded later is of course another matter. In factor analysis on the other hand, the number of factors k must be specified ahead of time to complete the model. In actual practice we are not always prepared to make a decision on the value of k ahead of time, so most of the standard statistical computer packages incorporate some quantitative criterion in order to automate this decision-making process. This also can be decided by looking at the number of eigenvalues which are greater than 1 in the previous PC where the first four components jointly explain 80% of variance. Mardia (1979) has given an excellent discussion on this aspect.

Classification Techniques

Discriminant Analysis

Discriminant analysis as a whole is concerned with the relationship between a categorical variable and a set of inter-related variables. More precisely, suppose there is a finite number, say k, of distinct populations, categories, classes or groups. In discriminant analysis the existence of the groups is known a priori, for example, in the case study considered here we know there are two (k = 2) types of companies, namely distressed and non-distressed.

In order to classify a particular individual as to which of the two groups it belongs, the procedure would be to compare the distance (Mahalanobis distance) of the particular individual of unknown origin from the mean of the respective groups. That is, after measuring the appropriate variables, compute the Mahalanobis distance of it from each group mean and classify the company as follows:

Rule: Allocate an individual with observation vector x to GP1 if

$$\left(x-\bar{x}_1\right)'S^{-1}\left(x-\bar{x}_1\right) < \left(x-\bar{x}_2\right)'S^{-1}\left(x-\bar{x}_2\right)$$

that is: $a_i'x + c_1 > a_2' x + c_2$ otherwise to GP2; where $\bar{x}_i (i = 1,2)$ is the group mean vector of the known two groups and S is the common covariance matrix and $a_i = S^{-1}\bar{x}_i, \quad c_i = \bar{x}_i' S^{-1}\bar{x}_i; \quad i = 1,2.$ Here we make a very strong assumption that the two groups have equal variance covariance matrix. The above rule will lead to a linear discriminant function (ldf), which is easy to handle. However, one can also examine the quadratic discriminant function (qdf) by relaxing the above strong assumption of equal variance-covariance matrix. For a detailed account of discriminant analysis, the readers are referred to McLachlan (1992).

Cluster Analysis

The techniques of cluster analysis are useful tools for data analysis in several different situations. They may be used to search for natural groupings in the data, to simplify the description of a large set of multivariate data, to generate hypothesis to be tested on future samples and for several other purposes.

In some investigations cluster analysis methods may be used to produce groups which form the bases of a classification scheme useful in later studies for predictive purposes of some kind. For example, in our financial data set, if we do not know which of the companies are facing financial distress and which are not, we can use cluster analysis to identify a natural grouping if any exists in the whole data set, thus enabling the investor to decide where to spend his money. Thus the problem that cluster analysis is designed to solve is the following one:

Given a sample of n objects, each of which has a score on p-variables, devise a scheme for grouping the objects into clusters (or groups) so that "similar" ones are in the same class. Here the number sought must be completely numerical. Discrimination pertains to a known number of groups and the operational objective is to assign new observations (members) to one of these known groups. Cluster analysis on the other hand makes no assumption concerning the number of groups or the group structure. Grouping is done on the basis of some measure of resemblance of individuals in the whole group. There are various clustering algorithms available, and for a detailed account the readers are referred to Gnandesikan (1977), Everitt (1978), and for an application of cluster analysis to cricket data, Ganesalingam et al. (1994). Ward (1963) proposes that at any stage of an analysis, the loss of information which results from the grouping of individuals into clusters can be measured by the total sum of squared deviations of every point from the mean of the cluster to which it belongs. At each step in the analysis, the union of every possible pair of clusters is considered and the two clusters whose fusion results in the minimum increase in the error sum of squares are combined. The dendrogram resulting figure using Wards' minimum variance method is called dendrogram. The dendrogram confirms the grouping obtained by PCA and factor analysis.

The other classification techniques are based on decision tree and rule induction.

Influential Observations

Influential observations or outliers are extreme observations and may exert greater influence on the estimation of model parameters. The outliers can enter the data either because of punching and data manipulation errors, or it may be caused by special circumstances, and the information it provides may be important.

According to Belsley, Kuh and Welsch (1980), an influential observation is one which, either individually or together with some other observations, has a demonstrably larger impact on the calculated values of various estimates. We must, therefore, pay special attention to outliers. If an outlier can be traced to an error in recording the data or to another type of error, it should, of course, be removed. On the other hand, if an outlier is not due to an error, it may have been caused by special circumstances, and the information it provides may be important. In this case we may use the robust method of estimation instead of ordinary least squares. We may be interested in seeing the impact with and without that influential observation on regression analysis.

Hence the most crucial question and challenge before the statistician is detection of influential or outlier observations. A simple scatter plot of dependent variable y against independent variable x may reveal an influential observation in simple linear regression. However, when we use multiple regression to investigate the simultaneous contribution of a set of explanatory variables, scatter plot may not reveal influential observations, because such plot may not stand out on any pair of coordinates. Atkinson (1981) has given two graphical displays based on half normal plots for detection of outliers and influential observations in regression. However, graphic displays usually suffer from the drawback that we require more judgment and usually it is user dependent.

A large number of statistical techniques besides graphical techniques have also appeared in the literature to study outliers or influential observations in regression analysis. Chatterji and Hadi (1986) have reviewed these techniques and described interrelationship among these techniques.

With the advancement of the Internet and World Wide Web, financial and economic data is available in abundance for research. However, the researchers in these areas with limited background in statistics need to use these data sets carefully as they may contain some outliers or influential observation which can distort the results of multiple regression analysis and may give a wrong confidence interval or hypothesis test. The software tools available now have made this job much easier, but still the burden of making an intelligent judgment is on the shoulders of the user. Using the regression techniques to plainly predict the values of the response variable, without paying attention to related hypothesis testing and observation playing extreme roles, may make the results meaningless.

There are several procedures in use to diagnose the influential observations. In the simple regression analysis, a fitted line on a scatter plot can easily show the influential observations. But in multiple regression, we have to rely on the numerical measures. There are several numerical measures that one can use to diagnose the influential observations.

Another method to find the observations which are influencing the model coefficients are the values of Cook's distances for each observation. A good discussion on this can be found in the detection of influential observations section in Applied Regression Analysis by Draper and Smith. An easy measure of the influence on the fitted values is the DFITS, which MINITAB will automatically calculate.

Forecasting Techniques

Forecasting is one of the important outputs of data mining. In forecasting the user can take past data on a variable or a given set of variables and project that in the future by building a suitable model. There are several techniques for forecasting available which range from naive methods to highly complex methods like neural net and econometric modeling. Forecasting techniques can be broadly classified into two parts: quantitative and qualitative techniques. Quantitative techniques can be applied when the information about the past is available in a time series and we assume that past pattern will continue into the future. Some of the important quantitative techniques are classical time series decomposition techniques, exponential smoothing, simple and multiple regression, Box-Jenkins approach, etc. Qualitative techniques of forecasting do not require data in time series and are mainly based on the judgment of the experts. A good review of different forecasting techniques can be seen in the book by Makridakis, Wheelwright and Hyndman (1998, 3rd edition).

SAMPLING TECHNIQUES FOR DATA MINING

Sampling techniques are essential tools for business data mining. Although there are several sampling techniques, simple random sampling is commonly used in practice. There are quite a few drawbacks of using simple random sampling and it may not be an appropriate technique in many situations. In this section we have reviewed various sampling techniques with their relative merits and demerits. We have also proposed a new sampling technique.

Sampling techniques play a key role in data mining. These techniques are also widely used in market research, economics, finance and system analysis and design. Sampling is the process of selecting representative elements of a population from a huge database. When these selected elements are examined closely, it is assumed that the selected sample will reveal useful information about the whole database.

For example, given a huge database of customers, it may be difficult to interview each and every one because of the enormous cost and also it will take a lot of time. Obviously the best way is to draw a small representative sample and interview these customers to assess the preferential pattern of consumers for different types of products, the potential demand for a new product, scope for any diversification in the production schedule, etc. Similarly the system analyst has to make a decision on two key issues: first to select the documents generated by the members of the organization; second, great many employees can be affected by the proposed information system. Which people should the system analyst interview, seek information from via questionnaire or observe? Obviously he will need a representative sample.

There are quite a few techniques available for selecting a sample, but only a simple random sampling technique is widely used in selecting a sample from a database. Although each unit in the population has equal probability of selection in the simple random sampling, it has many drawbacks. In this section we have reviewed various sampling techniques for industrial data mining. These techniques could be useful in different situations to draw a representative sample. Finally we have also proposed a new method of drawing a sample from a database.

Simple Random Sampling

This is the most commonly used sampling technique in data mining. In this technique each unit of the population has the same chance of being selected. The first step in taking a simple random sample is to assign a number from 1 to N to each element in the population. The next step is to pick a sample of n of these numbers by using any random number generator.

Stratified Random Sampling

In simple random sampling there is no guarantee that all the segments of the population will be represented in the sample. Stratified sampling, on the other hand, enables one to draw a sample representing different segments of the population to any desired extent. For example in market research one may be interested in drawing a sample consisting of males and females of different age groups, income groups, geographical region, etc. In stratified sampling population is divided in different strata and then a simple random sample is drawn from each strata. Choice of sample size in different strata depends either on the size of the stratum or based on the optimum allocation. In the first case, if the strata is big in size, we should draw a big sample from that stratum. In case of optimum allocation, we take into consideration not only the size of the strata, but also the stratum variability and cost of investigating a unit. This means we should choose a big sample from strata if the variability within the stratum is large. A small sample from strata can do the job if all the units are homogenous in nature. The cost of investigating a unit may not be relevant to some extent in case of questionnaire or telephonic interview, but personal interviews may involve travelling costs. We can ignore the cost factor in cases of surveys done on the Internet.

Systematic Sampling

In systematic sampling the first unit is selected at random, the rest being selected automatically according to a predetermined pattern. A simple pattern usually followed in selecting a systematic sample involves regular spacing of units. Assume that a database consists of N units, serially numbered from 1 to N. Suppose we want to draw a sample of size n. Assume that N is expressible as a product of two integers k and n, so that N=kn. In systematic sampling we draw a random number less than or equal to k, say i, and select the unit with the corresponding serial number and every kth unit in the population thereafter. Clearly the sample will consist of n units with serial number i, i+k, i+2k,., i+(n-1)k. In systematic sampling, the relative position in the population of the different units to be included in the sample is fixed. Consequently, there is no risk that any large contiguous part of the population will fail to be rejected. Indeed, an evenly spaced sample is, therefore, likely to give a precise estimate of the population mean than random sampling, unless the kth unit constituting the sample happens to be alike or correlated.

Cluster Sampling

The term cluster, when used in sample survey methodology, can be defined as any sampling unit with which one or more listings can be associated. The unit can be geographical, temporal or spatial in nature. This technique is particularly useful when a sampling frame that is the list of the individual enumeration units is not available. In cluster sampling the population is first divided into a number of non-overlapping clusters. A cluster is basically a collection of a number of smaller units, which are the ultimate objects of study. A simple random sample of cluster is first selected and all the units belonging to the selected clusters are surveyed. For example suppose we wish to select a sample of households in a medium-size city for the purpose of investigating utilization of health services among the residents of the city. A list of city blocks may not be available in the database but a list of city blocks can be obtained from various agencies like the U.S. Bureau of Census. This list of city blocks can serve as a sampling frame. Each city block can be considered as a cluster of households, and every household would be associated with a particular block. The sample of households can be taken by first taking a sample of blocks and then, within each of the blocks selected in the sample, we can list all the households. It is necessary to list only those households that are on the blocks selected in the sample of blocks.

Two-Stage Sampling

Earlier we discussed simple one-stage cluster sampling, which involves taking a simple random sample of clusters and then sampling every unit within each sample cluster. In some situations one would achieve greater efficiency if sampling were performed in more than one stage. An obvious situation is that in which clusters are too large for all units to be sampled conveniently. Also, when the listing units within clusters are very homogenous with respect to the variables being measured, there is no point in taking all the sampling units. In such situations it is often better to take a sample of listing units within selected clusters rather than to select all of them. In other words we draw the sample in two stages, with the first stage being a sample of clusters and the second stage being a sample of listing units within each sample cluster.

New Sampling Technique

Simple random sampling without replacement is the most commonly used scheme in practice. In this scheme, selection probabilities are equal for all units in the population. Consequently, all samples of size n from a population of size N have the same probability $1/_N C_n$ of being selected. In most of the practical situations population units vary considerably with respect to some characteristic, which is highly correlated with the characteristic under study. One such auxiliary characteristic may be the size of population unit. In this situation, simple random sampling may not be appropriate since it does not take into consideration the possible importance of the larger units in the population. In the use of simple random sampling, there is a loss of information available on the auxiliary characteristic. One simple method to incorporate such information is to utilize it for developing a suitable sampling strategy. The method that assigns unequal probabilities of selection to the different units in the population essentially fulfills this aim.

Sampling methods with unequal probability and without replacement are generally classified in two categories. The first category deals with those sampling methods in which the probability of inclusion for ith unit of the population into a sample of size n) is nP_I where P_I denotes the probability of selecting ith unit of the population in the sample at the first draw. In the second category inclusion probability is not proportional to size. In the first category Horvitz-Thompson (1952) estimator is commonly used. Hanif and Brewer (1980) have listed more than 40 unequal probability-sampling schemes. One of the simplest and most useful strategies for selecting sample with probability proportional to size was proposed independently by Midzuno (1952) and Sen (1952). This technique is commonly referred as the Midzuno-Sen method.

We have recommended a new strategy for sampling with varying probability. The proposed scheme is a mass-sample selection scheme. In the Midzuno-Sen sampling scheme, the probability of drawing a specified sample p(s) turns out to be proportional to the sample mean of the size measures of the units in the sample. But in practice, the population of x's is generally skewed and sample mean is not an appropriate measure of the central tendency. The proposed scheme assigns probabilities to the samples proportional to quantities, which could be taken as better measures of central tendency. Here due weighage is given to the skewness and variability of x values. We have shown in Kumar (1999) that in the majority of populations, the proposed scheme performs better than Midzuno-Sen scheme. Mathematical details and an algorithm to draw the sample using this method is given in Kumar (1999).

In this section we have reviewed various sampling techniques, which could be helpful in industrial data mining. Given a huge database (say census), these techniques could be used to draw a representative sample for the whole population. A sample is basically a subset of individual units selected from a large population. Variables or characteristics of interest are observed or measured on each of the sampled individuals. These sampled individuals can also be used in follow-up study. These measures are then aggregated over all individuals in the sample to obtain summary statistics for the sample. It is from these summary statistics or sample estimates that we can draw inference regarding whole population. The validity or reliability of these estimates depends on the fact of how well the sample was chosen and whether it represents the whole population or not. This shows the importance of sampling in data mining.

NEURAL NETWORK TECHNIQUES

Neural networks are very sophisticated modeling techniques, capable of modeling extremely complex functions. In particular, neural networks are non-linear, and moreover they are distribution free. For many years linear modeling has been the commonly used technique in most modeling domains, since linear models had well-known optimization strategies. Where the linear approximation was not valid, the models suffered accordingly.

Neural networks learn by example. The user gathers representative data, and then involves training algorithms to automatically learn the structure of the data. Thus the user needs only to have knowledge of:

- how to select and prepare data,
- how to select an appropriate neural network,
- how to interpret the results.

Thus the level of user knowledge needed to successfully apply neural networks is much lower than would be the case using traditional statistical methods.

The type of problems amenable to solution by a neural network is defined by the way they work, and the way they are trained. Neural networks work by feeding in some input variables, and producing some output variables. They can therefore be used where you have some known information, and would like to predict the value of some unknown information. For example, to analyze the form in horse racing, the factors to be taken into account might include times, weights, distance suitability, barriers, beaten and winning margins, the class of race and the overall field strength. The output information would be some guide as to the likelihood of success in a particular race (e.g., a prediction of the expected time that a given horse would take to run the race). There are a number of sites where this type of information is available for a fee. The user then has to decide which components of the data they will present to the neural network and the parameters of processing that they want the network to use (see below).

Neural networks have been successfully applied across a range of problem domains, in areas as diverse as finance, medicine, engineering, geology and physics. Indeed, anywhere that there are problems of prediction, classification or control, neural networks are being introduced. This success can be attributed to three key factors:

Power: Neural networks are very sophisticated modeling techniques, capable of modeling extremely complex functions. In particular, neural networks are non-linear. For many years linear modeling has been the commonly used technique in most modeling domains, since linear models had well-known optimization strategies. Where the linear approximation was not valid, the models suffered accordingly. Neural networks also keep in check the curse of the dimensionality problem that bedevils attempts to model non-linear functions with a large number of variables.

Ease of Use: Neural networks learn by example. The neural network user gathers representative data, and then involves training algorithms to automatically learn the structure of the data. Although the user does need to have some heuristic knowledge of how to select and prepare data, how to select an appropriate neural network and how to interpret the results, the level of user knowledge needed to successfully apply neural networks is much lower than would be the case using more traditional statistical methods.

Reasonable Processing Time: The key performance objective of the ANN will be to achieve the highest possible success rate. A further objective is to achieve this success rate without the ANN processing time being unacceptably slow. These two performance objectives may counteract each other but can often be traded off against one another through the design of the ANN.

Neural Network Parameters

Now we will give a brief description of the artificial neural network parameters.

Learning Rate: The learning rate determines the amount of correction term that is applied to adjust the weights produced by the equations on the linkages between inputs and the hidden layer when the error is back propagated during training (Haynes and Tan, 1993). The setting of learning rates controls the way the error is used in the neural network to correct the weights of the inputs for each training case.

A high learning rate, which is close to 1, may lead to unstable behaviour of the network. However a low learning rate of 0.25 or less means the network will take longer to train. If the learning rate is set too high, the network may become unstable; this means, the learning rate will need to be decreased if the network is taking too long to train or has become unstable. The learning rate of the optimal network is 70% or 0.7.

Momentum: The momentum value determines how much of the previous corrective term should be remembered and carried on in the training (Haynes and Tan, 1993). The higher the momentum, the greater the percentage of previous errors which are applied to weight adjustment in each training case. A high momentum smooths out the training process and prevents unusual data from throwing the training off track; however, a low momentum is only appropriate for data that is regular or smooth, that in the relationship to the learnt is simple. A moderate to high training rate will be set for the financial ratio inputs considered in our study.

Training Tolerance: The "training tolerance is the number representing the minimum value that each training must achieve, e.g., 0.2 means each item must come within 20% of the target range (Haynes and Tan, 1993).

By setting the training tolerance, the user determines how much training the neural network undergoes. Tighter training (or 3 or 0.4) helps alleviate marginal conditions. If the training tolerance is too close to zero, problems arise as training time becomes longer and the possibility of over training is increased.

Input noise: Input noise in the ANN is used to jolt the network out of local minima which may result due to the nature of the data or the back propagation algorithm being used. A very small input noise should be used, small enough to jolt the network out of local minima without causing changes to the data.

Back Propagation: Back propagation is one of the most popular artificial neural network algorithms currently in use as it is a good algorithm for any application which requires pattern mapping. The concept of BP is that if the network gives an incorrect answer, then the weights of the network are corrected (altered) so the error is decreased; thus the network is more likely to give the correct solutions in future predictions.

Back propagation is also a method for altering a network's weights by sending back the difference between the actual output and the expected output (i.e., the error) to the beginning of the hidden layer, where the weights are adjusted so that in the next iteration, the difference will be reduced (Haynes et al., 1993). The complex computations involved in back propagation networks often require a large number of iterations, which can introduce a severe time-cost.

DATA-MINING PROCESS

The flow diagram given in Figure 2 can be used for data mining. It illustrates the five steps mentioned in SAS Enterprise Miner:

Sample: The most important thing is to draw a representative sample from a large database. The details of drawing the sample were given earlier.

Explore: By exploring we mean calculating various statistics as mentioned earlier.

Modify: This consists of creating new variables or adding some new variables to clarify the data.

Model: This consists of choosing the best-available model for estimation or forecasting.

Assess: At this stage we need to make sure that various assumptions inherent in the model are satisfied.

Recent Developments in Data Mining

Data mining has become an essential analytical skill in e-Commerce. Business organizations are using data mining techniques to increase the profit. Some authors (e.g., Fayyad, 1997) see data mining as a single step in a larger process that we call knowledge discovery in database. Some other interesting open problems in data mining, for example, finding interesting patterns, spurious relationship, contaminated data, etc., is given in the paper by Hand (1998). A new journal named *Data Mining and Knowledge Discovery* covers recent developments in this area. Also

Figure 2: Flowchart of the data mining process

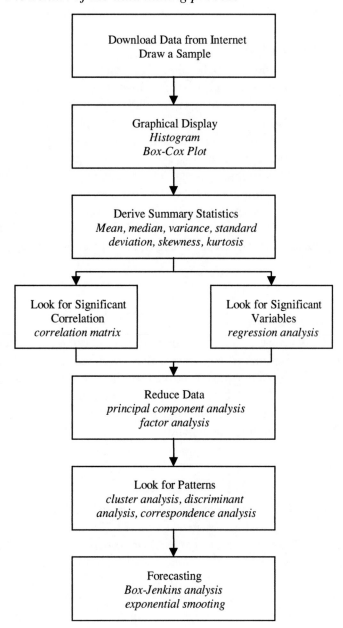

IEEE Intelligent Systems and Their Applications has a special issue on data mining (March 2000) which gives some important developments in special topics like knowledge design and feature mining. Kosala and Blockeel (2000) have given a survey of the research in the area of Web mining. Ma, Liu and Wong (2000) have presented a system called DS-Web that uses Web to help data mining.

Packages for Data Mining

As mentioned by Hand (1998), because of commercial interest in data mining, a number of software tools have appeared in the market. Some are general tools that are good enough to do statistical analysis like SPSS, SAS and MINITAB, etc., while others are special tools built for data mining, for example EXPLORA (Klosgen 1996), Interactive Data Exploration and Analysis Systems (Selfridge, Srivastava and Wilson 1996). These packages for example can segment market data and analyze the effect of new promotions and advertisements. Two special packages developed by Salford Systems are CART (Classification and Regression Trees) and MARS (Multivariate Adaptive Regression Splines). Some of the automatic forecasting packages, which do not require specialist knowledge, are AUTOBOX and FORECAST PRO. A review of these packages, including some other packages, is given in Kumar (1995).

CONCLUSIONS

Data mining is a very general term that refers to the things that people do to understand and explore data. In this chapter we have outlined some of the techniques for data mining. We have not looked at data mining from the point of view of database architecture and data warehouse. With the commercial interest growing in data mining, we feel that there is a good scope for developing an automated package, which could be easy enough to understand.

REFERENCES

Atkinson, A. C. (1981). Two graphical displays for outlying and influential observations in regression. *Biometrica*, 68, 13-20.

Belsley, D. A., Kuh, E. and Welsch, R. E. (1980). *Regression Diagnostics: Identifying Influential Data and Sources of Collinearity*. New York: John Wiley & Sons.

Chatterjee, S. and Hadi, A. S. (1986). Influential observations, high leverage points and outliers in linear regression. *Statistical Science*, 1, 379-416, with discussion.

Everitt. (1978). *Graphical Techniques for Multivariate Data*. London: Heinemann Educational Books Ltd.

Fayyad, U. (1997). Editorial. *Data Mining and Knowledge Discovery*, 1, 5-10.

Flury, B. (1997). *A First Course in Multivariate Statistics*. Springer Texts in Statistics.

Ganesalingam, S., Kumar, K. and Ganeshanandam, S. (1994). A statistical look at cricket data. *Proceedings of the 2nd International Conference on Mathematics and Computers in Sport*, 89-103 .Bond University, Queensland, Australia.

Gnanadesikan, R. C. (1977). *Methods for Statistical Data Analysis of Multivariate Observations*. New York: John Wiley & Sons.

Hand, D. J. (1998). Data mining: Statistics and more? *The American Statistician*, 52, 112-118.

Hanef, M. and Brewer, K. R. W. (1980). Sampling with unequal probabilities without replacement–A review. *International Statistical Review*, 48, 317-335.

Haynes J. D. and Tan, C. N. W. (1993). *An Artificial Neural Network Real Estate Price*.

Horwitz, D. G. and Thompson, D. J. (1952). A generalization of sampling without replication from a finite population in celebration of statistics. *The ISI Century Volume*. New York: Springer Verlag.

Klosgen, W. (1996). *Explora: A Multipattern and Multistrategy Discovery Assistant, in Advances in Knowledge Discovery and Data Mining*. In Fayyad, U. M., et al. (Eds.), 249-271. Menlo Park, CA: AAAI Press, Menlo Park, CA.

Kosala, R. and Blockeel, H. (2000). Web mining research: A survey. *Sigkdd Exploration*, 2, 1-15.

Kumar, K. (1999). Selection of sample with probability proportional to size. *Technical Report*, Bond University, Australia.

Kumar, K. and Bhatti, M. I. (1995). Experts systems in forecasting packages: A review. *Science International*, 7, 141-143.

Ma, Y., Bing L. and Wong, C. K. (2000). Web for data mining: Organizing and interpreting the discovered rules using Web. *Sigkdd Exploration*, 2, 16-23.

Makridakis, S., Wheelwright, S. C. and Hyndman, R. J. (1998). *Forecasting Methods and Applications*. Third Edition. New York: John Wiley and Sons.

Mardia, K.V., Kent, J. T. and Bibby, J. M. (1979). *Multivariate Analysis*. London: Academic Press.

Mendenhall, W. and Sincich, T. (1996). *A Second Course in Statistics: Regression Analysis*. Fifth Edition. New Jersey: Prentice Hall.

Midzuno, H. C. (1952). On the sampling system with probability proportional to sums sizes. *Ann. Inst. Math. Stat.*, 3, 99-107.

McLachlan, G.J. (1992). *Discriminant Analysis and Statistical Pattern Recognition*. New York: John Wiley & Sons.

Selfridge, P. G., Srivastava, D. and Wilson, L. O. (1996). IDEA: Interactive data exploration and analysis. In *Proceedings of SIGMOD 96*, 24-34. New York: ACM Press.

Sen, A. R. (1952). Present status of probability sampling and its use in estimation of farm characteristics. *Econometrica*, 20, 130-133.

Simulator, ANNES. (1993). IEEE Computer Society Press, USA, 354-357. Residential property ANN valuation system (private communication).

Ward, J. H. (1963). Hierarchical grouping to optimize an objective function. *Journal of the American Statistical Association*, 58, 236-244.

Chapter XVI

Fables of the Reconstruction: Characterizing Business Structures with Online Data Collection

David Bimler and John Kirkland
Massey University, New Zealand

INTRODUCTION

The '60s and '70s of the last century were effervescent with visions of a radical break between the past and the future. In their manifestos, Marshall McLuhan and the Situationist International (among others) foresaw a Global Village, a Society of Spectacle, post-literacy and nonlinear modes of consciousness evolving from mass media (e.g., Debord, 1977; McLuhan, 1964). More recently much of this rhetoric has been recycled, with similar claims made that contemporary communications and broadcast media (e-mail and the WWW) will lead to new paradigms, new business models, new economies. It remains to be seen whether current information technology will live up to these promises, or stay in a niche role, like shortwave radio or the Parisian pneumatic post. Examples of truly dead media are hard to find (Sterling, n.d.); even CB radio may retain a few adherents somewhere.

The authors' coffee tables are not graced by copies of *Wired*. But despite our reservations, we grudgingly admit that more people than ever before have access to communication that rivals the speed and reliability of Victorian penny post. The faster movement of information presents management with new challenges and demands. Niche markets develop with unprecedented speed. Geographical horizons are broader: not just globalized multinationals, but small, non-listed businesses may need to monitor conditions and consumer whims on the other side of the world.

At the same time, a company may be physically distributed, with its head office in one city and production staff in another and the call center God-knows-where. Here the WWW comes into its own. As a tool of consultation,[1] it allows performance to be monitored with insights and feedback gathered from throughout an organization (especially convenient if multiple sites are involved). It lends itself as well to surveying the public at large, for consumer perceptions of an organization's public profile. Another area of interest (not pursued here) is the online assessment of job applicants (Stanton, 1998). The opportunities of the Web are well-documented, as are its limitations, though less so. Below we return to the latter.

The focus of this chapter is on issues of organizational structure. Not many corporate entities in the public or private sector have the advantage of a structure that was carefully mapped out at the time they were established. Typically they evolve in an ad-hoc way as they grow. One may speak of an organizational lifecycle, in which the criteria for assessing an institution's performance depends on its developmental phase. Quinn and Cameron (1983) summarized nine models for organizational lifecycles and integrated them into their own framework (the Quinn-Cameron literature review is incomplete, omitting Lievegoed's (1973) 'developing organization' model). The time eventually comes when a corporate entity must take stock, must consider whether its internal divisions into sections and the interactions among these sections are optimal, and if not, how they can be improved.

Such considerations apply to government and local-body agencies as well as to private companies. For the most spectacular examples of mismanagement and organizational dysfunction, one looks to military history (Dixon, 1976). As a more recent case illustration, New Zealand has been somewhat of a laboratory for experiments in public-sector reform. When government bureaucracies were seen as sluggish and inefficient, often the response was to import business models and corporate cultures (thus, the health system, Social Welfare and Labor Departments). Contemporary New Zealand schools have adopted business models, with teachers organized into management teams.[2] The transplants were not always successful, and the phrase 'systems failure' has recurred in media reports ever since.

All this is leading up to the point that one cannot rely on a top-down, dirigiste approach to matching an organization's structure to its goals; to do so assumes that an elite echelon[3] holds a monopoly of wisdom, observational acuity and decision-making ability. The same top-down approach is present if consultants are called in to restructure, or downsize, or identify core business activities. An old joke defines "consultant" as "someone who borrows your watch to tell you the time, then charges you for the privilege." We accept the definition and argue that consultants should be equipped with suitable tools for horoscopy.

Note that we are not advocating a non-hierarchical structure for corporate entities, nor any other normative model, but rather a non-hierarchical process for monitoring structure and facilitating feedback. In what follows, our goal is an instrument for tapping the observations of staff, to assess a given organization's position on a small number of important organizational indicators or dimensions. It can then be compared with its optimal position. Ideally, the instrument could be administered through the Internet or intranets. But first it is necessary to identify those broad, molar dimensions. Candidates come to mind immediately: degree of centralization, openness to opportunity, adaptability, time-span of future planning.

A Better Clock-Face: Genesis of the Corporate Structure Q-Set

When the performance of government departments and private-sector organizations becomes the focus of media attention, certain phrases frequently occur: 'systemic failure' and 'structural failure.' Individuals being more willing to accept responsibility for successes, 'systemic success' receives less coverage, but presumably such a thing exists. This naturally poses the question, what features of a system or structure are linked to its success or failure? We are aware that blaming the system is an easy way of shifting responsibility away from individuals, so that 'we acted in good faith' has become another recurring phrase.

A number of tools already exist to quantify organizational climate and culture; to assess individuals' cognitive style or value system, for fitting them into organizational niches, to classify managerial system. In the future it may be fruitful to target these existing approaches (see Appendix A) with the same methods described below. They have one thing in common: they emphasize the individuals within an organization. Usually the role of management is seen as crucial, reflecting the higher remuneration that accrues to upper echelons.

In contrast, our interest is in how those individuals are arranged. In other words, in the aspects of a corporate entity that can be altered without replacing or retraining individuals (management qualities may not be susceptible to great improvement through training)... and conversely, the aspects that remain in place as individuals come and go.

We followed an exploratory approach, setting out without preconceptions as to what dimensions or aspects of structure are important. A 'concourse' of 62 items evolved, with the idea that any situation (actual, hypothetical or abstract) can be characterized by endorsing these items to a greater or lesser degree. They are designed to be observable generalizations about the interactions among departments (subsystems), or between departments and the environment. A second desideratum was generality to all scales: as well as large corporate entities, the instrument should be suited to describing small ones, or a single section of a large one. The statements were worded to be applicable to government administrations and agencies; confining them to private-sector corporations would restrict us to studying relatively competent, functional examples while excluding dysfunctional ones. The examples (below) include a school–these being ripe for a corporate-structure analysis, as noted earlier.

Some statements were drawn from media accounts, or the authors' experiences of different work environments. Others were inspired by a 'corporate' model of psychodynamics (see below), or adapted from a personality test that is in turn based on that model: the California Adult Q-set, or CAQ (Block, 1978). After generating about 80 statements, we whittled that number down to 62 (a mix of positive and negative statements) by eliminating any that merely duplicated others. Examples are included in the Results section, Table 1.

A corporate metaphor lies behind one influential school of psychology. Kurt Lewin (1935, 1936) imagined the personality as partitioned into many semi-autonomous functions or departments. The dynamics of these departments are the key variables: how they interact, how resources are shifted between them in moments of crisis ('permeability of boundaries'). Lewin's approach was prescient, and fits neatly into contemporary models of cognitive connectivity: the broad systems perspective is hardly limited to psychology. It is the basis of the CAQ, a widely used psychology assessment instrument. We did away with the metaphor and applied Lewin's insights directly. The key concepts in this context are:

Boundary Permeability: "Lewin suggested that permeability could be assessed by the degree of communication obtaining between systems. Boundaries that were relatively permeable would permit neighboring systems to mutually influence each other. Relatively impermeable boundaries would limit the 'spillage' from one system to another. Extremely impermeable boundaries would result in isolation or compartmentalization of psychological subsystems and lack of communication across systems" (Block and Block, 1980, p. 43). To summarize, permeability allows communication between internal systems and the external environment in response to environmental demands and distractions. It further allows the diffusion of tensions originating in one system to other systems.

Boundary Elasticity: "Elasticity refers to the capacity of a boundary to change the characteristic level of permeability-impermeability depending on impinging psychological forces and to return to its original modal level of permeability after the temporary, accommodation-requiring influence is no longer pressing" (Block and Block, 1980, p. 47-48).

Telling the Time, Online: Data Collection Considerations

It was tempting to translate our 62 items into 62 consecutive questions of the form, "How well does this apply to your organization, on a scale of 1 to 8? (where 1 = extremely inaccurately, 8 = extremely accurately)." But this would risk boring the respondents, when disengagement is a single keystroke away. The Web differs in many respects from a face-to-face encounter. Among them, respondents have no sense of the researcher as a real person who might be disappointed by incomplete or inaccurate responses, no sense of obligation (just as to the researcher, the hoped-for respondents are no more than faceless abstractions). This stands in contrast to the difficulty many people (most?) have in hanging up on a telemarketer or telephone surveyor. The politeness norms that still hold sway across the telephone do not operate in cyberspace.

Even in pen-and-paper questionnaires, scalar ratings in this familiar Likert-scale format are fraught with difficulty. It is hard to maintain consistent response benchmarks through a session (a level of applicability warranting a 5 at the start might receive a 7 at the end, as the criteria adapt to the context).[4] In an online questionnaire, this is exacerbated by the evanescence of one's responses, fading from memory as they scroll off the top of the screen.

In face-to-face data collection, a useful substitute for rating procedures is ranking, where the informant arranges items into order of applicability or accuracy. Often this is done by printing the items onto cards that can be sorted into piles on the desktop. Each item takes as its value the number of the pile it was consigned to, with the advantage that this value is explicitly compared with those of other items: "These items all apply more accurately than those, but less so than those others." Although the relative (ipsative) nature of ranking tasks leads to more consistent benchmarks, the method is not yet universally accepted.[5]

Clearly a purely Web-based strategy for recruiting and interrogating informants restricts the results to a select (often self-selected) group. In general it must be supplemented by interviewing or mailing to people unreachable by computer, if the results are to be representative of a broad population, and suitable for extrapolation. Thus Dillman (2000) has argued that to remain commensurate with their printed versions, online forms for data collection should resemble them as closely as possible. This may stifle the creativity of Web designers who would dearly like to use features, such as pull-down menus, unique to the HTML medium. Views on the use of state-of-the-art or Web-specific HTML features are mixed. "If the technology incorporated in a survey is too close to the cutting edge, we risk eliminating that population of users who lack the capability to participate. If an online survey is perceived as 'behind the times,' we potentially lack credibility with the user group we are trying to attract" (White, 1996, p. 57).

Given sufficiently clear instructions, the task of ranking by sorting can be self-administered. It can be posted to informants like a conventional questionnaire. And fortunately the desktop can be retained as a metaphor in the online implementation by a JavaScript program in the HTML page.[6] The items are initially presented, overlapping, in one large pile (see Figure 1); the informant reads them one by one, using keystrokes to consign each to the suitable sub-pile–typically with two options ("more applicable"; "less applicable") or three options (more, less or neither more nor less). The procedure is then repeated for each sub-pile (Figure 2). Two iterations, each with three options, sorts the items into nine rank-ordered piles; three iterations, each with two options, sorts them into eight piles. Other combinations are possible, of course. The dissection of the interminable list into shorter subtasks alleviates the boredom. Finally, the piles' contents are reviewed and shifted from pile to pile if necessary.

This is generically known as the Method of Successive Sorts (Block, 1978). One application arises in human development courses at Massey University: we assess students' comprehension of a key concept by asking them to rank a repertoire

Figure 1: Ranking the CSQ-set statements online, into nine piles (two three-way splits): near the beginning of the process

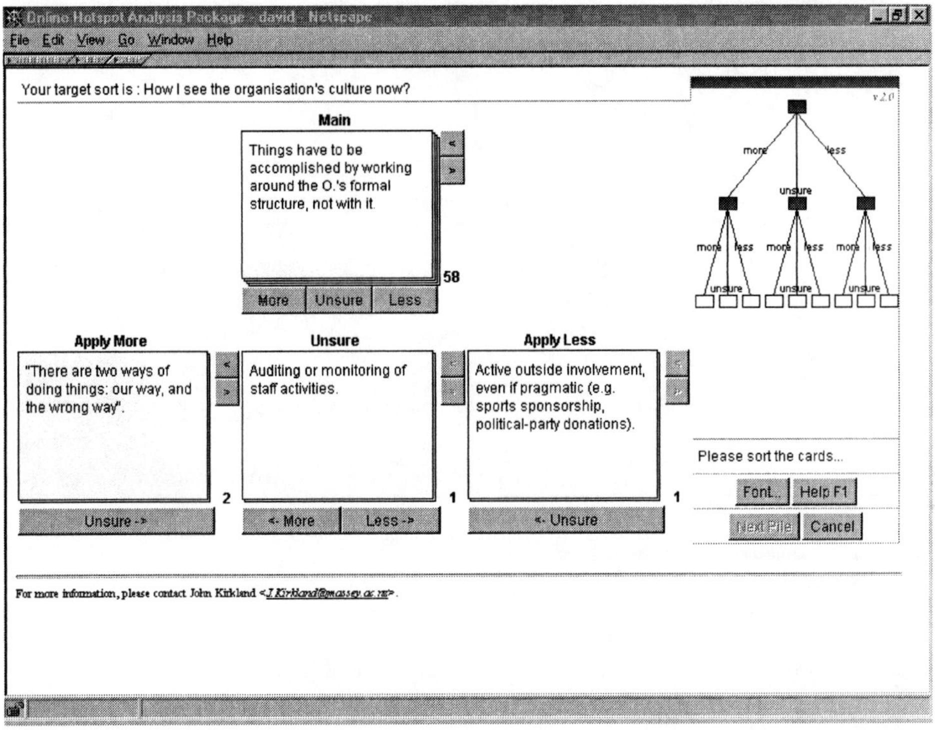

of behavioral items according to each one's association with the concept. A Web interface is a convenient vehicle for this, especially for distance students.

In the research reported here, informants were 29 volunteers from the staff of an IT company. They were divided between Wellington and Auckland, all with access to and familiarity with a Web-capable computer, so collecting their responses online was convenient (it was not essential: other groups have applied the CSQ-set by sorting cards manually). It did not escape us that the researchers were thereby relieved of the burden of data entry. The Web interface allows the pool of informants to be widened in the future to include clients or customers (if the company's public persona is of interest).

Staff were provided with the password to access the appropriate page (among several sorting applications) at the Massey University Web site. There, they ranked the items by applicability to "The Organization as it is now," following a sequence of three binary tree-splits (i.e., 8 piles). Each informant's data were identified by his or her name, with a firm commitment from the researchers that individual cases would remain anonymous when discussing the results with the management. Later the staff were invited to enter another rank description of "The Organization as it should be in three years' time" (i.e., its optimal structure). Nineteen fulfilled this secondary phase.

Figure 2: Towards the end of the online ranking process

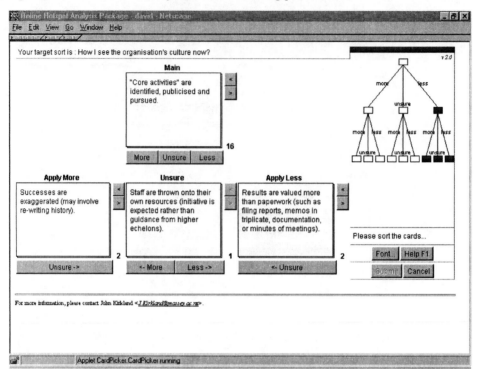

A similar JavaScript application is available in the form of WebQ (Schmolck, n.d.). This lists the items, along with columns of radio-buttons, in a frame occupying the screen's left-hand half. As buttons are clicked, identifying items as most applicable or least so or some intermediate level, the items are copied to rank-ordered panels on the right-hand half of the screen. The metaphor of pile-sorting is not so apparent in WebQ. Moreover, WebQ expects the number of items per pile to be predetermined by the researcher in a 'forced distribution.' The relative merits of forced versus free distributions are hotly debated by the cognoscenti (Block, 1978; Cottle and McKeown, 1981), but the claim of the latter to elicit interval-level data, as opposed to ordinal level, tipped the balance for us in the direction of unforced distributions.

Another package for rank-ordering items is Q-Assessor (Reber, Kaufman and Cropp, 2000), a free-standing program rather than a Web page add-on. Though not designed for online data collection, copies of Q-Assessor can be e-mailed to informants for them to operate, returning their responses later by e-mail–assuming that they are satisfied that the program serves no malign purpose. Q-Assessor is restricted to forced distributions.

Another promising procedure for ranking is "Random Ranked Triads" (modified from Shucker, (1959). Here the items are arranged in randomly into groups of three–20 triads for the CSQ-set, with two held over. The informant views each triad in turn, deciding which item is most applicable to the target, and which is least applicable. These receive scores of 1 and -1 respectively. By repeating the whole process several times, each item's applicability is judged in a number of different contexts. After three iterations, for instance, the total scores for the items range from -3 to +3. A Web interface to emulate this desktop process is being designed.

The next section explains how these data are interpreted within the framework of a spatial model–a three-dimensional 'map.' The map, representing similarities among items, is derived from a different set of data, this time consisting of the perceived relationships among items. These similarity data are only collected once; online collection is possible, but in this case was performed in person.

We used another form of sorting: the GOPA procedure (Bimler and Kirkland, 2001). Informants arrange items into piles, this time on the basis of similarity, grouping together items with similar meanings (and a high perceived likelihood of occurring together). On its own this grouping method is widely used in psychology and sociology (Coxon, 1999). Augmenting it by three further steps, to capture extra information and finer gradations of similarity, produces the GOPA method (short for Grouping, Opposites, Partition, Additive).

Two sets of informants took part: 45 staff from the IT company already mentioned, and 37 staff from a Hawkes Bay high school. To fit the school environment, items were edited lightly, substituting S[chool] for O[rganization] or using different examples. For confirmation of the map derived from these judgments, two subsets of 30 items each were examined in finer detail. Further similarity data were collected with an odd-one-out triadic procedure. Here, informants view the items in randomly selected triads, indicating the odd-one-out (least similar) in each.

Structural Horoscopes and Other Empirical Findings

Outcome 1

Given a number of points, and the coordinates defining their locations in space, the distances between points are easily calculated. The reverse operation is not so simple–starting with a matrix of distances, to reconstruct the coordinates–and to complicate matters, the distances are only known as approximations in real-world situations. A form of arithmetic voodoo is involved, known as "multidimensional scaling" (MDS). Details are omitted here. As with preparing sausages, a detailed recipe seldom increases the consumer's appetite.

From each set of GOPA-sorts (from IT and school staff), we derived a matrix of estimated dissimilarities among the statements. In fact two matrices were obtained. For a given pair of statements, one dissimilarity estimate comes from the number of times they were placed in separate groups (the G, P, A steps of the task). A second estimate, more informative about larger distances, comes from the number of times informants sorted the statements into separate groups and described those groups as 'opposite in meaning' (the O step).

Analyzing these estimates with Kruskal's algorithm for non-metric MDS resulted in a spatial model of the statements–a 3D 'map.' This model consists of 62 points, representing statements, arranged so that the distance between each pair of points reflects the dissimilarity between the corresponding statements. Three dimensions were retained, rather than two or four, on the basis of interpretability. Higher-dimensional solutions improve the match between dissimilarities and reconstructed distances, but it is a case of diminishing returns.

When two maps were derived from the IT and school participants separately, the correlation between them was over 70%, suggesting that participants shared a single cognitive scheme. Two further 30-statement maps were obtained from the triadic judgments using a different algorithm. This arranges points so that (as far as possible) each triad of statements corresponds to an isosceles triangle of points, with the 'odd-one-out' statement represented by the point that is furthest from the other two. The results agreed with the sorting-data maps.

Thus each statement is located by its coordinates on three orthogonal, bipolar axes. These coordinates capture much of the meaning of the statement. To give a feeling for the import of these axes, statements from both extremes are given in Table 1, along with labels. But no statement measures any single dimension in pure, unalloyed form.

The following points are worth noting:

i.   D2 and D3 are independent in the structure. Opportunism vs. conformity do not imply informality or formality–not in the participants' cognitive scheme, at least.

ii.   D2 and D3 are neutral; the qualities they represent can be good or bad. D1 is evaluative: resilience and flexibility are desired, normally…though not invariably. A rigid reluctance to adapt to changing circumstances receives a high value in some circumstances, within established religious organizations for instance.

iii.   Three dimensions have consistently emerged in studies of a range of fields. This does not establish an upper limit on the number of important organizational dimensions, since it may reflect a limitation of cognitive processing–a limit to how many forms of difference we can hold in our minds at the same time while assessing overall dissimilarity. Further axes might be revealed by experiments holding one of the first three dimensions constant.

iv.   D1 and D2 correspond to boundary elasticity and permeability respectively in Lewin's psychodynamics (1935, 1936). The Competing Values framework (Appendix 1; Quinn and Rohrbaugh, 1983) has a 'flexibility / control' axis, related to D2 here, and an axis of External/Internal focus, related to D3. The Competing Values framework does not evaluate companies on competence– its four quadrants include both well- and badly performing organizations–so D1 is missing. Analogous axes can be found underlying Thinking-Style items (Sternberg, 1988) and the CAQ (Block, 1978).

A three-dimensional model is awkward to present as a printed two-dimensional diagram. We find it convenient to start by projecting the points radially onto the

Table 1: Axes of MDS solution, with specimen statements from each extreme

Dimension 1. Resilience/rigidity.

D1- Rigidity, brittleness. Closed, nasty, insulated-righteous, denial.	D1+ flexibility, resilience, elasticity. Engaging, open, future-oriented.
39. Vindictive attitude held towards competitors, critics or ex-employees – perceived slights are not forgotten. 60. O. is always right – failures are blamed on someone (something) outside. 31. "There are two ways of doing things: our way, and the wrong way." 6. Hostility shown towards dissenting internal points of view (such as pessimism or devil's advocacy).	19. Important decisions are preceded by <u>genuine</u> consultation of all affected sectors within O. 51. Staff have access to the "big" picture, i.e., can see where their own contributions fit into O.'s overall goals. 41. O. inspires its members with a sense that all share responsibility for the overall performance. 45. O.'s recruitment policy looks ahead (long-term fit rather than short-term gain).

Dimension 2. Opportunism/conformity.

D2- Conformity. "Establishment," due recognition for obedience, due process.	D2+ Opportunism. Anything goes, seize the moment, "go out."
25. O. values its institutional memory, recognizing (even informally) the individuals who embody it. 48. Staff input is included when writing job descriptions. 28. Promotion is within departments/sections–vertically. 10. Seniority is achieved through length of service. 57. Staff need permission from above to set themselves tasks or initiate action.	2. O. has a broad definition of its scope or client base–"all is grist to the mill," "no job is too small." 32. O. is able to cooperate with other organizations and form alliances (e.g., multi-organization solutions). 54. O. is opportunistic and seeks to lever advantage from every situation. 11. O.'s planning features short-term expedients–"never mind the consequences."

Dimension 3. Informality/accountability.

D3- Formal accountability. Hierarchical internal structure.	D3+ Informal, practical autonomy. Flat internal structure.
38. Structure is reviewed often–whether productively or as window-dressing (e.g., renaming departments). 7. O. relies for evaluation of its performance upon auditing by some outside person or agency. 49. Accountability–people can be held responsible for the decisions they make, money they spend. 33. Organizational preference is for signing off one activity or project before starting another.	59. Results are valued more than paperwork (such as filing reports, memos in triplicate, documentation or minutes of meetings). 56. O.'s various units/sections have many different ways of communicating with each other. 50. For practical purposes informal communication channels (e.g., secretaries) have replaced formal channels. 37. If one department is overburdened then others will offer to relieve the pressure.

surface of a notional sphere centered at the origin. It turns out that relatively little distortion is produced by this projection, because the configuration approximates a spherical shell already: there is relatively little variance in the radial distances between the points and the origin. Then any of the standard map-making projections can be employed to flatten out that curved surface. In this case we divide it into 'resilient' and 'rigid' hemispheres (for positive and negative values of D1) and apply the stereographic projection to flatten each separately (see Figure 3).

The resulting split-hemisphere diagram (Figure 4) shows the arrangement of points as seen from the centre of the model. D2 and D3 become the horizontal and vertical axes in each hemisphere. The outer circle around each hemisphere indicates the 'equator,' where D1 = 0. Increasing proximity to the centre of each hemisphere indicates a higher (absolute) D1 coordinate relative to D2 and D3 coordinates, with "pure" D1 at the centre.

Figure 3: Representing a spherical model as a pair of flattened hemispheres; vectors become points

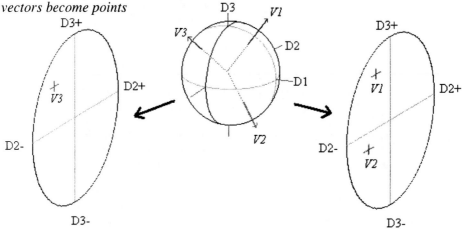

Figure 4: MDS solution for corporate-structure statements, viewed from the origin with radial distances from the origin suppressed. Left: negative, brittle hemisphere; Right: positive, resilient hemisphere. Italic letters denote hotspots (see text).

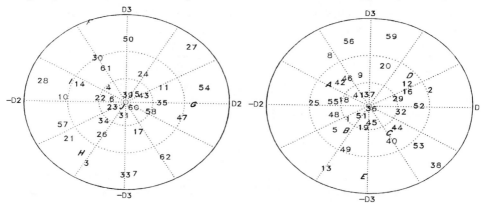

Outcome 2

The purpose of this map is to accommodate actual corporate-structure descriptions, acquired by rank-ordering the statements. According to how well it applies to the corporation, each statement receives a numerical value–the pile number, from 1 to 8. When these values are projected onto the statements' positions in the model, small values (least-applicable statements) tend to be on one side, with a gradient up to highest values for most-applicable statements on the side diametrically opposite. This gradient can be summarized as a vector, found using multiple regression (Figure 5).

Vector components correspond to positive or negative contributions from the respective dimensions. For instance, an organization showing bureaucratic stagnation as its primary feature would be characterized by a vector parallel to the D2- axis. Dysfunctional government administrations and agencies would have negative D1 components in the corresponding vectors. A D1-component (boundary rigidity) can be found in conjunction with negative or positive values of D2 (boundaries impermeable or permeable), the corporate equivalents of internalizing and externalizing personality problems. The former is perhaps more common. Extreme cases of the latter would be energetic but destructive 'delinquent' agencies, with the Inland Revenue bureaucracy coming to mind as an example.

The description can be a summation of an organization in its entirety, or relate to a single division or a single level of the hierarchy. One cannot rely on homogeneity within a corporate entity. In the software industry there is often friction between the marketing and technical divisions, when the enthusiastic promises of the former encounter the realistic reservations of the latter: a disparity of D2 components.

Figure 3 shows how a vector can be mapped as a point in a two-dimensional plot, like the statements themselves. It makes no difference whether the statements' numerical values are from one informant's description, or the average of several.

Figure 5: Using a vector to represent a distribution of rank-order values

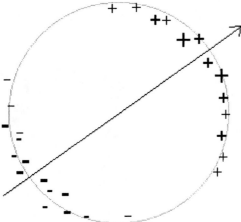

The description may be of a hypothetical situation as well an actual one: for instance, "This organization as it could be, performing its best," or "The structure I would personally find most congenial." The clock-like form of the plot creates an irresistible temptation to speak of an "organizational horoscope."

When we average the 19 "optimal structure" descriptions for the IT company and summarize them as a vector, it is identical to the D1 axis, i.e., to pure flexibility/ resilience. Individual descriptions of the optimal structure hew closely to the average, with individual vectors clustered around the centre of the D1+ hemisphere. The average value ascribed to each statement is proportional to its D1 coordinate. Perhaps this can be shown most clearly by plotting average values against the statements' locations in the map (Figure 6).

In contrast to this unanimity, the 29 "current structure" descriptions are spread more widely, reflecting the range of perspectives available to informants. When they are averaged, the summary vector is still dominated by D1+, but includes a significant D3+ component. This is the crucial point: the staff regard the company as deviating from its optimum state, in the direction of informality. It appears that they sometimes found themselves working in a vacuum, and would prefer more accountability and a better idea of what they should be doing (Figure 7). The opaque nature of the task should be kept in mind: the underlying dimensional framework is not apparent from viewing the items, nor is the link to vector components, so informants have neither incentive nor opportunity to skew results in some desired direction.

This observation met with a gratifying response from the CEO. Believing that the company had outgrown its early stage of unstructured informality in which staff were left to choose their own goals, he had considered introducing firmer guidelines

Figure 6: Values assigned to corporate-structure statements, averaged over 19 'optimal' rankings, plotted as circles at the statements' positions in MDS solution (shown as a split-hemisphere plot as in Figure 4). Negative and positive values are shown as open and solid circles respectively. Area of circles indicates absolute magnitude of values.

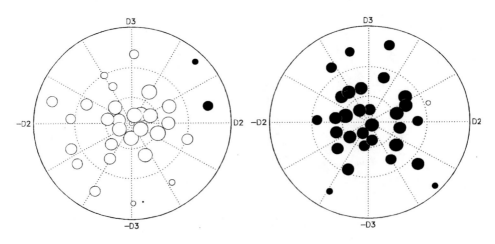

Figure 7: Twenty-nine descriptions of an IT company's current structure, summarized as vectors and plotted on the positive, resilient hemisphere of the MDS solution

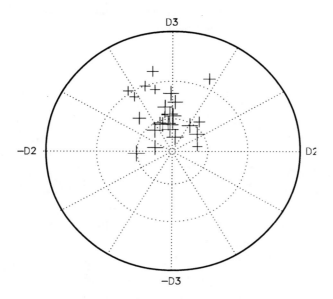

for their activities, but was concerned about the impact on morale. In this case, the CEO's intended changes coincide with staff desires. Moreover, since D3 is orthogonal to the 'conformity/opportunism' axis D2, the changes need not reduce initiative or the company's capacity to exploit opportunities.

A second application of the CSQ-set involved 33 teachers who described the secondary school where they taught, and also the school's optimal structure (in three years' time). These data are not reproduced here since the Internet was not involved in collecting them. The teachers' views of the optimal organization showed a pleasing degree of unanimity, and agreed with the earlier results from IT staff (i.e., the consensus coincided with D1, the 'resilience' axis). They saw the school at present as departing from that optimum, in the direction of excessively short-term opportunism, with a component of D2+ in their consensus vector. According to the principal, this reflected the opportunistic policies that the school had been forced to adopt in previous years, in order to survive within the "education market."

At this stage it is tempting to adjust the statement set for a separate assessment of each dimension–or rather, of the construct it represents. One long-standing psychometric tradition would create three distinct scales by selecting five or 10 statements from both extremes of each dimension. When an informant rates or ranks the statements, a score on each scale comes from the summed values of positive-extreme statements, minus the summed values of negative-extreme ones. The majority of statements are 'interstitial,' i.e., located by significant coordinates on two or more dimensions, and would be abandoned. This simplifies the task, but the approach amounts to asking the same question in a variety of guises (sacrificing the opacity between responses and scores); little intelligence is required to recognize the underlying leading question, "How resilient is the organization?" We would also be committed to the specific dimensions considered above...the complete, less redundant statement set keeps open the possibility of extracting additional information from response sets in the future.

Outcome 3

For another way of summarizing an informant's structure-descriptive ratings of the statements, retaining more detail than a vector, 10 'hotspots' were located within the map. Each represents a particular theme or 'key issue' and is shown as a letter (A to J) in Figure 3. For a given ranking of the statements, there is a score for each theme, in the form of a weighted sum of values given to statements in the neighborhood of that hotspot–the result is a profile of 10 hotspot scores. The weights involved in the weighted sums depend on proximity, ranging from 1 (for a statement that perfectly encapsulates the core meaning of the theme) down towards 0 as statements become more dissimilar and distance in the map increases.

The hotspots are listed in Table 2 with a few words of summary, and the closest statements to each (i.e., those contributing most to the score). Figure 8 shows the profiles for the descriptions of the IT company. The solid profile is the average of the optimal descriptions. It can be seen, for instance, that the current situation scores above the optimal level on 'loose informality' (hotspot F), while below optimum on 'external accountability' (E).

The hotspots are not positioned arbitrarily. They are located to capture as much as possible of the information within the rankings, by an algorithm detailed elsewhere (Bimler and Kirkland, 2001). However, they are only provisional, since there is not a great range of variation within the rankings. This should change as more data are collected, with government agencies, universities and the health system hopefully providing some disaffected observers.

Further Outcomes?

We have shown how the CSQ statements can capture a hypothetical (optimal) organization in observable terms. More speculatively, by Q-sorting the organizational correlates of concepts such as Internal Quality Management, TQM, Risk Management, Transformational or Transaction Leadership, it may be possible to subsume them within the same framework.

For instance, one might study the concept of "institutional creativity" or "innovative environment," since the three internal prerequisites for personal creativity (as laid down by Rogerian theory) can be generalized neatly to institutions. These prerequisites are:

(a) Openness to experience. Low degree of defensiveness; flexible, permeable boundaries in concepts, beliefs, perceptions and hypotheses; tolerance for ambiguity where it exists, ability to receive and integrate apparently conflicting information; sensitive awareness of feelings.

Table 2: Brief titles for the 10 'hotspots' (recurring themes), with the statements most closely associated with each

A. (mutual loyalty)

42 A sense of team spirit (identification with O.) is fostered: e.g., team-building exercises, uniforms.

55 O. recognizes member loyalty in tangible ways.

46 Staff may transfer between divisions/departments.

B. (internal accountability)

1 Fair and transparent systems are in place to evaluate staff performance, for promotion or reward.

36 Ethical standard is part of O.'s corporate culture.

5 Safe avenues exist for complaints for suggestions (i.e., internal whistle-blowing).

C. (means to an end)

44 O. has long-range corporate goals.

40 Potential problems and hazards are recognized, prepared for (i.e., contingency reserves, under committing resources to the task at hand).

53 "Core activities" are identified, publicised and pursued.

D. (resourcefulness)

12 O. rises to the occasion when challenged.

2 O. has a broad definition of its scope or client base.

27 O. has many balls in the air at the same time.

E. (external accountability)

7 O. relies for evaluation of its performance upon auditing by some outside person or agency.

49 People can be held responsibility for the decisions they make, money they spend.

38 Structure is reviewed often–whether productively or as window-dressing.

F. (loose informality)

56 O.'s various units/sections have many different ways of communicating with each other.

50 For practical purposes informal communication channels (e.g., secretaries) have replaced formal channels.

30 Staff are thrown onto their own resources (initiative is expected rather than guidance from senior staff).

G. (expedient opportunism)

54 O. is opportunistic as seeks to lever advantage from every situation.

47 O. seeks headlines–"any publicity is good."

11 O.'s planning features short-term expedients–"never mind the consequences."

H. (discouragement of initiative)

3 There are policies covering everything. When in doubt, consult the "policy handbook."

21 O. expects conformity in individual appearance, office décor, work style.

Continued on next page

Table 2: continued from previous page

I. (hierarchic incoherence)

14 Staff and units/sections are expected to stick to their own speciality, not stray onto one another's turf.
22 A 'need-to-know' policy keeps lower echelons ignorant of O.'s strategy.
4 Empire-building and private fiefdoms are commonplace within O.'s structure.

J. (closed denial)

60 O is always right–failures are blamed on someone (something) outside.
39 Vindictive attitude held towards competitors, critics or ex-employees.

Figure 8:Twenty-nine descriptions of an IT company's current structure, summarized as profiles (dotted lines). Solid profile represents the average optimal-structure description

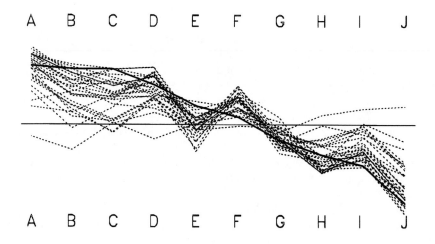

(b) Internal locus of evaluation. Evaluative judgment based primarily, not on outside standards or prejudices, but on one's own feelings, intuition, aesthetic sensibility, sense of satisfaction in self-expression, etc.
(c) The ability to 'toy' with ideas, colors, shapes, hypotheses; to translate from one form to another; to think in terms of analogues and metaphors.

CONCLUSION

The advent of the Web has greatly exercised the world of psychology. The prospect of a vast pool of potential informants, providing timely data–laying bare their souls through their computer connections without the one-to-one involvement of an interviewer–is evident to marketers, pollsters and pure researchers alike. Opinions have been traded in symposia and special journal issues on how best to exploit this resource. The conventional channels for recruiting informants seem obsolete: with so many people exploring the Web, enough would be lured to the researchers' sites and stick there like flies to be sucked dry at leisure. There are no obvious differences between Internet collection and pencil-and-paper methods in terms of the factorial structure of the data (e.g., Stanton, 1998). The need for a representative sample of the larger population is obviated if the data are for processing with Factor Analysis, or if Web services and features are themselves the subject of the study.

Examples of online research in practice are not found so easily. Investigating the appeal of a range of online shopping services, White (1996) appealed for informants in several ways. Eventually 301 were recruited of whom 166 (55%) provided at least some useful responses. Some respondents regarded the survey form as a kind of entertainment, akin to a game, and spent as much as an hour evaluating companies.

Brennan, Rae and Parackal (1999) report two studies. There were 220 participants in the first (recruited by e-mailing every address on a service provider's mailing list, an estimated 22% response rate), and 144 in the second (recruited by a message posted on five major New Zealand Usenet newsgroups). Eighty-five respondents completed both phases in the first study (with some useful data in 155 cases), and 62 completed both phases in the second. Among the reasons put forward for this attrition were the HTML forms being optimized for high resolution (800-by-640), and reliance on features unsupported by some Web-browsing software (Javascript and cgi scripts) or disabled by some users (cookies). Responses were far from timely, although the speed of online surveying has been cited as one of two advantages outweighing the small response rate–low expense being the other (Weible and Wallace, 1998).

Clearly there are problems in motivating enough respondents to bestow statistical validity on the conclusions. Dillman (2000) argues that offering incentives for participation (e.g., entry in prize draws worth $200 or $50 in the studies by Brennan et al.) is a misguided approach. Since respondents are essentially donors, of information and their own time, it may be that a framework of reciprocal obligation between researcher and respondent–a sense of freely exchanging gifts–is preferable to the transactional, marketplace framework created by offering a reward. The transactional framework does not guarantee high-quality, reflective data; to the contrary, the respondent is motivated to answer randomly or by rote, hurrying to complete the task: to complete it more than once (raising the spectre of skewed results) if the reward is more than a token one. The cautious researcher's distrust of purchased data works in both directions: respondents must take on faith the arrival of the promised reward.

Regrettably, commercial development of the Web has yet to foster a climate of trust. Most netizens have learned to be careful about divulging their e-addresses, for fear of winding up on yet another mailing list and adding to their deluge of electronic junk mail. This distrust has particularly corrosive effects for online research if identification, or personal demographic details, are sought from respondents. One phenomenon undermining the effectiveness of conventional market research is the promotional tactic of 'sugging': 'selling under the guise of a survey.' It's easy to foresee online research supporting a similar parasitical practice when it becomes widespread.

The Web displays a technological imperative towards higher-bandwidth multi-media interfaces. Conceivably this evolution will overcome depersonalized anonymity and restore politeness norms. If better graphics, streaming video and synchronized sound are not enough for a simulacrum of face-to-face contact, there remains 3D virtual reality. But text-only communication is compatible with social graces and a sense of community–we note the sense of personal contact reported by IRC habitués, and the past popularity of 'multi-user shared hallucinations' (e.g., TinyMOO). In theory, telephone customers should be demanding increasingly realistic telepresence with videophones as the Holy Grail, but at the time of writing, text-messaging is a cell phone success story: users are communing through text messages as cryptically abbreviated as anything from the days of costly cable telegraphy.

If the graphics in an HTML form for online surveying serve no purpose, they waste the informant's connection time. The purist design philosophy of modernism would consider them a form of dishonesty, a breach of trust… but perhaps this goes too far. How vital is a graphic accompaniment? The text-only French network, Minitel, has a popularity rivalling that of the Web (partly due to the availability of free terminals, and France Telecom's monopoly position), and a graphics-free interface has been designed for it by the e-company Yahoo.

We have no suggestions for dispelling this climate of suspicion, apart from the obvious one that it is a matter of self-interest as much as ethics for researchers to act openly about their objectives and scrupulously with the dissemination of data. All parties benefited from the research reported here. It provided the informants with a channel for voicing their views to the management, who in turn gained access to a perspective from which they might otherwise have been shielded. Nevertheless, informants were kept fully aware that we were working on management's behalf; they were informed about the goals of the research, as far as possible without jeopardizing the opacity of the statements they ranked; and their anonymity was maintained.

Recruiting online informants was not an issue in the cases described above. Nor need it be an issue in other applications of the CSQ to obtain a staff perspective. Recruitment could become a problem in extending the CSQ to a company's wider base of clients or customers.

One way that a Web site can acknowledge an informant's help is to provide immediate feedback for data collected (based, perhaps, on preliminary studies). Given the public's insatiable appetite for self-analysis pop-psychology tests, this is also a variety of motivation. In courses at Massey University, where the targets are not organizational structures but concepts of human development, students receive feedback in the form of hotspot profiles summarizing their rank-order descriptions. For the kind of data and analysis described in this chapter, two other forms of feedback are the components of a vector, and correlations with 'gold standards' (describing abstractions such as an optimal structure) obtained by averaging judgments from a number of experts. In turn this creates a danger that informants will participate repeatedly: seeing data-collection as a game and trying to achieve a 'perfect score.'

A detailed prescription for successful Web-based data collection lies outside our brief as well as our competence. Suffice to note that the basic principles of graphic design for communicating information (Tufte, 1983, 1997) apply with equal force to guiding informants through a survey form, to make their task easier rather than more confusing. For instance, color-coding the numerical response categories for each statement creates a distracting pattern of vertical stripes (Dillman, 2000). Tufte makes a strong case against empty illustrations ('chartjunk', eye-candy).

Considering the low resolution of a computer screen, many interfaces are profligate, wasting up to a third of the screen on the client's or the surveying company's trademarks. Administrative debris enjoys a higher priority than the questions. Tufte notes of this approach that "the information architecture mimics the hierarchical structure of the bureaucracy producing the design" (1997, p. 148)... which in a way is where we came in.

APPENDIX 1. EXISTING TOOLS AND INSTRUMENTS

- The Group Dynamics Q-Set (Peterson, Owens and Martorana, 1999) focuses on the dynamics within decision-making leadership groups. Though of interest because of its authors' understanding of the pathology of collective decision making ('group-think'), it is still tangential.

- The Multifactor Leadership Questionnaire (Bass and Avolio, 1989) measures two aspects of managerial behaviour, Transactional and Transformational Leadership. Comparable constructs have emerged from our research into the requirements of mentoring.

- The Competing Values Framework (Quinn and Rohrbaugh, 1983) is a complex theory-driven scheme, in which eight measurable axes are derived from two underlying dimensions of "flexibility/control" and "internal/external focus", which define four quadrants: the Rational Goal, Human Relations, Internal Process, and Open System Models.

- The Organizational Culture Profile (O'Reilly, Chatman and Caldwell, 1991) is a 54-item Q-set with the focus on values. It's been used to match people to jobs, by comparing individual value-systems with that of the organization, and to measure the extent of value congruence within teams, i.e., comparing individuals.

- Thinking Styles (Sternberg, 1988) identified 13 aspects or roles of 'mental self-government.' We found that these can all be subsumed in a general structure with three overarching dimensions (distinguishing Internal from External orientation; local from global focus; innovation from tradition). There are some parallels with organizational roles, but the Thinking Styles approach seems better-suited to describing a niche within a corporate entity–matching people to particular problems–than to the entity per se.

- The CRPR (Block, 1981) and the Maternal-Sensitivity Q-set (Pederson and Moran, 1995) are respectively designed for a parent's self-reported child-rearing attitudes and practices, and observed interactions with a child. Research points to three underlying dimensions in both cases: a general evaluative axis (good/bad), capturing aspects of empathy and supportiveness; activity; and encouragement of autonomy. The relationships characterizing adult life are thought to evolve from attachments involved in a child-to-parent bond. Thus, an analogous tool could be designed for describing administrative/managerial style (with comparable 'hands-on' and 'ability-to-delegate' dimensions).

- The Riverside Behavioral Q-Set (Funder, Furr and Colvin 2000) is a questionnaire for describing an individual's persona: in particular, his or her performance in a social interaction. It could be adapted for characterizing one particular aspect of a corporate entity: the public perceptions of it, how it interacts with the public (bearing in mind that 'person' is derived from 'persona,' and applies to collective entities as well as individuals).

Finally, a number of instruments purport to measure "organizational climate." The concept may have had a precise meaning when it was used in 1966, but it has since been blurred to include any non-tangible aspects of the work environment as perceived by employees.

ENDNOTES

1 Tangentially we note that just a modicum of consultation might have enabled managers to avoid mistakes like the movable-partition 'cubicle culture' style of office design that impaired the performance of white-collar staff through the '80s and '90s.

2 This is one of several interesting parallels between corporations and schools.

Eckert (1988, p. 190) observes, with regard to student activities: "The high school extracurricular sphere has the essential features of the adult corporate organization: strict delimitation from other communities, a hierarchical internal structure, action-set determination of personal relationships and role-determined identification of individuals."

3 Bureaucracy, cadre, dirigiste, echelon, elite: is it coincidence that so much of the lexicon of centralized incompetence is borrowed from French?

4 Shakespeare recognized the procedure's negative aspects, and his characters resent it being applied to them:
"Signior Antonio, many a time and oft
In the Rialto you have rated me...."

5 Creating a sense of persecuted evangelism among its adherents, as noted by W. S. Gilbert in Patience:
"Though the Philistines may jostle, you will rank as an apostle in the high aesthetic band...."

6 We are indebted to Andrew Drawneek for Web design and programming, and Tao Zhang for extensions.

REFERENCES

Bass, B. M. and Avolio, B. J. (1989). *Manual for the Multifactor Leadership Questionnaire*. Palo Alto, CA: Consulting Psychologists Press.

Bimler, D. and Kirkland, J. (2001). School truants and truancy motivation sorted out with multidimensional scaling. *Journal of Adolescent Research*, 16, 75-106.

Block, J. H. (1981). *The Child Rearing Practices Report*. Institute of Human Development, University of California: Berkeley.

Block, J. (1978). *The Q-Sort Method in Personality Assessment and Psychiatric Research*. Palo Alto, CA: Consulting Psychologists Press.

Block, J. H. and Block, J. (1980). The role of ego-control and ego-resiliency in the organization of behavior. In Collins, W. A. (Ed.), *Minnesota Symposium on Child Psychology*, 13, 39-101. Hillsdale, NJ: Lawrence Erlbaum.

Brennan, M., Rae, N. and Parackal, M. (1999). Survey-based experimental research via the Web: Some observations. *Marketing Bulletin*, 10, 83-92.

Cottle, C. E. and McKeown, B. F. (1981). The forced-free distinction in Q-technique: A note on unused categories in the Q-sort continuum. *Operant Subjectivity*, 3, 58-63.

Coxon, A. P. M. (1999). *Sorting Data: Collection and Analysis*. Newbury Park, CA: SAGE.

Debord, G. (1977). *The Society of the Spectacle*. Detroit: Black & Red.

Dillman, D. (2000). *Mail and Internet Surveys: The Tailored Design Method*. New York: John Wiley & Sons.

Dixon, N. (1976). *On the Psychology of Military Incompetence*. London: Jonathon Cape.

Eckert, P. (1988). Adolescent social structure and the spread of linguistic change. *Language & Society*, 17, 183-207.

Funder, D. C., Furr, R. M. and Colvin, C. R. (2000). The riverside behavioral Q-sort: A tool for the description of social behavior. *Journal of Personality*, 68, 451-489.

Lewin, K. (1935). *A Dynamic Theory of Personality*. New York: McGraw-Hill.

Lewin, K. (1936). *Principles of Topological Psychology*. New York: McGraw-Hill.

Lievegoed, B. (1973). *The Developing Organization*. London: Tavistock.

McLuhan, M. (1964). *Understanding Media: The Extensions of Man*. London: Routledge & Paul.

O'Reilly, C. A., Chatman, J. and Caldwell, D. F. (1991). People and organizational culture: A profile comparison approach to assessing person-organization fit. *Academy of Management Journal*, 34, 487-516.

Pederson, D. R. and Moran, G. (1995). A categorical description of infant-mother relationships in the home and its relation to Q-sort measures of infant-mother interaction. *Monographs of the Society for Research in Child Development*, 60 2-3, Serial No. 244, 111-132.

Peterson, R. S., Owens, P. D. and Martorana, P. V. (1999). The group dynamics q-sort in organizational research: A new method for studying familiar problems. *Organizational Research Methods*, 2, 107-136.

Quinn, R. E. and Cameron, K. (1983). Organizational life cycles and shifting criteria of effectiveness: Some preliminary evidence. *Management Science*, 29, 33-51.

Quinn, R. E. and Rohrbaugh, J. (1983). A spatial model of effectiveness criteria: Towards a competing value's approach to organizational analysis. *Management Science*, 29, 363-377.

Reber, B, Kaufman, S. and Cropp, F. (2000). Assessing Q-assessor: A validation study of Q-assessor computer-based Q-sorts versus paper sorts. *Operant Subjectivity*, 23.

Schmolck, P. *WebQ*. Available on the World Wide Web at: http://www.rz.unibw-muenchen.de/~p41bsmk/qmethod/webq.

Shucker, R. E. (1959). A note on the use of triads for paired comparisons. *Psychometrika*, 24, 273-276.

Stanton, J. M. (1998). An empirical assessment of data collection using the Internet. *Personnel Psychology*, 51, 709-725.

Sterling, B. (no date). *The Dead Media Project: A Modest Proposal*. Available on the World Wide Web at: http://www.deadmedia.org/modest-proposal.html.

Sternberg, R. J. (1988). Mental self-government: A theory of intellectual styles and their development. *Human Development*, 31, 197-224.

Tufte, E. R. (1983). *The Visual Display of Quantitative Information*. Graphics Press.

Tufte, E. R. (1997). *Visual Explanations*. Graphics Press.

Weible, R. and Wallace, J. (1998). Cyber research: The impact of the Internet on data collection. *Marketing Research*, 10, 19-23.

White, G. K. (1996). An online survey of food and beverage consumers on the Internet: An evaluation of the survey methodology. *Marketing Research Online*, 1, 39-59.

Section V

Internet Health and Banking Issues

Chapter XVII

E-Health and Online Medical Transactions

Alec Holt and John D. Gillies
University of Otago, New Zealand

INTRODUCTION

Electronic medical consultation as a means of health delivery is available worldwide. While only in its infancy in New Zealand, it is likely to gain momentum and acceptance, and will impact on both the health deliverer and consumer. Adoption of electronic consultation has the capacity to radically change the environment of healthcare. Emergence of new business models and social impacts are just two of the areas where there could be significant change. As technology is embraced by commercial, health and other interests, we see law and governance left struggling to keep up with the changes. Will the gap between the "haves" and "have-nots" widen or close? Has a beast been unleashed, or are we embarking into a brave new world where anyone can access the health information they need, regardless of socio-economic status, race or geographic situation? We discuss these questions with an emphasis on the New Zealand scene. In researching this chapter it seems that the positions about the future impact and appropriateness of telemedicine is polarized. At one pole are the "tele-evangilists" who think telemedicine will lead to a more patient-focused model. At the other pole are the "tele-luddites" who think that telemedicine introduces technology that complicates an already complex healthcare environment and will always come second to face-to-face interactions.

E-Health

Traditionally, patients and health providers have interacted face-to-face. The arrival of the telephone revolutionized communication; yet, it did not significantly alter the way health providers and patients interacted. The introduction of the Internet into the public arena throughout the 1990s has paved the way for significant advances in communication and information exchange in health. The facility of e-mail, via the Internet, allows transmission of a written message to a targeted receiver quickly and efficiently. This chapter predicts profound alterations in healthcare infrastructure, providing exciting opportunities at all levels of healthcare from individual providers to large multinational corporation initiatives.

E-mail consultation has numerous opportunities for patients including, for example, convenience, the ability to access second opinions and the ability to choose from a wide range of specialists who might otherwise have been inaccessible. Jones (2000) suggests that although there are many concerns over the rise of "Web doctors," numbers are likely to increase (Jones, 2000). A study analyzing requests for consultations at a free paediatric e-mail consultation service for parents concluded that: parents would rather use e-mail than face a "harassed" doctor for further explanations, and parents were not overly concerned about posting personal details that may not be secure. The authors concluded that e-mail was a legitimate form for patients to receive disease-specific information in a timely manner (Borowitz and Wyatt, 1998).

Apparently, many patients find it difficult to discuss embarrassing or "taboo" subjects with their doctors. Howe (1997) reports that this anonymous, faceless form of consultation can be at once personalized and anonymous (Howe, 1997). In New Zealand, Dr. Mulholland, a Taranaki general practitioner, operates a commercial e-health service called doctorglobal that is reported to be outstandingly successful. This type of enterprise is gaining the attention of professional medical associations who believe that some standards and protocols should be set (Coddington, 2000). Conversely, commenting on the launch of doctorglobal, Dr. Wiles, chairman of the New Zealand College of General Practitioners, described e-mail consultation as "dangerous nonsense" (Howe, 1997). However, there are publicly funded initiatives in New Zealand taking advantage of the possibilities offered by e-health include (Mandl et al., 1998): The Waikato Tele-Dermatology, The Waitemata Tele-Psychiatry, The South Island Tele-Medicine Project, The Christchurch Tele-Medicine Service and The New Zealand Tele-Paediatric Service.

The use of electronic signatures for prescriptions enhances the drive for a complete package of online health. It in effect activates the online consultation by allowing for the prescription and notes to be processed online. Ultimately the consultation can be achieved while the patient is at home and the prescription can be delivered to their front door. In New Zealand 68,000 prescriptions are filled each day. The latest Pharmac figures suggest 48 million scripts per year (Improving Our Health, 2000). Currently, health professionals write prescriptions on paper. The patient then gives the written prescription to the pharmacist who forwards it to Health Benefits Ltd. for reimbursement. There are major developments overseas to have prescriptions written and transmitted electronically. Even though electronic transmission technology is widespread in most businesses, there are unresolved technical standards and legal issues that delay its acceptance and implementation in the healthcare system.

The use of electronic prescriptions has the potential to benefit the healthcare system in many ways as it has advantages not only for prescribers and pharmacists, but also for patients. Patients are more likely to have error-free prescriptions, as the system would check drug dosages and drug interactions (Barber, 1995; Rolfe, 1995). The physician or pharmacist could provide medication education handouts to increase the patient's understanding of their treatment and improve compliance (Schiff, 1998). Prescriptions could be transmitted directly from general practices, hospital wards or clinics to a nominated pharmacy to provide more seamless care between hospitals, general practitioners and the community (Farrar, 2000; Siwicki, 1998). Electronic prescriptions may also reduce the pharmacist's difficulty in reading the prescriber's handwriting. This in turn should reduce the potential for disciplinary hearings and litigation arising from the interpretation of prescriptions (Middleton, 2000).

The downside of electronic prescriptions is that prescription fraud is on the increase due to the illegal use of scanners and laser printers to duplicate script letterheads (Ball, 2000). Electronic prescriptions would make stolen or forged prescriptions worthless. Obtaining the same prescription from various doctors would be more difficult as the patient's past drug history will be easily accessible (Winyard, 1997). However now built in checks can be used. The prescriber can instantaneously access background information about the drug, its side effects, drug interactions, formulary status and cost. The doctor and pharmacist could share the patient's medical and drug history through a centralized information registry and check any previous adverse reactions (Saunders, 2000). In the event of a drug recall, patient contact information will be readily available. The system could help with the collection and analysis of drug usage, and help formulate treatment protocols and care plans (Simmons, 1998; The Pharmaceutical Journal, 1999).

Social Implications

The arrival of e-Commerce has caught the health sector unprepared and without existing convention. The speed of the adoption of electronic medical consultation by innovators has proceeded ahead of the formalization of any frameworks or guidelines. This has provided a developmental environment relatively unfettered by any of the standards usually applied to a new form of treatment or service. It is likely that protocols and guidelines will evolve as emerging trends and patterns become more obvious or "pressing." However, due to a significant gap in the literature (particularly empirical work) related to social impact, predictions put forward remain as speculation. There are several relevant potential social effects of e-health, including issues related to equity, consumerism and altered relationships.

Equity

Most national health systems should develop equity policies for electronic medical consultation. While Internet connections are very accessible in New Zealand, computing resources should be made available to the consumer to ensure equity. The profile of the Internet-enabled consumer is significantly skewed to higher socio-economic and better-educated segments (Telehealth Applications–New Zealand, 2000; Milstein, 1999). Therefore, patient-initiated e-mail consultation may have entry barriers. As well as access to resources, the user must have adequate language, literacy and technical knowledge. This gives several groups, such as ethnic minorities, the elderly, poor and those with literacy problems a potential equity disadvantage with regard to electronic healthcare options. Some of these may be within. Eysenbach, who discusses a potential widening gap between the privileged "Internet-able" and underprivileged populations, who will not be able to participate in Internet-distributed healthcare, highlights this (Eysenbach et al., 1999).

Electronic consultation, however, can also offer significant benefit to some of those arguably disadvantaged in traditional models of healthcare. Telemedicine, for example, supplied to rural areas could dramatically reduce costs incurred in transfer to specialist care, whilst improving the speed of access. Health reforms have resulted in the closure of many regions' hospitals. Consequently patients may be faced with increasing difficulty in accessing healthcare. Along with this trend, rural New Zealand faces the loss of medical personnel. The Ministry of Health telephone pilot, serving parts of the East Coast District of the North island, is a pioneer service aimed to address some of these issues and if successful, may well pave the way for the formation of services utilizing more sophisticated technology. Public policy will eventually need to address these issues for the longer term, particularly as public health systems move toward greater use of e-health initiatives. This may mean the eventual supply of resources to selected individuals or groups–such as the provision of community Internet kiosks or centres–or make provision as Mulholland suggests through a contact person such as a community nurse, who has access to the Internet (Coddington, 2000).

Consumerism

Information technology gives the patient access to a wealth of knowledge and information (Jadad and Gagliardi, 1998). An informed patient is capable of participating more actively in healthcare decisions. This may mean, however, that providers feel faced with more aggressive and demanding patients, who require more time and explanation (Mandl et al., 1998; McCormick, 2000). Meeting these needs may be difficult within the usual length of commentary supplied in e-mailed responses. Attaching additional information as an accompanying file or document may also be time consuming to compile and find.

E-mail consultation services may be designed for patients that have an established relationship with a provider, or alternatively, offered as a means of attracting business. Egger suggests that because patients indicated access to their doctor by e-mail was important to them, the doctor would consider introducing e-mail to their practices (Egger, 2000). Feasibly then, offering this service may give future competitive advantage to a health practice.

The advent of the Internet has opened new opportunities for financial gain. In the space of only a few years, there has been a burgeoning number of both small and large e-health providers responding to the demands of a new wave of consumer-driven healthcare seekers. It is now possible for healthcare suppliers to create revenue unbounded by physical aspects, or even offer niche services on a global basis.

Provider-Patient Relationships

The extent to which consultation over the Internet will change the patient-provider relationship is unclear. Stevens compares the social impact of the Industrial Revolution with that of information technology (Stevens, 2000). Just as the Industrial Revolution ultimately re-ordered traditional relationships, such as how children related to parents or men to women, so it is feasible that the Internet may radically redefine traditional models. It seems likely that evolution of styles and frameworks will be a response to the many aspects that communication technology brings to the context.

Historically, a patient base would comprise those who lived or worked near a health practice. The Internet now provides the opportunity for a healthcare seeker to decide where to get information. This may be from a provider far from the patient's locality. A patient may even approach a provider from a different country who is considered a leading expert within a particular field (Coile, 2000).

The adoption of e-mail consultation is by no means the only factor that will influence how patients and practitioners interact in the future. There are other forces that will impact on this interaction, including:

- the vast array of information available through Web sites,
- the increasing financial imperatives for cost constraint; and
- the new generations of software and hardware that enable increasingly sophisticated systems of interaction, for example, *SendTalk*, *PowerTalk* and streaming video through *NetMeeting*.

Entering into e-mail consultation with an unknown online provider means the patients take on more responsibility for their treatment. Without the usual tangible evidence that bricks and mortar supply, patients will potentially be exposed to more risk and will have to invest extra time and effort researching questions to ask providers, assessing quality of responses and coordinating their own healthcare (MacStravic, 2000). There is also significant risk to patients of "surfing" providers and using advice in a piecemeal fashion. Currently it seems unlikely that a provider would happily become involved where multiple consultation and treatment trial is being undertaken, but in the future this might be normal practice.

With electronic prescriptions doctor-patient confidentiality is still at risk. Both the U.S. and British governments are considering a scheme called "key escrow"

(Mitchell, 1997) under which senders of professional or commercial e-mail must reveal their keys or passwords to a secure agency. Government officials producing a warrant could demand the key from this "trusted third party," and use it to monitor professional correspondence unbeknown to the clinician. If key escrow were adopted, patients' medical information would pass beyond the direct control of doctors, compromising the confidentiality principle. In the future intelligence services will be able to access information remotely without the knowledge of the medical practitioner. Governments say they need key escrow to help catch terrorists and track down paedophile rings, but in practice, keys might be sought for anything from managerial investigations into doctors' competence, to civil servants' checks on sick-pay claimants. The result could be severe damage to the doctor-patient relationship, with patients holding back information on mental illness, for example, for fear of official access. Because access by officials would be "secret," any subsequent breach of confidentiality could be blamed on the doctor.

Legal Issues

At present in New Zealand, there is no special legislation covering electronic consultation. e-Commerce laws are currently being finalized. These will be of a general nature and will need to be adapted to cover e-health (New Zealand Law Commission, 1998). The Health Act (1996) and Privacy Act (1993) are deemed to cover this area (Taylor and Leuven, 1999; Sloan, 1999). The Privacy Act is intended to promote and protect individual privacy in accordance with the OECD Guidelines (1980). Relevant to the health sector is the Health Information Privacy Code (1994) (http://www.privacy.org.nz/comply/hinfopc.html), which contains 12 rules regarding use and disclosure of health information. The theme of the code is patient empowerment and informed consent. Four rules of relevance to electronic consultation are Rule 3, Rule 5, Rule 10 and Rule 11.

Rule 3 requires that the consumer be fully informed about the fact that personal information is being collected. This is an area that appears to be poorly adhered to. Although no survey has been conducted to ascertain the level of compliance with the Privacy Act by New Zealand-based Web sites, an examination of more than 1,400 Web sites by the U.S. Federal Trade Commission found that although more than 85% of sites collected personal information from consumers, only 2% provided a comprehensive privacy policy (Pitofsky, 1998). The Privacy Commissioner has warned that he is prepared to act on any breach of privacy under this code (Sloan, 1999) although he would seem to prefer self regulation be introduced (Sloan, 2000). This despite the U.S. Federal Trade Commission concluding that "industry's efforts to encourage voluntary adoption of the most basic fair information practice...have fallen far short of what is needed to protect consumers" (Pitofsky, 1998). Rule 5 deals with security and storage, and therefore has particular relevance to electronic information. Some of the areas covered are password protection, screensavers, access control and secure intranets. Rules 10 and 11 limit health information use and disclosure. If browsing was considered 'use' of information, then there are interesting implications. The Privacy Commissioner has deemed that to constitute 'use,' data needs to be retrieved and some action taken.

Internationally, there has been the development of several non-profit organizations that aim to ensure ethical use of medical information on the Internet. These include the Intermountain Health Care (http://www.ihc.net/) and the Health On the Net Foundation (http://www.hon.ch/). The former, via the e-Health Ethics Summit, has drafted the International e-Health Code of Ethics, whilst the Health on the Net Foundation has elaborated a Code of Conduct for medical and health Web sites. These codes cover issues of quality, privacy, informed consent and confidentiality, as well as advertising, editorial policy, sponsorship and authorship. The vehicle for implementing the code has yet to be decided although various labelling techniques are under development using both cyber metrics and human ratings systems (Stephenson, 2000; Eysenbach and Diepgen, 1998).

The licensing of medical practitioners varies from country to country. In America a doctor is licensed to practice in one state only and cannot legally prescribe medication to a patient residing in another. The e-consultation is deemed to occur at the patient's computer terminal rather than the physicians. This restricts American doctors to providing consultations to patients living in their own state of practice. DrGlobal, a New Zealand-based Web-consulting group, has taken a different stand. They suggest that the consultation takes place at the physician's desktop, which is in the country where he is licensed to practice (Gillies pers comm.). The patient is regarded as a traveller who may require medical advice while on an overseas holiday. This raises concerns about how a patient may seek redress in instances of malpractice (Gillies pers comm.). It may also leave a physician open to exploitation by malevolent patients, who make a living from suing doctors. DrGlobal is addressing this problem by developing an international network of doctors. This will enable an e-consultation to take place by a physician licensed in a patient's country of residence.

The site of the consultation may be an arbitrary point, however, when a real issue is whether an e-consultation is legal or ethical, without a physical examination. The American Medical Association (AMA) clearly states that a doctor/patient consultation cannot take place without a physical examination, therefore an e-consultation can only be considered as expert advice (Barkham, 2000). Is the patient therefore paying for an informed opinion, when he can get the same advice for free from an "ask the expert" type of Web site? Porter thinks so, "I don't know of a decent doctor who reckons he or she could do a proper job during online consultation. To pretend you can and charge money for it is wrong" (Health On the Net Foundation, 2001). In order to meet legal and ethical guidelines, Web-based consultations should be an adjunct to an established doctor/patient relationship. This would allow for follow-up care, repeat prescriptions and any health advice to be delivered electronically to a patient following an initial physical visit.

A further major concern with the emergence of e-health is the online prescription of potentially dangerous "lifestyle" drugs, such as Viagra (to aid sexual dysfunction), Propecia (to promote hair growth) and Xenical (for weight loss). Obviously, there is an enormous demand for these drugs as attested to by the huge profits, which are being generated by Internet drug companies. These drugs are dispensed following an online consultation that is often no more than a health questionnaire, causing many companies to fall foul of the laws governing drug prescriptions. According to the Virginia Board of Medicine (Barkham, 2000), many of these sites have been closed down. Unfortunately, due to the nature of the Internet and the extraordinary difficulty in policing such activity, the sites soon surface elsewhere.

Currently electronic prescribing in New Zealand has no validity in law (Phillips, 1999). Regulation 41(b) of the Medicines Regulations 1984 sets out the requirements to be fulfilled relating to the form of every prescription and expressly provides that the prescription be signed personally by the prescriber with his usual signature not being a facsimile or other stamp (Greer, 2000). The fact that electronic transactions have no legal status in New Zealand was confirmed in the Crown vs. Wilkinson case early in 2000. The U.S. Justice Department is so concerned on this issue that they have offered us help to draft some basic cyber laws (Palmer, 2000). The Western Pacific Regional Office of the World Health Organization is awaiting legislative developments in NZ before it implements any policies (Yagami, 2000).

The NZ Law Commission has released two reports on Electronic Commerce (New Zealand Law Commission Report 58, 1999; New Zealand Law Commission, 1998) which discuss the legal implications of electronic signatures. The reports follow the overseas trend aiming to remove impediments to equivalence of electronic transactions and paper transactions as long as an appropriate "signature" is attached.

Ethical Concerns

While the legal aspects of Internet consultations are difficult to control, the ethical practices are almost impossible to monitor. Health practitioners are responsible for maintaining their own ethical standards. HON (Health on the Net) (Journal of Medical Internet Research, 2000) is a Geneva-based organization that serves as a watchdog of the ethical and legal principles of Internet health providers. It encourages health providers to adopt its code of ethics. The HON logo can be displayed on Web sites that have HON endorsement. Other groups such as the IHC (Internet Health Coalition) (Internet Health Coalition, 2000), AMIHA (American Medical Internet Health Association), IMIA (International Medical Informatics Association), government agencies and the telecommunications industry are all striving to achieve some sort of regulation of Internet practices.

The Internet has the potential to empower the health consumer by providing access to a huge range of information. Quantity of health information is, however, no substitute for quality. The onus is on the consumer to judge the quality of the information they receive. A patient seeking an online consultation must be able to ascertain the credentials of their e-physician, whether the physician is offering a full consultation or an informed opinion. A health Web site should therefore clearly state the qualifications and credentialing of its doctors, and the screening process used to choose them.

Security Issues

The Internet was designed by the scientific and academic communities to allow efficient and open information sharing among "trusted" entities, with little thought being given to security issues. It is therefore not surprising that security issues are emerging as a major concern of e-health. Confidential information transmitted via the Internet may be intercepted and read by unauthorized persons. Health information is particularly vulnerable and exposure can create irredeemable personal damage. For example, the disclosure of a positive HIV status, substance abuse or mental health record can change an individual's life forever, potentially affecting employment, financial and social status.

The doctor/patient relationship has always been sacrosanct in respect of confidentiality, but this may change with the development of online consultations. The security of an electronic medical record is the responsibility of the Web site administrator. Enormous profits can potentially be made from selling confidential patient information. The Guardian (Barkham, 2000) reported "...that many sites, including DrKoop, OnHealth and WebMD were sharing information about their users with third parties." If the appeal of Internet consultation is consumer anonymity, many customers may be deterred from using these services because of security breaches. It is the obligation of the individual health provider to protect the privacy its patients. If it fails to do this, consumer trust will be lost, and Internet health sites will lose credibility.

Pharmnet (Elsmore, 2000) has been established in New Zealand for the purposes of transmitted patient information and prescriptions through a VPN (virtual private network), using spread-spectrum radio links to connect all pharmacies and general practitioners in a WAN (a computer network that spans a relatively large geographical area). This is military standard equipment that changes its transmission frequency at random intervals (approx. 2 milliseconds) and almost impossible to listen into. It gives higher connection speed (up to 7 Megabits/sec) compared with 56k dial-up, or ISDN (integrated services digital network) lines. It is possible to run voice phone over the network, so talking to other professionals over the network is free.

The New Zealand Ministry of Health has been approached for a suitable standard for encryption, but there has yet been no reply. Pharmnet implements a 128-bit encryption and also uses IP address-specific passwords. This means that a password is only valid if it comes from a specific machine. The network is behind a firewall, and is held on two mirror sites. Five years of live data will be available for analysis, and the old data will be archived in compressed form onto CD-ROM. The Health Information Privacy Code 1994 specifies that the data must be kept for 20 years. The original system envisioned general practitioners transmitting scripts to a central server, as well as giving the patient a printed copy, which carried a bar code and an ID number. On receipt of the script the pharmacist would query the server and retrieve the script data. After making any changes necessary to meet HBL regulations, the pharmacist would dispense the script and write the changes back to the server.

Analysis of e-Health Consultation Sites

Four e-health consultation sites were identified to be evaluated–two from New Zealand, one from the UK and another from the USA. (1)DrGlobal (www.drglobal.com) is a New Zealand-based site. Queries are passed on to experts on that particular topic. A fee of $30-00 (NZD) is payable per consultation. (2)XtraHealth (www.xtra.co.nz/health/experts/) is a New Zealand based site. Queries are passed on to experts on that particular topic and answered within a number of days. This is a free service to the public. (3)AskDrGeorge (http://www.doctorgeorge.com) is a USA-chat-based site. Queries are posted in a chat format and the response is immediate. This is a free service to the public. (4)UKDoctorCall (http://www.doctorcall.co.uk) is a UK-based site. Queries are passed on to experts on that particular topic. A fee of $90-00 (NZD) is payable per consultation.

The following questions were compiled and posed to the e-health consultation sites:

Question 1

I sprained my right ankle two months ago whilst snowboarding. It was painful immediately and it swelled up on the outside of the ankle joint. I couldn't walk properly for a few days. I was seen at accident and emergency where they x-rayed my anklet and told me it was sprained and to rest it. Two months later it is still sore and it continues to swell up after even walking. I can't run anymore because of the pain and swelling. What do you think the problem could be? Should I see a podiatrist or a physiotherapist?

Question 2

I am writing on behalf of my 10-year-old son. He is currently quite well, I just have some questions I would like answered. I am concerned about him having becodisc for so long and I have the following questions: Is he going to have some side effects from long-term becodisc use? If he stayed on becodisc and was an Olympic contender (he is a good swimmer), would a blood test show that he was a steroid abuser? When he stops becodisc (usually over the summer months), he seems sniff constantly, which is extremely irritating. Is there any other treatment for this? Will he grow out of it, as he gets older?

Question 3

I have an 18-year-old daughter who has quite severe acne on her face. It is quite disfiguring and a major concern to her. So far she has tried some over-the-counter skin cleansing products and our GP has prescribed some lotions to apply but nothing has made any difference. She is otherwise fit and healthy and eats a healthy diet with not much chocolate. What should we do next in terms of treatment?

All three questions were posed to the first three sites, however, due to cost considerations, only the second question was posted to the UKDoctorCall site. Two general medical practitioners graded the responses using a 5- to 10-point Likert-type scale in terms of: response time, ease of access of the site, stated qualifications of the doctor, quality of the response in terms of: comprehensive, clarity, accuracy, usefulness (see Table 1 for the results).

Results

Response time. DrGlobal scored full marks with same-day response to all three questions. In the case of XtraHealth, the response time ranged from one-seven days. DrGeorge is an online chat format, therefore response is immediate. UkDoctorCall (one question only) response time was four days.

Ease of access to the site. DrGlobal, AskDrGeorge and UKDoctorCall all scored full marks for this section 60/60, as the sites were easy to access. XtraHealth was more difficult to access and only scored 36/60. The reason for this is that Xtra Health does not guarantee that all questions will be answered, and the response is posted to the Web page rather than directly back to the patient. This means that the patient has to check the site daily to see if their question has been answered.

Qualifications. Health care professionals who practice on the Internet have an obligation to identify themselves, their location and their professional credentials. In cases where the qualifications were not immediately apparent, questions were posed to the responders regarding their qualifications. Both DrGlobal and XtraHealth are upfront with regard to the credentials of the doctor answering the questions, and in both instances the doctors appear to be well qualified for the task. Out of a maximum score of 60, both DrGlobal and XtraHealth scored a total of 56 on this parameter. Both AskDrGeorge and UKDoctorCall failed to respond to requests for the qualifications/credentials of the doctor online, and thus both scored zero.

Comprehensiveness of the response. This variable relates to the extent to which the question was fully and completely answered. Out of a maximum score of 60, AskDrGeorge scored the highest at 58, with XtraHealth, DrGlobal and UKDoctorCall scoring 52, 51 and 51 respectively.

Clarity of the response. This variable relates to how clear and understandable

Table 1: Results

Criteria	XtraHealth	DrGlobal	AskDrGeorge	UKDrCall
Response time	30	60	60	40
Ease of access to the site	36	60	60	60
Qualifications	56	56	0	0
Comprehensiveness of the response	52	51	58	51
Clarity of the response	50	50	60	60
Accuracy of the response	60	57	46	60
Usefulness of the response	55	53	51	42
Total	339	387	335	313

the answer would be to the layperson. Out of a maximum score of 60, AskDrGeorge and UKDrCall scored the highest at 60, while XtraHealth and DrGlobal scored only 50. The DrGlobal responses were communicated posed in medical terminology, which might not be familiar to the average layperson.

Accuracy of the response. This variable relates to whether the response was in line with "best practice," scientific and up-to-date. Out of a maximum score of 60, both XtraHealth and UKDrCall scored 60, while DrGlobal scored 57 and AskDrGeorge had the lowest score at 46.

Usefulness of the response. This variable relates to the overall usefulness of the consultation in terms of time and where applicable, money invested. Out of a maximum score of 60, XtraHealth scored the highest at 55, with DrGlobal, AskDrGeorge and UKDrCall scoring 53, 51 and 42 respectively.

Key findings were:

- The response time varied considerably between the four sites.
- Three of the sites were easily accessible in terms of getting the answer back to the client.
- Only the two New Zealand sites clearly indicated the credentials of the medical staff.
- In terms of overall quality, the results of the four sites were very similar, and were generally rated satisfactory-to-high.
- The relatively high ratings for quality are in sharp contrast to existing perceptions where poor quality and questionable ethical standards are considered to be among major concerns for e-health.

Consumers should try and identify the following criteria (shown in Table 2 below) before they use a particular provider.

e-Health Case Study

A more detailed case study on healthcare for a specific topic (cancer) was also researched. Cancer is a term for a range of diseases; because of this it may be expected that a large number of affected patients will turn to the World Wide Web for information about their condition. A study was completed to evaluate the quality of a sample of health-related Web sites based in New Zealand using well-defined

Table 2: Criteria for the consumer to evaluate sites

Criteria	Options
Response time	immediate (online chat)/hours/same day/days
Ease of access to the site	results e-mailed back to the patient/posted to the Web page
Qualifications	providers identify themselves, their location and professional credentials
Comprehensiveness of the response	the extent to which the question was answered
Clarity of the response	how clear the answer would be to a layperson
Accuracy of the response	is the answer best practice, scientific and current
Usefulness of the response	overall usefulness in terms of time and money

standards (http://hein.otago.ac.nz/wwwHealth/E-health.html). Specifying a disease group of cancer (skin, prostate, gynaecological lung cancers and cancer in children) and limiting domain names to New Zealand (URL's ending with .nz) reduced the number of sites to be evaluated. Unfortunately, a review of New Zealand Web sites offering consumer health information about cancer highlighted a poor overall standard. This study of published medical advice on the Net highlighted the areas of ethics, legality, codes of medical practice, publishing codes, lack of authority, lack of objectivity and evidence of currency as being areas of concern. The study concluded in saying that health-on-the-Net sites may be innovative but should also comply with standards to allow those accessing them to make informed decisions about their healthcare.

DISCUSSION

As an emerging field, e-health offers many exciting prospects, to both the health professional and the health consumer. E-health has an enormous potential to make healthcare more accessible, affordable and convenient to the consumer. However, e-health has many latent pitfalls, particularly related to security, privacy, legal and ethical concerns.

Traditionally if a patient has a query related to a medical problem, they would need to make an appointment with the doctor. This can be a frustrating experience as well as a major disruption of one's daily schedule. By contrast, the e-consultation is flexible and requires minimal upheaval for the patient.

A major ethical concern with e-consultation is whether a doctor is able to make a diagnosis without physically examining the patient. Conversely, making a diagnosis is not only dependent on the physical examination, but also the patient history. Therefore as health information (for example, test results, radiology images, reports) is increasingly stored in Internet databases, these could be accessed by doctors to help in advising patients of possible diagnoses. However, it is unlikely that diagnostics will be the primary function of the e-consultation. Rather, the online consultation can serve to provide the patient with a second opinion, or to provide further information or clarification regarding an existing problem. A major attraction of the e-consultation is in its anonymity-particularly in terms of sensitive health problems the patient does not feel at ease to discuss in a face-to-face setting.

Maybe in the short term e-consultation should be viewed as an adjunct to conventional medical care, rather than as an alternative, and as particularly appropriate for the management of chronic health, relatively minor health problems or health behavior. At this stage e-health is not a substitute for emergency medical care.

A further concern of e-health is the mixed quality of information on the Internet. In this study four e-health sites were contacted and evaluated in relation to a number of predetermined criteria. Overall, the quality of the responses was satisfactory-to-high. One of the major concerns identified in this project was that two sites, contrary to the HON guidelines (Health On the Net Foundation, 2001), failed to disclose the credentials of the medical staff. While e-health is still in its infancy, it is a rapidly growing enterprise. On the one hand, there are the highly reputable sites, which provide a valuable service; on the other hand there are many disreputable and questionable sites. To the unsuspecting and naïve health consumer, there are many pitfalls and inherent dangers. Many of the sites are commercially oriented; others disseminate unscientific information, particularly in the field of alternative health. Often the information is presented in a manner that will appeal to the layperson as it offers a quick fix. Due to the boundless scope of the Internet, policing e-health is a practically impossible goal, thus sites will largely be responsible for maintaining their own ethical standards, under the auspices of organizations such as HON (Health on the Net) (Health On the Net Foundation, 2001).

While there is no way to stem the tide of e-health, it is foreseen that in the future, an important role of the health professional will be to educate the public to develop greater Internet savvy in order to become more discerning consumers of e-health.

Electronic signatures are currently allowed in New Zealand, for example, Health Benefits Limited use electronic claiming of General Medical Service schedules by general practitioners, and for ACC schedules using HealthLink (An Introduction to HealthLink, 2000) (an online extranet, based on a virtual private network) (Wilson, 2000). However the costs of pharmacies being continuously online may be too expensive to be viable and there is no satisfactory pharmaceutical coding systems that both pharmacists and general practitioners can as yet depend on (Yagami, 2000).

On the surface there seems be significant benefits in the use of electronic prescriptions. However this is not yet fully implemented in New Zealand because electronic service delivery is not just a technology issue. Legal and policy decisions in New Zealand need to clarify the legal status of documents that have been signed "digitally." The Minister for Information Technology for New Zealand, Paul Swain, has unveiled the program outline for the government's e-Commerce summit in November 2000, which will include a provision that a statutory requirement for a "signature" will be satisfied by an electronic signature (Swan, 2000). It will be the decision of the Ministry of Health as to whether this will include prescriptions. New Zealand is making steps to get its legislative framework in order, but it needs to combine this with its already good consumer protection and privacy laws to work with e-Commerce (Mitchell, 1997; Palmer, 2000; Elsmore, 2000).

ACKNOWLEDGEMENTS

...to all students on the post-graduate Diploma in HealthInformatics at the University of Otago, New Zealand, who have contributed to this research (http://hein.otago.ac.nz/wwwHealth/index.html).

REFERENCES

Ball, P. (2000). *Benefits, and Legality of Electronic Prescriptions in New Zealand*. A written communication with Dr. Patrick A. Ball, Senior Lecturer in Clinical Pharmacy, University of Otago.

Barber, N. (1995). What constitutes good prescribing? *British Medical Journal*, 310, 923-5.

Barkham, P. (2000). Is the Net healthy for doctors? *The Guardian*, June. Available on the World Wide Web at: http://www.0,3858,4026978,00.htm.

Borowitz, S. and Wyatt J. (1998). The origin, content and workload of e-mail consultations. *Journal of the American Medical Association*, 280(15), 1321-1324.

Coddington. (2000). Dot.com.docs. *North & South*, 64-67.

Coile, R. (2000). e-Health: Reinventing healthcare in the information age. *Journal of Healthcare Management*, 45(3), 206-210.

Egger, E. (2000). Market memo: How technology is changing the healthcare system. *Health Care Strategic Management*, 18(1).

Electronic Commerce Part Two: A Basic Legal Framework. New Zealand Law Commission.

Elsmore, K. (2000). Discussion paper sent to the Pharmacy Guild on Electronic Prescriptions in NZ.

Elsmore, K., (2000). *The Pharmnet Project in NZ*.

Ethical and Legal Issues in Interactive Health Communications: A Call for International Cooperation. (2000). *Journal of Medical Internet Research*, 2(1), e8, Available on the World Wide Web at: http://www.jmir.org/2000/1/e8/index.htm.

Eysenbach, G. and Diepgen, T. (1998). Towards quality management of medical information on the Internet: Evaluation, labelling and filtering of information. *British Medical Journal*, 317(28).

Eysenbach, G., Ryoung Sa, E. and Diepgen, T. (1999). Shopping around the Internet today and tomorrow: Towards the millennium of cybermedicine. *British Medical Journal*, 319, 1294.

Farrar, K. (2000). Can electronic prescribing increase the efficiency of the discharge process? *Hospital Pharmacist*, May, 7(5), 114.

Frequently Asked Questions on the Electronic Transmittal of Prescriptions (1999). *The Pharmaceutical Journal*, 263(7069), 698.

Greer, B. (2000). Legality of electronic and fax prescriptions in New Zealand, *Regulation*, 41(b), 1984.

Health On the Net Foundation. *HON Principles*. Available on the World Wide Web at: http://www.hon.ch/HONcode/conduct.html.

HealthLink. (2000). *An Introduction to HealthLink*. Available on the World Wide Web at: http://www.healthlink.co.nz/.

Hoffman, D. L. and Novak, T. P. (1998). Bridging the racial divide on the Internet. *Science*, 280, 390.

Howe, L. (1997). Patients on the Internet: A new force in healthcare community building. *Medicine on the Net*. Available on the World Wide Web at: http://www.mednet-i.com.

Improving Our Health (2000). *The Challenge for New Zealand–Media Release*. Available on the World Wide Web at: http://www.hfa.govt.nz.

Internet Health Coalition. (2000). *Finding Quality Health Information on the Internet*. Available on the World Wide Web at: http://www.ihealthcoalition.org/index.html.

Jadad, A. and Gagliardi, A. (1998). Rating health information on the Internet: Navigating to knowledge or to Babel. *Journal of the American Medical Association*, 279(8), 611-616.

Jones, R. (2000). Developments in consumer health informatics in the next decade. *Health Libraries Review*, 17, 26-31.

Katz, J. and Aspden, P. (1996). Motivations for and barriers to Internet usage: Results of a national public opinion survey. Available on the World Wide Web at: http://www.markle.org.

MacStravic, S. (2000). The downside of patient empowerment. *Health Forum Journal*, 43(1), 30-31.

Mandl, K. D., Mandl, I. S., Kohane and Allan, P. (1998). Electronic patient-physician communication: Problems and promise. *Annals of Internal Medicine*, 129, 495-500.

McCormick, L. (2000). Hey doc, I found this on the Internet. *Medical Economics*, 77(15), 6-8.

Middleton, H. M. (2000). Electronically transmitted prescriptions–a good idea? *The Pharmaceutical Journal*, 265(7107), 172-176.

Milstein, R. (1999). Telemedicine: Creating virtual certainty out of remote possibilities. *Department of Human Services* (State of Victoria).

Mitchell, P. (1997). Confidentialiy at risk in the electronic age. *The Lancet*, 349(9065), 1608(1).

New Zealand Law Commission Report 58. (1999). *Electronic Commerce Part Two: A Basic Legal Framework*, November.

New Zealand Law Commission. (1998). *Electronic Commerce Part One: A Guide for the Legal and Business Community*.

Palmer, G. (2000). Electronic commerce and the NZ consumer: A status report and a proposed NZ model code for consumer protection in the electronic age. In *PC World NZ*, 17-24.

Phillips, F. (1999). *Phillips Fox Focus on Technology Law, Electronic Signatures in New Zealand*. Available on the World Wide Web at: http://www.phillipsfox.co.nz/publications/111818389.htm.

Pitofsky, R. (1998). Federal Trade Commission. *Privacy Online: A Report to Congress*, June.

Rolfe, S. (1995). Ability of hospital doctors to calculate drug doses. *British Medical Journal*, 310, 1173-4.

Saunders, P. (2000). E-mail communication with Paul Saunders, Technical Analyst for the NZHIS, on electronic prescriptions in New Zealand.

Schiff, G. (1998). Computerized Prescribing: Building the electronic infrastructure for better medication usage. *Journal of the American Medical Association*, 279(13), 1024-9.

Simmons, D. (1998). Electronic prescriptions. *Journal of American Pharm Association* (Wash), 38(6), 776.

Siwicki, B. (1998). Electronic prescriptions: Just what the doctor ordered. *Health Data Management*, 3(10), 62-8.

Sloan, B. (1999). *A Practical Guide to Health Information and Privacy*. New Zealand Privacy Commission.

Sloan, B. (1999). *Privacy Protection: A Key to Electronic Commerce*. Paper by the Privacy Commissioner, Bruce Sloan, on the occasion of the APEC Electronic Commerce Steering Group Meeting, Auckland. NZ Privacy Commission.

Sloan, B. (2000). *Killing the Goose? Information Privacy Issues on the Web*. Notes for an address by the Privacy Commissioner, Bruce Sloan, to the Untangling Web Law Conference. NZ Privacy Commission.

Stephenson, J. (2000). National Library of Medicine to help consumers use online health data. *Journal of the American Medical Association*, 283(13).

Stevens, L. (2000). Changing relationships: How the Web is altering traditional healthcare models. *Medicine on the Net*, 6-12. Available on the World Wide Web at: http://www.mednet_i.com/.

Swan, P. (2000).The Minister for Information Technology Paul Swain unveils the program outline for the government's e-commerce summit in November. Available on the World Wide Web at: http://www.med.govt.nz/consumer/ elcom/summrel20000816.html.

Taylor, J. and Leuven, C. V. Electronic databases e-communication and privacy in the health sector. *Health Manager*, 7(2).

Telehealth Applications-New Zealand. (2000). *Australian New Zealand Telehealth Committee*. Available on the World Wide Web at: http:// www.telehealth.org.au/.

Wilson, M. (2000). *Electronic Claims of ACC Forms*. E-mail communication with ACC eBusiness Programme division.

Winyard, G. (1997). *Prescription Fraud*. Leeds: NHS Executive.

Yagami, A. (2000). WHO statement on the legality of electronic prescriptions and signatures in the Western Pacific Region, personal communication.

URLs Accessed

New Zealand Perspectives

* http://www.doctorglobal.com/
* http://www.enigma.co.nz/hcro_articles/9810/vol2no12_001.htm
* http://www.nzhealth.co.nz/nzdoc/archives.html

* http://www.cnn.com/2000/TECH/computing/04/25/nz.doctor.idg/index.html
* http://www.xtra.co.nz/homepage/health/main0,1439,Health%3AAsk+the+Expert%3A,00.html
* http://www.telemedtoday.com/
* http://www.telehealthmag.com/
* http://www.yi.com/mednet99/index.htm
* http://www.askyourdoctoronthenet.com/
* http://www.healthfile.co.uk/
* http://www.hon.ch/Conduct.html
* http://www.mdweb.com/
* http://www.la-doctor.com/main-directory.htm
* http://www.marketadoctor.com/index.html
* http://www.retina-doctor.com/namequery.htm
* http://207.198.253.192/default.htm
* http://www.ppdnet.com/content/netdisc/doctorcom.htm
* http://www.1-800-doctors.com/index.cfm
* http://www.e-med.co.uk/home.html
* http://www.dis.port.ac.uk/ndtm/
* http://www.ihealthcoalition.org/community/join.html
* http://www.atmeda.org/news/testimony04112000.htm
* http://www.cyberdialogue.com/resource/press/releases/1999/11-03-cch-ehealth.html
* http://www.dc.com/deloitte_research/featured/e-health/e-health.pdf
* http://tie.telemed.org/legal/
* http://telehealth.net/
* http://www.doctorgeorge.com/consultation_room/index.htm
* http://www.doctors.net.uk/
* http://www.nap.edu/html/networking_health/ch2.html
* http://intel.com/intel/e-health/whatisehealth.htm
* http://intel.com/intel/e-health/tips.htm
* http://intel.com/pressroom/kits/events/9810ihd.htm
* http://www.noie.gov.au/projects/ecommerce/ehealth/rise_of_ehealth/ehealth3.htm
* http://psychological.com/
* http://www.dr-ann.org/

Chapter XVIII

The Trend Toward Online Banking Services by Brick-and-Mortar Institutions: The Last Five Years

Dianne J. Hall, Ray E. Whitmire, Steven D. Hall and E. Leon Knight
Texas A&M University, USA

Five hundred financial institutions in the United States were randomly sampled each year for five consecutive years in order to examine Internet participation, both evident at the time of the survey and planned by the selected financial institutions. Each year the selected institutions were surveyed regarding the existing involvement of their institution with online banking and that institution's Internet plans for the following two-year period. This study examines changes over time in the responses of the surveyed institutions. The results show that, over the study period, the percent of respondents that had or planned an Internet present within two years of the survey increased from 52% in 1996 to over 90% in 2000, and that the number of online services offered to customers is increasing.

INTRODUCTION

During the last several years, e-commerce has emerged as a growing, apparently indomitable method of doing business. Some organizations have been founded solely as Internet companies (for instance, Amazon), while others have begun to cater to Internet-savvy customers by providing online retailing (for instance, K-

Mart) and service sites (for instance, Hewlett-Packard). The financial industry has followed suit, spawning both Internet-only banks (for instance, National InterBank) and Internet sites to supplement brick-and-mortar financial institutions (for instance, Bank of America). This study examines randomly selected traditional financial institutions over a five-year period for their usage of Internet technology and their intended usage in the near future.

BACKGROUND

Cyber Dialogue, an online market research company, reports that the number of people who conduct their financial transactions online is expected to more than triple in the near future, from 6.9 million in 1998 to 42.2 million in 2002 (Totty, 1999). Klinkerman (2000) estimates that 20% of household banking will be conducted online by 2003, and that half of retail banking transactions will be influenced by online information by the same year. The Internet is leveling the playing field among financial institutions and is allowing smaller financial institutions to become increasingly active and to provide an unprecedented array of services for customers. With partnerships such as FundsXpress Financial Network with CUNA (Credit Union National Association) and organizations such as Concentrex providing Internet banking solutions, these smaller institutions can offer a full array of online banking to their customers regardless of physical location or traditional banking hours.

Financial institutions, particularly community banks (generally non-corporate, local institutions), are recognizing almost limitless marketing opportunities available in cyberspace. Fiore and McDonnell (2000) estimate that 1200 financial institutions were online by June 2000; by 2003, more than 15,000 are estimated to be online (Fiore and McDonnell, 2000; Bielski, 2000). Clearly, the question has changed from whether services will be provided to what services will be provided and when.

Many financial institutions are developing sites that provide extended banking services in addition to more traditional services. Many Web sites are available through which to apply for small business loans and home mortgages (for example, Lending Tree). The First National Bank of Pryor in Oklahoma was reported to be using its Web site to offer small aircraft loans and provide information on the general aviation market (Bagwell, 1997). In 1995, Salem Five Cents Savings Bank became the first bank in New England to introduce Web-based banking services. It is now planning to offer free Internet access to anyone. Salem has identified a niche in the Internet banking arena (Power, 2000), but the largest Internet operation belongs to Wells Fargo. It grows by 100,000 customers a month and boasts 1.7 million active online users, which represents 25% of the bank's retail checking households (Power, 2000). Citigroup is extending its offerings to include the ability to access banking services from a variety of communication devices, including cell phones, PDAs, pagers and interactive television (Schmerken, 2001).

Fiserv, Inc., a banking service company that provides computer services primarily for financial institutions, stated that its rate of growth in the last year was much better than expected (Marjanovic, 2000). This company's sales of front-end Internet banking software and processing of online banking transactions generated revenue at an annual rate of $50 million in 1999, compared with approximately $15 million in 1998. Such services can be offered to either extensions of brick-and-mortar institutions or to Internet-only institutions.

Internet-only institutions are increasingly represented in cyberspace. American Banker conducted a survey among the (then) existing Internet-only banks to determine the perceived level of competition among these institutions; 9 of the 24 responded (Ptacek, 2000). The results from the survey indicate a confidence among Internet-only banks that there is room for everyone and that the niche strategy most Internet-only banks are pursuing will ultimately pay off. One such strategy is used by National InterBank, which targets "Web-savvy individuals, 18-44 years old," and has 6,500 customers, 500 of whom are Internet-only. Further, Ptacek (2000) states that "National InterBank is unique in that there are virtually no fees for traditional financial services: free bill-paying, free checking, free account research, free worldwide ATM withdrawal, free money transfers, free stop-payments, free cashiers' checks, free statement and check reprints, and a no-annual-fee credit card." Brick-and-mortar institutions must begin to compete in a new environment.

The definition of traditional financial services may in fact be changing. Entities largely unrestrained by banking regulation, such as investment companies, credit card companies and technology suppliers, may begin to control financial information with their ability to transmit and use data more quickly and efficiently than banks and credit unions. The payment system is the last vested monopoly of these latter institutions and could be replaced by the substitution of physical money with electronic equivalents that could be transmitted over the Internet by an assortment of institutions (Vartanian, 1997).

As an example of non-financial institutions offering financial services, Microsoft has joined other non-banks (specifically Intuit, makers of Quicken) in developing Web sites that give people the ability to consolidate all of their financial information in one place. Microsoft's MoneyCentral had 4.3 million visitors in March of 2000, and Intuit's Web site had 3.6 million. The largest Internet bank had only 2 million (Toonkel, 2000).

MoneyCentral became the first Web site to introduce OneSource Network account aggregation software from Corillian Corporation. MoneyCentral uses OneSource to collect information on bank and credit card accounts. Six brokerage houses–Fidelity Investments, Charles Schwab & Co., DLJ Direct Inc., Datek Online, TD Waterhouse Group and E-Trade Group Inc.–share information with OneSource. Using the Open Financial Exchange (OFE) standard, which enables the sharing of information between willing institutions, these non-banks can gather information from various sources. If an institution does not have OFE or does not want to participate, a controversial practice that uses screen-scraping techniques (lifting and recording data that is displayed on the screen) is used to get customers' data (Toonkel, 2000; Bennet 2000).

How are traditional financial institutions reacting to the diverse but encroaching competition from Internet-only banks and non-financial institution Web sites that offer financial services? Most are recognizing the need for an Internet presence, and are beginning development of interactive banking sites, or contracting such a service from an online banking services vendor. For example, many brick-and-mortar institutions, in response to this type of competition, have begun to facilitate data transfer between their institutions and their customers, allowing the customer to download data into formats compatible with personal finance packages such as Money and Quicken.

The research conducted over the last five years examined changes over time in the intentions of financial institutions to offer online banking and at what level of activity, and what, if any, obstacles to implementing online banking were perceived.

THE STUDY

It is rare that one can formulate a research design at the beginning of a perceived trend, but the explosion of Internet-enabled business in recent years has allowed such an opportunity, and the researchers chose to examine the propensity to offer online banking. Formally, the study focused on perceptions of executives in brick-and-mortar institutions regarding online banking practices, both real and planned, in their respective institutions and then followed the trends of practice and perception over five years. The users of such online services were not of interest and therefore may comprise either household or business customers or both. At the beginning of the study, it was determined that while a longitudinal study of the same financial institutions might be preferable in some respects, it would be difficult. The banking industry is currently in a volatile state, and the longevity of some institutions may be questionable. Also, it was the intention of the authors to examine industry trends, rather than actions of specific banks. By drawing a random sample from brick-and-mortar financial institutions each year, the authors felt that a more representative industrial trend would evolve.

Methodology

A single-page, two-sided questionnaire was developed and pilot tested using a control group of institutions of varying size in a large southwestern city in the United States. The instrument was designed to determine specific characteristics of the institution, including asset size, existing Internet sites (and sophistication), Internet plans (and sophistication) for the two-year period following the survey and perception of obstacles to Internet participation at any (or no) level. No anomalies were found and the instrument was determined to be valid. Some minor modifications were made to the instrument in response to recommendations from the control group, such as layout and instruction modifications. Additional modifications were made throughout the years in an effort to more closely address emerging trends, such as outsourcing and personal financial package interfacing.

Each year, address labels for 500 institutions were purchased from an outside research company that randomly generated the names of CEOs of financial institutions in the United States and its possessions. The survey instrument was numbered and sent to each institution in the sample in three different mailings, or until a response was received. The mailings were addressed to the CEO of each institution, as it was felt that CEOs were most likely to know the short-term goals and objectives of their institutions. The CEO was asked to complete the questionnaire, or to forward it to an individual who could provide the answers. Average response rate over the five years was 43%.

There was no effort made to ensure inclusion of any particular type or size of institution. Interestingly, however, the responding institutions represent a normal distribution curve when examined by asset size. Also, while the intention of the authors was to gather institutional responses regardless of the individual who completed the questionnaire, it was interesting to find that those individuals who requested a copy of the survey results were, in fact, the CEOs that were targeted.

Discussion

The respondents represent financial institutions of varying size and charters. Responses were examined for the institutions' existing or planned Internet presence over the five years studied. Also explored was the level of activity for the customer that any presence, existing or planned, would provide. If the respondents expressed no intention of developing an Internet presence, they were asked to give the reason or reasons. If the respondent expressed intention to develop an Internet presence, but did not intend to offer full-service banking capabilities, they were again asked to give the reason or reasons behind the decision.

General Classifications

The responding financial institutions were divided into three classifications of involvement. The first classification represents those institutions that reported an Internet presence of any level. The second classification represents those institutions that reported plans to have a presence within two years, and the third classification represents those institutions that reported no plans for an Internet presence.

Figure 1 shows the Internet presence level of the respondents for each of the five years. Sixteen percent of the respondents had an Internet presence in 1996, and by the year 2000 that number had risen to over 54%. Interestingly, the study shows that the percentage of institutions with plans to develop an Internet presence within two years of the survey time has remained fairly steady at one-third of the respondents on average, ranging from a high of near 38% of total respondents in 2000 to a low of 26% in 1997.

Figure 1: Internet presence of financial institutions (n=total number of respondent(s)

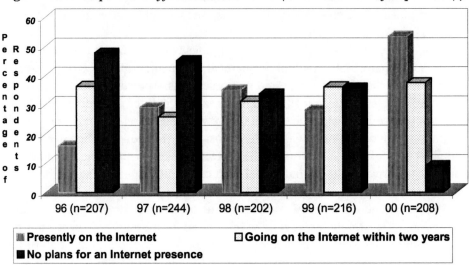

Percentages of Respondents

| | 96 (n=207) | 97 (n=244) | 98 (n=202) | 99 (n=216) | 00 (n=208) |

▦ **Presently on the Internet** ☐ **Going on the Internet within two years**
■ **No plans for an Internet presence**

Respondents who had no plans to develop an Internet presence began near 45% of total respondents in 1996, and plummeted to less than 10% in 2000, indicating without question that these institutions now see the Internet as an attainable, and possibly necessary, business tool. In addition, this dramatic decrease may be attributable to a development within the credit union industry. In 1998, the Credit Union National Association began to offer its members Internet space and service, enabling the smaller institutions to develop an Internet presence despite having fewer financial and personnel resources than larger financial institutions. Also, companies that provide online transaction site support are emerging (for instance, Concentrex).

The researchers were also interested in determining whether the self-reporting of Internet site development plans, combined with an existing Internet presence in a given year, would accurately predict Internet presence two years following. To test that informal hypothesis, the researchers assumed a conservative 10% demise rate for existing sites, and a 25% overstatement rate in planned Internet presence. These percentages were determined to be representative of situations including mergers or institution failures, unplanned delays, timing errors and plan changes, but in no way imply a formal model or a validated procedure. Such validation may be the basis for further research, however.

As an example of the calculation, the predicted Internet presence for 1998 would be the sum of 90% of the 1996 current respondents and 75% of the 1996 planned presence respondents, or a total of 41%. Table 1 compares the predicted Internet presence in 1998, 1999 and 2000 using the above adjustments to the reported percentage of current sites from the 1998, 1999 and 2000 surveys.

It was not surprising, given the approximate nature of the prediction, that actual growth rate fell somewhat below the predicted rate in both 1998 and 2000. However,

Table 1: Predicted vs. actual Internet presence (Percentage, rounded)

	1998	**1999**	**2000**
Predicted	41	46	54
Actual	35	28	53
Difference	6	18	1

the dramatic difference in the 1999 presence was unanticipated. It is assumed that these financial institutions, being somewhat overburdened with Y2K adjustments, put Internet plans on hold. Using the same formula for prediction as described above, it is anticipated that over 75% of brick-and-mortar institutions will have some level of Internet presence by the year 2002. Without this formula, the predicted rate is 91%. Analysts are currently predicting 86% (Bielski, 2000), which indicates that the model used here, while informal, does predict with a range of accuracy close to that of professional analysts.

Levels of Involvement in Online Banking

Four increasing levels of Internet involvement for financial institutions with an Internet presence are shown in Figure 2. All levels except Level 1 include capabilities from lower levels. A Level 1 Internet presence provides information about the financial institution but there is no interaction between the institution and the customer (possible contact information, such as e-mail hot links, are not considered to be interaction for level determination). Similar to a digital bulletin board, the Web site usually shows the name, address, services and other information concerning the institution. Level 2 allows the customer to submit information (e.g., a loan or credit card application) to the institution via the Internet. Level 3 allows sharing of information, such as the ability to check on a loan balance or to determine checking account activity (cleared checks, deposit amounts, etc.). Level 4 is the most sophisticated and allows the customer to process information that belongs to the institution, such as fund transfers or loan payments. Movement through each level during the last five years is clearly visible in this figure.

Over the last five years, institutions reporting Level 1 activity has dropped from a high near 79% in 1996 to a low of 40.5% in 2000, which may indicate that institutions begin with the first level, but move gradually toward higher levels of participation. Level 2 activity has an interesting drop from a steady percentage of low to mid-twenties between 1996 and 1999, to a level of less than 3% in 2000. This drop probably coincides with an overall increase in an institution's comfort with an Internet presence, improvements in technology and an increase in the number of service companies that either develop and host sites or provide contract employees

Figure 2: Level of Internet involvement (n=respondents with an Internet presence)

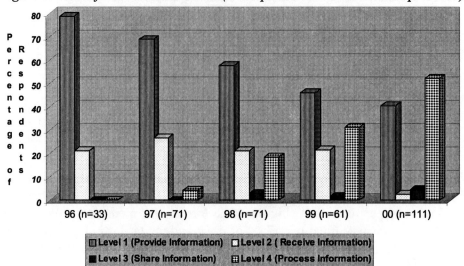

to the institutions. Level 3 activity has been largely unused, although it has risen from 0% in 1996 to almost 5% in 2000. Level 4 activity has shown the greatest strides, increasing from 0% in 1996 to over 52% in 2000. The results from the 2000 survey seem to indicate that financial institutions are either interested in providing basic service or full service, with very little activity in Levels 2 or 3. It is likely that brick-and-mortar institutions are beginning to fear competition from Internet-only institutions and are responding accordingly.

Figure 3 and Table 2 show institutions' Internet participation classified by asset size. Figure 3 shows only those institutions that reported an Internet presence in a survey year. As might be expected, larger institutions have a higher likelihood of existing or future planned involvement in online banking. By the year 2000, all respondents with assets of $500 million or more had an Internet presence, whereas less that 5% of respondents with assets of $10 million or less had or were planning an Internet presence. Table 2 shows only those institutions that did not have an Internet presence during the survey year and are separated by whether or not the institution had plans to develop an Internet presence. Institutions with assets in the $10 to $50 million range seem to consistently report no Internet plans. This percentage rose dramatically for 2000 (from an average of approximately 30% to nearly 79%), and may have been somewhat skewed by the relatively low number of institutions without Internet plans who responded to the 2000 survey. Institutions with assets above $50 million have consistently been gravitating toward developing an Internet presence. In 1996, 30% of the respondents with assets above $50 million had not planned a presence by 1998, whereas in 2000 the number of those respondents of that asset size not planning a presence had dropped to 10%.

Figure 3: Presently on Internet by asset size (millions) (n=respondents with an Internet presence)

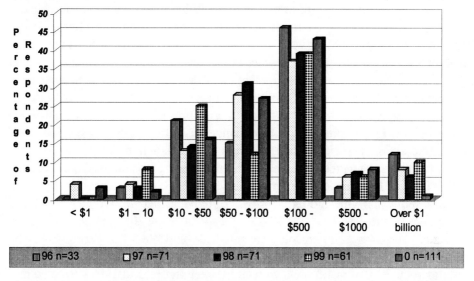

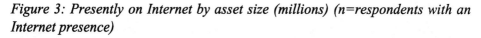

Table 2: Internet activity by asset size; Internet presence (percentage of respondents, rounded)

	Plan to be on Internet within two years (n = respondents with plans)					No plans for an Internet Presence (n = respondents with no plans)				
Asset size (millions)	96 n=75	97 n=63	98 n=63	99 n=78	00 n=78	96 n=99	97 n=110	98 n=68	99 n=77	00 n=19
< $1	8	2	5	1	4	11	17	15	22	5
$1 – 10	11	16	13	18	0	28	30	34	43	5
$10 - $50	25	20	38	43	44	31	34	32	32	79
$50 - $100	28	33	22	26	31	13	9	17	6	11
$100 - $500	20	24	17	9	21	16	9	2	4	0
$500 - $1000	1	5	3	3	0	0	0	0	4	0
Over $1 billion	7	0	2	0	0	1	1	0	0	0
Total	100	100	100	100	100	100	100	100	100	100

Internet Plans for the Next Two Years

Responding institutions were asked to delineate their institution's plans for Internet site activity level within the two years following the survey. This question was asked and recorded separately according to whether the institution currently had an Internet presence or was in the process of developing one. Among those institutions that had an Internet presence at the time of the survey, the biggest change in the last five years was in development of a Level 4 presence. The percentage of institutions predicting such a level rose from near 49% in 1996 to over 80% in 2000. Institutions in the planning stages for an Internet presence also showed an increase in predicting a Level 4 presence, but the change was not as large (almost 40% in 1996 compared to 66.7 percent in 2000). The results are shown in Table 3.

An interesting pattern emerges when investigating the results of the perceived future level of Internet activity versus the actual level. For instance, in 1998, only 7% of respondents with an Internet presence predicted that they would have a Level 1 presence by the year 2000, yet 40.5% of respondents in 2000 indicated a Level 1 presence. However, 27 percent of respondents in 1998 who were planning to develop an Internet presence predicted a Level 1 presence by the year 2000. In a similar vein, 70% of institutions with an Internet presence in 1998 predicted they would be at Level 4 by the year 2000, 41% of those planning an Internet presence predicted Level 4 and yet only 52% of respondents on the Internet in 2000 were at

Table 3: Future level of Internet involvement by financial institutions

Levels of Future Sophistication	Present Internet Presence (n = respondents with an Internet presence) (Percentage of Respondents)					Planned Internet Presence (n = respondents with plans for an Internet presence) (Percentage of Respondents)				
	96 n=33	97 n=71	98 n=71	99 n=61	00 n=111	96 n=75	97 n=63	98 n=63	99 n=78	00 n=78
Level 1 (Provide information)	9.1	18.3	7.0	3.2	9.9	22.2	38.1	27.0	19.2	15.3
Level 2 (Receive information)	33.3	14.1	12.7	13.1	4.5	26.9	17.5	20.6	14.1	9.0
Level 3 (Share information)	9.1	7.0	9.9	4.9	4.5	11.1	11.1	11.1	17.9	9.0
Level 4 (Process information)	48.5	60.6	70.4	78.8	81.1	39.8	33.3	41.3	48.8	66.7
Total	100.0	100.0	100.0	100.0	100.0	100.0	100.0	100.0	100.0	100.0

Level 4. This indicates that institutions may be overstating their ability to upgrade their online banking sites to full service capacity. Institutions that have not yet fully developed their presence may be slightly more accurate in their predictive ability.

Financial institutions that are presently on the Internet differ somewhat from institutions planning to enter the Internet in terms of planned capabilities. For instance, while less than 10% of institutions with a current online banking site predict Level 1, over 15% of those in development predict a Level 1 site in two years. Financial institutions typically enter the Internet at lower levels of sophistication and once on, move up to more sophisticated levels. In the future, it is likely that financial institutions will skip the lower levels of Internet involvement as technological capability increases and competition encourages more institutions to provide full service with their first Internet exposure. A presence limited to receiving and/or sharing information does not seem popular among financial institutions, either with current sites or in development. In 1996, of the institutions presently on the Internet, over 42.4% anticipated merely receiving and/or sharing information in two years. By the year 2000, this percentage had declined to less than 9%. In addition, only 18% of those moving onto the Internet plan to operate at these levels.

Perceived Obstacles

Institutions with no Internet plans were asked to indicate their reasons for not pursuing an Internet presence. The overwhelming obstacles perceived in all five years, as indicated in Table 4, were insufficient demand (average of 54%) and cost (average of 51%). Security of financial information (average of 28%) was also identified by about one-quarter of the respondents as an obstacle to Internet participation. The responding institutions did not seem to be overly concerned with a loss of personal contact, but programming difficulty was cited fairly highly in both 1999 and 2000 (54% and 21% respectively). The reasons behind the jump from 11% in 1996-1998 to the above percentages for programming difficulty are not immediately evident. It is possible that as institutions begin to watch other financial institutions' developed sites, they begin to recognize that the other obstacles as listed in the survey instrument are not impeding development by other institutions. Additionally, they may lack personnel with the expertise necessary to develop and maintain Internet sites, especially those operating at higher levels such as 3 or 4. The survey instrument also allowed for alternative responses, and insufficient personnel or expertise was cited most frequently, along with the institution being in the final stages of permanently closing their doors. Examining responses by asset size gave no appreciable new information, except that smaller institutions were more concerned with loss of personal contact than were the larger institutions.

Financial institutions with existing or planned Internet sites do not tend to identify any one obstacle to developing or maintaining a Level 4 site, although on average, cost is most cited. However, this average is largely driven by a surge in 2000 of almost 80%. It is likely that these institutions are beginning to feel the financial effect of operating an "alternative branch" that may not be cost effective. As shown in Table 5, there is no clear obstacle as stated by the responding institutions. Cited

Table 4: Obstacles indentified by financial institutions not going on the Internet (percentage of respondents)

	96	97	98	99	00
Insufficient Demand	65.9	53.7	75.0	37.7	36.8
Cost	41.0	35.2	47.0	74	57.0
Financial Security	33.5	32.8	32.4	20.7	21.1
Loss of Personal Contact	33.5	15.6	25.0	9.1	0.0
Programming Difficulty	11.6	11.1	11.8	54.6	21.1
Other Variables	16.8	7.0	20.6	24.7	10.5

relatively highly as an obstacle is security, although it too fluctuates from year to year. As with institutions not planning an Internet presence, programming difficulty appears to be increasing as an obstacle (32% in 2000). Insufficient demand as an obstacle has fluctuated substantially over the five-year period, ranging from a low of 3% in 1999 to a high of 88 percent in 1997. As Internet competency and trust grow among banking customers, it is likely that this obstacle will decline in importance. It is interesting to note that the financial institutions that are presently on or going on the Internet do not clearly identify insufficient demand as a formidable obstacle, whereas institutions not going on the Internet identify insufficient demand as the primary concern. Thus, there is a large disparity in perceived demand between Internet-bound institutions and those with no Internet plans.

Logically, insufficient demand is a reason for not going on the Internet, while financial security and cost appear to be the major concerns of those institutions that are on or going on. Financial institutions' concerns regarding financial security may be well founded. Dan Farmer (1997), co-author of the *Security Administrator Tool for Analyzing Networks (SATAN)*, recently tested more than 1,700 Internet sites and found that more than 60% of them–including banks and credit unions–could be broken into or destroyed relatively easily. Some firms failed to take even the most basic security measures to protect their server and files.

It is reasonable to speculate that demand for this type of service may grow significantly beyond today's anticipation, requiring that banks resolve the security issue so that demand can be met. This is especially true because of the growth of Internet access in households. Other variables cited by these institutions included failure to contract for a higher level of service and no track record on which to base the decision. As above, examining responses by asset size gave no appreciable new information.

Outsourcing

Beginning with the survey year 2000, the researchers began to examine who was developing and administering the Internet sites. It was anticipated that much of

Table 5: Obstacles identified by financial institutions on the Internet or going on the Internet for not seeking total interactive banking (percentage of respondents)

	96	97	98	99	00
Insufficient Demand	34.3	88.2	52.5	3.3	19.0
Cost	34.3	50.9	28.8	16.4	79.6
Financial Security	24.1	30.9	59.3	16.4	51.9
Loss of Personal Contact	13.9	21.8	17.0	1.6	0.0
Programming Difficulty	7.4	14.5	3.4	4.9	31.7
Other Variables	11.1	10.9	13.6	13.1	12.2

Table 6: Internet site development/administration

	Existing Internet presence (Percentage of Respondents)	Plans for an Internet Presence (Percentage of Respondents)
In-house staff	44.1	26.9
Outsourced	54.1	70.5
Both	1.8	2.6
Total	100.0	100.0

the work would be outsourced, as these types of capabilities are usually outside of the range of core competencies for banking personnel. Table 6 indicates the responses. It was surprising to note that, for institutions with an Internet presence, the use of outsourcing versus in-house staff was very close (44% to 54%). It was not surprising to see that over 70% of the work for institutions in the planning stages was being done by outsource staffing. It is suggested, therefore, that as institutions begin to feel comfortable with an Internet presence, they also begin to hire or train personnel to administer the site. It is likely that the large percentage of respondents who have outsourced development is also somewhat affected by the CUNA partnership noted earlier in this chapter, as credit unions are well represented among respondents.

IMPLICATIONS

In a conversation with top executives from four tech-savvy community banks with assets of under $400 million, bankers indicated that the capabilities available through the Internet are becoming as necessary for doing business as fax machines, pagers and cell phones (O'Connell, 2000), but not all financial institutions are able to design and implement Internet sites. Many financial institutions are choosing vendors to provide their online services. Managers must be aware of the criteria on which to evaluate these vendors. Several criteria identified by O'Connell (2000) are financial stability, commitment to ongoing enhancements, security, Internet connections, technical support, marketing support, training on the product, ease in interfacing data with the product, and cost.

The results of this study indicate that cost has become the primary perceived obstacle to providing all (or any) online services. However, because a banking Web site is inexpensive when compared to a branch site, banks should not worry about the budget to start up this type of operation (Agosta, 2000). Instead, the decision should be based more on customer needs and the type of banking services to be provided via the Internet. The results of this study indicate that insufficient demand and loss of personal contact are no longer considered obstacles. Rather than ask broad questions of their customers, managers should focus on specific needs and wants of both existing and potential customers. For instance, asking what Internet service is most important is likely to bring forth more information than simply asking if an Internet presence is of interest to the customer.

Most banks seem to believe in the need for some level of Internet presence, even though few believe that the majority of their customers were interested in such a site. In a study done by Chicago-based Grant Thornton LLP (Agosta, 2000), more than a third of small-bank executives who stated that they did not have Web banking believed they would by year-end. Yet, the Grant Thornton study found that only 29% of the banks surveyed said their customers wanted Internet banking service. (The research examined in this chapter is consistent with these findings. Lack of demand only declined as a perceived obstacle in 1999 and 2000.) Only 21% of those surveyed by Grant Thornton LLP offer bill payment, 11% loan applications and 30% cash management services. Those figures are expected to rise to 87%, 75% and 72%, respectively, by 2003 (Agosta, 2000). (Again, these findings are consistent with the findings discussed in this chapter.)

Planning and building an Internet presence is only part of the battle. The key to an effective Web site is to get people to come back, says Mark O'Brien of EDS (Totty, 1999). O'Brien suggests that financial institutions begin by offering a Web site that provides information such as balances, or perhaps receives information (such as transfer requests). Once such a site is established, the level of service can increase as demand for the service grows, ultimately ending with "all-inclusive" banking sites offering services such as bill payment. The research discussed in this chapter suggests that institutions are in fact progressing in this manner (see Figure 1).

Getting people to use Internet services, much less to come back to the site, may not be as easy as it appears despite the growing number of Internet-savvy individuals. A survey on Internet banking and consumer behavior conducted by Gerald D. Verdi & Co. found that Internet users continue to value brick-and-mortar banks (Robinson, 2000). This survey found that 70% of Internet banking customers had visited a physical branch in the past 30 days and that the average Internet banking customer visited a physical branch more than three times per month.

Robinson (2000) also found that customers of financial institutions who sign up for Internet banking have not abandoned other methods of banking. Banks have found that adding such a channel did not decrease business in other areas, but rather dispersed it. The Internet is only a single channel of a multiple-channel delivery system, but arguably one whose value is increasing. However, Robinson found that less than 5% of a bank's customers sign up for Internet banking, while more than 50% of the banking customers' households have PCs. He also found that half the people who attempt online banking do not log back on, which further supports O'Brien's (Totty, 1999) position.

Managers of financial institutions must begin to determine not only how to attract customers to Internet sites, but also how to keep those customers utilizing the sites as a regular course of action. By 2002, over 300 million people worldwide are expected to use the Internet on a regular basis (Hamlet, 2000); as comfort with Internet usage increases among financial customers, so will usage of Internet banking sites. Financial institutions need to plan their strategies by knowing who their market is, where they are located, what services they desire and what incentives can be offered. There appears to be a discrepancy in Internet banking usage that should be addressed.

The slow increase in Internet usage by the consumer may be the direct result of no material cash savings for the customer (Nadler, 2000). Internet banking can offer significant savings to the bank, but little if any of the savings is being passed on to the user, for instance, in the form of higher interest rates on savings accounts or lower costs on loans; therefore, there is little economic advantage for the traditional banking consumer to use Internet banking (Nadler, 2000). Other than the savings in time and possibly gasoline, no real advantage exists for the customer. Financial institutions may need to consider offering economic advantages to customers who use Internet sites if reduction of brick-and-mortar locations is a goal. Note, however, that some Internet-only banks have determined that physical locations are necessary. Canadian Imperial Bank of Commerce has contracted with grocery stores to offer banking services through in-store Internet pavilions (Lamb, 2000).

Managers who are planning or working through online banking implementation must prepare their strategy and be prepared to make changes. Peter Currie, vice chairman and chief financial officer of Royal Bank of Canada, and Toos Daruvala, a senior partner of McKinsey and Co., make the following suggestions (Klinkerman, 2000):

- Start preparing, move and take risks now.
- Prepare to commit 15-30% of a developmental budget to virtual banking without a matching revenue stream.

- Incorporate broadband technology.
- Get low-cost access devices out to customers.
- Build partnerships to provide cross-institutional account-aggregation capabilities.
- Combine mature judgment with the "ponytail and pierced-ear" perspective.

Managers of financial institutions can use the results evident in this chapter to gauge the progress of their institution against that of the industrial trend and seek to move beyond the mean. In the words of Currie, "... be totally dissatisfied in being a follower."

CONCLUSIONS AND FUTURE RESEARCH

Financial institutions are rapidly moving onto the Internet. In 1996, 15.9 percent of all respondents were on the Internet compared to 53.4% in 2000. However, financial institutions are not utilizing the Internet as quickly as they had anticipated, or at their anticipated levels. If expectations of the responding institutions are fulfilled, 91% of all financial institutions will be on the Internet by the year 2002. A more conservative figure, adjusted for over-anticipation, is around 75%.

As might be expected, smaller institutions have been relatively consistent in their rejection of an Internet presence or of an advanced level of participation. Conversely, larger institutions are finding it increasingly difficult to avoid the Internet. Smaller institutions are facing increasing competition and may find it impossible in the future to continue to avoid providing Internet banking services.

Those institutions currently on the Internet do not appear to be satisfied with the status quo, and are more likely to be moving to "full-service" banking than those that are not currently on the Internet but are in site development. In the future, it is likely that financial institutions will skip the lower levels of Internet involvement and provide full banking services with the introduction of their Internet site.

This research is limited in that it only examines financial institutions (banks and credit unions) in the United States or its possessions. However, as the Internet is a worldwide trend, it is likely that some of the findings would be replicated in another financial domain. Such research would be enlightening. Also, the results of a mailed survey, without opportunity to further question respondents, may be difficult to interpret.

It will be interesting to note the changes in perceived obstacles and in staffing for Internet sites in future surveys. It is anticipated that the only true obstacle in the future may be cost, as technological advances are likely to eliminate security concerns as well as level the playing field between large and small institutions. Insufficient demand as an obstacle is likely to decrease as the general population becomes more Internet savvy and trusting, and therefore more demanding of the convenience of online banking. Already there are several companies who provide site hosting, so it is also anticipated that programming difficulty as an obstacle will decrease and outsourcing (at least initially) will increase.

Future changes to this study will likely include questions to examine the perception of the impact of "Internet-only" institutions on the brick-and-mortar institution. Certainly, these institutions appear to be establishing themselves with ease and are becoming competition, especially for those brick-and-mortar institutions whose customer base is largely composed of individuals who are comfortable with, and prefer to use, Internet services.

Many banks that provide Internet service also provide the ability to download account information into available personal financial software packages, such as Quicken or Money. Other financial activities on the Internet include purchase of savings bonds, application for large-scale loans, student loans and other banking services. This study suggests that financial institutions not only begin to develop a sophisticated Web site, but supplement that site to include services that go beyond services traditionally offered at a physical location. It may be that to maintain the current customer base and to attract new customers, financial institutions must be able to outdo their competitors with Internet services. Free checking may no longer be enough!

REFERENCES

Agosta, V. (2000). Small banks won't be Web holdouts for long. *American Banker*, April, 165(78), 12a.

Bagwell, J. (1997). Community banks offer innovative Websites. *Bank Marketing*, October, 29(10), 13.

Bennet, A. (2000). June. Available on the World Wide Web at: http://www.money.com/money/depts/websmart/webwatch/archive/000615.html. Accessed April 2001.

Bielski, L. (2000). Online banking yet to deliver. *ABA Banking Journal*, September, 92(9), 11-16.

Bowen, C. (1998). Of interest at Rate.net. *Editor & Publisher*, May, 131(20), 34.

Chow, L. (1997). Pressure rising. *Far Eastern Economic Review*, September, 1690(39), 125-130.

Editor. (1996). An Internet banking boom is coming...really. *United States Banker*, June, 106(6), 20.

Fiore, P. and McDonnell, K. (2000). Careful decision-making must precede in-house, outsourced e-banking choice. *Bank Systems and Technology*, June, 37(6), 47.

Hamlet, C. (2000). Community banks go online. *ABA Banking Journal's 2000 White Paper*, March, 92(3), 61-65.

Kearns, D. (1997). Time for an NT security checkup. *Network World*, January, 14(1), 22.

Klinkerman, S. (2000). Mass movement. *Banking Strategies*, November/December, 76(6), 53-60.

Lamb, E. C. (2000). Delivery channels: What's the optimal mix? *Community Banker*, September, 9(9), 25-29.

Marjanovic, S. (2000). Fiserv wary of its e-commerce businesses, though they grow fast. *American Banker*, New York, May, 165(84), 11.

Muckian, M. (1995). Self-service at home. *Credit Union Magazine*, July, 61(7), 36-42.

Nadler, P. S. (2000). Fact and fiction in Internet banking. *The Secured Lender*, May/June, 56(3), 44-48.

O'Connell, B. (2000). Online: Seizing the opportunities in electronic banking. *American Banker*, June, 165(108), 15a.

Power, C. (2000). Salem five nurtures its online pioneer status. *American Banker*, June, 165(107), 1.

Ptacek, M. J. (2000). Online banking: Web teaming with banks seeking niches. *American Banker*, May, 165(96), 12.

Robinson, T. (2000). Internet banking: Still not a perfect marriage. *Informationweek*, Manhasset, April, (782), 104-106.

Schmerken, I. (2001). Citigroup strives for secure multi-device access. *Wall Street and Technology*, January, 19(1), 52.

Toonkel, J. (2000). New Microsoft challenge to banks: Account aggregation on MSN site. *American Banker*, May, 165(90), 1.

Totty, P. (1999). Internet levels the playing field for all CUs. *Credit Union Magazine*, July, 65(7), 77-99.

Vartanian, T. (1997). A cashless world. *Credit Union Executive*, February, 36(5), 38-46.

Verdi, G. D. (2000). Traditional banks should integrate Web banking with the branch network. *American Banker*, June, 165(116), 16.

Chapter XIX

Banks and Financial Consulting in the Internet Age

George Peters
Munich University of Applied Sciences, Germany

INTRODUCTION

In our analysis we concentrate on the effects of the Internet on private banking and abstract from other effects that may have changed private banking. We limit our analysis to the aspects of financial consulting; we do not discuss the pros and cons of traditional and online banks in the field of order placement. In the chapter we focus on the German private banking sector.

The private banking sector[1] has changed dramatically since Internet technologies have been introduced. Online banks have been founded and grown rapidly (Consors, Comdirekt, Direktanlage Bank, etc.). They do not have branch networks, but they offer their services via telephone and Internet. Most online banks do not offer financial consulting services (Advance Bank, a subsidiary of Dresdner Bank in Germany is an exception) but they provide extensive financial information on their Web sites. They are high-tech companies in comparison to the over-the-counter business of traditional banks.

In the business model of traditional banks, the private investors do not have to pay for the labor and cost-intensive, face-to-face financial consulting services directly. The order and depot fees for shares and funds not only cover the transaction costs but also consulting services. The consulting services of the traditional banks are fully subsidized by the order and depot fees.

It is often discussed how independent the advice of a bank really is. Banks not only sell and buy stocks on behalf of their private investors. They sell and buy stocks for themselves, they often deal with companies on the one hand and analyze the same company on the other hand. So some doubt whether the consulting service of banks is objective or if there is a certain bias in it.

Since online banks do not offer face-to-face consulting services like traditional banks, their order fees can be significantly lower–even traditional banks offer banking services without consulting and reduce their fees today.

In comparison to a branch network or even a call center the placement of an order via the Internet is less labor intensive. Obviously online banks have a high degree of automation and computerization. Therefore their transaction costs for the placement of an order of a private investor are much lower than the costs of traditional banks. The abandonment of consulting and the placement of orders via the Internet lead to order fees that are about 50%-95% cheaper than the fees of traditional banks.

In the chapter we argue that the traditional banks are facing the following challenge. While some traditional banks "force" their "poor" private investors to leave, they are very keen to keep their "rich" private investors. Normally the order fees generated by a "poor" private investor do not cover the consulting costs, while the order fees generated of a "rich" private investor not only cover the transaction costs of the bank but also the consulting services (Balzer, 2000).

But today all private investors, whether "poor" or "rich," have alternative ways to place orders and get consulting services. Today a private investor can have his account with a online bank, where he only pays for the transaction–without any "hidden" subsidy for consulting. If the private investor needs financial information and consulting, he can get it from independent sources.

In the following section we discuss the principle role of online banks. We then analyze the quality of financial consulting services and discuss traditional and advanced communication channels in private banking. That is followed by a section on traditional and Web-based financial consultants.

The Role of Online Banks

Since their introduction online banks have grown rapidly and gained a significant market share (afp, 2000a; Weber and Park, 2000). In some studies it is anticipated that in 2010 online banking will be fully established (Bongartz, 2000). Online banks offer lower fees in comparison to traditional bank. They can offer these low fees because they do not have an expensive branch network like traditional banks.

At online banks orders are placed via the Internet. Such an order process is highly automated and therefore cheap in comparison to the labor-intensive placement via telephone or over the counter. Online banks normally do not offer traditional financial consulting services (expensive face-to-face consulting). But they provide Internet-based information that is much cheaper to generate than face-to-face consulting.

Private investors leaving traditional banks must have decided that the financial consulting services of traditional banks do not compensate the higher fees. They can have several reasons.

The financial consulting might be bad (bad recommendations or too focused on the products of the bank). The financial service might be too expensive. Online consulting suits them better than traditional face-to-face consulting.

At an online bank the investor has the possibility to separate the order business and the consulting business and optimize both.

Some traditional banks seem to be afraid that their private investors are still interested in their free advice but trade at online banks. Recently Deutsche Bank introduced a "consulting lump sum" that has to be paid by the private investors independently whether they trade shares at Deutsche Bank or not (afp, 2000b, mtr, 2000).

The online presence even of traditional banks has become so important that the ratings of banks depend on it (Rössing, 2000). The question is no longer how much online presence is necessary for a bank but how much physical presence (branch networks) is still needed.

The Quality of Financial Consulting Services

The quality of the financial consulting services[2] comprises the quality of market research (equity research, exchange rates, macro-economic trends, etc.) and the quality of the communication between the financial consultant and the private investor.

The Quality of Market Research

The quality of the market research is assessed by various institutions. In Germany, for example, the University of Halle-Wittenberg, and the monthly business magazine *Manager-Magazin* assess the recommendations of banks (Hetzer and Seeger, 2000; Hegmann and Klusmann, 2000) twice a year. In America the *Institutional Investor* magazine, *Fortune* and many others assess the quality of research of analysts and investment houses.

The Independence of Research

One crucial point for high-quality research is how independent the analysts are. Are the analysts and banks only committed to research or do they have to take care of other goals?

Banks[3] not only have to publish high-quality research to demonstrate their expertise. They are also investors in equities themselves, they are underwriters in IPOs (initial public offerings) and they offer traditional banking and investment services to companies. Finally banks earn money when their private investors trade (order fees).

Therefore a conflict of interest may occur between the objective to deliver research and the other goals of the bank:

- *Banks as investors*. If a bank plans to buy shares of a company, a negative research report on this company could result in a lower share price. Consequently the bank could buy the shares at a better price. If a bank intents to sell shares, a positive outlook on this company could arise the share price and the bank could make a better bargain than without "supporting" research report.
- *Banks as underwriters for an IPO*. The profits of an underwriter for an IPO depend on how successful an IPO is. A higher demand for the new shares leads to higher share prices and consequently to higher profits for the underwriting bank. A bank with a successful record of history as underwriter can easily acquire new IPO projects. Therefore a positive research report on the company going public supports the business of banks as underwriter.
- *Banks as business partners of companies*. Some companies may expect positive research reports on themselves or at least no negative report when they deal with the bank. So positive research reports could help to acquire and keep companies as business partners.
- *Banks as intermediary between investor and stock market*. Banks earn money when their private investors trade. Their profits soar when their private investors trade more actively. So frequent changes in the sell and buy recommendations could stimulate the trading activities of their private investors and lead to increased profits of the bank.

We describe two cases, of Deutsche Bank and Goldman Sachs, related to a potential conflict of interests:

- In the year 2000 Deutsche Bank published an enthusiastic research report on EADS, a European aircraft company, shortly before its IPO. Deutsche Bank also was the lead underwriter for the IPO of EADS. The profits for Deutsche Bank generated out of the IPO depended on the success of the IPO. The positive research report helped to make the IPO a success and increased the profits of Deutsche Bank (Hetzer and Seeger, 2000; Hegmann and Klusmann, 2000).
- In January 2000 Goldman Sachs recommended to buy shares of the company Ixos, listed at the German stock exchange Neuer Markt ("market outperformer"). Less than two months later, Goldman Sachs sold 600,000 shares of its market outperformer Ixos (Nölting, 2000).

Of course we have no evidence and we explicitly do not assume that the research reports were wrong or written to support any other business of the banks. But without doubt both research reports came in handy for the banks. Recently a similar discussion has started in the U.S. (2001).

The main advantage of independent research institutions is that they do not have these potential conflicts of interests.

- They do not trade with equities. Therefore their research is independent of any intention to sell or buy stocks for themselves.
- Independent research institutions are no underwriters for IPO. So they have no advantage when they publish a positive research report on a company going

public. They do not experience any disadvantages when they publish a negative research report.

- They do not have any business relationship with the company they analyze. Therefore they can publish their reports regardless of any opposition of the analyzed company.
- They do not earn any money (order fees) when a private investor sells or buys stocks. They only earn money when they sell their research.

To stress the point again: the research of the banks may be fully independent from any other goal of the bank. The advantage of the independent research institution is that they do not even have the potential conflicts of interest the banks have. The only possibility to earn money for the independent research institutions is to sell their reports. So they have an essential interest that their research is of high quality.

THE QUALITY OF COMMUNICATION

Dimensions of Communication

While the quality of research is the central basis for excellent financial consulting, the communication between the financial consultant and the investor determines the quality of the advice and the performance of the portfolio of the investor.

We distinguish between the following dimensions of communication:

- Personalized and impersonalized information
- Information pulling and pushing
- Horizontal and vertical information exchange

Each dimension of communication plays an important role in financial consulting.

Personalized and Impersonalized Information

We define impersonalized information as information designed to serve a large number of people. The addressee of impersonalized information has to filter and arrange the information so that it suits his personal needs. Examples for impersonalized information are printed business magazines, newspapers or news on television.

Impersonalized information covers common needs of all investors. For example indexes like the American Standard & Poors 500, the Dow-Jones or NASDAQ index or important exchange rates like US$ to Euro or Yen are essential for almost all investors. Furthermore impersonalized information is important since it provides an inside to topics that are not covered by the concentrated focus of an investor. Therefore it helps to broaden his perspective, discover and investigate new investment opportunities (e.g., new trends in the optical sector or biotechnology).

In contrast to impersonalized information, personalized information is designed individually for one person. It serves the special needs of one investor. If an investor is heavily invested in American high-tech companies, he needs to have profound information about this industry and detailed and up-to-date information on Microsoft, Cisco and Sun Microsystems.

Another investor is invested in biotechnology. Therefore he looks for information on the biotechnology sector and especially, e.g., the company Biogen.

Information Pushing and Pulling

Pushed information is information that is sent to the addressee as soon as it occurs, an ad-hoc report for example: as soon as a public company has information that is important for the investor, it has to publish it.

Pulled information is information that will be provided on request only. When an investor is interested in a certain company, he can pull information and order a research report from his financial consultant.

There is a trade-off between information pushing and information pulling. In principle any information could be pushed. But because of the large amount of information, consequent information pushing would lead to an "information over-kill." The information could not be picked up and evaluated by the private investor anymore. But the private investor faces the problem that he does not know when crucial information occurs and consequently he does not know when he has to pull for information. Consequent application of information pulling would lead to a badly informed investor.

Therefore a certain balance between information pushing and pulling is essential for the investor. The individual balance for an investor is difficult to determine. It depends, e.g., on the time horizon of the investor. A day trader needs to have any relevant news immediately. Since there is no time for information pulling, he relies on pushed information. In contrast to the day trader, a long-term investor does not need any information on a company. He is interested in the long-term development of the company and the markets. So the daily monitoring of the market movements and all company news pushed to him would be contra-productive. He may prefer to pull information whenever he wants to control his investments.

Horizontal and Vertical Information Exchange

We define vertical information exchange as information flow between the financial consultant and the private investor. Horizontal information exchange is the exchange of information between private investors. A financial consultant is characterized as an institution that has the main task to produce and distribute financial information. The main role of a private investor is to invest and not to generate and distribute information.

Vertical information exchange is important to get objective and up-to-date information. But horizontal information exchange has increased over the past few years. For example Internet-based chat rooms have been heavily used for discussions on financial issues–and sometimes even for attempts to manipulate share prices.

Near-Real-Time and Accessibility of Information

Often near-real-time information is crucial even for a private investor. What does it help when a company reports a promising take-over or the approval of a planned merger by a monopoly commission but the investor receives the information some days delayed, e.g., reads about it in the newspapers the next morning.

What does it help when the information is somewhere but the investor cannot access it easily, e.g., a private investor would like to analyze the chart of a company. Some years ago there were only very expensive and time-consuming possibilities to get the chart: phoning the bank and asking for a letter with the information or stopping by at the bank and picking it up.

EVALUATION OF TRADITIONAL AND ADVANCED COMMUNICATION CHANNELS IN PRIVATE BANKING

Evaluation of the Traditional Communication Channels

The traditional communication channels between financial consultants and the private investors are face-to-face discussions and printed information like investor magazines and research reports. In the context of the dimensions of information, they primarily cover:

- *Personalized and impersonalized information*. The costs for personalized information has been high since it has been provided face-to-face. It has been very labor intensive and often slow since appointments have to be arranged, etc. In the field of impersonalized information, investors' newspapers and magazines cover interesting topics for the private investor. They are not real-time but cover medium- or long-term topics.
- *Information pushing and pulling*. Information pushing and pulling in the field of personalized information may only have worked for the important (rich) private investor. The costs and the complexity of personalized information pushing and pulling have been too high for normal private investors. The exchange of impersonalized information has been easier.
- *Vertical and horizontal information exchange*. Vertical information exchange has dominated in financial consulting. There have been some "investment clubs" organized by private investors (horizontal information) but they have not been very common.

Evaluation of Internet-Based Communication Channels

The Internet has dramatically changed communication in private banking. The costs of communication have decreased, the speed of communication and the accessibility of information have increased. We focus on the dimensions of communication again:

- *Personalized and impersonalized information.* The cost of personalized information has decreased dramatically. There are several financial Web sites on the Internet which can be customized by the user. At Yahoo!Finance (finance.yahoo.com), just to name one, the users can easily access important financial information (research, company news, insider trading, etc.). The signed-up user has the possibility to customize the site. The Web site Personal Wealth (personalwealth.com/businessweek.com) of the Standard & Poors offers extensive databases covering financial information, alerts and several other possibilities to adapt the site to the personal needs of the investor.

- *Information pushing and pulling.* The Internet offers a large amount of information on financial topics. The user can decide whether he wants to pull information and to what extent the information shall be pushed (normally by SMS and e-mail). The site Personal Wealth offers a daily newsletter by e-mail and an alert when their research team has changed its opinion on a share, just to name a few functions.

- *Vertical and horizontal information exchange.* While private investing has been dominated by vertical information exchange, the Internet offers the technology for discussion groups (horizontal information). The discussion groups are constantly very active although they are quite risky since one never knows who provides the information. But the horizontal information exchange has gained much importance since the Internet has offered the technology for discussion groups.

So traditional financial consulting has been supplemented or sometimes even replaced by new forms of Internet-based consulting.

TRADITIONAL AND WEB-BASED INDEPENDENT FINANCIAL CONSULTANTS

Independent Financial Consultants

Over the last decade the offers for independent financial consulting have increased. Some years ago the banks almost had some kind of information monopoly in the field of financial consulting. There were just a few newspapers and magazines covering topics for the private investor; some expensive newsletters of independent financial advisers could be subscribed to.

The private investor had no alternatives to the traditional banks offering the bundle product, high order fees and free consulting. In the last decade the number of independent financial consultants has increased:

- Driven by soaring share prices, more and more people began to be interested in financial news. So the demand for financial news increased.

- Private investors at online banks have been looking for alternative financial consulting. Again the demand for financial news increased.
- The Internet provides an ideal platform for financial consulting. So some companies started Web-based financial consulting services.

Traditional Independent Financial Consultants

Driven by soaring share prices and the rising interest of private investors, some publishers have introduced print magazines for private investors, and renowned newspapers like *Frankfurter Allgemeine Zeitung* and *Handelsblatt* have extended their coverage on private investing. On television the coverage of financial news has been extended; today the daily report from the stock exchange, the Dow Jones index and the exchange rate between US$ and Euro are regulars like the weather forecast. So there has been an extended coverage of private investment topics in traditional media.

Obviously the private investors have been looking for independent research to complement or even replace the financial consulting offered by their banks.

Internet-Based Financial Consultants

The Internet technology provides a platform that ideally supports the impersonalized and personalized information needs of private investors. It is fast, accessible anywhere anytime (especially in future when mCommerce is fully established (Poganatz, 2000)) and it can be adapted to the personal needs of the investor.

Therefore many financial consultants, banks and independent financial consultants have launched financial Web sites. Since the costs of information distribution are significantly lower in comparison to traditional media, the consultants can offer their expertise at competitive rates or even for free.

Independent financial consultants can be divided into two groups, the information editors and the independent research institutions.

The Information Editors

Information editors[4] collect financial information published by various news agencies, banks and others. They aggregate and republish them on the Internet. A well-known example is Yahoo!Finance (finance.yahoo.com).

The Web site informs not only about the stock quote, performance and fundamentals. It also provides information on the research of banks. Similar information can be found on the Web site of the American technology stock exchange NASDAQ (www.nasdaq.com).

Since information editors do not generate information by themselves, they rely on the information provided by third parties. They often offer the information for free since they use free or cheap information resources:

- They do not provide real-time data but delayed data. So the stock prices are normally up to 20 minutes delayed, information of news agencies are delayed too. Real-time data are important for institutional investors but the ordinary private investor suffers no great disadvantage when he only gets near-real-time data.

- They often do not provide detailed data of research institutions but aggregated information like buy and sell ratings.

The private investor must decide whether the aggregated and delayed information is acceptable for him or not. In comparison to traditional investment services, these sites provide a significant improvement with regards to speed, personalization, accessibility and completeness of information.

The main advantage of the information editors is that they provide concentrated information and opinions of several financial research institutions.

The Independent Research Institutions

Independent research institutions are not banks, so they do not have a potential conflict of interest between their research and the other businesses of their company. Standard & Poors, for example, offers independent research services for private investors (www.personalwealth.com, recently integrated into www.businessweek.com).

Renowned independent research institutions conduct high-quality research. Presently their Web sites offer more functionality than the Web sites of many traditional banks (compare Personal Wealth of Standard & Poors to any Web site of German banks). Maybe one reason for this is that the core business of Standard & Poors is information while the core business of banks is (still) banking.

In the long run the banks will improve their information supply on the Internet and offer similar functionality like Personal Wealth. This kind of financial consulting has only become possible by Internet technology. It will supplement or even replace costly face-to-face consulting of banks.

CONCLUSION

In this chapter we argue that Internet technologies have dramatic impacts on private banking. The change is driven by two developments, the success of online banks and the growth and automation of financial consulting services.

The online banks are highly computerized and offer no expensive personalized face-to-face financial consulting services. Therefore they can offer lower order fees in comparison to traditional banks.

The Internet technology enhanced the dimensions of communication dramatically so that traditional financial consulting (face-to-face, printed information) is only a possibility today. The new Internet-based forms and channels of financial consulting have become more and more important.

So traditional banks face the problem that more and more private investors do not accept the traditional product bundling any longer: they do not accept high order fees to subsidize the expensive face-to-face financial consulting services.

Enabled by Internet technology, they have alternatives to traditional banks. Today there are online banks that offer accounts without "compulsory consulting" and the extensive branch networks of traditional banks. Therefore they are much cheaper than the traditional banks.

So many private investors already have separated their transaction business and their needs for consulting and optimized both. The bundle-business of traditional banks, order fees cover expensive face-to-face financial consulting, antiquated in the Internet age.

ENDNOTES

1 Some basic information on the banking practice in Germany relevant for the chapter: In Germany private investors not only have a traditional account with their bank but also commission their banks to buy and sell shares at the stock market on their behalf (in New Zealand, for example, this is traditionally a function of stockbrokers. In the chapter we will refer to banks as institutions that deal as stockbrokers for individuals too). As additional service the most classical German banks offer financial consulting services that are "free" of charge. They finance these consulting services by high order fees when their customers trade shares.

2 We subsume under financial consulting services not only the services provided by banks but also services by anybody else (publishers of print magazines focusing on private investment, independent financial consultants, television and others).

3 We assume a universal bank system as in Germany.

4 Often the term "content aggregator" is used too for companies like Yahoo.

REFERENCES

afp. (2000a). Online-broker consors mit rasantem Kundenzuwachs. *Financial Times Deutschland*, March. Retrieved October 29, 2000, on the World Wide Web: http://www.ftd.de/ub/fi/FTDF9E3EC5C.html.

afp. (2000b). Tipps vom Anlageberater nicht länger umsonst. *Die Rheinpfalz*, October. Retrieved October 29, 2000, on the World Wide Web:http://www.ron.de/osform/cms_osmm?articleName=HERMES:20001023:14212 19&template=templates/cms_osmm/recherche/wirt/finanzen/meldung.oft.

Balzer, A. (2000). Wer fürchet sich vorm kleine Mann. Manager-Magazin, June. Retrieved October 29, 2000, on the World Wide Web: http://www.manager-magazin.de/magazin/artikel/fs/0,1153,77676,00.html.

Bongartz, W. (2000). Im Jahr 2010 hat sich online-banking etabliert. *Die Welt*, February. Retrieved October 29, 2000, on the World Wide Web: http://www.welt.de/daten/2000/02/24/0224ww153344.htx.

Hegmann, G. and Klusmann, S. (2000). Zoff zum Zeichnen. *Financial Times Deutschland*, June. Retrieved October 29, 2000, on the World Wide Web: http://www.ftd.de/ub/in/FTD961614764488.html.

Hetzer, J. and Seeger, C. (2000). Die besten Analysten. *Manager-Magazin*, July. Retrieved October 29, 2000, on the World Wide Web: http://www.manager-magazin.de/magazin/artikel/fs/0,1153,81931,00.html.

mtr. (2000). Neues Gebührenmodell für Detusche-Bank-Privatkunden. *Frankurter Allgemeine Zeitung,* 8. November.

n.n. (2001). *Merrill Lynch Policy Regarding Research Reports and Opinion Changes.* Retrieved March 25, 2001, on the World Wide Web: http://askmerrill.ml.com/corp/article/0,,16897_ask0000,00.html?ml.

Nölting, A. (2000). Unheilvolle Allianz. *Manager-Magazin*, May. Retrieved October 29, 2000, on the World Wide Web: http://www.manager-magazin.de/magazin/inhalt/fs/0,1153,523,00.html.

Poganatz, H. (2000). Aktien schwimmen auf wap-banking-welle. *Die Welt*, March. Retrieved October 29, 2000, on the World Wide Web: http://www.welt.de/daten/2000/03/09/0309fi156063.htx.

Rössing, S. (2000). Internet-Auftritt beeinflusst rating der banken. *Financial Times Deutschland*, February. Retrieved October 29, 2000, on the World Wide Web: http://www.ftd.de/ub/fi/FTD1GAQKO4C.html.

Weber, O. and Park, M. (2000). Silicon-valley-investor: Online-broker und andere cyberspace-highflyer. *Financial Times Deutschland*, October. Retrieved October 29, 2000, on the World Wide Web: http://www.ftd.de/pw/eu/FTD4ZZD1PEC.html.

The references are given as Internet links if possible. Nevertheless all references (except n.n.: Merrill Lynch Policy Regarding Research Reports and Opinion Changes) given as Internet links have been published in classical media (in printed form) also.

About the Authors

John D. Haynes is Professor and Chair in Information Systems at UCOL, Universal College of Learning, Palmerston North, New Zealand. He is also (resident August 2001 until May 2002) Visiting Professor of Management Information Systems at the University of Central Florida, Orlando, USA. Dr. Haynes has more than 30 published refereed journal papers/chapters in books/ conference papers and three published books, two as single author and one as editor. His research interests are e-Commerce and the Internet, information systems, systems analysis and design, artificial intelligence, the philosophy of information technology and phenomenology. He has five university degrees (alternating between computer science and philosophy) and his PhD (from Bond University in Australia) is in the area of Information Systems, Artificial Intelligence and the Philosophy of Phenomenology. He has had extensive experience as a consulting systems analyst in medical systems as Managing Director of Mediware (Australia) Limited from 1980–1989 (concurrent with the post of Head of Computing at the Hunter Institute of Higher Education, NSW, Australia). He was at Bond University, Australia, 1990-1998, where he was Head of Artificial Intelligence. He is Co-Chair of the Philosophical Foundations of MIS (Americas Conference on Information Systems), is reviewer for a number of international journals and Institutes, and is a panel member of a number of senior research forums both in New Zealand and Australia.

***

John Baker is Visiting Associate Professor at UCOL, Universal College of Learning, Palmerston North, New Zealand, and is Managing Director of Natural Learning Systems Ltd. in Australia. Dr. Baker has published, both as single and joint author, 38 books and more than 20 refereed journal papers, chapters in books and conference papers. He was a tenured Assistant Professor of Mathematics in the School of Information Technology at Bond University, Gold Coast, Australia, for seven years before his Managing Directorship of Natural Learning Systems Ltd., Australia, in 1996.

David Bimler received his BSc in Physics and his PhD in Mathematical Psychology. He is an Honorary Research Affiliate with Massey University in New Zealand. The common theme of his research projects is the application of multivariate procedures, multidimensional scaling in particular, to areas of psychophysics (with a special emphasis on vision) and psychology. Many of his publications are attempts to map the nebulous region where personality, development and motivation meet.

Deborah Bunker is a Senior Lecturer in the School of Information Systems, Technology and Management (SISTM) at UNSW and is a member of the University of Wollongong International Business Research Institute. She serves on the Editorial Board for the *Australian Journal of Information Systems*, has been a guest editor for the electronic journal *Philosophical and Conceptual Foundations of Information Systems* and is Secretary of IFIP TG8.6 on Transfer, Diffusion and Implementation of Technology. Professor Bunker has research interests that cover the management and diffusion of electronic commerce technologies in small and large businesses in relation to institutional culture. She also has wide-ranging experience as a senior consultant within the IT industry in the finance, transport, insurance and government sectors in projects that have included change management, end-user systems development, human resource and financial system development, and implementation and open systems architectures. She is currently responsible for the postgraduate courses in electronic commerce (EC) and is the Undergraduate Honours Program Director for SISTM.

Brian Corbitt was JADE Professor of Electronic Commerce and Head of the School of Information Management at Victoria University of Wellington until July 2001. He is currently Professor of Management Information Systems and Head of the School of MIS at Deakin University in Australia. He specializes in electronic commerce policy development, analysis and implementation and in business modeling and electronic commerce trade relationships. His published research includes reports to public and private agencies on smart cards, implementation of electronic commerce in SMEs in Australia, on intranets and on electronic commerce policy implementation. He has a great deal of experience in the implementation of e-Commerce solutions in developing countries and works with governments and business on developing policy and strategy for e-Commerce and e-Business.

James F. Courtney is Professor of Management Information Systems at the University of Central Florida in Orlando. He formerly was Tenneco Professor of Business Administration in the Information and Operations Management Department at Texas A&M University. He received his PhD in Business Administration (Management Science) from the University of Texas at Austin in 1974. His academic experience also includes faculty positions at Georgia Tech, Texas Tech, Lincoln University in New Zealand and the State University of New York at Buffalo. Other experience includes positions as Database Analyst at MRI Systems Corporation and Visiting Research Scientist at the NASA Johnson Space Center. His papers have appeared in several journals, including *Management Science, MIS*

Quarterly, *Communications of the ACM*, *Decision Sciences* and *Decision Support Systems*. He is also a member of the Governing Council of the Knowledge Management Consortium Institute.

Eric Deakins' early career was as a navigation officer in the British merchant navy. Upon completion of his Bachelor of Science degree, he taught naval architecture at the University of Plymouth. He has also managed a Computer Aided Design and Imaging Centre and a Maritime Research Centre, and has steered major IS projects to completion in the UK and the USA. Both his MBA and PhD focused on the simulation of dynamic risk in various management settings. More recently he has managed a dot-com start-up company, and his research interests include e-government practices, e-business systems alignment and Internet automization for smart e-business. He is currently Director of the Information Management for Managers (IM^2) Center based at the Waikato Management School at the University of Waikato in Hamilton, New Zealand.

William H. Friedman is Associate Professor of Information Systems at the University of Central Arkansas in Conway, USA. He has taught mathematics in the public schools of Philadelphia, and philosophy in several universities in Virginia. He has a BHL degree from Gratz College in Philadelphia, and BA and MA degrees (in logic and analytical philosophy) from the University of Pennsylvania. His PhD (philosophy) is from the University of Virginia, on the deductive logic of John Stuart Mill. Since then, he has published in the *Journal of Symbolic Logic* and the *Notre Dame Journal of Formal Logic*, and has presented many papers in other branches of philosophy, such as epistemology, philosophy of science and ethics. At the suggestion of his wife, he retooled in Information Systems at Virginia Commonwealth University and undertook a totally new career. At first, artificial intelligence and logic served to bridge the research gap between the disparate fields and he wrote about technical matters in systems analysis and design as well as programming. When he began teaching in the environment of a business school, he became interested in where management principles intersected computer practice and produced several articles on such business topics as the roles of user and sponsor in management information systems projects, implementing expert systems and accounting procedures for developing systems. He has presented several papers linking philosophy and MIS; his contribution to this book is a prime instance.

John D. Gillies (Course Director) is Paediatrician and Senior Lecturer in Health Informatics, Department of Medicine, Wellington School of Medicine, University of Otago. A medical specialist in paediatrics, he is also a Senior Lecturer and the Director of the school's Health Informatics program. Dr. Gillies is excited about the challenges of distance learning and distance teaching, and is continuously active in assessing new software packages to enhance this process.

Dianne J. Hall is a doctoral student in the Department of Information and Operations Management at Texas A&M University. She received her MBA at Texas A&M University-Corpus Christi. She has served as an instructor of management information systems, computer science and economics at Texas A&M University-College Station, Texas A&M University-Corpus Christ, Texas A&M University-Kingsville and Del Mar College, Corpus Christi.

Steven D. Hall is Professor of Accounting at Texas A&M University-Corpus Christi where he has been since 1981. He received his doctorate from Northern Illinois University in 1982 and has been on the faculty of accounting at the University of Wisconsin-Platteville and the University of Dubuque.

Alec Holt, BSc, DipSci, Mcom (Otago), MRSNZ, ANZCS, is Senior Teaching Fellow in Health Informatics, Department of Information Science, University of Otago. He is an information scientist with special interests in health and medical computing. Professor Holt has particular interests in geographic information systems (specifically for environment and health applications) and artificial intelligence, especially case-based reasoning. His research expertise is in the following areas: information technology and systems; geographical information systems; artificial intelligence–especially case-based reasoning, machine learning; spatial cognition; cognitive science especially analogy; health informatics. He has applied the above expertise areas to the following domains: public and environmental health; bio-informatics; e-health; information technology in tourism–especially modeling visitor movements; information technology for rugby analysis/prediction; image analysis. His main teaching areas are health informatics, spatial information systems and case-based reasoning.

Lucas D. Introna lectures in ethics, technology and organization in the Center for the Study of Technology and Organization at Lancaster University, United Kingdom. He is also Visiting Professor of Information Systems at the University of Pretoria. His research interest is the social dimensions of information technology and its consequences for society. In particular he is concerned with the way information technology transforms and mediates social interaction with specific reference to the moral dimension. He is Associate Editor of *Information Technology & People* and Co-Editor of *Ethics and Information Technology*. He is a founding member of the International Society for Ethics and Information Technology (INSEIT) and an active member of IFIP WG 8.2, The Society for Philosophy in Contemporary World (SPCW), and a number of other academic and professional societies. His most recent work includes a book, *Management, Information and Power*, published by Macmillan, and various academic papers in leading journals and conference proceedings on a variety of topics such as: theories of information, privacy, surveillance, information technology and post-modern ethics, autopoiesis and social systems, and virtual organisations. He holds degrees in Management, Information Systems and Philosophy.

Barry Jackson is a Senior Lecturer in the Department of Information Systems at Massey University in New Zealand. He has extensive experience in the teaching of systems development, systems thinking, interactive multimedia and information networks. His research interests include multimedia development, soft systems methodology and e-Commerce. He has a particular interest in the design, development and usability of Web-based interfaces. Within this area he has tended to focus on issues associated with the localization of Asian-based Internet sites.

John Kirkland is a Developmental Psychologist from Massey University, Palmerston North, New Zealand, who enjoys exploring alternative forms of data collection and analysis, and demonstrating that worthwhile research can be created outside the Atlantic rim. His primary general research interest area is socio-emotional development with a specific interest in attachment theory/application.

E. Leon Knight Professor Emeritus of Marketing at Texas A&M University-Corpus Christi where he served from 1976-2000. He received his doctorate from the University of Texas at Austin in 1974. He has also been on the faculty at the University of Kentucky and the University of Tampa.

Kuldeep Kumar completed his PhD in Statistics from the University of Kent at Canterbury, UK. He is currently Associate Professor in the School of Information Technology at Bond University, Australia. He is the winner of a Commonwealth Scholarship award, a Young Statistician Award (of the International Statistical Institute), the Commission of European Countries Post Doctoral Fellowship Award, a Bond-Oxford Fellowship Award and the Australia-Taiwan exchange programme Award. He has succeeded in receiving seven Australian Research Council (small) grants in the last five years. He has published more than 60 research papers in various international refereed journals/conference proceedings. His current research interests include data mining, applied statistics and multivariate analysis, time series analysis and forecasting and applications of artificial neural networks. He is on the editorial board of three journals and has refereed papers for internationally recognized statistical journals. He is currently chairman of the Statistical Computing Section of the Australian Statistical Society.

Kambiz Maani's professional and academic career spans over 24 years in the USA, South America, Asia, Australia and New Zealand. He is the president of Systems Thinking International, an educational and consulting firm and a Professor of Management Science and Information Systems at the University of Auckland. Dr. Maani is a frequent invited speaker on systems thinking, leadership and organizational learning. His executive courses on systems thinking have been offered internationally for the past six years, receiving rave participants' comments. His clients include Aetna Health, Unisys, Digital, Caterpillar, RAND, Babbage-Simmel, Fletcher Challenge, CHH, Ministry of Health, ACC, UniChem, Placemakers, Pacific Steel, TVNZ, MAF and Zuellig Pharma. His recent book (with Bob Cavana), *Systems Thinking and Modeling-Understanding Change and Complexity*, was published by Prentice Hall in 2000.

Ahmed Mahfouz is pursuing his PhD in Management Information Systems from Texas A&M University, College Station, Texas. He has an MBA and a bachelor's degree in Management Science (Computer-Based Decision Support Systems Option) from Virginia Polytechnic Institute and State University, Blacksburg, Virginia. His research interests include computer human interaction, electronic commerce, Web site design and research methodology. He has presented papers at conferences such as America's Conference on Information Systems (AMCIS) in Web site design, e-Commerce, multimedia and the philosophy of information systems. Mr. Mahfouz is also a graduate assistant lecturer and has received two awards for teaching excellence by doctoral students both at the departmental and dean's level. He is the recipient of the Texas A&M Regents' Graduate Fellowship. He has been a reviewer for journals, conferences such as HICSS and AMCIS, and for books dealing with e-Commerce and the philosophy of information systems. He is a member of the Association for Information Systems (AIS), Association for Computing Machinery (ACM), IEEE Computer Society and Association of Information Technology Professionals (AITP).

David Paradice is Associate Professor of MIS at Florida State University. He received his Doctor of Philosophy in Business Administration (Management Information Systems) from Texas Tech University. He has worked as a programmer analyst and consultant. He has published numerous articles focusing on the use of computer-based systems in support of managerial problem formulation and on the influence of computer-based systems on ethical decision-making processes. He has co-authored two books–*Database Systems for Management* (with James Courtney, Jr.) and *Application Development in Microsoft Access* (with Dirk Baldwin)–and co-edited *Ethical Issues in Information Systems* (with Roy Dejoie and George Fowler). He was previously on the faculty at Texas A&M University, where he also served as Director of the Center for the Management of Information Systems.

Ray J. Paul is Professor in the Department of Information Systems and Computing (DISC) at Brunel University, UK. He has been accused of empire building at Brunel, and proudly owns up. Dr. Paul is currently on loan from DISC as Dean of the Faculty of Science (which, however, includes DISC). He taught Operational Research and Information Systems at LSE before joining Brunel eight years ago. He has more than 200 refereed publications and 3 books. He is co-editor of the *European Journal of Information Systems*, which he co-founded in 1990, and is Series Editor of the Springer-Verlag Practitioner series, a collaborative venture with the BCS. His research interests are in business modeling, particularly simulation, and information systems development. He has held EPSRC, ESRC and MRC grants in the last few years and collaborates with a vast array of international talent too numerous to mention, exemplified by his Honorary Professorship in Community Medicine at Hong Kong University. More information (much more) can be found at http://www.brunel.ac.uk/~csstrjp/.

George Peters has postgraduate degrees in Telecommunication Engineering, Management Science and Business Administration and a PhD in Operations Research from Aachen University of Technology, Germany (RWTH Aachen). During his research towards the PhD, he worked at RWTH Aachen, the European foundation ELITE–European Laboratory for Intelligent Techniques Engineering and for the company MIT–Management Intelligenter Technologien GmbH in the field of data analysis. After his studies he joined IDS Scheer AG as a consultant in the field of business process reengineering and information systems. He worked for IDS Scheer AG for five years; his international exposure included projects in the UK, South Korea and Switzerland. In the year 2000 he spent one semester as Visiting Academic at the College of Business of Massey University, New Zealand. Presently he is Professor of Business Engineering at Munich University of Applied Sciences. He is also member of the supervisory board of the company HRW Factory Consulting AG.

Peter Raine is a New Zealander by birth. He has travelled and lived in many countries in Asia and the Pacific region. He began his working life as a horticulturalist, later moving into social work with Polynesian youth and polytechnic lecturing on the practical aspects of nature conservation. His academic career began with environmental studies, and he received first class honours at postgraduate level. He received his PhD in Environmental Studies from Massey University, Palmerston North, New Zealand. His recent research projects include work with Fijian forest dwellers, reconstruction of eutrophic lakes with Muaopuku Maori people in New Zealand, and work on a report on Tibet's environment and development with the Tibetan Government in exile at Dharamsala, India. He has published several articles on intercultural communication and indigenous peoples. Currently he is a researcher and adjunct faculty member for the International Honours Program (Boston, Massachusetts, USA).

Sandra M. Richardson is a graduate student in the Information Systems and Quantitative Sciences Department at Texas Tech University. She received a BS in Psychology (University of New Mexico) in 1997. She has published in *Information Systems Frontiers*, and presented papers at the 1999 and 2000 meetings of the *Americas Conference on Information Systems*, both published in the conference proceedings. She has more than 10 years experience in industry, including positions as Divisional Manager of the Public Service Company, New Mexico; Operations Manager at Imagimedia; and Accountant, University of New Mexico. She is experienced in design, implementation, operation and maintenance of accounting information systems. She has experience in project cost accounting, financial forecasting, budget preparation and preparing financial reports; project management; personnel management and human resources, market research and business plan development. Her research interests are in inquiring organizations, organizational learning, knowledge management and decision making, group processes, ecosystems management and accounting information systems.

Clarence N. W. Tan is currently Assistant Professor in Computational Finance at Bond and the Business Development Director of BlueSkyFrog, Australia's largest Mobile Internet Portal. He had worked for a number of MNCs, including Citibank's Foreign Exchange Strategic Positioning and Technical Trading Unit, Xerox Electronic Publishing Center, Citibank Asia Pacific Technology Group in Hong Kong and Citibank North American Investment Banking on Wall Street. Dr. Tan obtained his PhD from Bond University's Centre for Banking and Finance. He also holds a Bachelor's of Science in Electrical Engineering (Computers) from the University of Southern California in 1986, where he went on to simultaneously complete an MBA (Finance), and an MS in Industrial and Systems Engineering in 1989. Dr. Tan is an Associate of the Securities Institute of Australia (SIA); a Senior Associate of the Australian Institute of Banking and Finance; and a member of a number of professional bodies, including ATAA, ACS, IEEE, ANZIAM, Eta Kappa Nu, Omega Rho and Alpha Pi Mu. He is also a Fellow of the British Society of Commerce and Institute of Business Administration (UK). More details are available at http://w3.to/ctcv.

Tiok-Woo Teo obtained his Bachelor's of Accountancy from Nanyang Technological University, Singapore. He has garnered varied commercial experience in management information systems, end-user support and interactive media publishing prior to completing his Master's of Information Technology (Information Systems) at Bond University, Australia, where he is now a Postgraduate Fellow. His research interests include management information systems, supply chain management, electronic commerce and mobile Internet applications.

Theerasak Thanasankit is Lecturer in Business Information Systems in the Faculty of Commerce at the University of Melbourne. His PhD reported a detailed study of the impact of national culture on information systems and requirements gathering. He is widely published and is currently researching the social and cultural impact on information systems development and the application of those systems to electronic commerce. He is also researching the differential nature of trust and risk in electronic commerce as it is constructed in various national settings.

Neil Turnbull is currently senior lecturer in Social Theory at Nottingham Trent University in the UK. His current interests include the sociology and philosophy of technology. His current research is in the broad area of science and technology studies: investigating the way technologies are used by scientists in their experimental practices.

Catherine Wallace lectures in business communication, business writing and managing communications technology in Massey University's Department of Communication and Journalism. She is the Course Controller of the electronic commerce elective and teaches e-Marketing and Business Information Management in the MBA program. Her current PhD thesis investigates the impact of the Internet on business and explores issues of uptake and adoption, implementation and evaluation of Internet within organizations across a range of industry sectors. This enabled her to determine a list of critical success factors for Internet businesses. Professor Wallace was commissioned to write a brochure ("The Internet, Electronic Commerce and Your Business") and a guide ("e-Commerce: A Guide for New Zealand Business") by the Ministry of Economic Development in 2000. She has worked with a wide range of groups including Toyota managers, pilots, flight instructors and control tower operators, NZ Army, Telecom, Ezibuy, ANZ bank managers and social service administrators in teaching and consultancy situations. Her research interests include the human factors involved in technology transfer, language use in call centres, adoption and implementation of new communication technologies in the workplace, communication barriers, teleworking and virtual offices, and use of communication technology in organisations.

Ray E. Whitmire is Professor of Finance at Texas A&M University-Corpus Christi where he has been since 1973. He received his doctorate from the University of Texas at Austin in 1975.

Index